WAR MEMORIES

HUMAN DIMENSIONS IN FOREIGN POLICY, MILITARY STUDIES, AND SECURITY STUDIES

Series editors: Stéphanie A.H. Bélanger, Pierre Jolicoeur, and Stéfanie von Hlatky

Books published in the Human Dimensions in Foreign Policy, Military Studies, and Security Studies series offer fresh perspectives on foreign affairs and global governance. Titles in the series illuminate critical issues of global security in the twenty-first century and emphasize the human dimensions of war such as the health and well-being of soldiers, the factors that influence operational effectiveness, the civil-military relations and decisions on the use of force, as well as the ethical, moral, and legal ramifications of ongoing conflicts and wars. Foreign policy is also analyzed both in terms of its impact on human rights and the role the public plays in shaping policy directions.

With a strong focus on definitions of security, the series encourages discussion of contemporary security challenges and welcomes works that focus on issues including human security, violent conflict, terrorism, military cooperation, and foreign and defence policy. This series is published in collaboration with Queen's University and the Royal Military College of Canada with the Centre for International and Defence Policy, the Canadian Institute for Military and Veteran Health Research, and the Centre for Security, Armed Forces, and Society.

1 Going to War?
Trends in Military Interventions
Edited by *Stéfanie von Hlatky and H. Christian Breede*

2 Bombs, Bullets, and Politicians
France's Response to Terrorism
Christophe Chowanietz

3 War Memories
Commemoration, Recollections, and Writings on War
Edited by *Stéphanie A.H. Bélanger and Renée Dickason*

War Memories

Commemoration, Recollections, and Writings on War

Edited by

STÉPHANIE A.H. BÉLANGER
AND RENÉE DICKASON

McGill-Queen's University Press
Montreal & Kingston • London • Chicago

ISBN 978-0-7735-4793-3 (cloth)
ISBN 978-0-7735-4794-0 (paper)
ISBN 978-0-7735-4851-0 (ePDF)
ISBN 978-0-7735-4852-7 (ePUB)

Legal deposit second quarter 2017
Bibliothèque nationale du Québec

Printed in Canada on acid-free paper that is 100% ancient forest free (100% post-consumer recycled), processed chlorine free

This book has been published with the help of a grant from the Université Rennes 2 Research Group Anglophonie: Communautés, Ecritures (ACE) – EA 1796.

McGill-Queen's University Press acknowledges the support of the Canada Council for the Arts for our publishing program. We also acknowledge the financial support of the Government of Canada through the Canada Book Fund for our publishing activities.

Library and Archives Canada Cataloguing in Publication

War memories: commemoration, recollections, and writings on war/edited by Stéphanie A.H. Bélanger and Renée Dickason.

(Human dimensions in foreign policy, military studies, and security studies; 3)
Includes bibliographical references and index.
Issued in print and electronic formats.
ISBN 978-0-7735-4793-3 (cloth). – ISBN 978-0-7735-4794-0 (paper). – ISBN 978-0-7735-4851-0 (ePDF). – ISBN 978-0-7735-4852-7 (ePUB)

1. War and society. 2. War memorials. 3. War and literature. 4. Collective memory. 5. Memorialization. 6. Memory – Sociological aspects. I. Dickason, Renée, author, editor II. Bélanger, Stéphanie A.H., author, editor III. Series: Human dimensions in foreign policy, military studies, and security studies; 3

HM554.W37 2017 303.6'6 C2016-907151-0
C2016-907152-9

This book was typeset by Marquis Interscript in 10.5/13 Sabon.

Contents

Figures

Acknowledgments

Institutional support for this publication came from the European University of Brittany – Rennes 2 (France), in particular ACE (Anglophonie: Communautés, Ecritures) research unit, and from the Royal Military College of Canada (Kingston) to whom we are most grateful.

We owe particular thanks to our patient contributors whose commitment has enabled this collective to come to fruition and whom it was a pleasure to meet in Rennes in June 2014. The dedication of each one of them in reworking their book chapters in an integrative way brought meaning and harmony to the otherwise dislocated nature of the topic of war commemoration.

We are very happy to thank all our colleagues and friends, in France, in Canada, and worldwide, for their help and support. We are especially grateful to Yann Aubin for his administrative help with this project and to our faithful academic team in France, Alice Byrne, Nicole Cloarec, David Haigron, Delphine Lemonnier-Texier, and Sophie Mesplède, as well as to the ongoing support, in Canada, of the Canadian Institute for Military and Veteran Health Research Team, especially the director, Dr Alice Aiken, and the communications director, Ms Lauren Hanlon, as well as to our research assistants at the Royal Military College of Canada, Jérémie Fraser, Benjamin Fortier-Dion, and Luc Bilodeau.

Our most sincere thanks go to Ms Jacqueline Mason, from McGill-Queen's University Press, for her ongoing support and her exemplary energy in bringing this project to completion.

WAR MEMORIES

Introduction

STÉPHANIE A.H. BÉLANGER
AND RENÉE DICKASON

The idea of memory runs through contemporary public life at high voltage, generating polemic and passionate debate in the media, in the spheres of politics and in the academy. Yet although the contemporary "presentness" of memory is evident, how this is to be understood remains a matter of dispute. It is not clear what meanings attach themselves to the generic conception of memory itself; and while in the academy there is a common belief that memory is "everywhere," what this means remains an open matter.

Susannah Radstone and Bill Schwarz[1]

Collective memory is public remembrance but also private recollection. It is a patchwork, a complex composition of observations, initiatives, and experiences, which carries a natural subjectivity and which is blurred or revisited by the hindsight inevitably present when considering distant, or not so distant, events. The intricacies of fragments, traces, narrations, and images help in the search for truth and in the perpetual exercise of writing and rewriting history/histories. Commemoration is also part of the process of assembling scraps of what apparently happened and again implies subjectivity as points of view diverge according to various perspectives, whether social, cultural, political, or historical.

History has seen its fair share of notable events that have influenced successive generations, and the wars of the past have not all left the same imprint on collective memory. Wars of conquest or liberation have marked the history of the British Empire and its colonies in different ways. American foreign policy seems to be motivated by what is sometimes viewed as an imperialist vision which led the army into the quagmire of Vietnam and more recently into controversial involvement in the Gulf. Whether they end in victory or defeat, or are a source of patriotic pride or collective shame, wars are commemorated in museum exhibitions or through literature and the cinema, in which the threads of ideological discourse and the expression of subjective experience are intertwined. Some conflicts seem to attract "duties of memory" while others are simply forgotten. Military interventions across the last century have created new kinds of memories.

Recent wars, most notably World War I and World War II, have inspired and propelled historians to reassess the field of military history. Alongside them, researchers from various specializations, including war archeologists and cultural anthropologists, have enriched the tapestry of war memories by studying the perception and representation of wars among civilian populations at home and abroad. In the context of the one hundredth anniversary of the Great War and of the different commemorations of WWII, the links between memory and history are central to historiographical preoccupations.

This collective, which is divided into four parts, aims at encompassing the representations of wars in the English-speaking world during the past century. It presents an extensive and yet integrated reflection on various types of commemorations, interpretations of events, "theatres of memory" (to use Jay Winter's expression), and (re-)writing(s) of contemporary wars, adopting different angles and perspectives while keeping in mind the common theme of war memory: how and why do we remember war, and what does it tell us about the actors of war and about today's culture of war?

The first section of this volume presents a number of monuments and their significance in remembering the all-encompassing nature of wars. In the first chapter, Christine Knauer explores the remembrance of American veterans of the Korean War through different media. More specifically, she illustrates the use of monuments as a means to shed light on this complicated war and to increase the civilian population's patriotic feeling towards it. In a similar spirit, and offering a multitude of angles and perspectives, Judith Keene's study analyzes the issue of remembering the forgotten veterans of the same conflict, but focuses particularly on the groups responsible for raising the memorial to the American veterans of the Korean War in Washington, and how this monument and its design provide insight into the way these veterans are remembered today. Monuments and the politics surrounding their creation often embrace the values of the present rather than those of the past. It is in this spirit that Joan Beaumont presents an Australian and international perspective on the memorials dedicated to the fallen soldiers of the First and Second World Wars. Sam Edwards then discusses the political sensitivities around the erection of monuments, focusing on the construction of American war memorials on European soil (notably in France and Italy) as efforts to resolve tensions in fragile European-American relations during the Cold War.

The complexity of these relations, a result of the atrocities and sacrifices of war, have also been well documented through literature. The second part of this collective examines how books serve as tools to either commemorate war or condemn the act of remembering it. Isabelle Roblin analyzes Graham Swift's novel *Wish You Were Here* in a way that illustrates how medals, remembrance ceremonies, and memorials are unbearable burdens that should be eliminated to allow veterans to be able to move forward, as if remembering were not the best way for the survivors of war to cope. Struggles and recollections of war are further discussed by Subarno Chattarji who contrasts two texts, one from an American and the other from a Vietnamese immigrant to America. Both veterans are haunted by the war, but in different ways: one by memory and hurt and the other by its horrors. The recollection of war is a challenging subject for the soldiers trying to make sense of their experience. The next chapter by Stéphanie Bélanger and Michelle Moore uses interviews of Canadian soldiers from the recent war in Afghanistan to identify what stories they choose to tell about their experiences. Using the knowledge of Canada's particular national identity in relation to the trench warfare of World War I, they consider every generation's beliefs about previous wars and whether they were "truer" than their own. This suggests that the connection between identity and history may be stronger than the soldiers' actual experience of conflict. Although memories of war are rarely pleasant, some are more painful than others. Jeffrey Demsky and Melissa King address the imbalance in the memories of genocides in America. The Jewish Holocaust is common knowledge in the United States. However, the same cannot be said for the genocide of Armenian Christians. Americans' recollections and national identity associated with both world wars are the cause explored in this chapter. In the next study,

Raphaël Ricaud explores the fragmented recollections the American people have of the atrocities committed by American soldiers in My Lai, Vietnam. Ricaud examines how My Lai has been remembered over time in America: from shock, to neglect, to acknowledgment. Two Zimbabwean Liberation War novels are the subject of Annie Gagiano's analysis of the uses of war memories. She notes that both texts are complex in their depiction of war, but that, ultimately, the liberation struggle and its consequences were historically necessary. Laura Robinson discusses how the historical and political implications of war are also felt on the home front, through the examination of two novels by women writers. Her analysis suggests the significant blurring of male and female spheres in this context while revealing and honouring both the women who did not follow their gender role and the men who could not achieve their imposed ideal.

In its third part, this volume further considers the complexities of ideological representations promulgated through war by emphasizing how media and art such as comics, songs, paintings, and public discourse (re)narrate the experience of war and commemorate the fallen. Renée Dickason explores art in the form of comic strips and comic books in the WWII period in the United Kingdom. This chapter analyzes the politically motivated comics used to support the war effort at the time of the conflict and how, subsequently, they reflected and fulfilled the need for postwar reconsolidation. Just like comics, movies, documentaries, plays, and songs all aim to convey a message or express a feeling. John Mullen specifically addresses the issues of WWI British soldier songs created to fulfill the soldiers' needs to be vulgar and dissenting that were not satisfied by already existing, more often politically correct, music-hall songs. This study explores how the songs have been differently interpreted over time as either patriotic or anti-militarist. This tension is explored in the form of a paradox between what soldiers experience (war) and what they seek (peace) in Liliane Louvel's interpretation of Stanley Spencer's masterful paintings for the Burghclere Memorial. This dualism has also been exploited by American presidential speeches, especially for Veterans' Day and Memorial Day. Gilles Chamerois considers the treatment of war in Terrence Malick's *The Thin Red Line* from the highly philosophical perspective of Emmanuel Levinas's encompassing concepts such as infinity and totality, as opposed to hostility and fragmentation. Furthermore, Chamerois ponders the possible validity of an approach of dialogue rather than monologue or voice-over as a way to combat the dangers of alterity in war. In some documentaries, the first-person view nevertheless offers a closer look at the action, helping the public to better understand the soldier's experience, as illustrated in David Haigron's analysis of the award winning television series *Our War*. These moments of insight into the soldier's recollection of his time at war can be expressed between the waves of attacks, in the dull and idle moments of solitude. These burdens are commonplace in Georges Fournier's consideration of Peter Watkins's film about the eponymous *Diary of the Unknown Soldier*. He notes how, as days go by, hope and joy lose meaning and are swiftly replaced by pain and grief with the unalterable and probable reality of a sudden and inglorious death. There is no doubt that recollections of war vary according to the viewpoint from which they are remembered. Nicole Cloarec reflects on how two British films, *Oh! What a Lovely War* and *War Requiem*, use elaborate staging techniques as well as cinematic devices to create an antimilitarist spectacle. Moreover, even though the overwhelming message is one that opposes war, both films also include an underlying reverence for the fallen.

The fourth and final part of this collective expands on the role of native peoples in war memories. Corinne David-Ives considers the politics surrounding the effective integration of the Maori Battalion within the New Zealand Army and illustrates how this great achievement has helped to propel a positive image of the nation to the international community as well as to foster equality within the country. However, David-Ives mentions how the policy adopted in the early 1960s ended the existence of distinct indigenous units in the military, creating a generational gap. It is an unfortunate reality that not all of those who fought in wars are acknowledged. Until the early 1990s, this was the case for the so called Black Diggers, Australian aboriginals. Elizabeth Rechniewski explores the years of neglect followed by a recent surge in appreciation of these veterans in the context of a rapidly evolving and increasingly multicultural Australia. This volume concludes with Lorie-Anne Duech-Rainville's detailed study of how Joseph Boyden's *Three Day Road* interweaves the fate of Cree soldiers during the Great War and that of their ancestors after the signing of the James Bay Treaty. In both these related contexts, the concepts of home, the modern and traditional mind, residential schools, and the native circle are evoked as a means to better understand the true nature of indigenous reality.

The mediatization, performance, interpretation, and rewriting of facts and events during and after wars are central to the reflections in this volume. As we have seen, patriotic fervour, federating or demobilizing discourses, resistance, conscientious objection, injury and trauma, and propaganda and counter-propaganda contribute to the shaping of individual and collective memory and further the reconsideration of long-held truths in the light of new discoveries and with the benefit of hindsight. This collective illustrates how the art of commemoration in all its expressions influences how we remember war. The study of war memory is pluridisciplinary in essence, fragmented by definition, and impacts people's minds in a striking manner. The international contributions to this volume offer a rich tapestry of methodologies, interpretations, and specialities as can be seen from the biographical details of the authors. Despite their different academic backgrounds and experiences, they all share the same goal: to address the complexity and importance of war memories in order to better inform and hopefully highlight war through clear, accessible, and cutting-edge research.

NOTE

1 "Introduction: Mapping Memory," in *War and Remembrance*, edited by Jay Winter and Emmanuel Sivan (Cambridge: Cambridge University Press, 1999), 1.

PART ONE

Reappropriating History: Monuments and Commemorations

1

Their Forgotten War: Veterans and the Korean War in American Memory

CHRISTINE KNAUER

John Connolly, a Korean War veteran, once succinctly expressed what he and many other veterans felt about their status and that of the war in collective memory and history: "Most of the Korean veterans are very bitter, including myself, because nobody recognizes what they did as being very important. People didn't even know the Korean War was going on. They didn't know anything about it."[1] While the Second World War occupies an essential place in American memory and history in the best sense and the Vietnam War in the worst sense, the Korean War has maintained a problematic position. Indeed, Korean War veterans feel "caught between two wars. On the one side there are the World War II veterans who were well received when they came home ... At the other end of the spectrum are the Vietnam veterans who in many ways have been better able to verbalize something the Korean War guys secretly would like to do, which is to call attention to themselves and their plight."[2] Even before the Vietnam War had exhausted all the commemorative capacities of the public mind, remembering the Korean War in the United States had been a difficult task.

While both North and South Koreans are confronted with the war's devastating effects, its legacy, and memory, the Korean War in the United States has become known as the "forgotten war" among academics and non-academics alike. Although the conflict in Korea was the first "hot war" of the Cold War era (and a very violent and costly one at that), its status as a "limited war" – which President Harry S. Truman diminutively and repeatedly described as a "police action" – did not produce the same "allencompassing global threat

1

Their Forgotten War: Veterans and the Korean War in American Memory

CHRISTINE KNAUER

John Connolly, a Korean War veteran, once succinctly expressed what he and many other veterans felt about their status and that of the war in collective memory and history: "Most of the Korean veterans are very bitter, including myself, because nobody recognizes what they did as being very important. People didn't even know the Korean War was going on. They didn't know anything about it."[1] While the Second World War occupies an essential place in American memory and history in the best sense and the Vietnam War in the worst sense, the Korean War has maintained a problematic position. Indeed, Korean War veterans feel "caught between two wars. On the one side there are the World War II veterans who were well received when they came home … At the other end of the spectrum are the Vietnam veterans who in many ways have been better able to verbalize something the Korean War guys secretly would like to do, which is to call attention to themselves and their plight."[2] Even before the Vietnam War had exhausted all the commemorative capacities of the public mind, remembering the Korean War in the United States had been a difficult task.

While both North and South Koreans are confronted with the war's devastating effects, its legacy, and memory, the Korean War in the United States has become known as the "forgotten war" among academics and non-academics alike. Although the conflict in Korea was the first "hot war" of the Cold War era (and a very violent and costly one at that), its status as a "limited war" – which President Harry S. Truman diminutively and repeatedly described as a "police action" – did not produce the same "all-encompassing global threat to humankind" as the Second World War had undoubtedly done.[3] The Korean War has always been compared to previous or subsequent wars, and has hardly assumed a position or validity of its own. All too often, its veterans, like John Connolly, felt that their fates and the sacrifices they had made for the nation and for a foreign country were downplayed and ultimately overlooked.[4]

This chapter takes a closer look at the memory and commemoration of the Korean War in the United States. It examines how the United States has commemorated a war that did not correspond with the (alleged) triumphs of the preceding wars in which the country was involved. Specifically, it investigates how Korean War veterans in the United States have felt their war and their service have been remembered and how they should be remembered. In trying to shape the public memory of their war, Korean War veterans ultimately sought to differentiate themselves from Vietnam veterans and instead to close ranks with the victorious "Greatest Generation" of the Second World War.

WHILE THE WAR WENT ON

After the end of the Second World War, Korea was separated into an American-controlled South and a communist North under Russian jurisdiction along the 38th parallel. The ultimate goal was the reunification of the two parts; however, political and ideological circumstances made its realization improbable. On 25 June 1950, North Korean troops crossed the border into South Korea to attain unification by force. They advanced quickly and South Korean troops needed the support of their American patron.[5] After the United States entered the war under the UN flag on 30 June 1950, victories against the North Koreans were rare. Initially, General Douglas MacArthur, the UN commander, promised presumptuously to push back the North Korean troops "in the shortest possible time."[6] The reality, however, proved to be very different in the little understood conflict.[7] American troops lacked the training and combat readiness for ground combat with an unexpectedly well-trained and well-positioned enemy, who showed great fighting abilities and often relied on guerrilla warfare tactics that took American troops by surprise. Ultimately, the enemy outnumbered and overpowered the American troops. An American soldier stated in frustration, "I don't know where the hell they get them all. We kill them by the thousands and still they come."[8]

The superiority of American troops and equipment, which both the military leadership and the home front had anticipated, did not manifest itself in Korea. Owing to the lack of preparedness, equipment, and tactics, as well as racial arrogance and ignorance, the first two months of the war were an almost complete failure.[9]

As news from the war zone grew shockingly negative, the American public began to question whether American intervention in this distant Asian country was as easy a task as they had predicted or at least hoped it would be. With a series of defeats and a high number of casualties in the first few months of combat, the Korean War's rocky course soon disconcerted the nation. Yet, after a string of victories and the successful crossing of the 38th parallel at the Chinese border in the fall of 1950, a UN victory seemed imminent. General MacArthur boldly predicted that the troops would be home by Christmas 1950. Korea would then be unified under Western auspices and peace reestablished. However, the Chinese intervention in the Korean War in November 1950 marked a serious blow to the UN war effort as well as to the public's support for the war. By January 1951, a Gallup poll listed that 66 per cent of respondents favoured a US withdrawal from the war while 49 per cent believed the intervention in Korea was in itself a mistake.[10] China's intervention instigated a long stalemate with heavy fighting that exhausted both the troops in Korea and the American people's patience with the war at home. Beginning in July 1951, the peace talks between the two sides did little to alleviate Americans' concerns. In this turbulent course with few victories, the American public focused its attention on domestic issues. One somewhat disillusioned veteran commented, "You expect that the people would be more concerned about your service in Korea, but people showed indifference and were more concerned about their own interests."[11]

While the peace talks dragged on, press reports on the war decreased and disappeared from many newspapers, especially from front-page coverage. Increasingly, Americans wanted out of a war that many had lost interest in a long time before. In his 1952 election campaign, Dwight D. Eisenhower made use of Americans' frustration with a war that was going nowhere. Pledging to personally "go to Korea," the revered World War II general promised "to bring the Korean War to an early and honorable end," planning to eventually "Koreanize" the conflict and return the American troops home.[12] Following the speech, support for Eisenhower rose exponentially and he won the election. Thus, one of the most famous and respected US generals had seemingly answered Americans' longing for a swift end to a tedious war.[13] In April 1953, over half of the respondents in a Gallup poll wanted a peace settlement even if that meant that the UN troops had to make concessions.[14] The option of ending the war by returning to the status quo ante at the 38th parallel became increasingly acceptable among Americans.[15]

When in July 1953, after two years of deliberations, both sides finally agreed on the cease-fire and armistice, most Americans were certainly relieved that the fighting and dying had come to an end. However, there was no all-encompassing jubilation either in the press or in the streets. Ultimately, its less-than-victorious ending without real peace and a continued separation of Korea along the 38th parallel prevented the Korean War from being remembered as an unambiguous and heroic American triumph. Rather, awareness emerged that "the Korean armistice, important and vital as it is to us and the United Nations, will only be a curtain raiser for the bigger political problems that we will be facing in that immense area once the guns of the Korean war cease to roar."[16] At the end of the Korean War, more conflicts with active American involvement loomed on the horizon.

The public seemed increasingly reluctant to reflect on a war that did not live up to the imagined standards of the American victory culture which World War II had generated.[17] Neither the Korean War nor its veterans were cause for celebration. Little attention was paid to returning veterans, who were expected to blend into the "normal" life of the economically flourishing 1950s without many repercussions. Indeed, veterans felt that even the government did not show as much interest in them upon their return as it had for the veterans of the Second World War. "In response, some Korean War veterans 'quietly resumed their civilian lives … and set out to forget Korea,' determining that 'if we thought that we would receive any lasting public reward for our service, we were mistaken.'"[18] Their homecoming was not celebrated and did not make waves at a national level like the victorious returning soldiers of the preceding war to whom they were compared. People were ready and willing to move on quickly and leave the war behind. Even the creation of Veterans' Day only a year after the end of the Korean War did not result in a boost for Korean War commemorations and memorials. Knowledge, awareness, and memory of the fate of American soldiers, let alone that of Korean and

Chinese soldiers and civilians during and after the Korean War, have remained basic and problematic. The American victory culture that seemed to have permeated American society with the victorious end of the Second World War was disrupted by the unpopular war in Korea. However, the war could not fully put an end to this culture; rather the lessons it might have provided were neither learned nor taken seriously. "Korea became the war of lost lessons. Most conspicuously, we learned – and then forgot – that the commitment of American forces does not automatically assure victory."[19] Hence, remembering and commemorating the Korean War was a difficult task even before its end and before the Vietnam War began to dominate public discourse and memory.

THE FEAR OF COMMUNIST INFILTRATION

Accusations of "brainwashing" or of veterans falling prey to communism through powerful indoctrination at the hands of the enemy further tainted the memory of the war in the United States. "Brainwashing" was nothing new, as it ultimately encompassed "the studied application of systematic starvation, mental death threats and other hazards, filthy living conditions and a generally degrading treatment of the individual," meant to force the captives to cooperate with the captors.[20] Military officials were well aware that in all wars a number of prisoners of war collaborated with their captors to gain special treatment, which was often a strategy of survival. In that respect, the Second World War did not differ much from the Korean War. In its report on the POW question in 1955, the Secretary of Defense's Advisory Committee on Prisoners of War stated, "At the end of World War II the consensus of the experts was this: it is virtually impossible for anyone to resist a determined interrogator."[21] Furthermore, the military and the press reassured Americans that, "Out of 3,500 prisoners, only 90 have been identified as 'progressives.' Of these, Army officials believe that fewer than 30 showed themselves really susceptible to enemy propaganda, and some of the 30 had histories of pro-Communist leanings before induction. The vast majority of the US prisoners met the challenge well. They proved that the US soldier fighting indoctrinated Communists is a pretty well indoctrinated fighting man himself."[22]

Nevertheless, the issue of "brainwashing" and collaboration gained a life of its own and came to encompass "a near-magical process that turned victims into robots"[23] programmed to spread and protect communism abroad and upon their return to the United States. As POWs reported reeducation sessions in which they had to undergo teaching in communist ideology, many Americans at home began to panic. Tales of American soldiers cooperating with their captors for special treatment made the pages of newspapers all across the nation. The term "progressives" assigned to soldiers allegedly collaborating with their communist captors represented another powerful all-encompassing term that negatively penetrated public discourse on the war and its soldiers.

Suspicions and doubts about soldiers increased when twenty-one American POWs refused to return to the United States upon their release from POW camps in Korea. An essential part of the armistice agreement was that prisoners could choose whether they wanted to go back to their home country or stay with their captors.[24] Americans at home expected the thousands of captured American soldiers to return the US elatedly. Thus, it came as a complete shock to them that American soldiers stayed with communist captors voluntarily. The news that tens of thousands of North Korean and Chinese soldiers refused repatriation fell to the wayside amidst numerous reports on the American "turncoats"[25] who chose to stay in an "extremely backward, dreadfully impoverished" communist country.[26]

Many articles in the press spewed "alarmist language" on the indoctrination and subsequent response of American captives, which unsettled readers on the home front. This tone resonated profoundly with the American public and its deep-seated suspicions of external and internal subversion. The American defectors represented "weak-willed, malleable" individuals "unable to withstand the ordeal of captivity and the enemy's manipulation."[27] The reports confirmed America's greatest fear, fuelled by years of McCarthyism, that communists could subvert and instrumentalize regular American citizens, and more so, American soldiers.[28] The trial and execution of Ethel and Julius Rosenberg in 1953 seemed to reveal that communist spies had infiltrated the United States and lived unsuspected among regular American citizens. This made the threat all the more tangible for many Americans.[29] Everybody became a suspect, especially POWs under Chinese indoctrination.[30]

According to the tale of the seemingly omnipresent and powerful "brainwashing," POWs in Korea did not conduct themselves heroically. They appeared "inadequate and disappointing" in comparison to "World War II captives, who, at least in popular film and literature, never gave in to adversity and always comported themselves with exemplary courage."[31] Thus, while POWs returning from the Second World War did not garner much negative attention, soldiers coming home from Korea, especially POWs, came under close scrutiny for suspected communist infiltration.[32] In a later interview on his experience in and after the war, Robert Jones, a Korean War veteran, expressed his utter disappointment that "Those Americans interviewing us after we were liberated never seemed to be that interested in our wounds or diseases. They really weren't interested in a damn thing except did we collaborate?"[33] It seemed that POWs felt victimized yet again. This time, however, it was by their own people who should have celebrated their return.

For years, newspapers regularly reported on the twenty-one soldiers and their fate in the communist world.[34] Moreover, the American public as well as the American military worried about the political and ideological state of its soldiers. A veteran commented, "There had been some pretty bad press about prisoner behavior, and the Army was responding to these allegations. I believe they flagged our records for seven years."[35] Upon the return of these soldiers, the military investigated them more closely and launched courts martial. Although it ultimately found their behaviour "fine indeed," a new Code of Conduct was introduced in 1955, which inadvertently confirmed powerful and persistent rumours of "backsliding or weakness … among our prisoners."[36] The allegedly "disgraceful" behaviour of Korean War POWs had developed into a negative reference point for a growing number of military officials and American civilians.

The alleged weakness and susceptibility of American soldiers to "brainwashing" found its way into popular culture and public memory more than any other Korean War "myth." *The Manchurian Candidate*, a 1959 thriller novel that was turned into a popular movie starring Frank Sinatra and Laurence Harvey in 1962, encapsulated society's suspicions towards returning veterans.[37] The book and the movie tell the story of American Korean War soldiers brainwashed and used as communist sleeper attackers in the United States. Communist indoctrination had so altered one POW that, when shown the queen of hearts, he would act on command and kill without reflecting on or questioning the order. The plot managed to hit a nerve and captivate the minds of the public. A book review in the *Chicago Daily Tribune* called it "an exciting, brilliantly told story, peopled with characters symbolic of our times."[38]

The Manchurian Candidate was not the only film that dealt with the psychological state of American POWs in Korea. Five years earlier, the film *Prisoner of War,* starring Ronald Reagan, was screened in American theatres. Shot in twenty-eight days on a very limited budget, the film built upon and played with the theme of American soldiers in captivity showing weaknesses and collaborating with the enemy. In the title role, Reagan plays a US Army intelligence officer infiltrating a North Korean prison camp under cover as a collaborator to investigate the mistreatment of its prisoners. Although the movie was meant to reveal the atrocities that American soldiers and their allies had to experience, it still used and thereby confirmed the image of American POWs allegedly in collaboration with the enemy captor for their own advantage.[39] Despite their box office failures, *Prisoner of War* and the various adaptations of *The Manchurian Candidate* had a profound effect on the public mind and interpretations of the Korean War. The questionable image of American soldiers as impressionable and easily lured into the enemy's supposedly destructive ideology augmented the Korean War veterans' exclusion from celebratory and heroic discourses that were associated with soldiers of the Second World War. This further complicated the integration of the war and its soldiers into America's national myths. Fear of the "brainwashing" of not only unsuspecting civilians but also of trained soldiers who represented and defended the American nation remained strong in the memory of the war and its soldiers. As historian Charles S. Young points out, "Prisoners provided no way to see Korea in a more positive light; they were central to both the war and its dissipated memory."[40]

Unsurprisingly, veterans were aware of and shocked by the longevity of the allegations that books and the movies so persuasively perpetuated.[41] They felt obliged to fend off such assertions, which also threatened their identification with a masculine hero soldier. The "brainwashed" soldier seemed to prove an entire generation of soldiers' incapability to "man up" and stand up to an enemy who had allegedly managed to drain the military rank and file, and further weaken their already feeble fighting capacity. According to the *Los Angeles Times*, "cynical" Korean War veterans "say that Korea's greatest contribution to the world was the addition of the words *bug out* and *brainwash* to the English lexicon."[42] In an interview, Dr Glenn P. Smith, a clinical psychologist, commented on the frustration many veterans felt: "The Korean prisoners tend to feel a deep-seated resentment because of the labels that have been inappropriately ascribed to them – things like critics lumping them all together and calling them brainwashed and the whole thing about the forgotten war ... But the Korean War veterans were raised in a time when one didn't speak about what was going on underneath the surface. So they have trouble verbalizing their resentment."[43]

NOTHING TO SAY ABOUT THE KOREAN WAR

With its problematic course and tarnished reputation, the Korean War and its veterans lacked relevance in the public imagination and popular culture. In his award-wining book, *The Soldier's Tale: Bearing Witness to Modern War*, Samuel Hynes, a professor of literature and himself a war veteran, did not include the Korean War, cynically arguing, "I have nothing to say for example about the war in Korea, a war that came and went without glory, and left no mark on American imaginations – though nearly as many died there as in Vietnam."[44] In the wake of the forty-year commemoration of the war's beginning, the *Washington Post* called it "an inconclusive, ill-understood conflict" that "quickly faded in American memory."[45] The war garnered the reputation of being "forgotten" – a label that permeated popular as well as academic accounts. Almost every academic book or article on the conflict has referred to its allegedly neglected and forgotten status in American consciousness.[46] Although this reputation might now be a cliché, as noted by Leonard Bushkoff of the *Christian Science Monitor* in 1995,[47] or a construct, there remains more truth to the overused image.

While the Second World War and the Vietnam War managed to produce a plethora of cultural symbols, signifiers, or artifacts, the Korean War has remained underrepresented or represented negatively in American cultural memory. Korean War veterans have been especially affected by this lack of representation. Reflecting on the status of the Korean War, veteran and author James Brady stated: "World War I had Faulkner and Hemingway and *All Quiet on the Western Front* and 'Over There.' World War II had Mailer and Jim Jones and Mister Roberts and Irwin Shaw and all those great songs. Vietnam is a cottage industry. But except for a shelf of good histories and a wonderful memoir by Marty Russ called *The Last Parallel*, Korea didn't inspire many books or movies, and no great songs. We didn't even have a protest song, no Bob Dylan. All we had was … *M*A*S*H*."[48] Even *M*A*S*H*, the popular movie about a mobile army surgical hospital in the Korean War that was subsequently turned into a long-running television show, was and is often still interpreted as a mere artistic cover for reflections on the Vietnam War. In the words of sociologist James H. Wittebols, "In essence, *M*A*S*H* used the setting of the war in the past [Korea] as a means of commenting on the present [Vietnam]."[49] Compared to Vietnam and the two World Wars, only a limited number of movies have been made on the Korean War.[50] In public consciousness, the Korean War was not worth remembering; it was neither good nor bad, neither a total victory nor a complete failure.

Korean War veterans complained about their societal recognition and commemoration, or rather the lack thereof. Many felt that they had not received sufficient gratitude for the sacrifices they had made for a foreign people and the American nation during a war that took place in a country about which, ultimately, nobody really cared. In his memoirs published over forty years after the conflict, one veteran expressed what many others felt during and after the war: "The Korean War wasn't popular, and it was called a police action; war was never declared, even though it lasted for three years. People were enjoying the good life after the end of World War II and most weren't concerned, unless they had a loved one over there. After all, it was ten thousand miles away and not many were losing any sleep over it. Our war wasn't a war the American people could get behind and support, because most of them felt that the generals had their hands tied and weren't allowed to win … Heroes' welcomes didn't occur to us then [upon coming home], and they still don't to this day."[51] Whereas Second World War veterans were revered and Vietnam veterans gradually stylized as tragic and traumatized victims of circumstance in a horrible and unjust war, Korean War veterans felt that their image in the public mind remained hazy and suppressed.

Generally, it is not uncommon for soldiers or veterans to feel insufficiently honoured and commemorated by the people for whom they put their lives on the line. Veterans of the Second World War, who have received recognition locally and nationally since 1945, have also claimed to experience national ingratitude toward their sacrifices. In the wake of the opening of the Second World War Memorial in Washington, DC, in 2004, one World War II veteran noted, "I don't understand. Shouldn't it have been before the Korean War Memorial? Even Vietnam? I'm not anti those memorials. They deserve theirs, but I don't know why it took so long. At least some of us are left to see it."[52] Another contended, "They honored Vietnam. They honored everyone else but World War II."[53] These assumptions of not having been properly honoured, which Erika Doss calls "ahistorical" in the case of Second World War veterans, seem omnipresent among veterans. Factuality notwithstanding, the sense of being unappreciated or at least underappreciated is a reality for many veterans.[54] For those veterans of the Korean War, the war's recognition and commemoration has been less profuse, frequent, and less flamboyant. They have subjectively experienced their position in public memory as that of undervalued fighters for American values.

LEAVING A MARK

That the Vietnam War veterans received a memorial on the National Mall only seven years after the war had ended in disaster deeply upset many Korean War veterans, among others. For decades prior to the establishment of the Vietnam War Memorial, no suggestions for additions on the Mall had been made. With the opening of the Vietnam Veterans Memorial, campaigns for war memorials on the Mall resurfaced in quickly growing numbers. In the words of Gary Scott, chief historian of the National Park Service, a memorial represented "the expression of one generation trying to pass down their values to succeeding generations in durable materials: stone, marble and bronze."[55] Years later, journalist James Reston Jr sardonically commented in the *New York Times Magazine* on this somewhat jealous frustration: "Other wars are envious of Vietnam. It's as if that dirty little kid down the block slipped under the fence and stole all the glory. Now proper folks want their due."[56] Inspired by the success of the campaign for a Vietnam War memorial, veterans of the Korean War started their own campaign for a memorial on the Mall. They wanted "patriotic space"[57] to commemorate and honour the sacrifices they had made.

During the campaign for a Korean War memorial in 1986, Representative Stanford E. Parris from Virginia referred to the war's ignored state in American consciousness and memory, exclaiming before Congress: "It is deeply disturbing to me that, after 36 years, there is not yet a memorial in our Nation's Capital to honor these great Americans who served and sacrificed in the Korean War — the only group of war veterans not to be so honored. These individuals have been leap-frogged by time overlooked and ignored. It is within our power to see that this disservice is not permitted to go unremedied."[58] The *Washington Post*, among many papers, politicians, and interest groups, supported the endeavour: "Whatever – but get this project going now ... When it comes to service, courage, injury and death of these individuals, there should be no 'ranking' of wars by 'importance.'"[59] A manifestation of national gratitude and honour expressed in stone or steel was needed in order to make sense and assign national significance to the sacrifices made during the Korean War. One Korean War veteran from New York exclaimed, "If we don't have a memorial put up, no one will remember us, not only as individuals, but as a group, and what we have done."[60]

Korean War veterans felt deeply about finally being able to hand something meaningful to the next generations and therewith change history. Most veterans considered a memorial on the Mall to be the only appropriate and adequate way to commemorate, as it would "teach those who follow that we fought so they could live in freedom."[61] A monument honouring the war and its veterans was interpreted as the major force to establish a valid war memory and incorporate it into the personal and national identity construct. The campaigning paid off: ten years after Representative Parris's plea, the memorial was dedicated on the Mall in Washington, DC. Located southeast of the Lincoln Memorial, the Korean War Veterans Memorial consists of nineteen larger-than-life human statues that represent all military branches. Its central inscription reads "Freedom is not Free," reminding and calling on visitors to serve. In design and meaning, the memorial is "a complicated, multidimensional response to the Vietnam Veterans Memorial and the questions it raised on the Mall about remembering American wars and American soldiers."[62]

Architecture critics were mostly left unimpressed and partially appalled by the design. An article in *Architecture Magazine* called it "atrocious," while others complained about the apparent overcrowdedness of the Mall. In his *New York Times* article, Reston criticized the memorial as "a sign that we now have an entrenched quasi-governmental lobby advancing the cause of glorifying past American military conflicts."[63] Veterans, however, were mostly elated and praised it as a manifestation of the Korean War's changing status from a forgotten war into a war remembered and revered in American collective memory. The monument's rather traditional design, which ultimately celebrates heroism and the unquestioned righteousness of the war's cause, enticed and satisfied most veterans. Angus Deming, who had served in Korea, wrote in *Newsweek*, "That was us in Korea, the way we were, too ... But our mind-set was also different: we were closer to the World War II generation, and we answered the call simply because our country needed us. Our only anger, really, was that so much bravery, so much uncomplaining devotion to duty, went unrecognized for so long. Now that lingering bitterness has been laid to rest at last."[64] Deming's statement is representative of the attempt to extricate Korean War veterans and their war from the American defeat in Vietnam and to align it instead with victory culture and the "greatest generation" of the Second World War. To its veterans, the Korean War was to be remembered as a "good war," not as a futile mission that ended in a draw.[65]

The dedication of the Korean War Veterans Memorial was used as a (re)affirmation of values perceived to be innately American and as a method of discarding self-doubt. An editorial in the *Washington Post* exemplified this reinterpretation of the war: "But although the aggressor was not unseated (the goal of Gen. MacArthur's rollback strategy), North Korea was repulsed and South Korea saved. Time and space were bought for a competition of systems in which the South came to exemplify democratic and free-market growth, while North Korea stayed a stunted and dangerous hermit state. If there is yet a chance that things may go better, it is because the United States did what it had to in the war and then stayed the course, to this day."[66] The celebrations surrounding the dedication of the memorial and, five years later, the fiftieth anniversary of the war, turned the war and its ending into a success story. Furthermore, these celebrations were marked by interpretations of war and national identity constructs, which sought to make sense of past wars and the possible missions of future US wars. The transformation that South Korea underwent under American tutelage has been understood as proof of the superiority of capitalism and the American way of life. Moreover, the memorial turned the Korean War into a symbol of multiculturalism and racial understanding.[67]

By now, numerous states in the United States, from New York to Utah to California, have their own Korean War Veterans Memorials. Together, they are meant to show, in the words of a press release for the New Jersey Korean War Memorial, that "Finally the courage and sacrifice of so many will forever stand tall in our community."[68] The iconography of the Korean War Veterans Memorial in Washington has often been drawn upon in the creation of state memorials. Dedicated in 2000, the design of the New Jersey Korean War Memorial replicates the Washington-based design in its realistic depiction of resilient suffering and heroism. It consists of a 12-foot-high statue of "The Mourning Soldier" holding dog tags and a group of racially diverse soldiers "under fire." It also includes a wall upon which the names of the New Jersey dead are engraved and a statue of two soldiers carrying a wounded comrade.[69] For veterans, the memorials seem to have provided closure in the quest for recognition that they had envisioned for so long.

However, the fight over the appropriate way of remembering the Korean War is ongoing on both the local and national levels. References to the war's "forgotten" or relegated status in collective memory have reappeared frequently, imbuing the war with a singular mythology. The site of New Jersey's Korean War memorial has upset many veterans since its revelation in 1998. Tucked between casinos "within a short walk of a boardwalk pawn shop, a fortune teller, and vendors who sell sexually explicit T-shirts," the memorial found a place in Atlantic City, as no other community wanted to host it. While some argued that it was the best place for a memorial to be seen, others were incensed by the location and felt it was, yet again, a manifestation of their devalued position in society and its collective memory.[70] Furthermore, only two years after the grand dedication ceremony, and despite its enormous cost of $18 million, the memorial in Washington started to fall apart. The shading trees surrounding the memorial were dying. The memorial's pool pump was failing, filling the pool with algae and the fountain with dirty rainwater. Paving stones began to become uneven and sink into the ground. A war veteran indignantly described the memorial as "an insult to those men who are still suffering from the war."[71] Another veteran evoked the war's "forgotten status," stating, "That was the forgotten war and this is the forgotten memorial. Considering how long it took to build it, it will take another 20 to fix it."[72]

Since 2011, the Korean War Veterans Association has campaigned for an addition to the Korean War Veterans Memorial in Washington, DC. Invoking their forgotten status in the campaign for funding and approval, they point to clear shortcomings of the existing memorial "which clearly honors those who *served* in the Korean War, [but] it does not appropriately honor those who *sacrificed* so much in the war!"[73] They seek to add a "Wall of Remembrance" with the names of all who died in actions to finally "bring to the attention of the visitors the true cast of 'Freedom is not Free.'"[74] Reminiscent of the Vietnam Veterans Memorial with its long list of names etched into marble, the wall made out of laminated glass surrounding the Pool of Remembrance also plans to list the number of the wounded, listed as missing in action, and of the POWs, as well as the number of members of the Korean Augmentation to the US Army (KATUSAs), the Republic of Korea Armed Forces, and of the nations of the UN Command. While the addition to the memorial intends to reflect the Korean and international character of the war, a trait that the memorial's current design mostly lacks, it continues to remember predominantly "the magnitude of sacrifice made by Americans during this conflict."[75] But as American funding of the project remains scarce, "those looking for the necessary financing are feeling forgotten all over again."[76] After three failed attempts of passing a bill in Congress, the House of Representative on 24 February 2016 and the Senate on 16 June 2016 have voted for HR 1475, the latest legislation to initiate the construction of the "Wall of Remembrance." It now awaits consideration in the Committee on Energy and Natural Resources.[77] The veterans' search for recognition and closure seems far from over.

NOTES

1 John Connolly, veteran of the 23rd Infantry Regiment, the 2nd Infantry Division in Korea. Quoted in *European Intelligence Wire* (25 July 2003).

2 Lewis H. Carlson, *Remembered Prisoners of a Forgotten War: An Oral History of Korean War POWs* (New York: St Martin's Press, 2002), 226.

3 This assessment was first made in 1954 by Douglas W. Gallez, then an instructor of English at West Point and later an influential researcher in cinema studies. It was later rephrased by Ian S. Scott. Douglas W. Gallez, "Patterns in Wartime Documentaries," *Quarterly of Film Radio and Television* 10 (1955): 125–35; Ian S. Scott, "Why We Fight and Projections of America: Frank Capra, Robert Riskin, and Making of World War II Propaganda," in *Why We Fought: America's Wars in Film and History*, edited by Peter C. Rollins and John E. O'Connor (Lexington: University Press of Kentucky, 2008), 242–3.

4 Paul G. Pierpaoli states that the Korean War might have "'inherited' too much myth from World War II. And on the other hand, perhaps it 'generated' too little myth of its own." Paul G. Pierpaoli, "Beyond Collective Amnesia: A Korean War Retrospective," *International Social Science Review* 76, nos 3 & 4, 92–102. See also: Suhi Choi, *Embattled Memories: Contested Meanings in Korean War Memorials* (Reno: University of Nevada Press, 2014), especially chapter 4; Suhi Choi, "Mythologizing Memories: A Critique of the Utah Korean War Memorial," *The Public Historian* 34 (February 2012): 61–82. On the myths and memories surrounding the Second World War, see John Bodnar, *The 'Good War' in American Memory* (Baltimore: Johns Hopkins University Press, 2010).

5 Numerous books and articles exist on the military course of the Korean War. For a first overview, see: Clay Blair, *The Forgotten War: America in Korea* (New York: Times Books, 1987); Bruce Cumings, *The Origins of the Korean War I: Liberation and the Emergence of Separate Regimes 1945–1947* (Princeton, NJ: Princeton University Press, 1981); Bruce Cumings and Kathryn Weathersby, "An Exchange on Korean War Origins," *Cold War International History Project Bulletin* 6/7 (Winter 1995/96): 120–22; Bruce Cumings, *The Origins of the Korean War II: The Roaring of the Cataract 1947–1950* (Princeton, NJ: Princeton University Press, 1990); Allen R. Millett, "A Reader's Guide to the Korean War," *Journal of Military History* 61 (July 1997): 583–97; Millett, "The Korean War: A 50-Year Critical Historiography," *Journal of Strategic Studies* 24 (March 2001): 188–224.

6 General Douglas MacArthur quoted in "MacArthur Pledges Victory in 'Shortest Possible Time,'" *New York Times*, 17 July 1950, 1.

7 Revisionist historians like Bruce Cumings and John Merrill argue that the United States and its allies all too often ignored the internal and colonial aspects of the conflict, but viewed it solely through the prism of the Cold War and the fight against communism. William Stueck provides a good overview of revisionism and the Korean War in Stueck, "Revisionism and the Korean War," *Journal of Conflict Studies* 22, no. 1 (2002): 17–27.

8 Lieutenant Colonel Robert L. Wadlington quoted in Ralph Reatsorth, "Yank Tells of Struggle for Taejon," *Hartford Courant*, 23 July 1950, 16. On climate and territory see, for example, Hanson Baldwin, "Korea's Battle Picture: Our Defense Is Stiffer," *New York Times*, 23 July 1950, E5.

9 On racial arrogance see, for example, Michael S. Sherry, *In the Shadow of War: The United States since the 1930s* (New Haven: Yale University Press), 179–80.

10 George H. Gallup, ed., *The Gallup Poll: Public Opinion 1935–1971, Volume Two* (New York: Random House, 1972), 961. For a detailed study on the Korean War, public opinion, and its formation see Steven Casey, *Selling the Korean War: Propaganda, Politics, and Public Opinion 1950–1953* (Oxford: Oxford University Press, 2008).

11 Quoted in Melinda Pash, *In the Shadow of the Greatest Generation: The Americans Who Fought the Korean War* (New York: New York University Press, 2013), 186. See also Peter S. Kindsvatter, *American Soldiers: Ground Combat in the World Wars, Korea, and Vietnam* (Lawrence, KS: University of Kansas Press, 2003), 134.

12 Dwight D. Eisenhower, "I Shall Go to Korea." http://tucnak.fsv.cuni.cz/~calda/Documents/1950s/Ike_Korea_52.html (accessed 9 November 2014).

13 On the importancc of the speech, see Martin J. Medhurst, "Text and Context in the 1952 Presidential Campaign: Eisenhower's 'I Shall Go to Korea' Speech," *Presidential Quarterly* 30 (September 2000), 464–84.

14 Gallup Poll, 1140.

15 Gallup Poll, 1949–58.

16 Polyzoides, "Korean Armistice May Bring Crises," *Los Angeles Times*, 15 June 1953, 8. The article's author was Dr Adamantos T. Polyzoides, a professor of international relations and political science at the University of Southern California and regular columnist of the *Los Angeles Times*.

17 See for example Thomas Englehardt, *The End of Victory Culture: Cold War America and the Disillusioning of a Generation* (Amherst: University of Massachusetts, 1995).

18 Pash, *In the Shadow of the Greatest Generation*, 217.

19 Robert W. Gibson, "Korea: Remembering the War of Lost Lessons," *Los Angeles Times*, 18 August 1995, D2.

20 Anthony Leviero, "For the Brainwashed: Pity or Punishment?," *New York Times*, 14 August 1955, SM12.

21 "The Fight Continues after the Battle." http://military.laws.com/pow-report (accessed 10 October 2014).

22 "Tough Prisoners," *Time*, 21 September 1953, 30.

23 Charles S. Young, *Name, Rank, and Serial Number: Exploiting Korean War POWs at Home and Abroad* (New York: Oxford University Press, 2014), 143.

24 On prisoners of war in Korea and the armistice agreement, see Brian D. McKnight, *We Fight for Peace: Twenty-Tree American Soldiers, Prisoners of War, and "Turncoats" in the Korean War* (Kent, OH: Kent State University Press, 2014).

25 "Turncoats" was a regular epithet for the soldiers who refused repatriation. While historian Susan Lisa Carruthers references about 22,000 North Korean and Chinese soldiers refusing repatriation, Adam Zweiback references about 47,000. Susan Lisa Carruthers, *Cold War Captives: Imprisonment, Escape, and Brainwashing* (Berkeley: University of California Press, 2009); Adam J. Zweiback, "The 21 'Turncoat GIs': Nonrepatriations and the Political Culture of the Korean War," *The Historian* 60 (Winter 1998): 345–62.

26 Carruthers, *Cold War Captives*, 174, information on Korean War POWs and repatriation, 174–217.

27 Kyle A. Cuordileone, *Manhood and American Political Culture in the Cold War* (New York: Routledge, 2005), 81. On the three African American defectors, see Christine Knauer, *Let Us Fight as Free Men: Black Soldiers and Civil Rights* (Philadelphia: University of Pennsylvania Press, 2014).

28 Carruthers, *Cold War Captives*, 174–217.

29 See Ronald Radosh and Joyce Milton, *The Rosenberg File* (New Haven: Yale University Press, 1997).

30 See, for example, Pash, *In the Shadow of the Greatest Generation*, chapter 5.

31 Carlson, *Remembered Prisoners of a Forgotten War*, 3.

32 See, in detail, Carruthers, *Cold War Captives*. Young argues that the POW and repatriation issues played a, if not the, major role in forgetting the Korean War in the United States. Young, *Name, Rank, and Serial Number*, 175–81.

33 Carlson, *Remembered Prisoners of a Forgotten War*, 403; see also William Richardson, *Valleys of Death: A Memoir of the Korean War* (New York: Berkley Caliber, 2010), 312.

34 See, for example: "Turncoats Tell Visitors 'We Like It' in Red China," *Washington Post and Times Herald*, 12 September 1957, A9; "Turncoats Find a Limbo in China," *New York Times*, 19 November 1958, 5.

35 Carlson, *Remembered Prisoners of a Forgotten War*, 220.

36 "A Failure in Education," *Chicago Tribune*, 23 August 1955, 18; Carruthers, *Cold War Captives*, 206–13.

37 Matthew Frye Jacobson and Gaspar González, *What Have They Built You to Do? The Manchurian Candidate and Cold War America* (Minneapolis: University of Minnesota Press, 2006).
38 Richard Blakesley, "Human Time Bomb," *Chicago Daily Tribune*, 31 May 1959, C3.
39 Jacobson and González elaborate at length on the problematic message the film sends. Jacobson and González, *What Have They Built You to Do?*, 177.
40 Young, *Name, Rank, and Serial Number*, 182.
41 Jacobson and González, *What Have They Built to Do?*; Charles S. Young, "Missing Action: POW Films, Brainwashing, and the Korean War, 1954–1968," in *Cold War Culture and Society*, edited by Lori Lynn Bogle (New York: Taylor & Francis, 2001), 179–205.
42 Gibson, "Korea: Remembering the War of Lost Lessons," *Los Angeles Times*, 18 August 1995, D2. Emphasis in original.
43 Carlson, *Remembered Prisoners of a Forgotten War*, 227.
44 Samuel Hynes, *The Soldier's Tale: Bearing Witness to Modern War* (New York: A. Lane, 1997), xiv.
45 E.J. Dionno Jr, "Korea: The Bitter War Americans Forgot," 24 June 1990, A27; also quoted in Christine Knauer, "A Victory after All: Remembering the Korean War in the United States," in *We Are What We Remember: The American Past through Commemoration*, edited by Jeffrey L. Meriwether and Laura D'Amore (Newcastle upon Tyne: Cambridge Scholars Publishing, 2012), 154–74.
46 For "forgotten war" terminology in the press, see: Kate Stone Lombardi, "Belated Remembrance of the Forgotten War in Korea," *New York Times*, 26 May 1996, 13WC 1; David M. Shribman, "Remembering a Forgotten War," *Boston Globe*, 28 July 28 1995, 3; Dionno Jr, *Korea*, A27; Blair, *The Forgotten War*; Paul M. Edwards, *To Acknowledge a War: The Korean War in American Memory* (Westport, CT: Greenwood Press, 2000).
47 Leonard Bushkoff, "Beginning to Remember Korea," *Christian Science Monitor*, 8 August 1995, 20.
48 James Brady, "Last Call," *Washingtonian* 31 (December 1995), 76–7. Brady is the author of the Korean War memoir *The Coldest War* that television anchor Walter Cronkite, who coined the term "the Greatest Generation" for World War II soldiers, called "war reporting at its best – a graphic depiction, in all its horrors, of the war we've almost forgotten." James Brady, *The Coldest War: A Memoir of Korea* (New York: St Martin's Griffin), 2000.

49 James H. Wittebols. *Watching M*A*S*H Watching America: A Social History of the 1972–1983 Television Series* (Jefferson, NC: McFarland & Company, 1998), 16; Mike Budd and Clay Steinman, "M*A*S*H Mystified: Capitalization, Dematerialization, Idealization," *Cultural Critique* 10 (Autumn 1988): 59–75.

50 Tony Williams, "Beyond Fuller and M.A.S.H.: Korean War Representations: Film, Genre, and Comic Strip," *Asian Cinema* 20 (Spring / Summer 2009): 1–15. Williams also makes reference to *M.A.S.H.* as an "allegory of the Vietnam War."

51 Rudolph W. Stephens, *Old Ugly Hill: A G.I.'s Fourteen Months in the Korean Trenches, 1952–1953* (Jefferson, NC: McFarland & Company, Inc., Publishers, 1995), 11; see also William D. Dannenmaier, *We Were Innocents: An Infantryman in Korea* (Urbana: University of Illinois Press, 2000).

52 Eric Diller quoted in "After Years of Waiting and Wondering, World War II Vets Will Get Their Memorial," *Daily Breeze*, 23 May 2004, A1.

53 Unnamed World War II veteran quoted in Erika Doss, "War, Memory, and the Public Mediation of Affect: The National World War II Memorial and American Imperialism," *Memory Studies* 1, no. 2 (2008): 227–50.

54 Historian Erika Doss calls it the "ahistorical assumptions of postwar ingratitude" and states that these "drive today's mania to memorialize the "'greatest generation.'" Erika Doss, *Memorial Mania: Public Feelings in America* (Chicago: University of Chicago Press, 2010), 193. In his 2010 study on the Second World War, John Bodnar challenges more profoundly the notion of a hegemonic memory of the war. Bodnar, *The 'Good War' in American Memory*.

55 Quoted in Mary Leonard, "Monumental Efforts: The Battle Has Been Joined over Building a New War Memorial in Washington," *Boston Globe*, 13 April 13 1997, D1.

56 James Reston Jr, "The Monument Glut," *New York Times Magazine*, 10 September 1995, 6.

57 Steven Johnston, "Political Not Patriotic: Democracy, Civic Space, and the American Memorial / Monument Complex," *Theory & Event* 5, no. 2 (2001). http://muse.jhu.edu/journals/theory_and_event/v005/5.2johnston.html (accessed 12 May 2012). See also David Chidester and Edward T. Linenthal, eds., *American Sacred Space* (Bloomington: Indiana University Press, 1995): 1–42.

58 Stanford E. Parris, "Need for a Korean War Memorial," 26 June 1986, 132 Congressional Record, 99–2, H4309.

59 "Speaking of Memorials," *Washington Post*, 27 May 1985, A18.

60 Seymour Lehman quoted in Kate Stone Lombardi, "Belated Remembrance of the Forgotten War in Korea," *New York Times*, 26 May 1996, 13WC. Lehman made this statement in the context of a construction of a Korean War memorial in Lasdon Park, NY. However, it reflects the spirit a majority of veterans. For a short overview of the problematic development of the memorial, see Nicolaus Mill, *Their Last Battle: The Fight for the National World War II Memorial* (New York: Basic Books, 2004), 63, 66.

61 David A. Levine, "Letters to the Editor: The Monument Glut," *New York Times Magazine*, 1 October 1995, 12. Similar points are found in Joe Chung, "Letters to the Editor: The Monument Glut," *New York Times Magazine,* 1 October 1995, 48.

62 Kristin Ann Hass, *Sacrificing Soldiers on the National Mall* (Berkeley: University of California Press, 2013), 58.

63 Quoted in Reston Jr, "The Monument Glut." For harsh criticism of the memorial and plans to add others, see: Deborah K. Dietsch, "Memorial Madness: a War Memorial Competition Threatens to Diminish a Precious National Site," *Architecture* 85 (July 1996): 15; Roger K. Lewis, "Washington Monuments: Battles over the Mall: A Frenzy of Monument Building Is Sweeping through the Nation's Capital. Roger Lewis Takes Stock of the Latest Additions and What's to Come," *Architectural Record* 184 (1 January 1996): 17.

64 Angus Deming, "The Remembered War," *Newsweek*, 7 August 1995, 68.

65 Choi, "Mythologizing Memories," 61–82. Choi also underlines the importance of the "good war" analogy and makes the important point that war's public memory neglects "specificities and particulars of the Korean War; rather it promotes willful forgetfulness, a decision to remember the war as vaguely as possible." Ibid., 76. In her 2014 book, Choi identifies a predominance of the official narrative of the Korean War – "amnesic, ossified memories" – and the lack of "counter-memories" of the Korean War in the United States. See Choi, *Embattled Memories*, 4.

66 "Editorial: The Korean War: On the Mall," *Washington Post*, 26 July 1995, A22.

67 See: Knauer, "A Victory after All"; Hass, *Sacrificing Soldiers on the National Mall.*

68 Press release, "Official Dedication of the New Jersey Korean War Memorial Pays Tribute to Those Now No Longer Forgotten." http://

www.state.nj.us/military/korea/13nov00.html (accessed 12 October 2014).

69 For a description of the New Jersey Korean War Memorial see http://www.state.nj.us/military/korea/index.html (accessed 12 October 2014).

70 Mike Kelly, "Fitting Memorial: Want to Bet? Korea Vets Forgotten Again," *The Record*, 9 March 1998, A01.

71 Linda Wheeler, "A Shadow Has Fallen on Korean Memorial; Lost Trees, Loose Stones Upset Visitors," *Washington Post*, 10 May 1997, A1.

72 Linda Wheeler, "Neglected but Not Forgotten, Korean War Memorial Gets Help," *Washington Post*, 23 May 1997, D1.

73 William E. Weber, Colonel United States Army, retired, and Chairman Korean War Veterans Memorial Foundation, on H.R. 318, 10 June 2014, in Legislative Hearing before the Subcommittee on Public Lands and Environmental Legislation of the Committee on Natural Resources US House of Representatives (Washington: US Government Printing Office, 2015), 60.

74 "Help Us Get HR 1475 and S 1982 Passed to Authorize the 'Wall of Remembrance' to be added to our Korean War Memorial …" http://www.kwva.org/(accessed 18 June 2016).

75 Niki Tsongas, Massachusetts, "Korean War Veterans Memorial Wall of Remembrance Act of 2016," 26 February 2016, 162 Congressional Record, 114–2, H877.

76 Jada F. Smith, "Korean War Memorial Group Finds More Aid in Korea Than in US," *New York Times*, 10 November 2015, http://nyti.ms/1knwCCJ (accessed 24 June 2016).

77 "114 H.R. 1475 Referred to Senate Committee: Korean War Veterans Memorial Wall of Remembrance Act of 2016," 2016 H.R. 1475; 114 H.R. 1475.

2

Aesthetics versus Ownership: Artists and Soldiers in the Design of the National Korean War Veterans Memorial, Washington, DC

JUDITH KEENE

On 28 October 1986 President Reagan signed Public Law 99-52 that authorized construction of a memorial to the American veterans of the Korean War. It would be located on federal land within the District of Columbia and honour all American veterans who had fought in Korea: the living, the lost in battle, those taken prisoner, and the missing in action. The structure would be funded entirely by private contributions and the project was to be underway no later than five years from the date of signing. On 27 July 1995, President Clinton opened the memorial on the National Mall before thousands of elderly veterans and their beaming families. The decade between congressional approval and the memorial's completion was marked by a series of crises that revealed the complex interplay among the main players involved in the Korean War Veterans Memorial. While the veterans, the designers, and the members of the artistic commissions that oversaw public sculpture in the capital all shared a commitment to raising a Korean War memorial, every stage in its evolution was negotiated through a matrix of quite distinct and competing artistic, political, and institutional agendas.

Ostensibly, aesthetic differences were at the heart of the conflict. Arguments over monument and style, of course, are nothing new. Kirk Savage has documented the robust public disagreements that were integral to every stage in creating the commemorative landscape of the American capital.[1] The history of public sculpture throughout the twentieth century has been marked by the tension between realism and the modernist preference for non-figurative design.[2] War memorials offer a particularly fertile site for this contestation. Military supporters, in the main, expect representations of soldiers ornamented by a display of various military artifacts. Artists and designers, who favour a modernist aesthetic, tend to embrace the non-figurative form whereby the indexical relation to the commemorated event is metaphorical and indirect.[3]

Certainly, the aesthetic aspirations of those appointed to the Korean War Veterans Memorial Advisory Board (KWVMAB) were of military men from an earlier generation. Equally importantly, their design mission was driven by a larger project. The objective was to use the memorial as a means to expunge the odious tag of Korea as the "forgotten" war that for almost four decades had belittled the war service of those drafted there. With the national spotlight finally on these veterans, the figure of the Korean GI could be recast in the heroic mould of the American fighting man. From the earliest planning sessions to the final arrangements for the memorial unveiling, the strategy of the KWVMAB was to reconfigure the Korean War into America's "forgotten victory," and to re-script the role of the veterans of that war into hitherto unheralded heroes. Later the terms were stretched and re-historicized to claim Korea as the "First Victory," which had heralded the collapse of the Berlin Wall leading to America's greatest victory in the war against communism.

The largest group of stakeholders in the memorial's outcome were the "schmucks at the bottom," as ordinary veterans often bitterly referred to themselves.[4] For them, the promise of a monument signalled that they were now sanctioned to speak about their Korean War service and their perceived postwar mistreatment as "forgotten veterans."[5] Over the years, an initial truculence towards the US government among returned soldiers from Korea had gelled into a deep hostility towards everything associated with "Washington."[6] In the slow progress of raising the Korean War Veterans Memorial, many veterans came to include members of the KWVMAB in the reviled category of "DC functionaries." In turn, advisory board members, who saw themselves as leading the battle to restore the honour of the Korean War's "forgotten heroes," were flummoxed to be on the receiving end of veterans' hostility.

The artistic experts associated with the memorial design were focused on aesthetic questions but, not surprisingly, they also were influenced by other considerations of career advancement and professional esteem. The winners of the national design competition, the BL3 group of architects and landscape designers from Penn State University, envisaged a postmodern memorial that would function as a theatre of memory whereby visitors could experience a sense of combat along with a unit of American soldiers.[7] For these architects, the competition offered the opportunity to showcase their professional skills and, under normal circumstances, their validation in producing a design destined for the Washington Mall would have guaranteed fame and professional kudos. The Washington firm of architects, Cooper-Lecky, which took over when the winners were ousted, also had significant capital at stake, having been the architects of record responsible for building the Vietnam Veterans Memorial. Equally, the artistic experts on the national commissions that vetted the memorial designs brought to the tasks a brief that was distinct from the veterans' movement or professional architectural rivalries. The national Fine Arts Commissioners assessed form and footprint of the proposed Korean War Veterans Memorials as part of a larger view of public sculpture in the District of Columbia.

THE MEMORIAL DESIGN

The president of the United States had appointed a twelve-member Advisory Board to select the design and raise the necessary funds. It consisted of retired career soldiers from the Korean conflict, chaired by General Joseph Stilwell, the ex-commander of the American Infantry in Korea and later the head of the CIA's Eastern Division. His deputy, General Ray Davis, had headed the US Marine Corps. When Stilwell died in February 1992, Davis stepped into his shoes as chairman of the Advisory Board. With the exception of the recently formed Korean War Veterans Association, all the leading US veterans' organizations were included: the American Legion, American Veterans of Foreign Wars, the disabled and the paralysed veterans associations, plus retired officers now engaged in trade with Seoul. Rosemary T. McCarthy, a retired colonel in the Army Nursing Service, provided the lone female voice.

The strategy of the KWVMAB in all memorial dealings was to assert their authority to make all final decisions on the grounds that they were "old soldiers" and "battle-scarred" veterans. Chairman Stilwell regularly reminded critics that the Advisory Board was qualified for the job because three of the members had "left parts of their precious bodies on the Korean battlefield." And General Davis (Stilwell's deputy) had not only "been a commander at battalion level in World War II and of a division in Vietnam," but his "personal courage" in Korea had earned him the Medal of Honor. Even the sculptor, Frank C. Gaylord II, eventually commissioned to produce the memorial figures, had earned a place on the team by virtue of his having "served in World War Two."[8] Whenever they feared that they were about to be "outflanked" and "blindsided" (in the battlefield argot that peppers their correspondence) by civilians and "Washington insiders," the KWVMAB simply restated their war records, certain in the belief that battlefield experience always trumps artistic expertise.

At first all went well. Of several possible locations, the National Capital Memorial Commission assigned the Korean Memorial to a prime spot of seven and a half acres in Ash Woods, located just south of the Lincoln Memorial and across the reflecting pool from the monument to Vietnam Veterans. The next task was to select the memorial design. In a national competition open to all, the brief for the $20,000 prize was straightforward. The concept for the design would "express the nation's enduring gratitude" to all the American veterans in Korea, representing their "spirit of service, willingness to sacrifice, and dedication to the cause of freedom." The memorial's message should be "inspirational in content and timeless in meaning."[9] Strongly aware of the example of the Vietnam Veterans Memorial and keen to avoid the turmoil around Maya Lin's winning design, the Board added the rider that the American flag must be part of the composition and that the listing of names was not requisite. The twelve-member jury consisted solely of veterans, all drawn from Advisory Board members. This decision was also heavily influenced by the Vietnam Veterans Memorial experience where vehement opponents of Maya Lin's unadorned design had castigated the jury as misled by art experts.[10]

The competition closed on 1 May 1989. The 540 submissions were put on public display in the foyer of a Washington hotel.[11] What is striking about the images of these design concepts, viewed twenty years after the competition, is the number that replicate Maya Lin's walls, whether falling below or rising above the lay of the land. The small group of "amateur" submissions, most likely from veterans themselves, is also telling as they reveal what at least some of the veteran population saw as appropriate forms of war remembrance, though none of their designs made the final cut. [12] Several of the veterans' contributions take the theme of the downed plane. For example, the submission entitled "The Air Rescue" depicts a warplane that has nose-dived into a rice paddy. Another offers the adrenalin rush of combat through re-enactment in a site transformed into a battlefield theme park in which life-sized soldiers take and return fire.[13]

The most numerous submissions were from professionals – architects, landscape designers, and public artists. The runner up, which netted $10,000, came from a New Mexico architect, Ronald Nims, and drew on the much-used motif of the yin / yang from the Korean flag. Described as "unabashedly heroic," it stood high on the landscape. In third place, with prize money of $5,000, was Mark Fondersmith, a highly talented young artist who offered the only sculptural piece. It was a single large clay model presenting a striding infantryman, caped in the winter gear of poncho and helmet, and set in a landscape that suggests the mountains of Korea and, across the water, the United States, indicated by the Stars and Stripes. The jury of veterans were much taken with this figure that "captured the essence of the conflict," and they speculated that the sculptor himself might be a Korean veteran. The soldier's figure and his garb were later appropriated without permission as the final monumental figures on the Mall, and although the sculptor threatened a lawsuit, no acknowledgment was ever offered.[14]

The winning design came from an architectural group in Pennsylvania: Burns-Lucas, Leon, and Lucas, BL3, were academics at Pennsylvania State University. Don Alvaro Leon and John Paul Lucas were professors in the School of Architecture and Veronica Burns Lucas and Eliza Pennypacker Oberholtzer taught landscape architecture.[15] They researched the concept, "seeking patterns and relationships," speaking to old veterans and examining in depth the arresting images of David Douglas Duncan, the photographer who travelled with the Marine Corps in Korea.[16] The other theme their design highlighted was the indivisible link between war and the universal desire for peace. The memorial was a "theatre" in which the "visitor-participants" walked with a unit of thirty-eight 9-to-10-foot soldierly figures, almost like an additional member of the fighting unit. The representation of soldiers in combat carried resonances of the high realism of a traditional military monument while the visitor, cast in the role of participant rather than onlooker, was inflected by postmodernism. The path that the group would follow began at an entry plaza, a granite-paved area with a white marble square, then passed through a "bosque" of raggedly cut plane trees, suggesting the effects of battle, to move up a slight incline, from the highest point of which the Washington Monument was visible. From there the path fell away gradually to a second granite-paved space centred on an American flag at the base of which was a quote from St Augustine about the desire for peace. Planted along the full length of the path were barberries and holly, the bright red berries suggesting the blood of battle and the harsh prickles evoking the inhospitable Korean terrain.

BL3's conception was based on a carefully theorized view of the memorial as a "cultural text that has the potential to record and retain knowledge."[17] The metaphorical narrative incorporated the details of the surrounding landscape as symbolic elements that embellished the meaning of the whole setting. Equally, the form of the design was intended to avoid the isolation and the solipsism that often is associated with visiting memorials when the meaning of the memorial and the symbolism employed to convey that meaning is abstruse and far removed from the visitor's life and understanding. The design explication indicated that the group of soldiers had moved from peace to war and then finally would reach "ultimate peace," represented by the quiet space of the granite plaza where the American flag symbolized freedom and the safety of home. As the path moved gently upwards a shallow stream rippled over the soldier's feet, becoming smooth water as the soldiers drew closer to home. A circular walk at the end of the path took the visitor back to the beginning. The orientation of the space was laid out on axis lines in a triangle from the Lincoln Memorial and the Vietnam Memorial. Inscribed on a series of panels along the wall traversed by the path and facing the square were images and expressions from philosophers and commentators that encapsulated the essence of war and the necessity of peace. The thirty-eight ghostly figures symbolized the 38th parallel, where the conflict had begun and ended, and also the thirty-eight months of the war's duration. Thirty-eight was also the approximate number of soldiers in an American fighting unit.

It was indicative of future difficulties that BL3's explanatory material focused on the narrative and the symbolism behind the design components, whereas the jury's response was much more prosaic. As

General Davis explained, "To us [the design] was very realistic and we were surprised by all the symbolism the designers had in mind. They saw the figures as a passage of time whereas we saw a combat formation."[18]

In the Flag Day ceremony in the Rose Garden of the White House on 1 June 1989, with the beaming architects present, George H.W. Bush announced the winners and unveiled a mock-up model of the design. He commended the conception in glowing terms and showered fulsome praise on the valour of "America's uniformed sons and daughters who went to Korea not for themselves but, hating war, had sought only liberty and fought so that the enslaved might be free." Drawing on the KWVMAB briefing notes, President Bush also observed that now was the time to "remember an American victory that remains too little appreciated and too seldom understood."[19]

The preliminary step, before devising specific construction plans, was that the design concept was sent on the first round to the national gatekeepers that vet all proposals to install public art within the District of Columbia. The secretary of state held ultimate authority over all decisions to build but took advice from officials in the various advisory commissions. The National Battle Monuments Commission (NBMC), as its name suggests, was the overseeing body in proposing public art that deals with American soldiers. Created after the Great War, its first responsibility had been building cemeteries in Europe for the American fallen.[20] Made up of military people and appointed by the president, the NBMC exercised direct authority over the KWVMAB. Of all the federal institutions scrutinizing public design, the most powerful was (and still is) the Fine Arts Commission (FAC). The civilian commissioners, holding four-year renewable presidential appointments, are the nation's artistic and aesthetic guardians.

On the initial round, the responses to the aesthetics of the winning design concept overall were positive. There were some questions on practical matters of water table levels and paths and skateboarders raised by National Parks Service and the Army Corps of Engineers. The design, however, passed the main hurdle with flying colours. On 9 August 1989, the FAC declared itself "very pleased with the overall concept design." According to the commission's chairman, J. Carter Brown, "It had the potential of becoming a memorial of great power and dignity in its own right. While respecting the presence of the other nearby memorials, it has a heroic quality all its own." He also observed that a design as "complex" as this one will "naturally have a number of areas that will require additional study." But overall there was "great merit" in the design concept for a structure that could take its place with the major memorials in Washington.[21]

CONSTRUCTING THE KOREAN WAR VETERANS MEMORIAL

The construction of public sculpture is rarely straightforward and the design itself can bring a particular set of problems.[22] In light of the example of the Vietnam Veterans Memorial, Mary McLeod has argued that the "rapport between patron and client," so essential for a project's timely completion, is much harder to achieve when the memorial design reflects the tastes of a jury in a national competition.[23] As we have seen, the KWVAB had attempted to head off just such a conflict, but the all-veteran jury soon fell out with the winning designers and then with the artistic experts on the vetting commissions. The board members sought to modify the prizewinning design to one that would embody an idealized memory of men in active combat in Korea. Perhaps too in their intense involvement in refashioning the maquettes into heroic form they were also revisiting and rebuffing their own recalled lives as soldiers in combat.

There was no requirement within the conditions of the design competition that the winning architects should oversee the memorial's construction. Equally, it is not surprising that the BL3 architects assumed they would be closely involved. In the event, however, the Advisory Board hired the Washington firm of Cooper-Lecky, which had served as architects of record overseeing Maya Lin's design for the Vietnam Veterans Memorial, and they took on the Pennsylvania group as consultants. At an early stage, the Advisory Board indicated that they were unhappy with the ghostly nature of the sculptural figures, preferring a depiction of young, fit soldiers primed for battle. Stilwell requested that each of the thirty-eight figures be represented in accurate proportions to their actual occupations in the armed services in Korea.[24] Each soldier should be authentically kitted out, from the insignias on their collars to the lacing on their boots. Buckles, boots, and headgear must replicate the real thing and pieces in the possession of individual board members were collected and forwarded to the sculptor for reference.[25] Internal memos flew back and forth about which of the services was over- or under-represented. The

Advisory Board also required that the racial composition of the figures be made apparent and reflect their actual enlistment numbers and occupational assignments. Again, memos and tables were devised and circulated.[26] In the end, after months of intense investigation, the figures appeared in the unsurprising sequence: the majority were Caucasian, followed in diminishing numbers by African Americans, Hispanics, Asian Americans, and a lone Native American private.[27]

In an early design change Cooper-Lecky included a wounded soldier being assisted by two comrades. The Memorial Board response was swift and unequivocal. There were to be no injured GIs and no prisoners of war that might recall the earlier fears of brainwashed POWs returning home. Instead, all fighting men must stand unaided on their own two feet. Later, during a visit to the sculptor's studio, board members compiled a list of minute changes to be made to the facial expressions. For example, many faces were "much too harsh, too coarse and depicted a much older looking person;" a few even showed "terror!" which would "undermine the board's determination to portray gallant, victorious warriors."[28]

Within a very few months, the Penn State architects began to fear they were being cut out of the process.[29] When they presented a formal complaint, Cooper-Lecky replied that they had been paid the $20,000 prize money and the design now belonged to the US government. BL3 openly criticized the variations to their design as romanticizing and glamourizing war in the individuation of the combat figures. Veronica Lucas poured cold water on the unimaginativeness of the new design: the emphasis on the specifics of individuals and uniforms swamped the idea of the universality of war and peace.[30] John Lucas was reported in the *Washington Post* as having said that the prize-winning design had been turned from peace into a "GI Joe replica of war." This quote was picked up and widely reported in the press.[31] Infuriated, the Advisory Board distributed a statement that they were the battle-tried Korean veterans whereas the Penn State group were civilians, and their design "ignored the blood of the hundreds of wounded that had soaked the frozen Korean hillside."[32]

The Penn State architects hired a Washington lawyer and on 18 December 1990 sought an injunction in the US District Court against the US Battle Monuments Commission and the United States Army Corps of Engineers to halt all work on the "new, substituted memorial design." They filed for damages as well against the Korean War Veterans Memorial Advisory Board and Cooper-Lecky Architects for breach of contract.[33] It took courage, even bravado, to take on institutions attached to the US government, and when the cases failed, the three plaintiffs (Oberhacker had withdrawn) filed, again unsuccessfully, in the US Court of Appeals. In a press conference later, the Penn State team contended that "a small group of very powerful people has quietly and systematically acted to throw out the winning design" and replace it with one that "glamourizes and romanticizes the act of war."[34]

The veterans' community at large had welcomed news that their war service in Korea was to be commemorated, though support was most often qualified by a wary request for more information. The court injunctions and damages claims by the Penn State designers agitated veterans anew. Much to the chagrin of members of the Advisory Board, they were often included in the ordinary veterans' belief in the untrustworthiness of government officials. For example, the editor of *Canopy*, the magazine of the veterans of helicopter units, lambasted the Advisory Board who had "bilked" his fellow veterans into funding fat salaries and expenses-paid jaunts back and forth to Washington, where prestigious titles and deference were accorded those lucky enough to be appointed to presidential advisory boards.[35] In vain, General Stilwell assured the letter-writer who had peppered him with complaints that the members of the Advisory Board were soldiers and "not bureaucrats" and were unpaid except for expenses.[36] An ex-radio operator sounded off at the idea of one more "feather merchant monument" made by "people whose understanding of Korea came from watching *M.A.S.H.* and therefore wanted only to depict the Korean vet as a fool." He criticized the jurors who had chosen the design and therefore showed only "contempt for the military," demanding that the competition be held again with the stipulation that the judges be combat veterans, preferably from the Korean War.

The Advisory Board adopted an aggressive approach in advancing its side, prompted probably by the confidential knowledge that donations had plummeted. In a long piece in *Veterans of Foreign Wars*, Colonel Weber pulled no punches. He noted that many vets would have "heard some static from the pissing competition that the design team has started in Washington." He asked readers to make a choice, whether to trust the board, "all of whom are veterans" or "four people who have not heard a shot fired in anger." These civilian designers held a "wrong-headed premise" that they are "designated by God to decide a memorial for those of us who fought and died." Weber reassured veterans that the board was "busting its butt to do the best possible job" and signed off with a personal guarantee that he was "giving them the straight poop."[37]

The Korean War Veterans Association (KWVA), formed in 1986 to support the building of the monument, had been a strong memorial supporter, using the magazine *Graybeards* to publicize funding drives. The delays in construction and the legal tussle over the design, however, irritated the leadership. KWVA members began to express dissatisfaction and then anger at the memorial's rising cost.[38] In the January 1990 issue of *Graybeards*, they stated that since they were being asked for money they were entitled to receive honest answers. The question posed was, "Are cost-control methods employed or is the usual boon-doggling being followed?"[39] When the editor suggested that the amounts the Advisory Board claimed to have in their accounts did not add up to the total amount collected, General Davis and the chief executive officer, Bob Hansen, resigned in fury from the Veterans Association, and the Advisory Board cut them off official circulation lists.[40]

From 1990 to 1992, the KWVMAB and members of the Battle Monuments Commission with the architects of record unsuccessfully worked and reworked the replacement design for a series of appearances before the assessing commissions. On 8 November 1990, accompanied by the full membership of the KWVMAB, Kent Cooper presented their first revised plan, by then called the Delta scheme. In this and subsequent appearances, the architects of record made frequent references to their experiences in the construction of the Vietnam Memorial. Perhaps influenced by that practice, a highly polished wall, stretching alongside the path, had been given much prominence.[41] The thirty-eight figures, a Cooper-Lecky spokesman explained, were of the same height and scale as Hart's *Three Soldiers*.[42] Each soldier now had a different pose and was engaged in a different aspect of combat: there were infantry soldiers but also Marines, Navy and Army aircraft spotters, Navy artillery, and Korean service personnel with the traditional carrying frame strapped on their backs. Asked by a commissioner whether this constituted a "GI Joe scene," Cooper stated evenly that it was a carefully conceived column of troopers that any Korean veteran would find plausible. A major change was that the original granite material of the core figures had been abandoned as not conducive to the realism and the faithful rendition of the figures and their equipment that was now the central element in the design.

The Advisory Board members had taken up with gusto their expanded responsibilities in the design process. They gave specific instructions to the New York muralist Louis Nelson, hired to etch the polished granite.[43] Its composition would consist of two-thirds telling a "coherent story" of the three years of war.[44] Another section, covering the men and women in support services, should include the tools and equipment they manned, and be shown in "operational mode." The last third of the mural was dedicated to those killed in action, still missing, or held as POWs. Somewhere too there should be a section where the Armed Forces of the Republic of Korea, and the medical and military contributions from the other twenty countries, were each portrayed in a manner that reflected the scale of their participation. They also wished that "map(s) of Korea with appropriate detail and narrative should be incorporated into the site for visitor information and orientation." As well, the pool had been extended and centred and a separate commemorative grove added, which the Korean War Advisory Board referred to as "the open chapel."

On 14 December 1990 the chairman of the Fine Arts Commission asked the American Corps of Engineers to peg out the memorial site showing the precise height and span of the design for a joint meeting of the planning commissions, the National Parks Service, and the KWVMAB.[45] At that gathering, J. Carter Brown commented that what was "attractive about the Vietnam veterans memorial was that you couldn't see it" because it "didn't wave its hand at you."[46] Five days after the stakeout, on 22 January 1991, members of the Fine Arts Commission voted unanimously to "disapprove" the Cooper-Lecky design, recommending more "concentration, condensation, containment, and focus." Brown reported that the commissioners all shared a "pervasive feeling that there was just too much going on."[47]

A month later, on 17 February 1991, the FAC deemed the subsequent design submitted by the board and the architects of record to be "too big, too high, and too diffuse." A combined FAC and National Capital Planning Commission (NCPC) task force, with advice from the National Parks Association, had been formed after the stakeout. At their meeting on 21 February 1991, several members of the FAC were more positive about the design possibility, though there were several references to "GI Joe" action figures. In this iteration, the footprint of the memorial had been scaled back: the path was reduced to 180 feet and the etched history lessons were replaced by images of ordinary military personnel using a photo-engraving process devised by the New York muralist. Brown was very keen on the inclusion of support units and ordinary enlistees; he liked the originality of this "new idea" because it contrasted nicely with the nineteenth-century monuments of "the general on horseback." However, the FAC asked to see more detail about the final product.[48]

On 19 March 1991 Kent Cooper returned to the FAC and the NCPC task force with further design revisions. Stilwell introduced the presentation, reminding the assembled commissioners that the KWVMAB had already spent $2 million on revisions and redesigns from money donated by Korean War veterans, their widows, and their families. He also argued that the success of the American troops in the Persian Gulf and their imminent homecoming made this the perfect time to construct the memorial to soldiers in Korea who had "fought under incredibly more difficult conditions and against greater odds."[49] In this latest version, although the height of the parallel wall had been lowered and the sculptured figures had been reduced to just over 7 feet, neither the FAC nor the NCPC were convinced. They gave conditional support as long as the sculpture figures were "less representational in character," and the wall height even lower and with less formal landscaping.[50] In mid-June, Cooper-Lecky built a 35-foot scale model in the studio and invited Advisory Board and FAC members to a viewing. The latter were underwhelmed. Their unanimous response was that with the figures and the wall "it was all too much."[51] At the FAC's scheduled meeting on 25 June, the chairman stated that "nothing has changed in the design," the architects had simply "tinkered with it but are not ready to come up with a fresh approach." In an interview in the Penn State student newspaper, the secretary of the FAC likened the Cooper-Lecky design to a "menu or a meal with too much to digest." Brown had later explained that the design was overloaded, "excessive and confusing," and the freestanding figures simply do not work. Brown's preference was for a frieze, as on the Pantheon, or a bas-relief similar to that which encircled the nearby Pension Building. In any event, in his assessment, it was time for all involved to "step back and re-examine the situation together," especially as the capital with scarcely an empty space was in danger of suffering "monumentitis."[52]

Behind the scenes, the KWVMAB was made frantic by the signals of an imminent final rejection. The five-year time frame for the Advisory Board's appointment was to expire in three months, at the end of October 1991. Some members suggested moving on to the second or third prize-winning designs, but Stilwell and Kelley feared that as the fundraising had centred around the publicity of a column of soldiers, any change would set off a media storm that would further agitate veterans. General Kelley wrote to Brown that the Advisory Board had been "stunned and perplexed" at the FAC's rejection of the thirty-eight figures which was in "stark contradiction" with the "previous conceptual approval" and without explanation or due regard for what could be "incalculable, adverse consequences." While the Board unanimously endorsed the column of troops, members were willing to halve the number of soldiers in the column in order to reach a "middle ground."[53]

In the meantime, angry veterans who had been writing letters to the Advisory Board also began to contact the commissioners in Washington. At the FAC's meeting in 27 August 1991, Brown read into the minutes that he objected very strongly to the letters from "certain veterans and so forth that the commission is anti-veteran and anti-Korean war." This was not true as each redesigned submission had been unsuccessful on its own terms. By this meeting of the FAC, the memorial had undergone significant change. The number of figures had been halved and the details of uniforms, in the choice of which Korean board members had invested so much attention, were now covered with windblown ponchos, adapted from Fondersmith's sculptured maquette. Despite the scaling back, several members of the FAC observed that three to five figures would be even better, and there was the possibility that an understated bas-relief in bronze would be much more effective than the multitude of figures etched on the wall. The word around Washington was that it was time to abandon the design and start again, perhaps with a new competition.

For the final showdown with the Fine Arts Commission, scheduled for 24 October 1991, the KWVMAB lobbied the House and Senate and called on sympathetic veterans to do the same.[54] In planning for the last-ditch stand, the board agreed they could cut back the number of figures even further, but they also were determined to call the FAC's bluff to make it clear that this was their absolute and final concession. General Davis's address was rewritten and reworked into a fine piece of rhetoric.[55] It laid out the contradictions confronted: the "containment" favoured by the FAC versus the NPC's demands for "horizontal openness." Yet, they had conscientiously attempted to meet every request.[56] Also, thousands of veterans and the Korean businesses Samsung and Hyundai had donated money in good faith and could not understand why the memorial made so little progress. Davis rounded up with the fact that the KWVMAB's appointment would extinguish imminently and if the matter of the monument was not solved there and then it would be the end of the project.

Chairman Brown responded tartly that the commission's constituency comprised "the people of the United States and all those Americans yet to be born." Commissioners used their "best professional judgement on basis of what [they] are shown, whether it is a new or a revised design or a totally fresh concept." So far the opinion was that the design was not "airborne." In response, Davis warned that since the KWVAB was "up against the block" if the design was not passed, the board intended to tell veterans that the FAC was responsible. Brown's reply was that "we can live with this," and he added that with the threat of the deadline Congress would grant an extension if it wanted this design. When the motion was put to disapprove the design several commissioners had shifted towards the Delta design and this time the vote was tied. As a consequence, a decision was postponed until the following month.

In anticipation of what was assumed to be the final chance for the memorial, Cooper-Lecky made further changes. The walkways were narrowed, strips of highly polished granite were laid between the soldierly figures, and the previous connections from the pathway were blocked to discourage visitors from walking among the figures. The length of the wall was reduced by a further 55 feet. The muralist, Nelson, had demonstrated his creative acumen in responding to the criticism of the etching's "super-realism" by reduced the size of the images and their coverage, which now appeared as though on an unrolling Chinese scroll. Although none of the Advisory Board was "enamoured" with this idea, it proved to be a clinching detail.[57] At the FAC's gathering on 16 January 1992, the war on the Korean Veterans Memorial front ended. The commissioners voted three to one to pass the Cooper-Lecky design. On 28 May 1992, Memorial Day, the preliminary plans for the design were finally approved and on 14 June

1992, in front of some 5,000 invited veterans and family members, President Bush used a gold-plated shovel to turn the first sod.[58]

CONCLUSION

There is little written about the Korean War Veterans Memorial, certainly nothing like the literature on the memorial to Vietnam veterans. Barry Schwartz and Todd Bayma, perhaps echoing G. Kurt Piehler's broad view that the American trend is to more pluralistic monuments, have read the range of ethnicities and the inclusion of women in the Korean memorial (in the final iteration of the wall) as a sign of the memorial's pluralism and inclusiveness in the service of the American state.[59] My analysis leads to a different conclusion and one that is closer to Kirk Savage's comment. Savage's assessment, when set within the broad landscape of American monumental examples, is that the Korean War Veterans Memorial is a "jumble of elements."[60] In my view, it could hardly be other than a hybrid structure given the competing claims to ownership of the structure, whether by virtue of the claimants' combat experience or the aesthetic expertise of the designers. The memorial footprint, the layout, and the core of moving soldiers constitute an amalgam that represents the series of outcomes from profound and often acrimonious differences between the stakeholders despite their shared commitment to the enterprise of raising a national memorial to Korean War veterans. In light of all of this, the dry comment of the final unconvinced member of the Fine Arts Commission is telling. Despite the rigours of the series of submissions and design re-workings, for her the memorial reminded her most of a "football game in the rain" whereby what was left of the National Mall was "Mr Lincoln and the three soldiers from Vietnam, now joined by nineteen more from the Korean war memorial."[61]

ACKNOWLEDGMENT

I am glad to acknowledge the research materials and comments from John Paul Lucas, Mark P. Fondersmith, and Don A. Leon and the permission from the latter to use materials he has placed in the State University of Pennsylvania Archives. The paper has benefited from comments by Robert Aldrich, Ann Curthoys, Elizabeth Rechniewski, and the anonymous reviewers for this volume.

NOTES

1 Kirk Savage, *Monument Wars: Washington, D.C., the National Mall and the Transformation of the Memorial Landscape* (Berkeley: University of California Press, 2005).

2 Erica Doss, *Memorial Mania: Public Feeling in America* (Chicago: University of Chicago Press, 2010), 123–31.

3 Patrick Hagopian warns against too simplistic a division between advocates of realism and modernism but also provides telling examples of both. Hagopian, *The Vietnam War in American Memory: Veterans, Memorials, and the Politics of Healing* (Amherst: University of Massachusetts Press, 2009).

4 Memo from Bob Hansen to All Advisory Board Members, 22 May 1991, "Draft Presentation for Advisory Board Members and others." National Archives and Records Administration (NARA) RG 220, Records Temporary Committees, Commissions and Boards (RTCCB), Korean War Veterans Memorial Advisory Board (KWVMAB), box 7.

5 According to Erica Doss, contemporary American memorials function as "archives of public affect" that serve as "repositories of public feeling and emotion." Doss, *Memorial Mania*, 13.

6 Judith Keene, "Lost to Public Commemoration: American Veterans of the 'Forgotten' Korean War," *Journal of Social History* (Summer 2011): 1099–117.

7 Postmodern commemorative forms consciously highlight the link between present experience and the events of the past, and re-enactment provides a powerful memory technology. See Marita Sturken, *Tangled Memories: The Vietnam War, the AIDS Epidemic, and the Politics of Remembering* (Berkeley: University of California Press, 1967), 12–17, 19–43.

8 R.G. Stilwell to Col Michael E McGuinn III, 4 February 1991. NARA, RG 220, RTCCB Korean KWVMAB. Minutes of Board Meetings, 1987–95, box 6.

9 The Korean War Veterans Memorial in the Nation's Capital, "Concept." The Don A. Leon Collection, Penn State University Archives, Pennsylvania University Libraries.

10 Hagopian details the choice of the Vietnam memorial jury and its opposition in *The Vietnam War in American Memory*, 93–110.

11 "Photographs of Designs Submitted for the Korean War Veterans Memorial Competition," American Battle Monuments Commission (1989). NARA RG 117.

12 Hagopian discusses amateurs and professional design submissions in *The Vietnam War in American Memory,* 95–7.

13 "Photographs of Designs Submitted for the Korean War Veterans Memorial Competition," American Battle Monuments Commission (1989). NARA RG 117.

14 Mark Fondersmith, not a veteran, submitted a design that received high praise though individual jurors and the architects of record later made the unlikely claim that the figures that grace what became the present-day memorial had not been influenced by Fondersmith's concept but had been designed independently. See the 1989 correspondence from Colonel Weber, General Davis, and General Stilwell, in the possession of Mark P. Fondersmith, copied to the author.

15 Richard Robbins, "State College Architects Design Memorial," *Tribune Review,* 1 April 1990, Design / B1. NARA RG 220, RTCC&B KWVMAB, 1987–95, box 4.

16 "Design Statement of the Korean War Veterans Memorial by V. Burns Lucas, D.A. Leon, J. P. Lucas, and E. Pennypacker Oberholtzer." Don A. Leon Collection, Pennsylvania State University Archives, 275148 AX/CATO/PSUA/M/07.17.

17 "A Brief Account of the Theoretical Frame of the Korean War Veterans Memorial by V. Burns Lucas, Don Alvaro Leon, John Paul Lucas, and Eliza Pennypacker." Don A. Leon Collection, Pennsylvania State University Archives, 275148 AX/CATO/PSUA/M/07.17; Sturken, *Tangled Memories,* 12–17, 19–43.

18 Quoted in Johnson, "Granite Platoon," 2.

19 Frank J. Murray, "The Korean War 'Silent Veterans' Will Get Memorial" and "Dedication Ceremony Korean War Veterans Memorial," *Washington Times,* 14 June 1989, d01.

20 James Reston, "The Monument Glut," *New York Times,* 10 September 1995; George F. Will, "The Status Sweepstakes," *Newsweek,* 26 August 1991, 64.

21 J. Carter Brown, The Commission of Fine Arts to Mr Stanton, National Parks Service, 9 August 1989. NARA, RG 220, RTCCB, KWVMAB, box 2.

22 See the essays in Hélène Lipstadt, ed., *The Experimental Tradition: Essays on Competition in Architecture* (Princeton: The Architectural League of New York, 1989).

23 Mary McLeod, "The Battle for the Monument: The Vietnam Veterans Memorial," in *The Experimental Tradition,* 121.

24 See Don Kent Cooper's presentation to National Capital Memorial Commission, 8 November 1990, 11–13.

25 General Ray Davis to General P.X. Kelley, USMC (ret), 18 April 1994; Bob Hansen to Ad Hoc Design Committee, "Trip report to inspect current status of statues at foundry." NARA, RG 220, RTCCB, KWVMAB, 1991–95, box 5.

26 Part of the problem was that there seemed to be no official record of such things and the National Archives could offer no assistance. See RG 220 Records of Temporary Commissions, Committees, Boards, KWVMAB, 1991–95, box 2.

27 KWVMAB Memo from Bob Hansen, "The Dispersed Column Update #2," 20 March 1992, with map indicating race and position. NARA, RG 220, RTCCB, KWVMAB 1991–95, box 2.

28 The instructions were precise. For example: number three, "face looks too sweet"; number five, "overall face looks too tired, dead in the water, totally panicked, ok to be stressed but should show more determination"; number eight, "face too old"; number ten, "remove beard"; number eighteen, "remove pock marks on face." Attachment to number one to report, Ad Hoc Committee, 15 November 1994. W. Kent Cooper, Memo Review of Sculpture at Tallix [in response to Advisory Board requests]. NARA, RG 220, KWVMAB 1991–95, box 5.

29 Burns Lucas, Leon, and Lucas Architects, "The Korean War Veterans Memorial. A Statement of Concern," 25 September 1990. NARA, RG 220, RTCCB, KVMAB, Early History Files, Design Concerns, box 4.

30 T. Leith, "Monumental Conflict: Contest Winners in Dispute over Design of Korean War Memorial," *NCSU: The Alumni Magazine of North Carolina State University* (June / July 1991), 31–3.

31 Benjamin Forgey, "Architects Sue over Redesign of Memorial: Team Seeks to Halt Plan for Korean War Monument," *Washington Post*, 19 December 1990, C01; John Paul Lucas has observed that he had been misquoted in the GI Joe reference. Communication with the author, January 2015; Lucas was also quotaed as stating that the revised design embodies the way certain generals like war to be viewed. Kristin Huckshorn, "Monuments: Cornerstones of Controversy," *USA Today*, 6 November 1990.

32 The gist of the press release was drafted by Jan Jackson for General Stilwell in response to BL3's press statement in "My 2 C + worth." Her ideas were reused in replies to veterans' enquiries and to the press. NARA, RG 220, RTCCB, KWVMAB, "Early History Files 1986–91," *Design Concerns*, box 4.

33 "Memo from Bob Hansen to Mike McKevitt, "Historical Summary and Current Status of Litigation," 11 June 1991. NARA, TCC KWVMAB, box 7.

34 Benjamin Forgey, "Architects Sue over Redesign of Memorial: Team Seeks to Halt Plan for Korean War Monument," *Washington Post*, 19 December 1990, C01.

35 Gene Yarnell, "Prop Blast," *Canopy* 7 (October 1990).

36 General Stilwell to Kenneth Meier, 4 February 1991. NARA, RG 220, RTCCB, KWVMAB, 1986–91, box 4.

37 Col (ret.) William E. Weber, "Weber on the Wire," *VFW* (Winter 1990): 4.

38 The initial estimated cost of $5 million had increased steadily to a final cost of $18 million.

39 See "You Wrote It" and "You Said It" in *Graybeards* 6, no. 5 (June 1991): 15–16.

40 See *Graybeards*, June 1991, and *Korean War Educator*, Korean War Veterans Association News, KWVA Accomplishments (2002). http// www.koreanwareducator.org/kwva/p_accomplishment_korea (accessed April 2010).

41 It is worth noting that the polished black walls in Maya Lin's design had particularly irked the design opponents.

42 See: Cooper-Lecky's presentation to the National Capital Memorial Commission, 8 November 1990, 11–48; KWVMAB, "Meeting of November 8 1990," NARA, RG 220, RTCCB, KWVMAB, box 6.

43 Memo to KWVMAB from Office of the Executive Director, "Board Consensus on Walled Depiction and Related Matters," 3 January 1990. NARA, RG 220, RTCCB, KWVMAB, 1986–91, box 4.

44 In elaborate detail Stilwell described the essential elements of the war story in ten main battle episodes. Stilwell, "Pertinent Extracts from General Stilwell's memo dated December 18, 1989 on Major Historical Events To Be Included on the Wall," Attachment no. 2, KWVMAB, 3 January 1990. NARA, RG 220, RTCCB, KWVMAB, 1986–91, box 4.

45 Benjamin Forgey, "More Salvos in Memorial Fight: Commission Delays Decision on Korean War Monument," *Washington Post*, 14 December 1990, B02.

46 *New York Times*, 15 December 1990.

47 Benjamin Forgey, "Memorial Design Rejected: Commission Wants the Korean Monument Scaled Down," *Washington Post,* 18 January 1991, C03; J. Carter Brown to Colonel Badger, 22 January 1991. NARA, RG 220, RTBCC, KWVAB, box 6.

48 Sarah Booth Conroy, "Korean Memorial Praised: Revision Includes Mural of Support Troops," *Washington Post*, 22 February 22 1991,

bo2. A number of the Advisory Board members initially were not enthusiastic, presumably because the detailed military history of the war had made way for these images. "Memo to all Advisory Board Members from Bob Hansen," "Schedule," 22 May 1991. NARA, RG 220, RTBCC, KWVAB, 1987–95, box 7.

49 Chairman's Notes, Stilwell and Associates, 19 March 1991. NARA, RG 220, RTBCC, KWVAB, 1987–95, box 7.

50 NCPC, "Korean War Veterans Memorial, Report of the Task Force," 4 April 1991, 6pps. NARA, RG 220, RTBCC, KWVAB, box 2; Sarah Booth Conroy, "The Korea Memorial's Slow March," *Washington Post*, 5 April 1991, bo3.

51 Barbara Gamarekian, "The Korean War Memorial: Another Review, Another No," *New York Times*, 29 June 1991.

52 Quoted in Lisa Loeffler, "No Peace for Korean War Memorial," *The Daily Collegian*, 2 July 1991. http://www.collegian.psu.edu/archives/article_bdb1fc56-24fd-5ee1-8677-d72a72d364f6.html.

53 P.X. Kelley, American Battle Monuments Commission to The Honourable J Carter Brown, 27 August 1991. NARA, RG 220, RTBCC, KWVAB, 1987–95, box 1.

54 See National Commander of the American Legion to the Chairman of National Parks, 11 October 1991. RG 220, RTBCC, KWVAB Temporary Committees, 1988–95, box 1.

55 General Raymond G. Davis, "Introductory Remarks Before the Commission of Fine Arts," 24 October 1991, 7; Draft Immediate Press Release from Bob Hansen, 24 October 1991 [not issued], 2; J. Carter Brown to General Kelly, ABMC, 31 October 1991. NARA, RG 220, RTBCC, KWVAB, box 7.

56 Commission of Fine Arts, 24 October 1991, [Minutes] 121. RG, 220 RTBCC, KWVAB Temporary Committees, 1988–95, box 1.

57 Memo to All Advisory Board Members from Bob Hansen, "Status of Approval Strategy," 18 November 1991. NARA, RG 220, RTBCC, KWVAB, box 7.

58 The report of the ground breaking refers to the sixteen figures that will comprise the core of the memorial. "Korean War Memorial Moves a Step Forward," *Washington Post*, 15 June 1992, do3.

59 Barry Schwartz and Todd Bayma, "Commemoration and the Politics of Recognition: The Korean War Veterans Memorial," *American Behavioral Scientist* 42, no. 6 (March 1999): 946–67; G. Kurt Piehler,

Remembering War the American Way (Washington, DC: Smithsonian Books, 1995), xiii; Savage, *Monument Wars*, 282.

60 Savage, *Monument Wars*, 282.

61 Sarah Booth Conroy, "Arts Panel Approves Korean War Memorial," *Washington Post*, 17 January 1992, C01.

3

Australia's Memorial Building on the Western Front, 1916–2015[1]

JOAN BEAUMONT

The Roll of Honour at the Australian War Memorial, Canberra, lists over 102,000 men and women who have died serving with the Australian defence forces since 1901.[2] Almost all of these deaths occurred in conflicts in other countries, often as a function of alliance diplomacy. As a consequence, there are many sites across the globe in which Australians, individually and collectively, have invested meaning and significance, by virtue of the fact that they, or their family members, fought and died there. As Matthew Graves has put it, "The memorial geography of Anzac [now] straddles the globe from France, Belgium and Turkey, via the Mediterranean and Middle East through Thailand, Malaysia, Korea, and Vietnam, to Papua New Guinea and New Caledonia."[3]

The processes whereby Australians imprinted this memory footprint around the globe have changed over time, varying according to the mix of individual and collective agency in memory-making and the role played by the Australian state in national commemoration. But in almost all cases, given that Australian sites of war memory are extra-territorial, there has had to be an accommodation and negotiation with the foreign countries and communities that host them. This chapter considers these negotiations in relation to the installation of Australian war memorials on the Western Front: firstly, in the immediate post–World War I period; and then in the "second generation of memory" from the 1980s on.[4] By tracing the history of Australia's memory footprints in France and Belgium, the chapter illustrates the growing importance in recent commemoration of a sense of a shared, possibly transnational, memory, a memory which transcends national boundaries and plays a key role in the "memorial diplomacy" of contemporary international relations.[5]

THE SITES OF THE FIRST AUSTRALIAN FOOTPRINTS

Australian war memorial building in France began during the war itself. In 1917 the 1st and 2nd Divisions of the Australian Imperial Force (AIF) erected two crosses in the ruins of Pozières where they had suffered huge casualties in July and August 1916. A 4.5-metre-high Celtic cross honoured the 1st Division, and stood on this site until 1932 when it was dismantled and sent to the Australian War Memorial.[6] Another wooden cross, erected in memory of the 2nd Division, lasted until it was destroyed by a storm in 1930.[7]

These seem to have been unofficial memorials, in the sense that they arose from "first-hand experience in small-scale communities rather than the 'imagined communities' of a large nation."[8] Within months of the war's ending, however, a more officially coordinated process of Australian commemoration on the Western Front began. Early in 1919 the Australian government decided to erect memorials at various points in the battle zone "to commemorate the deeds of the A.I.F." After planning meetings of senior leaders of the Australian Corps in Belgium and London, it was agreed to build two memorials to the Australian Corps, one in France and one in the Ypres salient, and to erect a memorial to each of the five infantry divisions which had fought in France and Belgium.[9] The memorials, in the form of obelisks, were to be funded by the government to the tune of £12,000.[10]

The choice as to the particular site for each divisional memorial was delegated to the divisions themselves, or at least to their senior leaders.[11] There were some guiding criteria: firstly, the memorials should commemorate battles; secondly, they should be on sites "where the greatest number of men fell."[12] In addition, the memorials should be "in the most commanding view points" so that they could be seen from many locations.[13] No one was to be left in any doubt about Australians' exploits. Rather, "the famous deeds of the 'Aussies' [were to] be marked for all time on the Battle Fields."[14]

Pozières was the unanimous choice for the 1st Division's memorial.[15] Not only was this already established as a site of remembrance, but it was the first operation on a large scale undertaken by the 1st

Australian Division in France. Three Victoria Crosses were awarded during this operation, and Charles Bean, war correspondent, official historian, and pre-eminent agent of Australian war memory, later called the Windmill at Pozières "a ridge more densely sown with Australian sacrifice than any other place on earth."[16]

The sites chosen by the other divisions, however, come as something of a surprise today. The 2nd Division chose Mont St Quentin. This hill, overlooking Péronne, had been captured in a dramatic assault between 31 August and 3 September 1918, and this operation had been widely lauded at the time. The British commander of the Fourth Army, General Sir Henry Rawlinson, declared it to be "a feat worthy of the highest praise."[17] Interestingly, the 2nd Division memorial was not the standard obelisk of other divisional memorials. Instead, the division's commander, General Charles Rosenthal, took it upon himself, even before the war ended, to commission "a first class Australian sculptor," Web Gilbert.[18] The statue Gilbert created was unveiled on the seventh anniversary of the Mont St Quentin attack in 1925 by French Field Marshal Ferdinand Foch. Depicting a towering Australian soldier plunging his bayonet into a prostrate German eagle, it was not so much a memorial as a triumphant monument to the slaying of Imperial Germany. Unsurprisingly, the statue disappeared in the Second World War, when Péronne was again occupied by the Germans.

Meanwhile, in 1919 the 3rd Division chose for the site of its obelisk Sailly-le-Sec, on the northern bank of the Somme, east of Amiens. It was here that the division had played a role in halting the spectacular German offensive of March 1918. According to General John Monash, the divisional commander at that time, this represented "literally, the end of the great German advance in this part of the field."[19] The 4th Division, for its part, chose another 1918 battlefield: Bellenglise. Here, in September 1918, the division had helped break the Hindenburg Outpost Line, earning an accolade from a German battalion commander to the effect that "Your men are so brave and have so much dash that it is impossible to stop them."[20] It is significant that the 4th Division chose Bellenglise in preference to other battles in which it had been involved, particularly Bullecourt, during which the casualty rate had been as high as 78 per cent in one brigade.[21] The surviving records state that an initial decision by the division in favour of Bullecourt was reversed after "2 long and wordy meetings" in 1919.[22] Possibly it mattered that the Bullecourt "was not what be [*sic*] termed a successful operation."[23] Finally, the 5th Division chose Polygon Wood, one of the more successful operations within the long Third Ypres campaign of August to November 1917.

It seems clear from the sites chosen for these divisional memorials that the leaders of the AIF preferred locations were "reminiscent of their greatest achievements."[24] They wanted to be remembered for their victories, not for catastrophic defeats – and particularly not for war's traumatizing effects which have been a central trope in the post-1980s incarnation of the Australian national memory of war, the Anzac legend.[25]

NEGOTIATING THE MEMORIAL SITES

Choosing where to install the divisional memorials was only the beginning of the process of Australian memorialisation. After this, Australian authorities had to gain approval for their claims from the British authorities under whom the AIF had served. Since Australian units had always formed a small part of a vast imperial and multinational war effort, there were other claims to "ownership" of particular battlefields. Such potential disputes were moderated through the London-based Battle Exploit Memorials Committee, which required "properly documented evidence" to back Australia's case.[26] In the end, the committee did not block any of the claims made by the five Australian divisions. It was probably to Australia's advantage that these claims were made early in the post-armistice period when much of the decision-making surrounding imperial war graves and memorials was still fluid.[27]

Another challenge was acquiring the land upon which the Australian memorials would stand. Faced with a tsunami of memorial plans from its allies, the French government declared in April 1919 that it was willing to accept proposals for permanent memorials. However, it insisted on dealing with one central authority.[28] This was agreed to be the Imperial War Graves Commission (IWGC), whose charter gave it responsibility for acquiring land for the purposes of cemeteries, erecting permanent memorials in cemeteries and elsewhere, and maintaining all British Empire military cemeteries and graves.[29] Australia, of necessity, had to work within this framework of imperial memorial diplomacy, since it had no independent diplomatic service at this time. However, Australian authorities were keen to use the labour of the AIF as it awaited repatriation to build the divisional memorials, so they initiated negotiations for land purchases with the local stakeholders. These purchases were referred via the IWGC to the French and Belgian governments for approval.[30]

By late 1919 four of the five divisional memorials had been completed.[31] In addition to these, a plaque was installed in Amiens Cathedral in November 1920 to mark the role the AIF had played in defence of the city in 1918.[32] Meanwhile, to the north at Hill 60 near Ypres, a monument to the 1st Australian Tunnelling Company had been erected by the company itself in April 1919.[33] This marked the site of a spectacular explosion of subterranean mines which killed some 10,000 Germans prior to the Allied attack at Messines on 7 June 1917.

THE AUSTRALIAN NATIONAL MEMORIAL, VILLERS-BRETONNEUX

After this burst of memorial building in 1919 had ebbed, the focus of Australian commemoration on the Western Front turned to the construction of war cemeteries and memorials to the missing. These were essentially imperial commemorative activities, led by the IWGC on which Australia, like the other dominions, was represented. It was not until 1938 that the Australians finally erected their national memorial at Villers-Bretonneux.

Why this memorial was so delayed is not entirely clear. As mentioned, the decision was taken early in 1919 to build two memorials to the Australian Corps. The Belgian option, on Broodseinde Ridge, was soon abandoned; it seems it was thought that the 5th Division memorial at the nearby Polygon Wood would serve this function.[34] Meanwhile, the location for the other memorial, Villers-Bretonneux, was chosen by mid-1919. This was again a site of Australian victory, the much vaunted recapture of the town of Villers-Bretonneux from German occupation on the night of 24–25 April 1918. The fact that this action occurred on the second anniversary of the landing at Gallipoli in April 1915, Anzac Day, gave it almost instant mythic status for Australians.

A ten-acre site outside Villers-Bretonneux was purchased by the Australian government in 1919, but thereafter progress on building the memorial slowed.[35] This was possibly because the French government was becoming uneasy about populating their sovereign landscape with massive British memorials.[36] It was only in 1938 that the Australian national memorial was finally unveiled. Its design, by the British imperial architect Sir Edwin Lutyens, was a tower 31 metres tall, flanked by walls inscribed with the names of more than 10,000 Australians missing in France. The unveiling of the memorial in 1938 was presided over by King George VI, with Queen Elizabeth and the French President Le Brun in attendance. Since budgets were tight in the post-Depression years, the Australian prime minister did not come – an absence unthinkable at any major commemorative ceremony today.[37] Instead the Australian delegation included the high commissioner in London, former prime minister Stanley Bruce, and those cabinet ministers who happened to be in Britain already on government business. Hundreds of veterans and nurses made the journey to Villers-Bretonneux, although the only government financial assistance they received was for travel from London.[38]

THE SECOND MEMORY "BOOM"

After the installation of the national memorial, there was a long hiatus in Australian commemorative interventions on the Western Front. With Australian formations not being deployed to land fighting in Western Europe during the Second World War, there were few new sites on the continent that commanded Australian attention. After 1945 the main concern was with repairing the damage inflicted on First World War memorials as a result of battle or the German occupation of France and Belgium.

Primary among these sites was Mont St Quentin, where the 2nd Division memorial had disappeared. In 1947–49, the Australian government decided, after consulting Rosenthal, not to replace the statue, partly because it was not possible to find the cases of the original, and partly because it was conceded that this "might in the years to come be regarded as offensive." Only the panels on the base of the statue were replaced at this time.[39] In the mid-1960s, however, a constellation of veterans of the 2nd Division, the lobby group the Returned and Services League (RSL), and Australian ambassadors to France pressured the Australian government to install a new memorial.[40] Unveiled in 1971, this took the form of a consciously more subdued statue, depicting an Australian soldier in a slouch hat with his head cast slightly down.

The real impetus for a wave of new memorial building came, however, with the remarkable resurgence in memory of war from the mid-1980s on. The reasons for this phenomenon, which was global as well as Australian, are beyond the scope of this chapter.[41] Suffice to say that memorial building on the Western Front shifted from being, as it had in 1919, the preserve of a relatively small political and military elite, acting with no reference to audiences at home, to the domain of multiple agents playing out their memory-making in very public performances, at home and abroad. Concurrently, memorial diplomacy, which in the immediate post–First World War period had been an instrument whereby Australians secured their claims on sites of memory, became itself a force of international relations. With this, the nationalist impulse behind commemoration, though still dominant, became infused with the rhetoric and rituals of a supposed shared or transnational memory between Australia and its former allies.

All of this became manifest in a proliferation of new memorials, mostly at the initiative of the Australian government, and a reorientation in Australia's commemorative focus towards catastrophe rather than victory. Of course, the five divisional memorials of 1919 remained in place, but at least two of them, Sailly-le-Sec and Bellenglise, slipped to the margins of commemorative practice. Sailly-le-Sec, in particular, was eclipsed by two other sites in its vicinity: one, the well-established national memorial at Villers-Bretonneux; and the other, a new site of memorialisation, Le Hamel.

Villers-Bretonneux's continued prominence has owed something to its having a mix of attributes that attract battlefield "pilgrims," as those undertaking such tourism are now routinely called. It is reasonably accessible from Paris and close to the town of Villers-Bretonneux, which has creatively constructed its own identity around a shared memory of its liberation in 1918 and a history of postwar collaboration with Australians.[42] However, beyond this, the status of Villers-Bretonneux in the Australian memory hierarchy has been affirmed strongly by ongoing interventions by the Australian government and Franco–Australian memorial diplomacy. The national memorial was the site of a transnational ceremony in 1998 when, in recognition of the eightieth anniversary of the end of the war, the French bestowed the Legion of Honour on four very elderly Australian veterans.[43] Ten years later, more than 5,000 Australians attended an official Anzac Day dawn service at Villers-Bretonneux, an event which has been seen by one scholar as something of "a commemorative take-over"[44] in the sense that the established commemorations by the local citizens were overtaken by a more orchestrated ritual on the part of the Australian government. In the aftermath of this event, the Australian authorities decided to make an official dawn service an annual event at Villers-Bretonneux.[45]

Le Hamel's new status similarly reflected a more intense level of Australian commemorative intervention in France. Overlooked as a site of memorialisation for many decades, Hamel was "discovered" as part of a flurry of new memorial building under John Howard (prime minister, 1996–2007). Howard, whose father and grandfather had both served in the First World War, embraced the opportunity to mark the eightieth anniversary of the end of the war with a memorial honouring not just the Australian Corps but all Australians who had served in France. This was part of Howard's wider agenda of refocusing Australian war commemoration on Europe, as opposed to the Asia-Pacific orientation of his political arch-rival, Paul Keating (prime minister, 1991–96), in the early 1990s.[46]

Unveiled in 1998 (and rededicated in 2008 after major repairs necessitated by poor design), the Hamel memorial again spoke to the way Australia's memory footprint was being reshaped by memorial diplomacy. Its unveiling was attended by delegations from several nations, among them France, Britain, and the United States (some of whose forces had fought under Monash at Hamel). The occasion was an exemplar of those "carefully choreographed public ceremonies on the anniversaries of historic occasions at selected sites of memory, long established or of recent invention," to quote Matthew Graves.[47] Conscious of the French audience, the Australian Minister for Veterans' Affairs, Bruce Scott, chose to depict Hamel rather improbably as a fusion of the Anzac and French revolutionary traditions: "No longer cannon fodder, sheep driven into the bloody slaughter of years past, but free men, partners in the enterprise before them. In the fight for France's liberty, equality, and fraternity found new form at Hamel."[48]

While Hamel and Villers-Bretonneux were being reinvented, other sites of memory, notably Bullecourt and Fromelles, also gained a new prominence in Australian commemoration. Memorial diplomacy played a role in their rediscovery but primarily their memorialisation testified to the complexity of contemporary memory formation and, in particular, the way in which pro-active individuals created a memorializing context into which the Australian state was drawn. Passed over by the 4th Division in 1919, Bullecourt was for decades on no remembrance trail other than that of veterans and their enquiring families. However, from the 1970s, intrigued French residents created a museum and raised funds for a memorial. This was soon capped with a bronze slouch hat funded by the Australian War Memorial, the Returned and Services League, and the Australian Department of Foreign Affairs. Progressively, the Australian government became fully woven into this tapestry of local remembrance. A new Australian memorial park was opened in 1992, in which was installed a bronze statue of a digger by the sculptor Peter Corlett.[49]

Fromelles too was "forgotten" for decades, even though it was one of the worst battles for the AIF on the Western Front: some 5,533 Australian casualties were incurred in twenty-four hours on 19–20 July 1916. However, it was not until the 1990s that an Australian memorial park was created here, at the centre of which was another Corlett statue, Cobbers. Depicting an Australian staggering under the weight of a wounded soldier draped across his shoulders (an actual event from 1916), this was a reflection of the degree to which compassion, sacrifice, and mateship were becoming the distillation of the Australian national memory of war in the age of "post-heroic warfare."[50]

The Fromelles memorial park was a government initiative but far more important in the projection of Fromelles to a dominant place in the commemorative hierarchy was the activism of a small group of Australians, headed by a retired school teacher from Melbourne. Intent on finding a mass grave in which they believed that many missing Australians of Fromelles were buried, they initially met with official scepticism. But their persistence won out – thanks, in part, to advocacy by the popular media whose role in the construction of contemporary memory can be critically important. Eventually a mass grave containing the remains of around 250 soldiers, most of whom were Australian, was excavated near Fromelles.[51] These remains were then reburied in 2010 in a newly created cemetery, the first to be built by the Commonwealth War Graves Commission in fifty years.

The missing of Fromelles provided a platform for yet more memorial diplomacy. The former head of the French army claimed at the first of many Fromelles burials that "Memory is only alive when nations are brought together. Memory is only alive when it unites generations."[52] But Fromelles also spoke to two of the phenomena that have fuelled the growth of Australian war memory in recent years: firstly, the explosion of genealogy and, with it, the desire to set family stories "in a wider, at times, universal context"; and secondly, the centrality of victimhood in contemporary memory of war.[53] The very fact that Fromelles was *not* a victory, but rather a manifestation of the worst of British almost criminal incompetence, resonates with today's popular understanding of the First World War much more effectively than does Polygon Wood or Bellenglise, the successful operations with which the 4th and 5th Divisions chose to be identified in 1919.

CONCLUSION

The early twenty-first-century imprint of Australia's national memory on the landscape of France and Belgium is manifest in the Australian Remembrance Trail, which has been developed by the Department of Veterans' Affairs for the centenary of the First World War.[54] This includes four of the 1919 memorials – Bellenglise, Mont St Quentin, Pozières, and Villers-Bretonneux (the latter of which is being enhanced by an interpretive centre) – and the more recent sites of memorialisation – Fromelles, Bullecourt, and Le Hamel. These are joined also by Péronne, Ploegsteert (near Messines), Zonnebeke, and Ieper (Ypres). Most of the latter have an intrinsic historic importance, but their inclusion also owes something to the fact that they have established local museums on the First World War.[55] The Australian government can invest in these, at relatively little financial cost, while accruing significant capital in international collaboration.

These "stations of the cross" of the secular religion of Anzac would be familiar to the men of the AIF. All were sites of great struggle and loss in the war years and they align with the battle honours on the national memorial. However, the soldiers who fought the war might question the reordering of the priorities within these sites of memory, and the emphasis on victimhood and sacrifice in the discourse that accompanies contemporary rituals of commemoration. They would also surely be astounded at the centrality of war memory in the Australian national political culture and in international diplomacy, and the commodification and trivialisation of war commemoration that accompanies this. What this dissonance between the memories of the men of 1919 and Australian national memory today confirms is the now axiomatic lesson about collective memory formation: that it is dynamic and contingent, and its rituals enshrine the values of the present rather than of the past. For this reason alone, Australia's memory footprint in France and Belgium will continue to be the subject of ongoing renegotiation and reinvention in the changing political landscape that will prevail in the decades after the centenary commemorations have ended.

NOTES

1 This is a shorter version of the article by Joan Beaumont, "Australia's Global Memory Footprint: Memorial Building on the Western Front, 1916–2015," *Australian Historical Studies* 46, no. 1 (March 2015): 45–63. The Version of Record can be accessed at Taylor & Francis Online at http://dx.doi.org/10.1080/1031461X.2014.998246.

2 Australian War Memorial (AWM). https://www.awm.gov.au/encyclopedia/war_casualties/(accessed 20 August 2014).

3 Matthew Graves, "Memorial Diplomacy in Franco–Australian Relations," in Shanti Sumartojo and Ben Wellings, eds., *Nation, Memory and Great War Commemoration: Mobilizing the Past in Europe, Australia and New Zealand* (Bern: Peter Lang, 2014), 182.

4 Jay Winter, *Remembering War: The Great War between Memory and History in the Twentieth Century* (New Haven: Yale University Press, 2006), 26.

5 I borrow this term from Graves, "Memorial Diplomacy."

6 Photos EZ0131, E02059, AWM collection, AWM. http://www.awm.gov.au/collection/REL29088/(accessed 20 August 2014).

7 Memo to Fabian Ware, Imperial War Graves Commission (IWGC), 18 January 1930. A458 P337/6 pt 2, National Archives of Australia (NAA).

8 John Bodnar, "Public Memory in an American City: Commemoration in Cleveland," in *Commemorations: The Politics of National Identity*, edited by John Gillis (Princeton: Princeton University Press, 1994), 75.

9 Minutes of conference at Ham-sur-Heure, Belgium, on Battle Memorial Scheme, 14 March 1919. AWM27 623/3, AWM; "Australian War Memorials in France," 14 March 1919. AWM27 623/4, AWM; Australian Battle Memorials and Soldiers' Graves (ABM&SG) Committee, Minutes, 20 March 1919. A2909 AGS6/1/5 pt 1, NAA.

10 Department of Defence to Prime Minister's Department, 7 October 1919. A461 D370/1/15, NAA.

11 ADC Australian Corps, Lieut. Temperly, "Re War Memorial," 4 April 1919. AWM27 623/3; Brig-General I. Mackay, "Australian War Memorials," 16 March 1919. AWM27 623/4, AWM.

12 Meeting of GOCS [General Officers Commanding] Divisions and Brigades, "Australian War Memorials in France," 14 March 1919. AWM27 627/3, AWM.

13 ABM&SG Committee, 20 March 1919. A2909 AGS6/1/5 pt 1, NAA.

14 Captain S. Keesing, Australia House, "Proposed A.I.F. Memorials in France," 27 February 1919. A2909 AGS6/1/5 pt 1, NAA.

15 "1st Australian Divisional Memorial," AWM27 623/4, AWM.

16 "1st Australian Division," "1st Australian Divisional Memorial," AWM27 623/4; C.E.W. Bean, *Anzac to Amiens: A Shorter History of the Australian Fighting Services in the First World War* (Canberra: Australian War Memorial, 1946), 264.

17 "2nd Divisional Memorial," December 4, 1918. AWM27 623/5, AWM.

18 Sir Charles Rosenthal diary, November 3, 1918. MLMSS 2739, vol. 1, State Library of NSW, Sydney; Memo, Charles Rosenthal, "Second Australian Division," December 4, 1918. AWM27, 623/5.

19 John Monash, *The Australian Victories in France in 1918* (London: Hutchinson & Co., 1920), 29.

20 "4th Divisional Memorial," AWM27 623/7, AWM.

21 John Coates, ed., *An Atlas of Australia's Wars* (Melbourne: Oxford University Press, 2001), 60.

22 General E.G. Sinclair-MacLagan to General T. Hobbs, 28 March 1919. AWM27 623/7, AWM.

23 Commander 12th Australian Infantry Brigade, Ref. G53, 13 March 1919. AWM27 623/7, AWM.

24 "War Memorials in France and Belgium," A461 D370/1/15, NAA.

25 Christina Twomey, "Trauma and the Reinvigoration of Anzac: An Argument," *History Australia* 10, no. 3 (December 2013): 88.

26 Appendix to Paper no. 2, Battle Exploit Memorials Committee (BEMC), April 1919. A2909 AGS1/3/1, NAA.

27 Army Order, 12 April 1919, AWM27 623/7, Appendix to Paper no. 2, BEMC. The only claim about which there was any hesitation was Polygon Wood, but this was approved by the end of May 1919. Minutes of 2nd Meeting of the Battle Exploit Memorials Committee, 24 April 1919. A2909 AGS1/3/1, NAA.

28 War Office, Army Order, "Memorials on Battlefields," 12 April 1919. AWM27 623/9, AWM.

29 Fabian Ware, *The Immortal Heritage: An Account of the Work and Policy of The Imperial War Graves Commission during Twenty Years 1917–1937* (London: Cambridge University Press, 1937), 25–41.

30 The Australian representative, Captain A.H. Bardin, made recommendations to ABM&SGC which forwarded these to the IWGC for action with the French government. Minutes of ABM&SGC, 17 July 1919, A2909 AGS 1/2/1, NAA. All sites were formally transferred back to the French State in 1937. Minute for Prime Minister, "Australian War Memorials in France," October 1937, A461 A370/1/15, NAA.

31 The 5th Division memorial at Polygon Wood had then to be reconstructed in 1920 because of insufficient filling-in of tunnels and dugouts underneath. CO Australian War Graves Services, "Australian Memorials," 17 December 1920. A2909 AGS 6/1/6, pt 1, NAA.

32 "Australian Memorials," 17 December 1920. A2909 AGS 6/1/6, pt 1, NAA.

33 The Hill 60 memorial was replaced in 1923 by a granite obelisk after the original fell into a state of disrepair.

34 Meeting of ABM&SG Committee, 29 May 1919. A2909 AGS 1/2/1, NAA.

35 "Australian Memorials," 17 December 1920. A2909 AGS 6/1/6, NAA.

36 See, for example, Report on Meeting of Anglo-French Mixed Committee, 16 July 1926; Minutes of 7th Meeting of Anglo–French Mixed Committee, 25 June 1926. A461 H370/1/15 pt 1, NAA.

37 Prime Minister J. Lyons to Minister for Repatriation, 7 February 1938. A461 H370/1/15 pt 3, NAA.

38 "Villers Bretonneux War Memorial," 18 March 1938. A461 H370/1/15 pt 3, NAA.

39 Letter J.D. Anthony to Senator Edward Mattner, 18 March 1964. A463 1964/4940, NAA; Appendix to Cabinet Submission on Australian Divisional Memorials in France and Belgium, 16 January 1947. A2700 1208A; Second Australian Division 1st A.I.F., Circular no. 2, April 1970. A3211 1971/1087 pt 8, NAA.

40 K. Pallor, Commonwealth War Graves Commission to A.D. Watt, Australian High Commissioner, London, 15 April 1971. A3211, 1971/1087 pt 8, NAA; The RSL initially opposed the change but then advocated for a new statue to mark the anniversary of Mont St Quentin in 1968. Anthony to PM Harold Holt, 21 July 1966. A463 1964/4940, NAA.

41 For a recent engagement with this question, see Carolyn Holbrook, *Anzac: The Unauthorised Biography* (Sydney: University of New South Wales Press, 2014).

42 Linda Wade, "'By Diggers Defended, By Victorians Mended,' Searching for Villers-Bretonneux" (PhD thesis, University of Wollongong, 2008);

Linda Wade, "The Reconstruction of Villers Bretonneux, 1918–22," in *Anzac Legacies*, edited by Martin Crotty and Marina Larsson (Melbourne: Australian Scholarly Publishing, 2010), 146–65.

43 Minister for Veterans' Affairs Media Release, 17 June 1998, supplied by Department of Veterans' Affairs under special access.

44 Romain Fathi, "'A Piece of Australia in France': Australian Authorities and the Commemoration of Anzac Day at Villers-Bretonneux in the Last Decade," in *Nation, Memory and Great War Commemoration*, edited by Shanti Sumartojo and Ben Wellings, 280.

45 *The Age* (Melbourne), 25 April 2008.

46 Holbrook, *Anzac*, 179–94.

47 Graves, *Memorial Diplomacy*, 170.

48 Address by Minister for Veterans' Affairs, supplied under special access by Department of Veterans' Affairs, file reference 990975.

49 See Joan Beaumont, *Broken Nation: Australians and the Great War* (Sydney: Allen & Unwin, 2013), 305–7.

50 See Joan Beaumont, "Remembering the Heroes of Australia's Wars: From Heroic to Post-Heroic Memory," in *Heroism and the Changing Character of War: Towards Post-Heroic Warfare?* edited by Sibylle Scheipers (Basingstoke: Palgrave Macmillan, 2014), 344–6.

51 For a full account see P. Lindsay, *Fromelles* (Melbourne: Hardie Grant Books, 2008).

52 *The Australian*, 1 February 2010.

53 Winter, *Remembering War*, 40.

54 Department of Veterans' Affairs, "Australian Remembrance Trail along the Western Front." http://www.dva.gov.au/commems_oawg/OAWG/Pages/art.aspx (accessed 25 August 2014).

55 Local museums include Bullecourt, L'Historial de la Grande Guerre at Péronne, the Memorial Museum Passchendaele in Zonnebeke, and In Flanders Field Museum, Ieper.

4

Monument Missions: Remembrance, Reconstruction, and Transatlantic Memory in Postwar Europe, 1945–1962

SAM EDWARDS

"The plan requires a certain amount of ingenuity and audacity," said Colonel Charles E. Johnson, chief of staff of the US 3rd Infantry in an order sent to the division's head of logistics in September 1945. He continued:

> Send one 2.5 ton truck with a competent engineer officer … to the above sites [Licata, Anzio, St Tropez]. Have Officer [*sic*] pick suitable locations, not necessarily on the beach, but rather a main thoroughfare near beach. Have him then contact local mayor … and get permission to put this small compact memorial on selected spot … After the erection of all three monuments he returns, where upon you (G-4) turn all papers over to the G-1 (monuments officer) who writes a letter to the French and Italian Governments … and requests that this real estate and monument be allowed to remain forever as a monument not only to the 3rd Division but to the everlasting bond of friendship between the two great countries … As to how you will erect the monument at Fedala [North Africa], I haven't the slightest, but recommend that a letter be sent thru [*sic*] channels stating that we have this bronze plaque that we would like the French government to erect for us … as a symbol of the beginning of the struggle of brother nations – The U.S. of America and the Republic (?) of France as represented by the Free French Patriots against the German tyrant.[1]

Over the next few months, and for reasons that are difficult to determine, no action seems to have been taken with regard to Johnson's order. Nonetheless, towards the end of July 1946 the order was reissued by the adjutant to Major General Parker, the commanding officer of the division. In other words, this time the order came straight from the top. Consequently, on 26 July 1946 Captain James Eakin left the headquarters of the 3rd Division in Bad Wildungen, Germany, and, making use of a truck like that suggested by Johnson, set out on a journey that would take him through much of war-torn Europe. On 31 July he arrived in St Tropez in the south of France, built a simple stone monument (upon which was attached a small bronze plaque) commemorating the division's role in the liberation of the Rhone Valley, and, by 12 August, he was able to move on. A few days later, on 19 August, Eakin arrived in Anzio, chose a suitable location, came to an agreement with the town mayor, built another small monument and, once again, went on his way. A similar situation followed when he arrived in Licata, Sicily, on 1 September, and this time the monument, which was almost identical to the two that preceded it, was completed by the 13th. This monument mission then concluded at the end of September 1946 with a quick trip across the Mediterranean to North Africa. By 15 October a stone marker commemorating the 3rd Division's role "in the long, hard struggle that terminated in the liberation of France and the defeat of Germany" was in place on the North African coast at the town of Fedala, just south of Casablanca. Eakin returned to Marseilles shortly after. He was safely back in Bad Wildungen by 4 November, and a few weeks later was able to report to division headquarters that "monuments of the design approved by the Commanding General of the Third Infantry Division have been erected ... to commemorate the beachheads which the Third Infantry Division established against hostile defences during World War II."[2]

In many respects, Captain Eakin's journey through battle-scarred Europe was amongst the final missions of the war; the heroic dead of the 3rd Infantry were memorialized, their sacrifices venerated, their passing mourned. But, in another sense, Eakin's three-month monument mission also marked a beginning: the first "act" in a postwar theatre of memory which saw soldiers and civilians, Americans and Europeans, veterans, town mayors, religious leaders, and agents of the American government commence work to mark the war's costs on the European landscape. This essay compares and contrasts this postwar memory work with reference to two specific regions of Europe, each of which had a similar yet also distinct war experience: northern France and northern Italy. In doing so, I show how local context and concerns frequently inflected the memorial projects of American veterans' groups, so many of which were initiated amidst the tensions of the early Cold War. As such, American commemoration was Europeanized, with many of the established memorials becoming forums in which contemporary transatlantic relations were constructed, celebrated, and, at times, contested.

TO CENSOR AND CONTROL: PRIVATE MEMORIALS AND THE AMERICAN BATTLE MONUMENTS COMMISSION, C. 1918–1945

The immediate post-1945 period witnessed a flurry of commemorative activity similar to that undertaken by Captain James Eakin as representatives of the Allied military endeavoured to mourn their fallen comrades.[3] For those in the federal government tasked with developing ordered, organized, and suitably national memorials, these privately sponsored commemorative projects were a source of real concern. Indeed, the organisation responsible for all overseas war commemoration – the American Battle Monuments Commission (ABMC) – had been established in 1923 partly in an attempt to control, censor, and if necessary *prohibit* such private memorial building. For the officers of this organisation, then chaired by the former commander-in-chief of the American Expeditionary Force, General Pershing, one of the key motives driving their work was to ensure that the fields of Flanders and northern France did not become overwhelmed by scores of artistically questionable markers and monuments, so many of which, they feared, would be abandoned once the troops returned home.[4] Left to become derelict and decayed, these crumbling structures would surely reflect poorly on the United States government, which would no doubt have to step in and provide for maintenance and repair at public expense. Shaping these concerns were the still-fresh memories of the post–Civil War period. At locations such as Gettysburg, for example, numerous veterans' groups built monuments of variable artistic merit, and some even engaged in what amounted to a commemorative competition "for the biggest and most attention-getting memorials ... even if this distorted the historical record."[5]

This was the precedent hanging over the actions of the ABMC after 1918; order, unity, clarity, and cohesion lost to distinction, difference, and competition. Thus, instead of the disorderly memorial theme parks that characterized so many Civil War battlefields, and keen that American military sacrifice not be overshadowed by that of their wartime allies (the British were planning a significant commemorative project under the auspices of the newly created Imperial War Graves Commission), the United States government intended to commemorate the fallen in France with a small number of nationally sponsored memorials. In doing so, the commission intended these commemorative landscapes to provide aesthetically arresting reminders of what the United States had given in the name of European freedom. Commemoration, in short, was to be one of the key mechanisms through which the United States would communicate its arrival as world power and celebrate its role as guarantor of European liberty.

In several respects, the ABMC achieved its objectives. By 1937, the commission had established eight national cemeteries in northern France and Belgium, together with eleven national memorials dedicated to those battles and campaigns considered particularly significant.[6] Yet, in other respects, the commission's success was partial, a point connected to another government policy. When offered the choice of leaving their lost loved ones in Europe or having their bodies returned home at government expense, the vast majority of American families chose the latter, thus depriving the ABMC of the quantity of bodies necessary to make a more powerful political statement (the British, in contrast, decreed that all those killed overseas would be buried where they fell).[7] Equally important, the commission's attempts to regulate private memorial projects similarly met with failure. Just as after the Civil War, American soldiers, often with enthusiastic local support, built numerous monuments marking their sacrifices and successes. Veterans of the 4th Division erected three memorials, one for each of the major battles in which they were involved, whilst the Society of the 1st Infantry Division erected five monuments at various locations in France and Belgium as well as a large memorial column in the nation's capital.[8] Elsewhere, the 2nd Infantry Division successfully erected no less than twenty-two memorials in Europe, although even this was outdone by veterans of the 5th Division who came closest to realizing the ABMC's worst fears: by 1920 they had constructed twenty-eight memorials in northern France and Belgium.[9]

Despite these visible – and recent – affronts to their authority, the very same impetus to control and censor still dominated the federal government's approach to commemoration a generation later. If anything, the post-1945 period witnessed an even more heightened awareness of the importance of appropriate memorial forms and sites: the United States had emerged as a global superpower; the American Century had dawned; and a new ideological enemy loomed on the horizon, just beyond the Urals. Thus, aware of the changed global political climate, and conscious that unlike in 1918 the European victory of 1945 was much more an American affair, the federal government once again initiated plans to produce an organized landscape of national memory that would honour the American dead whilst also reminding Europeans of their blood debt to the United States.

Reports from the ground in Europe further hastened efforts in this direction. In September 1945, for instance, Secretary of War Henry Stimson and Secretary of the Navy James Forrestal wrote to President Truman to inform him that "Certain of our troops overseas are planning to erect memorials to the achievements of their units and have requested approval of the theater commander. Some memorials have already been erected … General Eisenhower's staff have asked the War Department for guidance in these matters."[10] Clearly concerned, Stimson and Forrestal then requested that the ABMC once again oversee all American commemorative activities, for as they recalled: "The monuments erected by our troops before they returned from World War I were, in general, poorly designed and constructed." Indeed, as far as Stimson and Forrestal were concerned, these monuments had become "a source of embarrassment both to their authors and to the Representatives of our government in France and Belgium."[11] President Truman responded in March 1946 by issuing an executive order outlining the regulatory "Functions of the American Battle Monuments Commission," an act followed three months later by congressional approval of a bill authorizing the commission to assume responsibility for all overseas commemoration connected to World War II.[12] At General Eisenhower's headquarters these actions were welcomed; whilst still a junior officer, Ike had served on the staff of the ABMC in the 1920s, gaining what historian Steven Trout has called a "crash course in the often complex political and social dimensions of memory."[13] As a result, Ike understood "how modern wars are memorialized," and he was personally supportive of the commemorative agenda of the ABMC.[14] Therefore, in the White House, at the Pentagon, and at Supreme Headquarters Allied Expeditionary Force Europe (SHAEF), American leaders were committed to ensuring that the federal government controlled the memory of the war, at least in terms of how it would be marked on the European landscape.

But as the activities of Captain Eakin already suggest, and much as after 1918, those ever-persistent agents of private commemoration – American veterans – again outflanked the federal government, and privately sponsored monuments dedicated to the American military again marked the villages, fields, and lanes of Europe. Crucial to the success of such endeavours was the active support and assistance provided by local European communities. As such, these memorials provide a record of contemporary transatlantic relations, affirming the argument of Richard Pells that the artifacts of an expanding American culture were not simply imposed upon reluctant Europeans in the postwar period; instead, Europeans adopted, adapted, and Europeanised those features of American culture which they imported.[15] So too, then, were the structures of American commemoration altered by the involvement of European communities. Let us take two examples in turn: one from France, and the other from Italy. As we shall see, the success of each American memorial depended on whether local concerns connected with the wider transatlantic context; success depended on whether the monument matched the moment.

MONUMENT ON THE MARNE: THE 3RD INFANTRY DIVISION AT CHATEAU-THIERRY, C. 1918–1961

After 1918, and just like their counterparts in the 1st, 2nd, 4th, and 5th Divisions, the veterans of the 3rd Infantry Division initiated plans to establish a monument to their dead (a fact that also no doubt inspired their divisional descendants, led by Captain Eakin, in 1945). The division had fought several important engagements, most notably in the summer of 1918 during the Second Battle of the Marne, during which it had been committed to the Allied line at Chateau-Thierry, to the northwest of Paris. In July, as other Allied troops fell back in retreat before an aggressive German assault, the soldiers of the 3rd, particularly those in the 30th and 38th Regiments, stubbornly held their positions on the banks of the River Marne, duly earning their divisional nickname "Rock of the Marne." By the war's end, four months later, the division had suffered 16,000 casualties, of whom just over 3,000 were killed in action.[16]

Plans to erect a monument at Chateau-Thierry in memory of those killed, and to mark the division's role in stemming the last great German offensive, emerged shortly after the armistice. Members of the division then on occupation duty on the Rhine provided the resources necessary to identify an appropriate site as well as to commission an architect and construct a suitable monument. Funds to cover the total cost of $25,000 were in place by the summer of 1919, in time for Major General Robert L. Howze to lay the foundation stone in August.[17] Resistance from the ABMC and negotiations with the French authorities briefly delayed plans.[18] The local community was keen to ensure the site chosen connected with its plans for reconstruction; the newly formed commission, meanwhile, intended to secure for itself the right to commemorate American military sacrifice, and plans were already afoot for a nearby national memorial as well as a national war cemetery. For the officers of the ABMC, therefore, the memorial planned by the veterans of 3rd Infantry Division risked muddying the clarity of their commemorative message in the very way they most feared. Instead of an ordered landscape of memory suggestive of American power and national purpose, a monument specifically dedicated to the 3rd Infantry would fracture and fragment a unifying narrative. Indeed, it would surely produce a commemorative response from members of other American units who fought in and around Chateau-Thierry, much as was the case at locations like Gettysburg towards the end of the nineteenth century. Nonetheless, the ABMC once again failed to prevent the veterans of the 3rd Infantry from building their monument at Chateau-Thierry. Progress was slowed, to be sure, but with the assistance of the local community the project continued.[19] By 1927 the monument was complete (just in time for the grand return to Europe organized that year by the American Legion), and in 1929 members of the Society of the 3rd Infantry made their first official visit to the site.[20] It was an arresting structure, dominated by two large obelisks, one of which carried the date 1914, and the other 1918. Next to these, a low wall of the same white stone carried the division's insignia and the names of the dead.

This was the first monument established by veterans of the 3rd Division at Chateau-Thierry. But this is not the monument that stands there today. The current structure was not dedicated until 1961, and it is the story of how this came to be which draws our attention here. Even more than the first monument, this later memorial demonstrates the extent to which the success of privately sponsored American monuments depended on local support *and* on the transatlantic political climate. This story begins in 1940, during the Second World War.

Exactly what happened remains a point of conjecture, but one thing is certain: the monument to the 3rd Infantry erected at Chateau-Thierry after the First World War was damaged during the fighting connected to the German Blitzkrieg attack that stormed through France in the summer of 1940. During the course of these battles, one of the two tall "shafts" dominating the memorial's design was accidentally hit by German shell fire, or perhaps by aerial bombardment, or, worse still, the Germans might have deliberately ordered the monument destroyed in order to expunge the legacy of earlier defeat. The details were (and still are) a little unclear.[21] Indeed, whilst the monument certainly suffered battle damage, a few in the division thought responsibility for this lay elsewhere. For instance, some veterans believed it was destroyed by the French decision to demolish a nearby bridge in order to halt the German drive on Paris, although one senior officer, who claimed to have seen the still-standing monument in 1944, understood the damage to be the result of even greater negligence. Writing several years after the war, this officer remarked that the monument had actually suffered "due to the criminal carelessness of the French who removed the memorial [after it was damaged] from its old site to its present location on the hospital grounds."[22] One president of the Society of the 3rd Infantry even developed the theme further, contending that following accidental battle damage, the monument was in fact "saved from complete destruction on orders from one of the German generals in command of the invading forces in World War I out of respect for the fighting ability of the Division."[23] In short, it was either the fault of the Germans, who by accident or intention had hit one of the shafts and pock-marked the other, or it was the French, who due to various shades of neglect and disregard had damaged part of the structure and then compounded the problem by careless attempts to protect and preserve it.

This unresolved issue of responsibility lingered in the background for some time. By 1955, however, when the mayor of Chateau-Thierry first suggested to the division's veterans that the monument might be rebuilt,[24] the idea of French culpability was increasingly marginalized, and responsibility for the monument's demise became rather more impersonal; the product not of willful human agency or distracted neglect, but simply part of the collateral damage that accompanies "war." Gone, then, was blame; its place was taken by calm acceptance: war destroys, combat damages.

Meanwhile, that same year, the society's annual convention affirmed these early initiatives by establishing a memorial committee consisting of several former senior officers.[25] At this stage, the committee had a broad remit, which included establishing a memorial to the division in Washington, DC, *and* checking the status of the division's damaged monument at Chateau-Thierry. Reconstituted at the 1956 and 1957 annual conventions, by 1959 the society's executive voted the committee into permanent existence in order to ensure that its plans were not delayed by the rather rapid turnover in leadership.[26] The chairman of the committee and the driving force throughout this period was Frederick Winant, a former commander of the division during World War II. With Winant at the helm, the committee's remit was refined, and already by 1957 a subtle but significant shift in purpose had emerged. No longer was the committee intended to simply check the "status" of the Chateau-Thierry memorial as a preface to its ultimate resurrection. Rather, after a local architect had made it clear that the old monument was too badly damaged to be restored, Winant's committee – with the keen support of the mayor of Chateau-Thierry – decided an entirely new monument should be commissioned.[27] This new monument was to be dedicated to the division's dead from *both* World Wars. As a senior member of the society and then commanding general of the active duty 3rd Division (based in Europe), Major General Roy E. Linquist explained after an inspection tour of the proposed monument site in the summer of 1958: "By including World War II as well as World War I motifs in the monument, the appeal can be broadened without detracting in any way from the glory won by the heroic Marnemen of July 1918."[28] By refining the project in this way, the monument had become absorbed into the work of municipal reconstruction. Indeed, this idea came to the fore when the memorial was incorporated into a wider local endeavour to make right still lingering war damage. The site chosen for it was a new park, close to the original site that had been damaged during fighting in 1940. The funds necessary to undertake the work were even sought – and granted – from the French Ministry for War Damage.

As is often the case with projects of this sort, various challenges emerged which threatened to delay (if not derail) the society's monument mission. The French government only offered $9,000 of the estimated $18,000 necessary to the project, a deficit that had to be made good by donations from the society's membership as well as from active duty Marnemen.[29] And then there were the logistical details: the precise location required discussion and debate, and the Army Historical Branch had to be consulted regarding the names of the battles that could be legitimately included in the memorial's inscriptions.[30] Most challenging of all, however, were the problems offered by language and distance.[31] The memorial committee did not have a fluent French speaker, nor did they have an agent on the ground who could contract for and supervise the work. In an attempt to respond to this problem, Winant requested that ABMC officers in France provide on-the-ground assistance. Given their long-established institutional antipathy to private memorial building, however, the commission politely declined, reminding Winant of their constitutional role and responsibilities.[32]

This issue of on-the-ground assistance might have been a bridge too far for the Society of the 3rd Infantry Division. At the very least, plans might have been delayed due to misunderstandings and miscommunication, especially when we recall that these were years of increasingly tense Franco-American relations and, at times, rising anti-American sentiment in Europe. In 1958, Charles De Gaulle assumed the presidency of the French Republic, and what followed in the subsequent years was an attempt to reassert French power and rebuild French grandeur, acts often interpreted in Washington as a concerted campaign of anti-Americanism.[33] Such Gaullist "posturing," as many in the American government saw it, included establishing France as an independent nuclear power in 1960, formal recognition of communist China in 1964, a state visit to the Soviet Union in 1966, and public criticism of American policy in Vietnam.[34] Most damaging of all to Franco-American relations was De Gaulle's decision to withdraw the French military from NATO's integrated command structure in 1966 in order to maintain French sovereignty. De Gaulle then rubbed salt into the wound by demanding that all

American troops leave French soil within one year. As a result, 26,000 American soldiers and 37,000 dependents stationed at thirty different American military bases were evacuated (many to Britain and West Germany), and NATO headquarters was relocated from Strasbourg to Brussels.[35] A Gallup poll conducted that same year suggested that De Gaulle's "anti-American" policies had a significant degree of popular support: 41 per cent of respondents declared that they thought the presence of US military bases in France was a "bad thing"; only 29 per cent believed they were "good" for French security.[36] Thus, by October 1961, as Winant and company explored ways to ensure the completion of their memorial, Franco-American relations had already begun their descent into a "deep freeze."[37]

This was hardly a climate conducive to helping American veterans erect a war memorial just north of Paris (a memorial indeed, which commemorated the American defence of French liberty in the twentieth century – twice). Little wonder that members of the ABMC, as agents of the federal government, were concerned that De Gaulle's reign would frustrate some of *their* plans. In the late 1960s, for instance, the secretary of the commission, General Thomas North, expressed real concern that contemporary Franco-American relations threatened to hinder his efforts to establish a new American memorial at Utah Beach in Normandy, where the first American troops waded ashore on the morning of 6 June 1944. At one point, North even wrote to Lieutenant Colonel ver Hulst, the commission's officer in Paris, expressing his concerns "as to whether the moment is propitious for proposing the erection of an American World War II memorial in France in view of the reputed attitude of President De Gaulle toward America and its activities in France."[38] Clearly aware that the proposed structure would publicly inscribe an American victory upon the French landscape, an action that hardly tallied with contemporary Gaullist attempts to mythologize the heroic French Resistance or similar attempts to rebuild French grandeur, North's concern is entirely understandable.[39]

Similar tensions might well have hindered the plans of the Society of the 3rd Infantry at Chateau-Thierry, or at the very least have added to the problems of communication and comprehension. In actual fact, however, the situation was quite the opposite; if anything, contemporary transatlantic politics helped channel a route through what might have been an impasse. Two issues were crucial. First, whilst

Franco-American *diplomatic* relations were descending into a deep freeze, elsewhere many French regional and municipal leaders seemed keen to reassert their ties with the United States. After receiving Thomas North's worried communique from Paris, for example, Lieutenant Colonel ver Hulst was happy to reply that "There was nothing to worry about from the Government nor especially from the people of the Manche who are 100% pro-American and still keenly feel their gratitude for the liberation of their department and France."[40] A few days later, the mayor of the nearby commune of St Marie du Mont similarly informed Thomas North "in the strongest possible terms that the people of his department and the whole coastal region were very favourably inclined towards us."[41]

The very same "favourable" inclinations were apparent in communications between Winant's memorial committee and the mayor of Chateau-Thierry. As early as 1956, the mayor had let it be known that the "City of Chateau-Thierry greatly desires to see the monument in honor of its veterans reconstructed and that our inhabitants will never forget the sacrifices made by the sons of the United States in order to liberate our soil from the yoke of the enemy and are always ready to prove their gratitude to them."[42] Local support remained throughout. In the summer of 1958 the president of the Society of the 3rd Infantry was informed that the "Mayor of Chateau-Thierry is enthusiastic about the project,"[43] and by 1959 – despite the language problems – the latter had effectively assumed responsibility for supervising much of the work. Thus, municipal memories of Franco-American common purpose, first expressed by the erection of the original memorial in the 1920s, trumped contemporary diplomatic tensions.

The second issue crucial to the successful completion of the memorial was equally a product of the moment. For whilst De Gaulle would later demand the departure of US troops in order to assert French sovereignty, their *presence* in 1961 helped ensure that the Society of the 3rd Infantry could complete their project. As such, when the ABMC first declined the role of agent on the ground, the society turned instead to the active duty 3rd Division, which, by a quirk of fate, had just been deployed to Europe. In due course, two successive commanding generals of the division provided informal assistance and liaison with the municipal authorities in Chateau-Thierry, and active duty personnel helped plan the dedication ceremony.[44] Moreover, when the ABMC did finally become involved in the monument's realisation, their key agent on the ground was Colonel William Himes, recently of the 3rd Division. In October 1961, veterans joined with the local community to dedicate the completed memorial, which consisted of a solid and angular obelisk decorated with a large bronze sword and flanked by a low stone wall recording the division's campaigns.

The Society of the 3rd Infantry Division succeeded in erecting a new memorial at Chateau-Thierry in 1961 due to two key factors. First, by expanding the project into a combined commemoration of the division's dead from both World Wars, they were able to co-opt local initiatives towards municipal reconstruction. Second, whilst the Franco-American diplomatic context was not necessarily favourable to the construction of an American war memorial in France, it was nonetheless outflanked by a *local* desire to commemorate transatlantic ties as well as by the demands of the contemporary Cold War Atlantic Alliance, demands which had seen the active duty 3rd Division deployed to Europe to guard the free world's frontier. And whilst the principal purpose of this deployment was to keep watch on the Rhine, aiding the construction of a solid stone reminder of the division's previous sacrifices for Europe was certainly in keeping with their broader assignment. In this sense, a monument mission with origins in the past became a means to make a powerful – and reassuringly permanent – statement in the present. Indeed, the transatlantic politics of the moment were more than apparent during the dedication ceremony, attended by a variety of Franco-American dignitaries as well as fifty-man contingents from the US Army and French Army.[45] In the weeks before the ceremony, the organizers paid considerable attention to ensuring that the proceedings were a suitably "Franco-American" affair,[46] particularly as East-West relations worsened with the construction of the Berlin Wall, begun just two months earlier in August 1961.[47] It is little wonder that earlier in the year Winant had perceptively noted that the dedication ceremony would constitute a much-needed expression "of cordial American-French relations."[48] Nor should we be surprised to learn that the visiting American veterans and dignitaries agreed to round-off this demonstration of transatlantic brotherhood by marching to the nearby *Monuments aux Morts* (the memorial to Chateau-Thierry's Great War dead) and there lay a wreath of remembrance.[49]

RE-FORTIFYING THE GOTHIC LINE: THE 363RD INFANTRY REGIMENT AT SCARPERIA, C. 1945–1957

In northern France, therefore, the (re)establishment of an American war memorial in 1961 provided a forum in which contemporary Franco-American tensions were negotiated, and in which a Franco-American community of memory was realized just as Cold War tensions heightened. In contrast to the federally funded memorials of the ABMC, the 3rd Infantry Division's private memorial was the product of rather more intimate transatlantic contact and connections, and was thus indicative of the broad dynamics of contemporary transatlantic relations. Whilst initiated by Americans and paid for (in part) with American dollars, the design was French, the landscaping was French, and the French War Ministry as well as the local community provided the energy and effort to ensure completion. Here was the Europeanisation of American culture in action. But Europeanisation of this sort was still determined by place, people, and politics. At other locations in Europe the response could be rather different. At the small town of Scarperia, for example, just north of Florence, attempts to establish a memorial to the US 363rd Infantry Regiment soon after the war are suggestive of some of the differences between postwar Italy and postwar France.

Between the summer of 1944 and the spring of 1945, the 363rd Infantry – amongst many other Allied infantry units – fought a series of bloody and brutal battles in order to breach Field Marshal Kesselring's final line of defence in Italy, the so-called "Gothic Line." The mountainous terrain of this part of Italy, dominated by the northern summits of the Appenines, proved ideal ground for a defensive war of attrition, and a nightmare for attacking infantry. By the battle's end, the 363rd had suffered 2,245 casualties, including 489 killed in action.[50] A sergeant quoted in the regiment's official history provides a vivid sense of the nature of the combat. Writing of an attack intended to break the Gothic Line near Monticelli, the sergeant's description is reminiscent of war diaries from the Western Front a generation earlier. He explains that soon after the attack was launched, "Heavy casualties were inflicted. All the officers, all the platoon sergeants, two section sergeants, and five squad leaders were either killed or wounded."[51]

Understandably, and just like their counterparts in the 3rd Infantry Division at Chateau-Thierry, once the battle was over and the war won the veterans and victors of the 363rd similarly initiated efforts to commemorate their fallen comrades with a battlefield trophy.[52] Plans first emerged in the first weeks after the war's conclusion in Europe, and by August 1945 an Italian architect had already been approached to design a suitable memorial and a local landowner had agreed to donate an appropriate site.[53] The architect was Professor Raffaello Brizzi of the University of Florence. Upon accepting the commission, Professor Brizzi expressed his "heartfelt thanks to the Command of the 363rd Infantry Regiment for the honor given me and my school by entrusting me with the task of drafting the project for the monument."[54] Brizzi's design was ambitious: made of white stone, he envisaged a memorial centred on the figure of a silent sentinel, uniformed and standing at ease, rifle in hand with stock resting on the ground. Behind this figure was to be a tall, curving stone wall, whilst on either flank, at a much lower level, were to be two "wings" listing the names of the 436 members of the 363rd Infantry killed nearby. The site chosen was just to the north of Scarperia, close to the tiny hamlet of L'Uomo Morto, the point at which the 363rd had launched their to attempt to break the Gothic Line, and not far from the area at which one of their number, Private First Class Oscar G. Johnson, won the Medal of Honor.[55] The regiment estimated the total cost for the project at 1 million lire (US$11,000).[56]

Like so many other American memorial projects in postwar Europe, plans then moved remarkably quickly. By November 1945, veterans of the regiment had raised almost $10,000 in funds, and an official of the nearby American Consulate had agreed to act on behalf of the regiment in order to ensure timely construction and completion. Much as at Chateau-Thierry, locally based active duty American troops also aided the project by providing the transportation of the construction materials. By the spring of 1946, the monument had been completed, and soon after its dedication the mayor of Scarperia signed an agreement accepting communal responsibility for its future upkeep and maintenance, as well as establishing special regulations intended to ensure that future construction work would not compromise the integrity or character of the commemorative space. The mayor explained his reasoning for these actions: "It is an act of courtesy toward the Allied Government and even more for a sense of gratitude toward the memory of the soldiers of the American Army who died offering their lives for the liberation of Italy and of this town."[57]

In the space of a year, therefore, the soldiers of the 363rd Infantry Regiment had breached the Gothic Line, contributed to the allied victory in Italy and Europe, constructed a monument to their dead, and demobilized to head home. Stories of similar American monument missions might be had from many other locations in postwar Europe, especially in France and England.[58] But of interest to us here is what happened next. For whilst at Chateau-Thierry the local community assimilated the memorial to the 3rd Infantry into their own landscape and history, at Scarperia, in contrast, the local community quickly lost interest in the "memory of the soldiers of the American Army."

Problems first emerged in the spring of 1946, shortly before the monument's dedication. Professor Brizzi, who had assumed responsibility for design and execution, sadly passed away.[59] Soon after, it became apparent that he had not secured, as promised, the deed to the land upon which the monument was built. This caused concern amongst veterans of the regiment, for without the deed they could not ensure the structure's future, a fatal blow to a stone monument (which is often intended to be a buttress against forgetting).[60] Just as importantly, without the deed the regiment's memorial association could not "pass" the monument into the care of the ABMC.[61] Acting on behalf of the regiment's memorial association, therefore, the American consulate in Florence contacted the landowner to request confirmation that the deed would be forthcoming, as was originally agreed. Efforts to resolve this situation continued into 1947, but in July the landowner made it known that he no longer wished to cede the land in question.[62] Following this, he then became uncommunicative, and by early 1948 the consulate was sorry to report that "The owner of the property, where the monument is located, does not reply to the letters which have been sent to him."[63]

But worse was to come. For despite the fact that the memorial's authors believed the initial support of the local community had "eliminated the fear that the monument might fall into a state of neglect through the years,"[64] as it turned out this proved to be no such guarantee. Indeed, whilst visitors to the memorial in 1947–49 were very impressed by its beauty and location,[65] by the early 1950s signs of disrepair had become all too apparent. In 1952, one English tourist reported that a recent visit to the memorial had left her "horrified to see the state of that beautiful memorial." As she explained in correspondence with an Italian friend, "The steps are overgrown with grass and weeds. The grass near it does not appear to have been cut for years and the whole thing looks desolate and neglected."[66] A year later, William Magill, the regiment's wartime commanding officer and the man who was to become the driving force behind later efforts to maintain the memorial, made a tour of inspection. He, too, was disappointed by what he found, later noting that the memorial was surrounded by "high weeds," and that there were some "minor depredations" as well as a "somewhat run-down and depressing condition."[67] Keen to do what he could to initiate the necessary repair and maintenance work, Magill drove to nearby Scarperia and sought out a meeting at the town hall. He reminded the mayor of his community's promise to provide for the monument's upkeep, but the latter seemed "completely uninterested and disclaimed any responsibility for the ordinance previously passed."[68]

The remarkable issue here is the sheer speed at which the monument was conceived, completed, and cast aside. It was commissioned and dedicated – in the presence of local people – within twelve months of the war's end. The mayor of Scarperia provided an official ordinance acknowledging responsibility for future upkeep soon after, and visitors in 1949 still commented on its design and beauty. But by 1947 the landowner had changed his mind and refused to cede ownership to the memorial association, by 1948 he was entirely uncommunicative, and by 1952 the local community seemed resolutely uninterested in the monument's present condition or future state. Even the ABMC proved less than helpful in finding a workable solution to provide for the monument's future. Following precedent and procedure, the commission initially declined to assume responsibility for the monument, explaining that it had been built in direct contravention of their authority and in disregard of orders issued by SHAEF in 1945.[69] At one point, the ABMC's officer in Rome actually offered to "effect the permanent removal" of the memorial so that its state of disrepair "would not reflect unfavourably on the United States and members of the Armed Forces."[70] Only with reluctance did the commission later agree to supervise some repairs, but on the condition that the 363rd's memorial association send a cheque providing the $1,440 necessary to complete the work.[71]

The records remain unclear as to exactly why the 363rd's memorial at Scarperia fell so quickly into disrepair in the early 1950s. However, like the memorial dedicated by the 3rd Infantry Division at Chateau-Thierry in 1961, the broader transatlantic context *and* local conditions suggests an answer to the riddle. At Chateau-Thierry, souring Franco-American relations in the late 1950s and early 1960s did not prove an obstacle to completion because the local community, with the support of American veterans, took it upon themselves to be a conduit for improved transatlantic contact and connections. Such an initiative was a product of the lived experiences of the twentieth century, experiences that had seen the American military fight on behalf of the community's liberty *twice*. At Scarperia, in contrast, whilst the soldiers of the 363rd were, by 1944, fighting to liberate Italy from German occupation, the narrative of Italy's – and Scarperia's – war experience also included several challenging complications. First, there was the problem of the fascist government's earlier commitment to the Axis cause.[72] Second, there was the very nature of the Allied campaign of liberation, a campaign which saw Italian cities devastated by Allied bombs, and Italian heritage levelled by Allied artillery (for instance, at Monte Cassino).[73] Neither of these aspects of the Italian war experience was particularly conducive to enthusiastic commemorations of liberation, or of the liberators. Added to these problems in the past were the problems met by Italian-American relations in the Cold War present. In fact, as early as 1946, Magill had already expressed concern that contemporary tensions between the United States and Italy might prove an obstacle to successful completion. In correspondence with the US consulate in Florence, for example, Magill noted that "There has been some anti-American sentiment in Italy because of the Trieste situation." He went on to express his hope that "The reports are exaggerated and that our efforts to commemorate the deeds of our men in Italy shall not be jeopardised by the actions of some hotheads."[74] For Magill, therefore, there were real concerns already in 1946 that the ongoing crisis regarding the border of Italy and Yugoslavia at Trieste – a crisis which had seen the United States and United Kingdom assume military authority over the city rather than return it forthwith to Italian control – might impact plans to dedicate the newly completed memorial that summer. Moreover, a year later, in May 1947, the extent to which Cold War tensions were affecting US-Italian relations became even more apparent following the decision of Prime Minister Alcide de Gasperi – under American pressure – to expel from the government members of the Communist Party of Italy (PCI) on pain of losing future American economic and financial support.[75] In northern Italy, the industrial stronghold of Italian communism, many were outraged by what they perceived to be such an obvious and heavy-handed application of American power, feelings that were accentuated a month later following the announcement of the Marshall Plan for European Recovery. For many European communists, especially in France and Italy, this plan, which in due course saw the United States provide $13 billion in aid, smacked of economic colonization rather than disinterested altruism. US-Italian tensions then increased even further in April 1948 during the Italian general election, an event that, in the words of one historian, "took place in an atmosphere of total left-right confrontation, each side financed and armed clandestinely by its respective superpower sponsor."[76] At one point, the American ambassador even became concerned that the PCI was still sufficiently strong to secure power legally, a concern that led the newly created CIA to launch a covert propaganda campaign in Italy in order to prevent such a communist victory (an act unprecedented in American foreign policy).[77] On occasion, American officials – motivated by what was now defined as a policy of "containing" perceived communist expansion – even went so far as to contemplate a formal military intervention.[78] In response, the PCI launched its own vigorous propaganda campaign, seeking to draw special attention to what they argued was unacceptable and illegal American interference in Italian affairs. Little wonder that by the early 1950s some American visitors noted that the streets of places like Rome and Milan were "littered with anti-American posters."[79]

In Scarperia, in short, contemporary tensions in US-Italian diplomatic relations were not always countered by a local community keen to declare their continued fidelity to the American liberator. Indeed, if anything, the situation was the exact opposite, with some local politicians – especially the mayor – happy to forget their earlier promises, now frustrated as they were by American interventions in domestic Italian politics as well as American leadership of the capitalist, anti-communist West. It is hardly surprising, when seen in this context, that Magill could note after a visit to Scarperia in 1953 that the "gratitude of the Italian people has cooled." Whilst following a disappointing meeting at Scarperia's town hall, his Italian interpreter simply explained – with disgust – that the problem with the mayor was all too apparent; he was just "[a]nother Communist."[80] Significantly, this was the very same year in which one American ambassador in Europe warned Washington that a "'flash-fire of anti-Americanism' was sweeping through" the continent.[81]

It seems that just a few years later, to Magill's relief, the situation had somewhat recovered, with Italy now a firm member of NATO. By 1957 the American consulate at Florence reported that the "continual problem regarding upkeep and appearance" of the monument had been resolved. He went on to explain to Magill that his consulate had "finally succeeded in having the 363rd Infantry monument put into good condition through the efforts of the active duty US military in Europe, as well as the authorities in Scarperia who now agreed to resume 'full responsibility for future upkeep.'"[82] But this was not the case between 1947 and 1954. At this time, as American power in Europe was consolidated, as "containment" was initiated and Marshall aid dispatched, and as Cold War tensions increased following a series of international crises,[83] an American war memorial in the foothills of the Apennines lost the support of a local community which, like so many in northern Italy in this period, became dominated by representatives of the PCI, the very organisation that the CIA was so keen to eliminate from Italian politics. Unlike at Chateau-Thierry, where the local community used the memorial to the 3rd Infantry as a forum in which to demonstrate their continued fidelity to the American liberators, at Scarperia there was no such sentiment, at least not during the period from 1947 to 1954.

MONUMENTS, MEMORY, AND TRANSATLANTIC RELATIONS, C. 1945–1962

Much has been written recently about the efforts of the American military to preserve the monuments of European culture from the depredations of war – the actions of the so-called "monuments men."[84] Yet relatively little is known about how representatives of that very same military also sought to *create* their own monuments. The memorials at Chateau-Thierry and Scarperia record this creative effort; they offer a window on a lost history of World War II, the history of how American veterans sought to inscribe their sacrifices on the European landscape. Second, these memorials are, in many respects, an irony of history, for according to military regulations they were not supposed to have been built, as their unofficial nature risked undermining a federally sanctioned memory of American military sacrifice, a memory that the ABMC was tasked with controlling and constructing. For the ABMC, commemoration was an invaluable forum in which to promote transatlantic unity in the confused and chaotic early Cold War. Where better for Allied generals and diplomats to make declarations of faith in the Atlantic Alliance than in an American military cemetery in Europe? As General Marshall, the chairman of the ABMC and former secretary of state, remarked during a 1952 meeting discussing the commission's memorial building plans: "With some thought we should be able to dramatize these memorials, thereby conveying not only to our own people, but to the people of European nations that we made a great contribution in the war." He went on to explain that "Europeans, particularly are apt to respond to the great artistic triumph which the memorials constitute."[85]

The problem was that despite Marshall's vision, these nationally funded memorial landscapes did not involve much one-to-one transatlantic contact in their construction, nor were they always suggestive of American and European common purpose. They were large projects, built by local Europeans, but requiring (or allowing) very little in the way of European input with design or form. Indeed, as Ron Robin has identified, the cemeteries and memorials built by the ABMC attempted to assert a distinctly American form of institutional architecture.[86] They might have been intended as expressions of transatlantic brotherhood, but they often impressed as statements of *American* power and prestige.

Private memorials, in contrast, were generally the work of smaller, more localized networks of memory constituted by American veterans and European community leaders. The former were often the instigators, frequently providing the funds; the latter were often the facilitators, identifying a suitable site and securing the necessary official permission. As such, these networks were, in the words of Jay Winter, "fictive kinships" – small-scale groups of commemorative agents joined by a common past and driven by a common endeavour to see that past commemorated in a particular way.[87] Here, therefore, was the irony, for these kinships of memory actually ended up contributing to the broader agenda of post-1945 American foreign policy in Europe. Private memorial projects, after all, produced the very sort of one-to-one transatlantic contact that contemporary American officials – as the Marshall Plan and Fulbright Program both attest – considered so crucial to maintaining Western unity in the face of Soviet aggression. Thus, where the memorials and cemeteries of the ABMC inscribed an American *national* memory on the European landscape, monuments like those at Chateau-Thierry and Scarperia inscribed, in contrast, a *Europeanized* American memory. Put differently, their origins, construction, and completion resulted in the creation of what might be reasonably termed *transatlantic* memory. Such political objectives were certainly not lost on those who instigated these private memorials. As one of those involved in the 363rd memorial at Scarperia noted to William Magill in the spring of 1949 (as the latter was struggling to win the help and support of the ABMC): "You might also include the point that the memorial was constructed by Americans, in memory of Americans, and that it establishes a much better reputation for Americans in the eyes of Europeans. The higher echelon is very conscious of the reputation of Americans these days."[88] Marshall would have approved of the sentiment, even if the action troubled him.

Nonetheless, as we saw, the successful cultivation of such transatlantic memory still depended on the place, the people, and the politics. At Chateau-Thierry, Franco-American diplomatic tensions failed to derail plans for a monument to the US 3rd Infantry Division. The lived experiences of two world wars, and the contact and connections that these experiences had bequeathed, ensured that community leaders at Chateau-Thierry remained committed to realising the memorial to their defenders and liberators. At Scarperia, meanwhile, initial local sympathy and support for the memorial to the 363rd Infantry Regiment quickly gave way to disinterest, at best, and active disregard, at worst. Here, local politics, combined with the complexities of the Italian war experience as well as the challenges to the postwar economy, produced an environment in which community leaders lost interest in maintaining a memorial to the agents of a government which some now saw as a capitalist behemoth trampling on European sovereignty. As such, the history of the monument missions uncovered here points to the importance of situating these memoryscapes firmly in their local, national, and transnational contexts. In doing so, they provide a stone and marble record of those early postwar efforts to define and describe a newly forged Atlantic Alliance. Moreover, in their own small way they provide visible confirmation of what Jon Davies has persuasively argued about war memorials: that they are the boundary markers of the West, delineating "us" from "them," ally from enemy.[89] These Europeanized American war memorials fortified the frontier of the free world in the early Cold War.

NOTES

1 United States Army Military History Institute (hereafter USAMHI), Lucian K. Truscott, Jr photograph collection, United States 3rd Infantry Division's Beachhead Monuments of World War II.
2 Ibid. Memorandum, Captain J. Eakin to Commanding General, 3rd Infantry Division, 15 December 1946.
3 For details about activities in eastern England and in Normandy, see Sam Edwards, *Allies in Memory: World War II and the Politics of Transatlantic Commemoration, c. 1941–2001* (Cambridge: Cambridge University Press, 2015).
4 G. Kurt Piehler, *Remembering War the American Way* (Washington: Smithsonian Institution Press, 1995), 98; Lisa Budreau, *Bodies of War: World War I and the Politics of Commemoration in America, 1919–1933* (New York: New York University Press, 2010); Ron Robin, *Enclaves of America: The Rhetoric of American Political Architecture Abroad, 1900–1965* (Princeton: Princeton University Press, 1992), 30.
5 Jim Weeks, *Gettysburg: Memory, Market and American Shrine* (Princeton: Princeton University Press, 2003), 61.
6 For details about these cemeteries and memorials, see the ABMC's website: http://www.abmc.gov/.
7 Piehler, *Remembering War the American Way*, 97.
8 Rose E.B. Coombes, *Before Endeavours Fade: A Guide to the Battlefields of the First World War* (London: Battle of Britain Prints International, 1976), 156; American Battle Monuments Commission, *American Armies and Battlefields in Europe: A History, Guide, and Reference Book* (Washington, DC: United States Government Printing Office, 1938), 523.
9 For information about the 1st Division memorials at Vigneulles and Buzancy, see Coombes, *Before Endeavours Fade*, 155, 133. For details about the 2nd and 5th Division memorials, see Coombes, *Before Endeavours Fade*, 161–2, 140; ABMC, *American Armies and Battlefields in Europe*, 522, 523.
10 National Archives and Records Administration II (hereafter NARAII), RG 117, Proceedings of the ABMC, Secretary of War Henry Stimson and Secretary of the Navy James S. Forrestal to the President, 20 September 1945.
11 Ibid.
12 NARAII, RG 117, Memorials and Monuments Correspondence, President H.S. Truman, Executive Order 9704, 14 March 1946; See

also S. 2141 Bill, "Extension of ABMC," 5 March1946, enacted 26 June 1946; For further details, see Edwards, *Allies in Memory*, 90–8.

13 Steven Trout, *On the Battlefield of Memory: The First World War and American Remembrance, 1919–1941* (Tuscaloosa: University of Alabama Press, 2010), xvi; Stephen Ambrose, *Eisenhower: The Soldier* (London: George Allen and Unwin, 1984), 82–6.

14 Ibid.

15 Richard Pells, *Not Like Us: How Europeans Have Loved, Hated, and Transformed American Culture since World War II* (New York: Basic Books, 1997). See also: Elaine Tyler May and Reinhold Wagnleiter, eds., "*Here, There and Everywhere*": *The Foreign Politics of American Popular Culture* (Hanover, NH: University Press of New England, 2000); Heide Fehrenbach and Uta G. Poiger, eds., *Transactions, Transgressions, Transformations: American Culture in Western Europe and Japan* (Oxford: Oxford University Press, 2000); Geir Lundestad, *The United States and Western Europe since 1945* (Oxford: Oxford University Press, 2005).

16 For details about the 3rd Infantry Division's war, see the official history: Jeffrey Gaul, *History of the Third Infantry Division: Rock of the Marne* (Paducah, KY: Turner Publishing, 1988).

17 For the origins of the World War I monument, see Tim Stoy, "A Condensed History of the 3rd Infantry Division Memorial in Chateau-Thierry." http://www.warfoto.com/3rdsocietyHistory.htm. A few details about the broader context can also be found in Budreau, *Bodies of War*, 134–40. I should like to thank Mr Stoy here for the advice and information he provided as I drafted this essay.

18 Full details about the origins of the post-1945 memorial can be found in the USAMHI, "3rd Division Papers, 1917–1961." For reference to negotiations with the French over the site, etc., see "Added Note to Memorial Committee's Report of July 13, 1959."

19 For a discussion of wartime Franco-American relations, particularly near the front line, see Jennifer Keene, *Doughboys, the Great War, and the Remaking of America* (Baltimore: Johns Hopkins University Press, 2005), 106–11.

20 See Stoy, "A Condensed History of the 3rd Infantry Division Memorial in Chateau-Thierry." http://www.warfoto.com/3rdsocietyHistory.htm. One source actually suggests that the memorial was completed much earlier, in 1923. But this is more likely the date at which the ground was symbolically "broken." See USAMHI, "3rd Division Papers,

1917–1961," W.W. Eagles, Society of the 3rd Infantry Division to Colonel Mage, American Battle Monuments Commission, Paris, 28 May 1957.

21 Various ideas and theories about the origins of the damage to the World War I monument feature in the correspondence connected to the post-1945 monument in USAMHI, "3rd Division papers, 1917–1961." See, for example: Memo to Chief, Maintenance Division (ABMC), 27 August 1957; Col Jack D. Mage, ABMC, to Mr John R. Wood, American Consul, Paris, 19 August 1957; General W.W. Eagles and Captain F. Winnant, Society of the 3rd Infantry Division to Major General Thomas North, ABMC, 5 September 1957; Edward J. Butler, President for the Society of the 3rd Infantry Division to Major General Roy E. Lindquist, 28 January 1958; Major General Roy E. Lindquist to Edward J. Butler, 3 July 1958; Major General T.J. Cross to Major General Roy E. Lindquist, 31 July 1958; Lt Colonel Paul S. Lindberg, HQ, 3rd Infantry Division, Europe, to Commander in Chief, US Army Europe, 27 April 1959.

22 USAMHI, "3rd Division papers, 1917–1961"; Major General T.J. Cross to Major General Roy E. Lindquist, 31 July 1958.

23 Ibid. Edward J. Butler, President for the Society of the 3rd Infantry Division to Major General Roy E. Lindquist, 28 January 1958.

24 Ibid. "1961 Convention Report by the Memorial Committee," 6 July 1961.

25 Ibid. General W.W. Eagles and Captain F. Winant, Society of the 3rd Infantry Division to Major General Thomas North, ABMC, 5 September 1957.

26 Ibid. Winant, "Report by the 3rd Division Memorial Committee," 13 July 1959. See also "Resolution No. IV," 40th Annual Convention 3rd Infantry Division, 15–18 July 1959. Significantly, amongst the key members of this committee was Major John S.D. Eisenhower, Korean War veteran and son of then President Eisenhower. Thus, the Memorial Committee, which later ran into some resistance from the ABMC regarding its plans (which were, we recall, contrary to the commission's aims and authority), contained within its number the son of the man who had himself upheld the commission's regulatory authority in the 1920s and reasserted that authority whilst Supreme Commander of the Allied Forces in Europe in 1945. Whether this was mere coincidence or strategic skill is unclear (given we are dealing with senior military officers, one suspects the latter).

27 Ibid. Major General Roy E. Lindquist to Edward J. Butler, 3 July 1958. See also Winant, "Report by the 3rd Division Memorial Committee," 13 July 1959.

28 Ibid.

29 For the costs, etc., see ibid. Winant to Major General Watson, Commanding, 3rd Infantry Division, 1 November 1960. See also Winant to Watson, 28 September 1960.

30 Ibid. Brigadier General James A. Norrell, Chief of Military History, to Mr Frederick Winant, 21 October 1961.

31 Ibid. Winant, "Report by the 3rd Division Memorial Committee," 13 July 1959.

32 The ABMC had communicated their unwillingness to be involved with the monument as early as 1957. See USAMHI, "3rd Division Papers, 1917–1961," Major General Thomas North, ABMC, to Major General William W. Eagles, Society of the 3rd Infantry Division, 12 December 1957. However, in the spring of 1960 the commission's attitude softened a little and they did provide some informal, albeit limited, help.

33 Henri Rousso, *The Vichy Syndrome: History and Memory in France since 1944*, trans. by Arthur Goldhammer (Cambridge: Harvard University Press, 1996), 82; Robert Gildea, *The Past in French History* (London: Yale University Press, 1994), 112–34.

34 Richard Kuisel, *Seducing the French: The Dilemma of Americanization* (London: University of California Press, 1996), 131–53.

35 Frank Costigliola, *France and the United States: The Cold Alliance since World War II* (New York: Maxwell Macmillan, 1992), 144–5.

36 *The Gallup International Public Opinion Polls: France, 1939, 1944–75*, 1, 1976, 530–1.

37 Costigliola, *Cold Alliance*, 118–59.

38 NARAII, RG 117, Memorials and Monuments Correspondence, General Thomas North to Lt Colonel G.M. ver Hulst, Officer in Charge, ABMC, Paris, 18 April 1967.

39 For more details about this project, see Edwards, *Allies in Memory*, 168–76.

40 Ibid. Lt G.M. ver Hulst to General Thomas North, 28 April 1967.

41 Ibid. Memorandum for the Officer in Charge from General Thomas North, 5 July 1967.

42 USAMHI, "3rd Division Papers, 1917–1961," Mayor of Chateau-Thierry to Colonel Jack Mage, ABMC, Paris, 26 September 1956.

43 Ibid. Major General Roy E. Lindquist to Edward J. Butler, 3 July 1958.

44 Ibid. Edward J. Butler, President for the Society of the 3rd Infantry Division to Major General Roy E. Lindquist, 28 January 1958; see also Winant, "Report by the Memorial Committee," 30 June 1958; For details about the involvement of active duty 3rd Division troops at the dedication ceremony, see Memo, Division Sergeant Major's Visit to Chateau-Thierry, 30–31 August 1961; See Major John L. Jennings, HQ, 3rd Infantry Division, Memo for Division Commander, 5 September 1961.

45 Ibid. Memo for 3rd Infantry Division Sergeants' Major, 2 September 1961; see also: *L'Union* (local paper for Chateau-Thierry), 9 October 1961; *Watch on the Rhine* (periodical of the Society of the 3rd Infantry Division) 43, no. 1 (December 1961): 3–9.

46 See USAMHI, "3rd Division Papers, 1917–1961," Winant to Mayor of Chateau-Thierry, 29 August 1961; Memo, Dedication of the Chateau-Thierry Memorial, 5 September 1961; Winant to Major General William W. Dick, Commanding, 3rd Infantry Division, 5 September 1961.

47 At one point, Winant was even concerned that tensions between East and West Germany might make travel to the dedication ceremony impossible. Ibid., Memo, Dedication of the Chateau-Thierry Memorial, 5 September 1961.

48 Ibid. Frederick Winant, "Report by the Memorial Committee," 8 March 1961. For a similar expression, see also Winnant to General Watson, 6 February 1961.

49 Ibid. Colonel William J. Himes to Major Jennings, HQ, 3rd Infantry Division, 14 September 1961.

50 For the official history of the regiment's campaign, see Ralph E. Strootman, *History of the 363rd Infantry Regiment: One Regiment of the 91st Infantry Division* (Washington, DC: Infantry Journal Press, 1947; Kessinger Publishing, 2007).

51 Ibid., 84.

52 Full details about the memorial's origins and realisation can be found in USAMHI, "William Fulton Magill Papers, 1945–1957." See file "Correspondence on 363rd Infantry Regiment Monument."

53 Ibid. Major George C. Kotchik, 363rd Infantry to "Owners of proposed monument site," 14 August 1945.

54 Ibid. Prof. Raffaello Brizzi to Major George C. Kotchik, 16 August 1945.

55 See Strootman, *History of the 36rd Infantry Regiment*, 76–7, 250–1.

56 USAMHI, "William Fulton Magill Papers, 1945–1957." See file "Correspondence on 363rd Infantry Regiment Monument," Professor Raffaello Brizzi to Major George C. Kotchik, 16 August 1945.
57 Ibid. "Town of Scarperia, Province of Firenze, Extract from the General Register of the Deliberations of the Communal Board, of December 12, 1945" (translated 15 April 1946).
58 See Edwards, *Allies in Memory,* 39–43, 90–111.
59 Ibid. Walter W. Orebaugh, American Consul, Florence, to William F. Magill, 28 March 1946. See also Magill to ABMC Washington, 5 July 1949.
60 Ibid. Magill to Orebaugh, 13 July 1946.
61 Ibid. Magill to Lt Colonel Long, 9 June 1947; Lt Colonel Long to Magill, 6 August 1947.
62 Ibid. Orebaugh to Lt Colonel Glen C. Long, HQ, Zone Command, Austria, 6 August 1947.
63 Ibid. See Magill to J.A. Collins, US Vice-Consul, Florence, 14 November 1947; Orebaugh to Lt Colonel Long, 25 February 1948.
64 Ibid. Magill to Orebaugh, 16 April 1946.
65 Ibid. See, for example, Magill to Orebaugh, 20 January 1947; Magill to Orebaugh, 5 February 1947; General Keyes to Magill, 3 July 1947.
66 Ibid. Naomi Jacob to Casa Micki, 30 October 1952.
67 Ibid. Magill to Floyd V. Pinnick, 31 August 1954.
68 Ibid.
69 A presidential order and a general order from Eisenhower's HQ outlawed unauthorized private commemoration. See NARAII, RG 117, Memorials and Monuments Correspondence, President H.S. Truman, Executive Order 9704, 14 March 1946. See also S. 2141 Bill, "Extension of ABMC," 5 March 5 1946, enacted 26 June 1946. For a reference to the unauthorized nature of the memorial, see Memo, "Responsibility for War Monument at Scarperia, Italy, US Consulate, Florence, to Department of State, Washington, 27 June 1950."
70 Ibid. Ogden J. Martyn, ABMC, Rome, to Lt Colonel Floyd V. Pinnick, 22 June 1953.
71 Ibid. Brigadier General Thomas North, ABMC, to Magill, 4 September 1953.
72 For a discussion of this issue, see Claudio Fogu, "*Italiana brava gente:* The Legacy of Fascist Historical Culture on Italian Politics of Memory," in *The Politics of Memory in Postwar Europe*, edited by Richard Ned Lebow, Wulf Kansteiner, and Claudio Fogu (Durham: Duke University Press, 2006), 147–76.

73 For a discussion of the allied bombing campaign against Italy, see Richard Overy, *The Bombing War: Europe 1939–1945* (London: Penguin, 2014), 510–46.

74 USAMHI, "William Fulton Magill Papers, 1945–1957." See file "Correspondence on 363rd Infantry Regiment Monument," Magill to Orebaugh, 13 July 1946.

75 For details about the tensions in postwar US-Italian relations, see John Lamberton Harper, *America and the Reconstruction of Italy, 1945–1948* (Cambridge: Cambridge University Press, 1986). See also Alessandro Brogi, *Confronting America: The Cold War between the United States and the Communists in France and Italy* (Chapel Hill: University of North Carolina Press, 2011).

76 D.W. Ellwood, "The 1948 Elections in Italy: A Cold War Propaganda Battle," *Historical Journal of Film, Radio and Television* 13, no. 1 (2006): 20.

77 Ibid.

78 Ibid., 21.

79 Pells, *Not Like Us,* 156.

80 Ibid. Magill to Floyd V. Pinnick, 31 August 1954.

81 Costigliola, *Cold Alliance,* 79.

82 USAMHI, "William Fulton Magill Papers, 1945–1957." See file "Correspondence on 363rd Infantry Regiment Monument," W.D. Fisher, American Consul, Florence, to Magill, 22 November 1957. The memorial remains today, although the soldier that once dominated the design has since been replaced with a pedestal and a bronze relief. For details, see http://www.uswarmemorials.org/html/monument_details.php?SiteID=74&MemID=134.

83 See, for example: the crisis in Greece; Soviet testing of a nuclear bomb; the "loss" of China to communism; and the Berlin Air Lift.

84 See: Robert Edsel, *Monuments Men: Allied Heroes, Nazi Thieves and the Greatest Treasure Hunt in History* (London: Arrow, 2010); Robert Edsel, *Saving Italy: The Race to Rescue a Nation's Treasure from the Nazis* (London: W.W. Norton, 2014).

85 NARAII, RG 117, Proceedings of the ABMC, 63rd Meeting, 5 December 1952.

86 Robin, *Enclaves of America,* 116–22.

87 See Jay Winter, "Forms of Fictive Kinship and Remembrance in the Aftermath of the Great War," in *War and Remembrance in the Twentieth Century*, edited by Jay Winter and Emmanuel Sivan (Cambridge: Cambridge University Press, 1999), 147–50.

88 USAMHI, "William Fulton Magill papers, 1945–1957." See file "Correspondence on 363rd Infantry Regiment Monument," Lt Col Long to Col. Magill, 4 March 1949.

89 Jon Davies, "Reconstructing Enmities: War and War Memorials, the Boundary Markers of the West," *History of European Ideas* 19, no. 1–3 (1994): 47–52.

PART TWO

War Narratives: Recollections and (Re)writings

5

The Time Has Come to Talk of Many Things: Wars, and Deaths, and Remembrance in Graham Swift's *Wish You Were Here*

ISABELLE ROBLIN

Wish You Were Here, British writer Graham Swift's ninth novel, is in some ways quite different from his previous ones. First, in his earlier novels Swift had usually opted for autodiegetic, sometimes multiple first-person narratives (*Last Orders,* Booker Prize in 1996, being the most famous example), which allow the reader to see events only from one narrator's point of view at a time. Swift had said in an interview in 2005: "Who knows if one day I might produce a third-person novel? It's a thing which I've always felt isn't me, but it might be a good thing if it happened. You have to surprise yourself" (2010, 376). This is exactly what he did in *Wish You Were Here*, and he duly commented upon this unwonted narrative choice: "Unusually for me, the novel is written in the third person. Its 'voice' isn't Jack's, even though it might sometimes seem that it is. I think I wanted it to be the kind of third person that's so intimately close to the character that it almost melts into the first person. Nonetheless it's third person and this allows for a degree of stepping outside Jack (and other characters) and commenting upon them" (Ruppin). Even though the "Jack" character is the main centre of consciousness, the omniscient, heterodiegetic third person narrator, with an insight into the characters' thoughts and feelings, knows in fact much more than he and the other characters do, and thus "the novel might be said to evoke a collective psychic wound that is expressed variously in various characters" (Ruppin).

Even though the author himself was born in 1949, many of Graham Swift's characters in novels such as *The Sweet-Shop Owner* (1980), *Shuttlecock* (1981), or *Last Orders* are traumatized by World War II and its aftermath. Not so in *Wish You Were Here*, where World War II is hardly mentioned at all. Set in November 2006, another conflict takes centre stage: the "war on terror" and its bloody consequences, one of them being the death of Corporal Thomas Luxton, killed in action by a roadside bomb in Iraq.

The fate of Tom Luxton is explicitly linked to that of two of his great uncles, both killed on the same day on the Somme in 1916. Even if there are some similarities in the ways their deaths are commented upon, they are commemorated in a totally different way. The World War I heroes are memorialized every Remembrance Sunday in what has become over the years a well-established, familiar ritual for the Luxton family and the small community of Marleston in rural Devon, centring on the village war memorial. But it falls to Jack Luxton, as Tom's only remaining next-of-kin, to make a crucial journey from his caravan park on the Isle of Wight to attend the official "repatriation" ceremony for his younger brother Tom at an air base in Oxfordshire, and then his private burial in Devon. As this journey unfolds, Jack confronts his most troubling and secret memories as he remembers his past and has to find a way to lay both its traumatic events and the ghost of his brother to rest. The basic diegetic story covers just three days and frames "a journey to a funeral (of sorts)" (Broening).[1] The novel itself, by its refusal of linear chronology and shifts in points of view, deals as much with the past as with the present, which are seen as intrinsically linked together.

"LIEUX DE MÉMOIRE" IN *WISH YOU WERE HERE*

The French historian Pierre Nora defines what he calls *lieux de mémoire* (translated into English as "realms of memory" by Arthur Goldhammer) as "any significant entity, whether material or non-material in nature, which, by dint of human will or the work of time, has become a symbolic element of the memorial heritage of any community."[2] There are two such *lieux* in *Wish You Were Here*. One, classically, is a public monument: the war memorial in the imaginary Devon town of Marleston. "It was anyway for all to see that among the seven names, under 1914–1918, on the memorial cross outside All Saints' church in Marleston village there were two Luxtons: 'F.C.

Luxton' and 'G.W. Luxton', and after 'G.W. Luxton' were the letters 'DCM'" (9), for Distinguished Conduct Medal which, the reader is told, is "only one medal down … from a VC [Victoria Cross]" (11). The heroic status of the soldiers killed during the Great War whose names are carved in the memorial stone is not questioned by the inhabitants of the village. Not only the Luxton brothers "were both heroes who'd volunteered and died for their country," but moreover "it was the general, unspoken view of the slowly diminishing group who gathered every November around the Marleston war memorial that all those seven names on it were the names of heroes" (11). Remembrance Sunday is what binds the small community together and the dead brothers' posthumous prestige rubs off on their descendants: "George Luxton and his DCM were the reason why – even long after another world war – many residents of Marleston village and its vicinity had turned up in November with their poppies when otherwise they might not have done. The Luxtons themselves, of course, were always there. George Luxton … was the village hero and no one … could deny that he was the Luxtons' claim to fame" (10–11).

There is also a smaller and more private *lieu de mémoire*, the medal itself ("silver king's head with a red-and-blue ribbon," 9) awarded to George Luxton for his exceptional bravery and passed on in the Luxton family from generation to generation. However, the distinction between public and private *lieu de mémoire* is blurred, ritually, every year on Remembrance Sunday, when the medal is taken out of its box for "the inescapable annual attendance at the remembrance service" (13–14): "Michael [Luxton] was an unsentimental dairy farmer, uncomfortable at, but grudgingly empowered by, having a hero in the family. He made a display of both feelings. He'd put on his suit with an air of unwillingness, as if the whole performance only deprived him of time better spent, even on a Sunday morning, on the farm. He'd pin on his poppy; then he'd take the medal, which Vera [his wife] would have polished, and slip it almost furtively into his breast pocket" (15).

After the ceremony, the participants repair to the local pub where the showing off of the medal to the community has become a sort of party trick: "There'd usually be someone who'd ask … 'So – do you have it with you, Michael?' And his father … would … dip his hand into his top pocket and take it out again, clenched round something. And only after more time had passed and while he still looked at the air in front of him would he open his hand, just for an instant, above the surface of the bar, and then return the medal to where it had come from. It was a performance his dad was good at and one worth its annual repetition" (19).

The function of these *lieux de mémoire* is, as Pierre Nora wrote, to stop time and prevent oblivion through the endless repetition of the same ritual.[3] Moreover, as Selma Van de Perre, a survivor of Ravensbruck Concentration Camp, pointed out, commemoration is deemed important because "things that have happened in the past must be remembered so that future mistakes are not made," and also to "thank the people who have given their life." For her, the function of public commemoration is to help the relatives of those who died "because it reduces some of the grief" and "it lessens the sufferings to be with like-minded sufferers" (Van de Perre 2014).

However, not only are the lessons of history definitely not learnt in the novel, but the very act of remembrance, far from having a cathartic effect on the relatives of those who died in the wars, turns into an unbearable burden, preventing the characters from moving on and trapping them in a vicious circle of violent repetition. The emblem of remembrance and commemoration, the medal, becomes itself a constant reminder and witness of death. When Michael Luxton, a farmer pushed out of business by the mad cow disease, commits suicide on the night after Remembrance Sunday, 1994, he has the medal with him in his shirt pocket, which prompts the third-person, omniscient narrator to conclude in a pun that "The fact was that Michael had died wearing, so to speak, the DCM" (239). When Michael's son Jack finally decides to sell the farm and all the family heirlooms and start a new life with his wife on the Isle of Wight, he cannot resign himself to getting rid of the medal and he takes with him that toxic emblem of his family history. When Jack's brother Tom, who had run away from the farm on his eighteenth birthday to join the army, is repatriated after being killed in a roadside bombing in Iraq, Jack first repeats his father's last Remembrance Day ritual: he too wears the medal in his shirt pocket at his brother's burial in the village churchyard, just next to the war memorial, and he too contemplates committing suicide (after killing his own wife) with the very gun his father had used. Only on the ferry back to the Isle of Wight, when he decides to get rid of the medal, can he break the destructive cycle of what has become the mindless repetition of a meaningless ritual and free himself of a past and of memories which have become unbearable and a threat to his own survival: "A few [hardy souls] would have noticed … a large, strongly built, even rather intimidating man, feel for something in the region of his breast pocket, then, clutching it tightly for a moment in his fist, hurl it into the sea. Though it was small, it must have been metallic and relatively heavy, since, catching a quick, coppery gleam from the sunset, it sliced cleanly through the wind into the waves" (333).

At the very end of the novel, Jack cannot still quite come to terms with his momentous decision and cannot publicly admit to his almost sacrilegious act: "He'd have to explain that too, sooner or later: the absence of the medal. He'd say that he'd taken it with him – which was true – and had thrown it in Tom's grave. It was a lie, but it was a white lie" (352). His decision to divest himself of his father's gun in the same way acts as a kind of liberation, for him as well as for his dead brother, and marks to a certain extent the end of his mourning: "The thought would come to him that he would simply get rid of all this weaponry, he'd get rid at last of the gun and that when he did so, Tom would finally be laid to rest" (352).

"LIEUX DE MÉMOIRE" AS LIES

Moreover, the medal itself as *lieu de mémoire* is in fact more or less deceptive. The reader is told by the narrator, in a voice reminiscent of the history teacher Tom Crick in *Waterland*, the "real" story of the medal, something the characters themselves cannot possibly be aware of:

> Once, most of a century ago … along the valley of the River Somme, two Luxton brothers had died on the same July day. In the process, though he would never know it, one of them was to earn a medal for conspicuous gallantry, while the other was merely ripped apart by bullets. Their commanding officer, Captain Hayes, who had witnessed the act of valour himself, had been eager, that night, to write the matter up, with his recommendation, in the hope that something good – if that was a fair way of putting it – might come of the day's unspeakabilities. But though he knew he had two Luxton brothers under his command, George and Fred, he had never known precisely which was which. In their full kit and helmets they looked like identical twins. They all looked, he sometimes thought, like identical twins.

> But the two Luxton brothers were now equally dead anyway. So he had opted for George (it was the most patriotic name), intending to corroborate the matter the next morning, if he had the chance, before his dispatch was sent ... But he never did have the chance, since by seven am ... not long after blowing his whistle yet again, and only obeying a futile order that elsewhere along the line had already been cancelled, Captain Hayes too was dead.
>
> So it was George, not Fred, who got a DCM ... and neither brother would ever dispute it. No then-surviving or subsequent member of the Luxton family ever had cause to challenge what was set down in the citation and carved in stone. (10–11)

This could be a very relevant illustration of Pierre Nora's point[4] about the opposition between memory (and its realms) and history: in Swift's novel, the characters' memory – and memories – of past events are based on a very partial knowledge of the actual facts and grounded in a sometimes quaint or sentimental family folklore (as for instance, Jack and Tom's mother's invented story about their great-uncles Fred and George sharing the medal). Therefore, it is up to the narrator-as-historian to reclaim for the reader the historical truth about the brothers' deaths, even if by doing so he undermines and contradicts the family's received version of events. This conception of fiction as "more true" than history echoes Norman Mailer's, who in *The Armies of the Night* (1968), subtitled "History as a Novel. The Novel as History," stated that "the novel ... is, when it is good, the personification of a vision which will enable one to comprehend other visions better" (Mailer 219) than history, which according to him and especially in that case, tends to be blinded by "a forest of inaccuracy" created particularly by the mass media.

The narrator's role is also in this case to provide a critical viewpoint on World War I. Not only is the attribution of the DCM to George completely arbitrary (his first name is considered "the most patriotic" by Captain Hayes), but also like so many others, the two brothers' and their commanding officer's deaths were totally useless, the result of "a futile order that elsewhere along the line had already been cancelled" (Swift 2011, 10). In keeping with many historians today in the ongoing debate about the colossal butchery that was World War I, the narrator debunks the *cliché* carved in the *lieux de mémoire* that are the stone memorial and the silver medal of the heroic death of the young men, who like countless others were in fact the docile victims of inept commanders. Is that what heroism is really about, the narrator seems to ask the reader? Weren't these young men's lives scandalously wasted? The narrator echoes many contemporary historians, such as the Canadian Margaret MacMillan or the American David Fromkin who, while insisting on the responsibility of the German High Command in the outbreak of hostilities, also highlight the nationalist fervour and the desire for war in the various European countries involved, which may partly explain the docility of these ordinary soldiers, at least until 1917.[5]

Heroism is always suspicious or at least problematic in Swift's novels, the most obvious example being Robert Beech in *Out of this World*, who at the end of World War I lost his arm but won the Victoria Cross for picking up an unexploded grenade and throwing it away from his wounded and unconscious commanding officer. Was it "an act of unqualified stupidity" (Swift 1988, 195)? Was it "an act of unquestionable heroism, meriting nothing less than a Victoria Cross" (1988, 195)? Was he following "the highest principles of valour" he had been taught at Sandhurst (1988, 197) or was he trying to commit suicide after hearing that his beloved wife had died while giving birth to their son? The same suspicion is to be found at the core of *Shuttlecock*: was Prentis senior the daring hero portrayed in his memoirs or did he in fact break down when tortured and eventually tell the Nazis the names of the members of the Resistance network who were later executed? Unlike in *Wish You Were Here*, however, in these first-person narratives there is no omniscient narrator to tell the reader (and the other characters) what "really" happened and questions remain unanswered. It is then up to this reader to decide (or not) on the interpretation s/he prefers.

As in many other novels by Swift, in *Wish You Were Here* history also more or less repeats itself (not as a farce, but as another tragedy, with all due respect to Karl Marx) a couple of generations later, with another conflict, the "war on terror" (149, 206) unleashed by the events of 11 September 2001. These are never explicitly mentioned in the novel, but clearly, albeit elliptically, alluded to: "[Tom]'d watched those cattle burning on the telly … in the spring of 2001. And it wasn't so long afterwards that a couple of planes had flown into a couple of big towers … giving a whole new meaning to the act of suicide and having a range of consequences, including ones for British soldiers, which would make a spot of cow disease seem piddling" (203). This rather enigmatic comment echoes the narrator's terse (and somewhat provocative) description of the preparations for the Normandy landings and D-Day itself seen from the point-of-view of William Chapman, the main character in *The Sweet-Shop Owner*: "The roads up and over the downs were thick with traffic. Lorries, tanks, bulldozers. Troops being moved to sealed-off training areas ... The skies buzzed. Something was happening. Then, one day in June, it was still" (Swift 1983, 82). It is up to the reader to fill in the narrative blanks, dot the i's and cross the t's and more generally make the connection between the text and what s/he knows about history.

Once again, in the end, the reader of *Wish You Were Here* knows more about the circumstances leading to Tom Luxton being killed while "'on active duty' in Iraq, in the Basra region of operations, on 4th November 2006" (78) than his brother Jack. Jack's frequent wonderings about the manner of his brother's death will never be truthfully answered: "His brother's death was a mystery" (273); "He knew that he would never ask (though he would certainly wonder) exactly how – let alone why – his brother had died (he knew that the army would prefer him not to ask such questions)" (122). Indeed Major Richards, "the sensitive army officer appointed as a by-the-book regimental angel of death" (Tonkin), has nothing but platitudes and clichés to offer as explanations: "He'd said that Corporal Luxton was a brave and exemplary soldier who'd done his duty to the utmost, so that the army was proud of him, and that it was a great blow to everyone" (89).

Moreover, the reader retrospectively realizes that Major Richards had in fact lied to Jack when he had told him that "he could confirm that Corporal Luxton would have died instantly, on active, front-line duty" (91). Chapter 23 is reminiscent of the famous short and enigmatic "Jack" chapter in *Last Orders*, when the dead man is given a say, as it is entirely told with Tom as centre of consciousness. In that chapter, the third-person narrator reveals Tom's real reasons for joining the army: "We come to learn that Tom's departure was a long-deliberated act of revenge against his father for the father's callous dispatching of Tom's beloved dog, Luke" (Broening) and that Tom had then realized "he had the killer instinct in him" and, had he stayed, he would probably have killed his own father (Swift 2011, 209). We share Tom's last thoughts as he understands that "he wasn't going to die by any nice clean sniper fire, but was going to be burnt to death" (208), trapped under mangled metal in his armoured vehicle. We witness his last moments as he remembers some of the key events the reader has already been told about from another point of view, for "as in many of Swift's novels, information is provisional, and events are initially told in fragments, and then, eventually those fragments are pieced together into a more complete picture" (Broening).

Furthermore, the question of what exactly is left of Tom's body after his horrible death is avoided by Major Richards who, because of Tom's reluctance to ask too many questions, "was spared from explaining … that next of kin had the right to view the body while it rested in the coroner's care. In this instance it would be between Jack and his undertakers. But Major Richards hoped it had never entered Jack's head" (121). The comforting lies the major had been feeding Jack about his brother's supposedly instant death are therefore not exposed, but nonetheless Jack has his suspicions: "Jack didn't like the idea of cremation; it called up bad pictures. Being a farmer, he naturally went for burial. And he had the distinct feeling that Tom might have been half-cremated already" (123). Once again, because of the choice of an omniscient narrator, the reader knows more than Jack does.

Both Tom and Jack refuse the idea of parallels to be drawn between the two generations of Luxton soldiers who died at war. For example, Tom wanted to make a clean break with the past and so "he'd never once said to anyone that he'd had a great-uncle who'd got the DCM (Posthumous). When he'd walked, that icy night, with his backpack, past the war memorial, he'd never turned his head" (203–4): that particular *lieu de mémoire*, linked to his family history, no longer meant anything to him. As for Jack, when Brookes, the parish rector, thinking about Tom's funeral, asked "if he wanted him, in his own address, to say anything in particular – possibly something about those two Luxton brothers on the memorial outside?" he "had thought for a while and said that no, he didn't want that" (263). However, he was at first ready to say whatever he thought might have been expected of him at the repatriation ceremony and even to lie: "He thought of how if he was required following this ceremony to make a speech, he would say how Tom, his little brother Tom, had always wanted to be a soldier ever since he'd learnt about his two great-uncles who'd died in the First World War and how one of them had won the DCM. Or some such crap. He'd say it" (170).

As often in Swift's novels, the statement is revisited and expanded a few pages later: "But it wouldn't have worked anyway, would it? If he'd had to get up and make a speech and said that Tom had always been stirred by those two Luxton boys of long ago. Because that would have been like saying that Tom had actually wanted to go off and get himself killed as well. As he had done. And what kind of war, exactly, had Tom been going off to fight when he'd slipped out of Jebb's Farm thirteen years ago? What kind of war, exactly, had he even been fighting now? At least those two Luxton lads had known the score. Maybe. It wouldn't have worked because it wasn't true" (178). However, Jack, who anyway "could never have got up to make a speech – before lords, ladies and colonels – even to save his own damn life" (178), cannot stand the repatriation ceremony and hurriedly walks away before the end, overwhelmed by conflicting emotions.

THE BODY AS A NEW *LIEU DE MÉMOIRE*

The readers of Swift's novel are probably familiar with the official repatriation ceremony, as described on the MOD website under the heading "Repatriation of the dead," which Swift followed closely in *Wish You Were Here*:

> The repatriation is a formal military ceremony and the exact arrangements for repatriation vary from case to case, but in general terms the following apply:
>
> - When a soldier is killed overseas, his or her body will be flown back to the UK by RAF aircraft.
> - The aircraft will usually land at RAF Lyneham in Wiltshire.
> - The repatriation ceremony will take place during normal working hours.
> - A band may occasionally be present, as may the media, although only with Ministerial consent and dependent on circumstances.
> - In some cases a military bearer party will convey the coffin from the aircraft to the hearse.
>
> The wishes of the deceased's family will be noted and adhered to as far as possible. Families are under no obligation to attend a repatriation but as it is a solemn affair, all aspects of the process are carried out with due respect and dignity regardless of family attendance.[6]

The ceremony, or at least the public part of it, was unfortunately a regular feature of the six o'clock news in the 2000s. In March 2011 (the very year when *Wish You Were Here* was published), the granting of royal patronage to the town of Wootton Bassett in Wiltshire ("the first royal patronage to be conferred upon a town since 1909") by Queen Elizabeth II "in recognition of its role in the early 21st century military funeral repatriations, which passed through the town,"[7] is but one more proof of its unfortunate notoriety. It also clearly makes the town a new *lieu de mémoire*.

However, this is a fairly recent development in the way the army deals with its casualties: "Until the late 1960s, when repatriation of bodies to allow a privately funded funeral in the UK was introduced, the policy of Her Majesty's Government was that Service personnel who died overseas should be buried close to where they fell. Up to that date, funeral arrangements for a deceased Serviceman overseas would have been a matter for the formation concerned and burial would have taken place locally with no relatives present. Now, if a Serviceman or Servicewoman dies overseas, the remains may be repatriated and buried in a cemetery chosen by the family at military expense."[8]

This is in fact the main difference in the novel between Tom Luxton and his World War I ancestors. Even though all three died a violent and useless death, George and Fred Luxton were but names on the war memorial as they had been buried "close to where they fell," far away in Flanders field, whereas Tom's actual bodily remains are for his brother the disturbing reminder of the young man he had been and of their shared memories. Furthermore, during the journey from the Isle of Wight to Devon, Tom keeps appearing to Jack as a sort of ghost, and it is only in the very end when Jack has decided to put the past behind him (his decision being symbolized by his getting rid of the DCM and his father's gun) that he can definitely lay his brother to rest: "Tom was here, in this cottage. How Jack's muscles had frozen, then melted. How he'd lowered the gun, for which, he knew, the cost would be the disappearance of his brother … How … he'd felt that though Tom had vanished he was still with him, and how he might even have groaned out loud, 'For God's sake help me, Tom'" (351).

In Swift's novel, the organization of the repatriation ceremony is explained in great detail beforehand to Jack by Major Roberts, and chapter 20 is entirely devoted to it. The formality and the solemnity of the proceedings remind Jack of "those Remembrance Days" (170) and therefore attempt to link Tom to his forebears. The ritualisation process, though different because of the repatriation of the bodies, is in operation. However, as the author himself writes in a very unusual "note" at the end of the novel, "This is a work of fiction that does not aim to give a documentary account of the repatriation process of dead British servicemen and any specific similarities to any such actual repatriation are unintended and coincidental." In Swift's case, the deliberate and assertive fictionalisation of the repatriation ceremony is absolutely not a way to "exonerate the writer from any real obligation to the truth, allowing his or her imagination to roam freely, altering or inventing events to suit their own purposes" (Kossick 8). Rather, as Norman Mailer had done it before him, it is an article of faith in the capacity of the novel to reflect human experience better than factual reality.

As we have seen, *Wish You Were Here* may mark a turning point in Graham Swift's novels in terms of narrative technique (use of a third-person, omniscient narrator) as well as themes. Indeed, the defining moment for his characters is no longer grounded in the context of WWI or WWII, but in much more recent and equally traumatic events, that is to say the consequences of George W. Bush's "war on terror" in the aftermath of the 9/11 attacks on the World Trade Center in New York City and the Pentagon in Washington, DC. It is also one of the very few novels by Swift with a definitely happy ending. Indeed, Jack Luxton finally overcomes, with the help of the ghostly figure of his brother Tom, the urge to repeat the cycle of violence which has already destroyed a significant part of his family. After a gruelling suspense, it is finally with an umbrella and not with a gun that he greets his wife's arrival in the pouring rain. As the old prophet said, "They shall beat their swords into ploughshares, and spears into pruning hooks; nation shall not lift up sword against nation, neither shall they learn war anymore" (Isaiah 2:4). The novel may also be read as a vindication of the vanity, and even the deceptive nature, of official commemorations and *lieux de mémoire*. Only fiction, it seems, can do the victims of wars and their families justice.

NOTES

1 The parallel with *Last Orders*, Swift's 1996 Booker Prize–winning novel about the journey undertaken from London to Margate by four men (three of them WWII veterans) to scatter the ashes of their friend, is quite striking.

2 Pierre Nora, "Preface to the English Language Edition," in *Realms of Memory: Rethinking the French Past*, edited by Pierre Nora,

trans. by Arthur Goldhammer (New York: Columbia University Press 1996), xvii.

3 "La raison d'être fondamentale d'un lieu de mémoire est d'arrêter le temps, de bloquer le travail de l'oubli, de fixer un état des choses, d'immortaliser la mort, de matérialiser l'immatériel" (Nora 1984, xxxv).

4 For example when he writes: "Parce qu'elle est affective et magique, la mémoire ne s'accomode que des détails qui la confortent ; elle se nourrit de souvenirs flous, télescopants, globaux ou flottants, particuliers ou symboliques, sensible à tous les tranferts, écrans, censures ou projections. L'histoire, parce que opération intellectuelle et laïcisante, appelle analyse et discours critique. La mémoire installe le souvenir dans le sacré, l'histoire l'en débusque" (Nora 1984, xix).

5 See for example the different articles in the recent sixteen-page dossier in *Books* magazine looking at the "desire for war" in June 1914, "juin 1914: le désir de guerre," *Books*, 24–40.

6 http://www.army.mod.uk/welfare-support/23204.aspx.

7 http://en.wikipedia.org/wiki/Royal_Wootton_Bassett.

8 http://www.veterans-uk.info/remembrance/repatriation.html.

REFERENCES

Broening, John. 2012. "Death and Remembrance: *Wish You Were Here* by Graham Swift." *The Denver Post*, 5 June. Accessed February 2014. http://www.denverpost.com/books/ci_ 20543959/book-review-graham-swifts-wish-you-were-here.

Charles, Ron. 2012. "Graham Swift's *Wish You Were Here*." *The Washington Post*, 17 April. Accessed February 2014. http://articles.washingtonpost.com/2012-0417/entertainment/35452741_1_bookreview-new-book-mad-cow-disease.

d'Erasmo, Stacey. 2012. "An Island of One: *Wish You Were Here*, by Graham Swift." *The New York Times*, 22 April. Accessed February 2014. http://www.nytimes.com/2012/04/22/books/review/wish-you-were-here-by-graham-swift.html?_r=0.

Gallix, François. 2003. *Graham Swift. Écrire l'imagination*. Pessac: Presses Universitaires de Bordeaux.

Kossick, Shirley. 2004. "Fact into Fiction: A Discussion of Recent Fictionalized Treatments of Real Life Figures and Events." *Cape Library*, May–June, 8–13 Accessed September 2014. http://www.westerncape.gov.za/text/2004/8/may2004_08-13.pdf.

Mailer, Norman. 1968. *The Armies of the Night: History as a Novel, the Novel as History*. New York: Plume (1994).

Markovits, Benjamin. 2011. "*Wish You Were Here* by Graham Swift." *The Observer*, 12 June. Accessed February 2014. http://www.guardian.co.uk/books/2011/jun/12/graham-swift-wish-you-here.

Morel, Michel, Jean-Jacques Lecercle, Jean-Louis Picot, and Marc Porée. 1996. *Graham Swift ou le temps du récit*. Paris: Ed. Messène.

Nora, Pierre. 1984. "Entre Mémoire et Histoire." In *Les lieux de mémoire*, vol. 1, *La République*, edited by Pierre Nora, xv–xlii. Paris: Gallimard.

– 1992. "L'ère de la commémoration." In *Les lieux de mémoire*, vol. 3, *Les France, 3. De l'archive à l'emblème*, edited by Pierre Nora, 975–1012. Paris: Gallimard.

Robson, Leo. 2011. "The Novelist Graham Swift Has, in *Wish You Were Here*, Produced an Elegant Chronicle of Quiet English Lives." *The Telegraph*, 20 June. Accessed February 2014. http://www.telegraph.co.uk/culture/books/bookreviews/8579300/Wish-You-Were-Here-by-Graham-Swift-review.html.

Ruppin, Jonathan. "Interview with Graham Swift." Accessed February 2014. http://www.panmacmillan.com/author/grahamswift.

Swift, Graham. 1980. *The Sweet-Shop Owner*. Harmondsworth: Penguin (1983).

– 1981. *Shuttlecock*. Harmondsworth: Penguin (1986).

– 1988. *Out of This World*. London: Penguin.

– 1996. *Last Orders*. 1996. London: Picador.

– 2009. "Local History and an Interview." In *Making an Elephant*, 347–77. London: Picador.

– 2011. *Wish You Were Here*. London: Picador (2012).

Tonkin, Boyd. 2011. "*Wish You Were Here* by Graham Swift." *The Independent*, 17 June. Accessed February 2014. http://www.independent.co.uk/arts-entertainment/books/reviews/wish-you-were-here-by-graham-swift-2298489.html.

Van de Perre, Selma. 2014. "Commemoration." In *Something Understood*, edited by Mark Tully, BBC Radio 4, 9 November. http://www.bbc.co.uk/programmes/b04nqs3y.

6

"The Distant Shores of Freedom": Recollecting and Rehabilitating Vietnam in America

SUBARNO CHATTARJI

Forty years after the fall of Saigon, American memories of the Vietnam War have coalesced around certain identifiable and dominant frames: that of the "quagmire," the "noble cause," the US as "victim" (of the war, media, members of Congress, or the anti-war brigade), the heroic, innocent soldier, the corrupt politician/REMF/bureaucracy, and so on.[1] These memories have been created and facilitated by Hollywood, mainstream media, some historians, Vietnam veterans and writings by them, and the Vietnam Veterans Memorial in Washington, DC. The memorializations are not, of course, simplistic, discrete, or homogenous, and the battle over the remembrance of Vietnam has been joined by an increasingly visible and vocal Vietnamese diasporic community in the US. Their representations take the form of memoirs, novels, poetry, ethnic enclaves, beauty pageants, concerts, and videos. This paper discusses two memoirs: The Van Nguyen and David Lynn Hughes's *When Faith Endures: One Man's Courage in the Midst of War* (2004), and Quang X. Pham's *A Sense of Duty: My Father, My American Journey* (2005). Both memoirs are concerned with aspects of redemption: while the former is located within the redemptive contexts of the Church of Jesus Christ of Latter-Day Saints, Pham's memoir outlines his quest as a US Marine to redeem himself, his father, and South Vietnam. The use of redemption as cathartic closure is similar to the trauma model's need for closure and is fraught with particularly American redemptive narrative schemas. The accounts are variegated and complex in their nostalgic reconstitutions of a lost nation, the problems of acculturation in the US, and creations of diasporic identities.

The two narratives create seemingly non-ideological discursive spaces in their recollections of the conflict, sometimes erasing inconvenient facts or strategically eliding discomfiting pasts and presents. The memoirs, while questioning particularly liberal US representations of the Vietnam War and the role played by former South Vietnamese allies, end up consolidating conservative remembrances of the conflict in the US as well as within the Vietnamese diasporic community. In their reiteration of clichés about the war and its aftermath, both texts participate in a wider rewriting of pasts and futures that fits in nicely with certain ideological remembrances of the Vietnam War within the US. Such recontextualizations are closely linked to narrative perspectives in both texts. For instance, Nguyen claims that "The United Nations, led by the United States, resolved to intervene in the conflict and try to prevent South Vietnam's fall to the communists."[2] The myth of benign intervention revises history, and both Nguyen and Pham construct memories of South Vietnam in turns as idyllic, heroic, and occasionally traumatic. In Nguyen's telling, the trauma arises from his incarceration in re-education camps; in Pham's, his father's experience of re-education is intermixed with his own conflicted sense of shamed identity: "For more than twelve gruelling years, and indeed for the rest of his life, my father would pay dearly for being on the losing side. His North Vietnamese captors called him unpatriotic, traitor, blood-debtor, American puppet, pirate pilot, and cheap mercenary … Former officers and soldiers of South Vietnam are not 'traitors' and 'American puppets.' They were simply doing their duty for their country."[3] To redeem his father is to redeem himself and his birth country, and the memoir constructs a linear narrative for father and son, a desire indicated in the sub-title, *My Father, My American Journey*, wherein the telos of American arrival is mediated through his immigrant/refugee "alien" status and his father's shamed past. "Now that my father is gone again, I realized I had joined the Marines for him and for South Vietnam, as much as I did for any sense of patriotism to America. I wanted to relieve him of a loser's guilt, a husband's regret, a father's remorse."[4] Arguably "loser's guilt" haunts US narratives as well and this ideological congruence is not entirely surprising. What is interesting are the ways in which Pham's narrative repeatedly dwells on betrayal, abandonment, and victimhood in ways that are reminiscent of mainstream American representations such as *Platoon* or *First Blood*. "We abandoned him [Milou], the same way the United States left South Vietnam, like a dog that just didn't fit into its plans."[5] There are unmistakable echoes here of Chris Taylor at the end of *Platoon*: "We did not fight the enemy. We fought ourselves." Jack Kugelmass's suggestion "that American society increasingly attributes a positive valence to victimhood" is appropriate for Pham's memoir and its writing of the self into existent American narratives of victimhood during and after the Vietnam War.[6]

The category of victimhood is not equally or un-problematically open to all – women veterans for instance – and just as American veterans had earlier staked a claim to victimhood, so too now Pham inserts his narrative within an accepted trajectory. Victimhood, however, was not universally desired by all veterans, some of whom protested the war when they returned. Vietnam Veterans Against the War (VVAW), for instance, was an organization of ex-soldiers who spoke out against US involvement in Vietnam as early as 1967. In January and February 1971 VVAW organized the Winter Soldier Investigation to provide testimony to the horrors and atrocities of the American war in Vietnam. The narratives of veterans-as-victims aided by Hollywood as well as the Vietnam Veterans Memorial in Washington, DC, developed in sharp contrast to the witnessing of V.VAW. As Harry Haines observes, the memorial has become "a sign of national expiation": "The Vietnam War is normalized in terms consistent with American political ideology, the deaths are made rational, and the veterans are whole again, stronger for their expiated guilt."[7] Within oppositional possibilities of belonging, the veteran-as-victim has acquired cultural and political legitimacy whereby "collective guilt is evaded through the medicalization of individual experience. The overall result has been a shift in moral focus from collective obligations to narratives of individual suffering."[8] Antze and Lambek are referring here to Allan Young's comments on the ways in which post-traumatic stress disorder (PTSD) was medically legitimated as a means of entry to victimhood, which then served to obscure political responsibility.[9] The gestures of belonging in Nguyen and Pham's memoirs are strategically comparable in that they too highlight victimhood. Viet Nguyen comments on the importance of victim narratives in the rendering of Asian Americans in the US: "One of the most important representations of the Asian American body politic in the post-Vietnam War period is that of the victim.

Historically, the role of the victim is one of the few 'sympathetic' representations of Asians and Asian Americans in dominant American discourse. Subsequent to the Vietnam War, the representation of the victim assumes particular importance as a mode of rendering Asians visible."[10] Pham clearly places his father, himself, and South Vietnam within the space of "sympathetic" victimhood within which he can recuperate all three in terms acceptable to dominant discourse.

The valorization of victimhood is, of course, not unique to Vietnam. Writing of post–Second World War memories, Martin Shaw observes that "heroic struggle in the context of defeat and victimization ... forms the stuff of myths of war. Defeat and victimization are, of course, a large part of what war is about for individual combatants and their families, even in the most successful of campaigns. When they are the collective experience of peoples and nations, they are equally potent."[11] In influential political and cultural domains, America and its veterans are construed as victims of the Vietnam War, and the veterans' lack of agency allows for the elision of troubling imperial pasts and presents along with individual and collective responsibility. These elisions permit the remembrance of Vietnam as a "noble cause" and the continuance of imperial foreign policy interventions under the (dis)guise of duty or the role of saviour. "Vietnam" becomes a "syndrome," a disease that may only be cured by telling stories of the war and by more muscular military and political engagements. In writing himself into these narratives, Pham not only participates in and contributes to wider cultural formulations but he also wishes to indicate departures and ruptures in asserting that the Americans are not the only victims – he and his abandoned peoples are victims too, and their stories must be told and heard with equal respect.

James Banerian's response to the PBS series *Vietnam: A Television History* is emblematic of a counter-narrative, an attempt to reorient South Vietnamese pasts to recreate a heroic nation that has been nonexistent since its demise after April 1975. "Some Vietnamese have lamented that in a few years the program may be shown to their children in schools, giving the children a poor impression of their parents' role in the war and their reasons for being in the United States. These refugees are afraid that in the future there will be no one to dispute the information presented in the series, that its influence will extend beyond 1983, when it was first shown, and continue to trouble them in the future."[12] The battle for memory rests on the imperative to wrest control of the past so as to shape the future, and it is this ideological landscape that Pham wishes to inhabit and influence. Jon Thompson's conclusion to a study of Michael Herr's *Dispatches* speaks of the troubled, intimately linked histories of America and Vietnam, histories which neither is willing to confront: "Vietnam: America's ghost; America: Vietnam's ghost. Each haunting the other, making of the other a powerful, spectral no-man's land of memory and hurt, memory's badlands that know no border with the here-and-now."[13] Arguably the US seems more haunted by the spectre of Vietnam, but Pham's memoir is haunted precisely by "memory and hurt," memories of hurt selectively retrieved or erased, and the narrative shifts between victimhood and heroism are reflective of inevitable contraries within these troubled landscapes of memory and history.

Alongside tropes of abandonment and betrayal, Pham draws on American immigrant histories and myths, a trajectory of hope and achievement played out in his joining the US Marines. "I wanted to be a real American because I could no longer be a true Vietnamese, since my country of birth no longer existed." "A real American" equals being a Marine rather than "a perpetual foreigner with mediocre grades."[14] His belongingness is shattered when his sergeant instructor asks: "What the fuck are you doing in my Marine Corps? Are you a Viet Cong spy?"[15] The interplay of the desire to be a "real American" and to validate ARVN (Army of the Republic of Vietnam, i.e. South Vietnam) heroism and thereby Vietnamese worth is problematic and crucial as it creates interstitial spaces for the narrating/narrated self. These two narrative strands, one of becoming American, which draws on immigrant desires of acculturation, and the second of redeeming his father and remembering South Vietnam, intersect throughout the memoir creating (un)conscious gaps in the narrative wherein reside resentment, betrayal, anger and shame at racism faced, and gratitude. "The United States provided my family a second chance to live in freedom and peace and to get to know each other again, it did not forget about my father and his fellow detainees. And for that we are indebted."[16] Amidst the confusing/confused narrations, rhetorical questions on "who really won and who really lost" indicate the difficulty of acknowledging contemporary postwar contexts in the US as well as communist Vietnam with its particular histories, struggles, and oppressions.[17] Pham's primary points of entry into these vexed domains are his father and himself. "This is simply a story about a refugee boy who grew up without his father and became confused by an enduring nostalgia for Vietnam."[18] Of course, it is not that simple and it might be worth considering why this (and Nguyen's) story is being told. At issue here are the differences between morally "easy" morality readings of war such as World War II and the Holocaust and the "moral" reading of conflicts with their more complex intermixture of motives, responsibilities, and aftermaths.[19]

In his essay "Landscapes of Memory: Trauma, Narrative, and Dissociation," Laurence Kirmayer argues that individual memories draw significance "from *meta-memory* – implicit models of memory which influence what can be recalled and cited as veridical. Narratives of trauma may be understood then as cultural constructions of personal and historical memory."[20] Pham's memoir circulates within certain "implicit models of memory" available to the Vietnamese-American community: the heroic ARVN; a nation betrayed by the US; a feckless leadership responsible for loss of the nation; communist Vietnam as a travesty of being Vietnamese; and the need to preserve Vietnamese identity and history in ethnic enclaves in the US. These models are not only "cultural constructions" but also modes of justification of the war, of being South Vietnamese, and of being a refugee. Pham's narrative lays claim to the lost nation, an ownership if not of land then of its memories, histories, and cultures, and this claim is an exclusivist one which must be guarded against liberal American and communist Vietnamese claims.

The de-legitimation of post-1975 Vietnam is also evidenced in critical commentaries such as Nguyen Hung Quoc's essays "Vietnamese Communist Literature (1975–1990)" and "Vietnamese Literature in Exile (1975–1990)" wherein he argues that communist literature and literature written within Vietnam have little or no literary or political value.[21] As a "narrative of trauma," Pham's story is engaged not just in a personal quest but in a rehabilitative history of his people. For instance, he recalls a meeting with Eddie Adams who expressed his regrets at taking the photograph of General Loan shooting a suspected Viet Cong operative in Saigon. In Pham's telling, "In a fraction of a second, a South Vietnamese military hero would be forever transformed into a barbarous symbol of the war."[22] The enemy in this and other immigrant accounts is not only the Viet Cong or the communists but the anti-war movement in America and its handmaiden, the liberal media. The memorial push-back is thus not only against mainland Vietnamese accounts of the conflict but of mainstream American ones that sometimes valorize their former enemy and see Vietnamese immigrants/refugees as evidence of loss and waste.

Pham and Nguyen inhabit what Kirmayer calls "a public space of trauma" which, he writes, "provides a consensual reality and collective memory through which the fragments of personal memory can be assembled, reconstructed, and displayed with a tacit assumption of validity."[23] Kirmayer's insights highlight the operation of a sleight of hand in validation of the trauma/memory and narrative (which is always selective) such that only certain traumas are validated. Pham's effort is to claim validation of his trauma and for this he repeats the already available narrative clichés in an effort to inscribe into them his own experience. But in doing this, he inadvertently augments the dominant narrative of trauma/collective memory and its ideological force fields. Pham's recuperation of his heroic father and the ARVN, in its refusal to place that wartime participation within larger networks of the civil war in Vietnam as well as American imperial violence, serves to de-historicize his father's role, as if he were a prototypical Vietnamese hero. Pham does not make nuanced distinctions between South Vietnamese such as his father, anti-communist nationalists in the South, communists fighting for independence and unification, and US interventionism with its complex reasons for participation. In Pham's tale the only true Vietnamese patriots are those who fought for and lost their homeland.

The Van Nguyen's memoir traces his journey from re-education camp to freedom in the US, but is interwoven with prior journeys to the US and a complex reunion with his family. When he is one of twenty five selected for advanced language training at Lackland Air Force Base in San Antonio, Texas, he is ecstatic: "To visit the distant shores of freedom I had heard and read so much about, the country to which we owed our present liberty, for me outweighed the inconvenience of a long separation from Lien and Vu."[24] Although Nguyen does offer accurate catalogues of American responsibility for social and economic realities in wartime Saigon, he qualifies the descriptions in terms of the necessity of freedom: "I will always believe that their [the Americans'] cause was just. Our freedom was no less worthy that that of a Filipino or a Frenchman in World War II, or later on, that of a Korean, a Kuwaiti, or an Iraqi."[25] The elisions in such accounts are obvious; no histories of the American empire – particularly ironic in the context of the 2003 US invasion of Iraq – and no alternative possibilities of freedom whether Vietnamese nationalist or Vietnamese communist are considered.

Conjoined with this idea of benign US intervention is the redemptive promise of the US which underlies both texts: "The Book of Mormon declaration that this land, because of its inspired Constitution, is a land of promise, a land of choice above all other lands, a land destined to prosper if righteous, was made clear to me."[26] Nguyen's narrative is inflected by his religious beliefs and it is a source of strength in captivity as well as a means of drawing implicit parallels with communist dogma: "No one could escape his sins against the communists. If your sins were hard to discover, they would provide some for you."[27] Nguyen's memoir draws upon and adds to the genre of Vietnamese-American re-education camp memoirs as well as narratives of redemption achieved through struggle – in re-education and refugee camps, in perilous journeys by boat, and finally in becoming "American" – and in his reunion with his wife Lien he accentuates the difficulties of cultural assimilation.[28] "The cultural gap was real and difficult to bridge. That is why I compare her trials in America to my trials in re-education camp. In a way, both my communist captors and her American benefactors attempted to re-educate us by changing our way of life and teaching us a new way of living. At the same time, they discounted or discarded our former ways of doing things. Although her helpers were kind, while mine were brutal, the process of change was hard on both of us."[29] This is an acute assertion and, given the redemptive teleology of journeys and experiences, a startling analogy that highlights the contradictions of arrival at the "distant shores of freedom": arrival as forever deferred and not really a spatial category at all, that freedom from re-education camp and communism is only partial in contexts of new un-freedoms related to race, memories of Vietnam and the war, and economic hardship. The constant deferral of freedom could be read as a critique of the cliché of redemptive closure and the possibility of complete cultural assimilation as well as the idea of liberty and its baggage of liberal politics that the US notionally stands for. The all-embracing looseness of liberal ideals of liberty and freedom barely masks troubling ambiguities – ones which Nguyen faces but seeks to resolve within predictable narrative contexts.

Nguyen articulates a transition from elation to anxiety noted by the anthropologist Nazli Kibria in her study of inner-city Vietnamese immigrants in Philadelphia from 1983–85. She writes: "The Vietnamese immigrants recounted feelings of euphoria in the days immediately following arrival in the United States. There was excitement at being in a country that carried images of great material wealth and personal freedom ... But this initial elation soon dwindled. It was replaced by often overwhelming anxieties about the task of building a new life and of regaining the middle-class status that had been lost in the years following 1975."[30] Along with class anxieties were gender ones as Vietnamese men found that their "migration to the United States had impoverished the social and economic resources ... The high sex ratio, cultural challenges and a shift in the scope and significance of women's homemaking activities all reflected and deepened men's losses."[31] Pham chronicles this transition in terms of class and social status as well as the incompatibility of "traditional" Vietnamese family hierarchies with opportunities offered by America. "My father accomplished a much more difficult challenge by surviving years of captivity, only to become a *nobody*, a cipher in this country. That's what happens when you lose a war and your country. The winners take away your family, your people, and your flag."[32] The winners are not identified, an ambiguity tellingly glossed over by the author. Identity is located and defined by the "family," one's "people" and "flag," and the enemy is responsible for stripping away these markers so that loss in war is not merely a military defeat but precursor to a more fundamental existential crisis, one that culminates in the divorce of his parents. "As I had envisioned during my deployment, my parents' marriage lasted only one year after my father arrived in the United States ... My father was hungry for life, to regain the prime years that had been taken away. My mother had become fiercely independent; my sisters grew to be equally autonomous, each achieving her own personal and professional successes, totally contradicting Hollywood's depictions of Vietnamese women."[33]

Since the narrative is focused on his and his father's journey, the mother and sisters exist primarily as antidotes to Hollywood cliché and acknowledgement that Vietnamese women were not all victims. Within the larger narrative frame of victim selves betrayed by the US and South Vietnamese leadership, the agency achieved by women is refreshing, and yet there seems to be an undertow of resentment as if the women failed their husbands and fathers in not recognizing his sacrifices and pain. In his estimation, the challenge faced by his father was a more difficult one precisely because it is made invisible, and his dismissal of women's hardships contrasts with Nguyen's acknowledgement of his wife's trauma. His mother's and sisters' struggles are made visible in success (although the details of achievement are irrelevant), and for his father failure has to be highlighted and recognized as heroic. There is a curious feminization of his father in the erasure of his public heroic-warrior role as well as private irrelevance as head of family or Confucian law giver. This is a feminization that mirrors the manner in which American policy makers and soldiers often perceived the Vietnamese as effeminate and/or "queer" and therefore unworthy or sneaky enemies, engaging in guerrilla war rather than "manly" direct combat. The taint of unmanliness and cowardice, however, stuck more to the South Vietnamese as American soldiers expressed admiration for the courage and determination of the Viet Cong and contempt for their allies during the war and in peace.[34] As narrator, Pham takes on the role of the dutiful, honourable son who will recuperate masculinity stripped in war and peace time, and Pham's own induction into the Marines is an exercise in redeeming manhood.

Such masculinities value the inevitable yet highly simplistic and problematic response to taunts of effeminacy/loser's status, closing the door to alternative, more creative responses by women in his family who are not lauded. Robert Jay Lifton writes of Marine training: "Confirmation as a Marine and a man were one and the same ... To graduate from contemptible unmanliness – to be confirmed as a Man-Marine sharing the power of the immortal group – one had to absorb an image of women as a lower element."[35] While Pham sees the women in his family as antithetical to Hollywood stereotypes, he seems to place them outside the pale of male narratives which they cannot comprehend and indeed disrupt by their independence and success. The image of the initially "foreign," yet quintessentially American, independent woman feeds into the ideological cliché of American freedom, thereby partially justifying, as in the case of Afghanistan in 2001, US invasions to liberate oppressed women. The complex situation of women fighting for freedom in Vietnam is not considered. In his strenuous attempts to resuscitate the "honour" of South Vietnamese armed forces, Pham reiterates a homosociality, a male comradeship disrupted by a lost war and immigration. Describing his father's comrades-in-arms, Pham writes: "The men in this small linoleum-floored eating place had also served their country,

South Vietnam, with honor, but they were a long way from a comfortable retirement. Even so, the VNAF veterans eating their three-dollar bowls of spicy noodles were as honorable as the Marine brass sipping Merlot at the O' club."[36] Moments of narrative redemption are haunted by irredeemable memories of displacement, dishonour, decay, and dissolution.

In its struggle between lost pasts and vacant presents, Pham's memoir conjures a community of heroic forbears. Nguyen conflates re-education camp with cultural assimilation, asserting an equivalence of violent change that reflects ambivalence in the telos promised by the transition to America. Nguyen is a father and husband and, unlike Pham's father, he finds a home in the Mormon community where he works as a translator. He and Lien are reunited in and through their respective "re-education" traumas. The latter offers space for a process of community based on trauma, its mutual acknowledgement, and gender balance which differs from the generally accepted solipsistic notions of trauma. Pham leaves the Marines after seven years only to rejoin the Reserve Marines after his divorce. He visits Vietnam and on his way back to the US writes: "This time I was really going home, back to America, as an American."[37] The visit to Vietnam magically "completes" the process of Americanization. It cements not only gratitude (at not being on the streets of Saigon, for example) but identity based on service and sacrifice and narrative distancing. The utopic desire is expressed in narrative assertion which barely camouflages the conflicts that have been articulated and silenced in the course of the memoir.

In their transitions from Vietnam to the US, both memoirs refer to the American presence in their former country. Nguyen describes "parts of Saigon" as "vulgar, counterfeit versions of America" catering "to the needs of men whose lives were reduced by the war to the lowest levels of moral behaviour." Later he cites President Bradshaw of the LDS: "He also realized that some Vietnamese were angry because America's military had contributed to the moral decline of the city ... There were also many young children, amputees missing arms or legs, selling cigarettes on the streets of Saigon for their survival. Abandoned mixed-race Amerasian children wandered the streets, homeless and shunned by both races ... President Bradshaw was aware that this resentment for Americans, however misplaced and however widespread, might make the missionaries targets for someone's idea of revenge."[38] The catalogue of war flotsam is accurate but its emotional registers are muted. There are dissociations from Vietnam and Vietnamese compatriots both in Vietnam and in the US where Amerasian children were "shunned." The US contribution to social and economic realities is hinted at but within a frame of "misplaced" resentment and the safe functioning of missionary work. That Vietnamese resentment may be justified, or that migration to Saigon is linked to American bombings in the countryside or policies such as the Strategic Hamlet Program, or that arguably the United States had destroyed most of South Vietnam in the name of making it safe for democracy, or that communist and nationalist Vietnamese were engaged in a battle for the future of Vietnam is all outside the ideological ambit of the narrative, for the narrator asserts that America's "cause was just." Nguyen gestures toward the possibility of American responsibility only to write out US violence in South Vietnam, and that sleight of hand is visible in Pham's memoir as well.

In attempting to stake out a seemingly non-ideological space, Pham's desires are revealed: "This book is not a personal condemnation of six US presidents, the US Congress, arrogant Pentagon leaders from the supposed 'greatest generation,' or hippie antiwar protestors for their roles in the multisided quagmire known as 'Vietnam' ... Neither will these pages vindicate former leaders of South Vietnam for losing their country in such a rapid, public, and humiliating way ... South Vietnam did have its share of cowards, draft dodgers, and deserters. There were dishonest, incompetent, weak men in the Republic of Vietnam armed forces ... They held the highest ranks of leadership."[39] Through the memoir, Pham proceeds to vindicate his lost nation and its leaders. For instance, when he meets Generals Nguyen Cao Ky and Nguyen Ngoc Loan, he does not condemn them, and refers to the latter as a "military hero" "forever transformed into a barbarous symbol of the war," not by his acts but by a photograph which the photographer Eddie Adams tells the narrator he regrets having taken. The ideological space that the photograph opens goes beyond the claim made on it by the photographer and takes it into the realm of collective memory. The narrative here is perhaps claiming part-ownership of the photograph by inserting oppositional claims as to the manner in which the photograph has been instrumentalized so far. Within such narrative claims, American soldiers "weren't wrong. Their leaders were wrong," thereby absolving them of responsibility just as some mainstream narratives do in their iteration of the soldier-as-victim.[40] Ideologically, the notion that American leadership was/is wrong can also open up a space of critique of US militarism as embedded in a larger schema at the level of policy rather than simply that of the foot soldiers. Ultimately, it probes the notion of responsibility for war crimes and might perhaps seek to move beyond notions of responsibility as embedded only in foot soldiers or the absolution of foot soldiers as "mere instruments." In Pham's narrative, the absolution of American soldiers and South Vietnamese has a curious effect on history and memory: it erases American violence, the historical and ideological contexts for that violence, and it transforms the Vietnam War into a conflict inflicted by the communists on freedom loving South Vietnamese whom generous Americans came to defend.

Pham and Nguyen's memoirs are "pitched" at and contribute to mainstream US post-Vietnam recollections. Both texts function as identity claims – a typology of US identity that eschews the bi-racial or "homelessness" literally and figuratively played out on the streets of Saigon and Little Saigon, Orange County, California. Both narratives lay claim to citizenship, and their "applications for citizenship" are stripped of ambiguity, as if driven by the "need" to "betray" or at best forsake one's original homeland. This is a fairly standard narrative from a particular ideological standpoint, and what is fascinating and troubling are the ways in which Vietnamese-American memoirs ventriloquize a dominant set of ideas. The recuperation of South Vietnam and the creation of a hyphenated identity in America seems to be predicated on a refusal to interrogate myths of benign intervention, or America's imperial pasts, or contradictions at the heart of America's "Ruthless Democracy," or the possibility of valuing anti-imperial struggles such as the one in Vietnam. It is not as if the memoirists are blind to these networks and histories – Pham, for example, refers to Orange County's Republican pedigree and how it "made a perfect fit for the anticommunist residents of Little Saigon"[41] – but these moments of revelation cannot be pursued for what they may reveal and upset.

It is possible to argue, as Jay Winter and Emmanuel Sivan suggest in the context of World War I, that Vietnamese-American memories are akin to lamentation, and lamentation is not the same as critique because in the former blame is put elsewhere: US presidents, US Congress, antiwar protestors, the Pentagon, cowardly leaders, communists, and others.[42] Within frames of lamentation, the memoirs carry a burden of creating and consolidating one set of memories and identities over another set, and this moral relativism allows for the erasure and/or confabulation of facts and events. Paul Antze and Michael Lambek focus on this aspect of burdened memories: "When memories recall acts of violence against individuals or entire groups, they carry additional burdens – as indictments or confessions, or as emblems of victimized identity. Here, acts of remembering often take on a performative meaning within a charged field of contested moral and political claims."[43] Arguably, all memorial acts are performative ones, but this argument has particular resonance within the context of Vietnamese-American memory in that it sets out to create a distinct category (Vietnamese-American) of war and postwar remembrance at odds with and critical of already existent and normative categories such as American men and women veterans, communist victors, Hollywood wars, antiwar representations, and policy debates in the State Department and Pentagon, in Congress, and in Democratic and Republican parties (John Kerry and John McCain as presidential candidates, for instance). In these memoirs, Vietnamese-Americans constitute a category, the South Vietnamese, who were and are victims of war, communism, refugee camps, and racism but not of imperialism or capitalism or hyper-militarism. In fact, the mirroring of hyper-militaristic acts such as the need to join the US Marines, if read critically, problematizes the category of victim versus perpetrator or the traditional psychoanalytic argument that victims of abuse can also turn perpetrators. The two texts discussed here seem to complicate the binary by a process of selective narration and memorialization that is also a forgetting. What is elided are the particularities of war in Vietnam, the jettisoning of discomfiting pasts to mould oneself into not entirely comforting presents. The agency that Nguyen and Pham claim for themselves by writing the self into dominant American ideological traditions is circumscribed by the need to belong, which is predicated on the imperative to erase. The ventroquilization mentioned earlier performatively creates an honourary American perpetrator that seems to cast itself as victim, forgetting the victimization engendered by the Vietnam War. Pham does not consider the possibility of refusing to be a perpetrator, instead perceiving his position as victim to be the final validation of further acts of violence embodied in his joining of the Marine Corps as well as a refusal to question structures of militarism and military violence.

In conclusion, it is worth considering the lamentation versus critique frame that Antze and Lambek articulate. This notion of lamentation is also part of a liberal tradition of seeming dissent which allows for the status quo while fashioning the self as oppositional. Critique on the other hand can look towards a radical destabilization of the status quo if compounded with political action. Here, it seems lamentation becomes another cliché articulated for cultural assimilation. Alternately, one could think of lamentation versus celebration, as loss is registered (especially in Nguyen's text) indicating value in Vietnam that cannot be recuperated in the US. Yet even that "belonging" or identification with Vietnam is not unproblematic as it is nostalgia for what preceded cultural loss or theft (since the communists are illegitimate heirs to Vietnam) or sacrifice or deprivation. Pham's location of nostalgic pasts in the figure of his father is an example of this problematic. "Re-education" is not only the actual site of imprisonment but of re-fashioning selves and pasts in an "alien" land one now calls "home."

NOTES

1 See Richard Nixon and W.H. Allen, *No More Vietnams* (London: W.H. Allen, 1986) and Guenter Lewy, *America in Vietnam* (Oxford: Oxford University Press, 1978).

2 The Van Nguyen and David Lynn Hughes, *When Faith Endures: One Man's Courage in the Midst of War* (American Fork, UT: Covenant Communications Inc., 2004), 22.

3 Quang X. Pham, *A Sense of Duty: My Father, My American Journey* (New York: Ballantine Books, 2005), xii–xiii.

4 Ibid., 32.

5 Ibid., 25.

6 Jack Kugelmass, "Missions to the Past: Poland in Contemporary Jewish Thought and Deed," in *Tense Past: Cultural Essays in Trauma and Memory*, edited by Paul Antze and Michael Lambek (New York: Routledge, 1996), 205.

7 Harry Haines, "Disputing the Wreckage: Ideological Struggle at the Vietnam Veterans Memorial," *Vietnam Generation* 1, no. 1 (Winter): 141–56.

8 Antze and Lambek, eds., *Tense Past*, xxiv.

9 Allan Young, *The Harmony of Illusions: Inventing Post-Traumatic Stress Disorder* (Princeton, NJ: Princeton University Press, 1995).
10 Viet Thanh Nguyen, *Race & Resistance: Literature & Politics in Asian America* (New York: Oxford University Press, 2002), 27.
11 Martin Shaw, "Past Wars and Present Conflicts: From the Second World War to the Gulf," in *War and Memory in the Twentieth Century*, edited by Martin Evans and Ken Lunn (New York: Berg, 1997), 192.
12 James Banerian, *Losers are Pirates: A Close Look at the PBS Series "Vietnam: A Television History"* (Phoenix, AZ: Sphinx Publishing Inc., 1985), 8.
13 Jon Thompson, "Ferocious Alphabets: Michael Herr's *Dispatches*," *The Massachusetts Review* 3, no. 4 (Winter 2002/2003): 601.
14 Pham, *A Sense of Duty,* 135.
15 Ibid., 138.
16 Ibid., 13.
17 Ibid., 10.
18 Ibid., 4.
19 This is not to imply that readings of World II or the Holocaust are intrinsically "easy" but that they are often construed as such. I am grateful for this and several other insights to Annie Gagiano. I am also grateful to Swatie for her comments on a draft version of this paper.
20 Pham, *A Sense of Duty*, 4; Laurence J. Kirmayer, "Landscapes of Memory: Trauma, Narrative, and Dissociation," in *Tense Past*, ed. Antze and Lambek.
21 See Nguyen Xuan Thu, ed., *Vietnamese Studies in a Multicultural World* (Melbourne: Vietnamese Language and Culture Publications, 1994).
22 Pham, *A Sense of Duty*, 68.
23 Kirmayer, "Landscapes of Memory," 190
24 Nguyen and Hughes, *When Faith Endures*, 71.
25 Ibid., 140.
26 Ibid., 74.
27 Ibid., 175.
28 See, for example: Nguyen Long with Harry Kendall, *After Saigon Fell: Daily Life under the Vietnamese Communists* (Berkeley: University of California, Institute of East Asian Studies, 1981); Edward P. Metzner et al., *Reeducation in Postwar Vietnam: Personal Postscripts to Peace* (College Station, TX: Texas A & M University Press, 2001); Kien

Nguyen, *The Unwanted: A Memoir* (Boston: Little, Brown and Company, 2001).

29 Nguyen and Hughes, *When Faith Endures*, 225.

30 Nazli Kibria, *Family Tightrope: The Changing Lives of Vietnamese Americans* (Princeton, NJ: Princeton University Press, 1993), 73.

31 Ibid., 130.

32 Pham, *A Sense of Duty*, 12 (italics in original).

33 Ibid., 222.

34 Susan Jeffords, *The Remasculanization of America: Gender and the Vietnam War* (Bloomington, IN: Indiana University Press, 1989).

35 Robert Jay Lifton, *Home from the War: Vietnam Veterans, Neither Victims nor Executioners* (London: Wildwood House, 1974), 242–3.

36 Pham, *A Sense of Duty,* 229.

37 Ibid., 247.

38 Nguyen and Hughes, *When Faith Endures*, 74, 97–9.

39 Pham, *A Sense of Duty,* 4, 7

40 Ibid., 247.

41 Ibid., 192.

42 Jay Winter and Emmanuel Sivan, *War and Remembrance in the Twentieth Century* (Cambridge: Cambridge University Press, 1999).

43 Antze and Lambek, *Tense Past,* viii.

7

Frame Stories of War Narratives in Contemporary War Testimonies: How the Canadian Soldier Tells His Own Experience of War through the Lenses of Historical War Narratives

STÉPHANIE A.H. BÉLANGER
AND MICHELLE MOORE

The First World War plays a major role in Canadian culture as it was the first war fought under Canadian national orders instead of the British Crown. It is often seen as a pivotal moment in formations of national identity and it plays a major role in military culture and soldier identity. An analysis of the representations of WWI in the war stories of contemporary soldiers reveals how trench warfare is represented in the soldiers' testimonies, and what role it plays in their perception of war and of their own identities as soldiers.

In our fragmented world where ideologies progressively fade from the atrocities they evoke, truth has become relative. As a result, the study of testimonies becomes the study of multiple identities: individual, social, and national.[1] The study of testimonies is a modern approach that has not yet reached its centennial. It was first theorized by Jean Norton Cru, a French scholar. Cru served in the First World War out of an ideological urge, inspired by his reading of exalting novels. He desired to take part in the great event that is war.[2] Unfortunately, his expectations of a great battle differed significantly from the horrors he experienced. He published two books on testimonies at the end of the conflict, one of which cumulated close to 1,000 pages and one hundred testimonies.[3] In his other book, a shorter fascicule, Cru theorized testimonies as a genre and explained his approach. His hope was to undermine the use of heroism to glorify these brutal events. Researchers overlooked the impact of testimonies, primarily based on the lack of objectivity involved with relaying events, the incompatible multiple points of view they bring to light, and the inconsistencies in the quality of their narration.[4]

But at the heart of this subjectivity and these contradictions, testimonies all share a common characteristic: the contamination between narratives. This phenomenon can also be defined as a matter of intersubjectivities, when the self is penetrated by social discourse, such as geopolitical vectors (Canada's political position on the national and international scene), personal experience (fight for this, fight against that), and perceived expectations from the readers (Do I look like a victim? Do I complain too much? Will they understand a soldier's life? Will they remain indifferent?). The justification to act becomes the core of the soldiers' motivation to write, and also functions in many ways as a cornerstone in their return to the regimental and core identity.[5]

A schematic analysis of the micro-narratives of Canadian soldiers who deployed to the recent war in Afghanistan will identify how the soldiers perceive WWI and how these perceptions influence the way they describe their own participation in contemporary warfare. How have these war memories of WWI influenced their lived experience, and how did their own experiences of warfare influence their representation of this past war? How does this representation shape their soldier identity? This chapter will focus on what remains of WWI in the collective memory of contemporary soldiers and, subsequently, how this morsel memory influences the perception of their soldier identity.

WHO IS TELLING A STORY?

The following reflections are based on recent publications of testimonies as well as a research project comprised of seventy-five interviews of Canadian Armed Forces (CAF) soldiers in combat arms returning from Afghanistan between October 2010 and October 2011.[6] The sample is considered as representative of the overall population of soldiers in combat arms as it is in many ways comparable to the various nationwide surveys on serving members run by the project "My Say."[7] From this sample, 45 per cent of the soldiers had not deployed to a peace mission and 75 per cent were enrolled after Rwanda/ Somalia. The average soldier who participated in this project was enrolled at the end of the 1990s, is a sergeant, did three missions (two combat), and has a high-school diploma. The sample used here is much smaller and, as such, imposes much more interpretative restrictions. The advantage of data based on interviews as opposed to surveys is that they allow for a much deeper, more complex understanding of a soldier's experience of war.

The study of testimonies allows us to identify, interpret, recognize, and appreciate the impact of war on soldiers – more precisely on the soldiers' multiple "identities" as opposed to a singular "identity."[8] It allows us to better understand the construction of these identities after war has deconstructed, or at the very least questioned, the perception that military members have of themselves, of their roles, and of their identity. Nevertheless, testimony as a genre became a way of expressing oneself in the twentieth century that transcends, at the dawn of the twenty-first century, all media of expression: from oral to written and from documentaries to video streaming. In a world where all is fragmented and where truth is relative, the study of testimonies becomes the study of an entire culture's identity.[9] Jean Norton Cru, himself a veteran of WWI, published hundreds of testimonies from the so-called *poilus*, a French concept used to refer to the soldiers of WWI who experienced trench warfare.[10] Cru was convinced without a doubt that the collection and diffusion of testimonies would help stop the war by showing the reality of war and its horrors. Of course, not too long after his books were published the world saw the burst of a second international conflict. Despite weaknesses based in the testimony's subjectivity characteristic of the genre, testimonies continued to captivate the public's attention.

Testimonies are now mainly studied through the experience of the Holocaust as an approach to traumatism.[11] More specifically, the research tends to focus on the mechanisms that human beings undertake to survive an extreme experience. In this sense, the comparison between soldiers and survivors of the Holocaust, while studying the hermeneutic of testimony[12] (individual) and the culture of commemoration[13] (social), shows how these narratives help give a meaning to a life experience that has lost its meaning. However, there are numerous limitations with the analogy between the soldier and the survivor. Soldiers are not only survivors of violence, but they are also often users of the recourse to violence. The majority of soldiers who lived what can be categorized as a traumatic, stressful, or extreme experience do not see themselves as traumatized, and even relate their experience as an adventure.

> Sitting on the side of my hole I was watching my comrades with bravado despite the fact that the kneecap of one of my knees was furiously and incessantly trembling even if I firmly held onto it … I tried to calm myself down but I was still scared. Facing death with your eyes wide open is certainly the greatest adventure in life and I was snapping my teeth furiously. All intelligent life reeked of fear, there was no way to mistake it for anything else. I was trembling and it was not of cold.[14]

In that sense, very few references are made to the Holocaust in modern testimonies. Interviewed military members in this study will make a reference to some uncle, grandfather, or other family member who was killed in action or who went missing in action during the war, but without explaining what it was or what it means to them.

> Yeah, because they are, their belief, my father was in World War II. He finished his service and he got out, went on with his life. My uncle was in Korea, on my mom's side and he enjoyed it but he did it for a while and he left. I was, I've been making a career out of it, which is something that's different in the family.[15]

The above comment is anecdotal and very different from the following one made about fighters of WWI.

> Internationally, huh, I think we, we command a lot of respect internationally. Hum, I have spoken to soldiers of many different nations and – now Canada has always had this reputation within the military community, the global military community, of being unconventional and, hum, hum, unpredictable. So, they, they, we've always been, from the First World War forward, we've always been viewed as, as, huh, serious, serious soldiers. We've, we've always brought a lot to the table. And, hum, even today, they're, you know, we're regarded as, as tough, professional soldiers. Now within the, the global community at large, everybody, hum, I think Canadians, huh, get a lot of respect as being, hum, quiet professionals.[16]

As such, past wars serve as the lenses through which soldiers understand, express, and compare their own experience of war. We stipulate that the different references to past wars chosen by the interviewed military members relate to their own modern sensibilities. The hesitation in the voice illustrated by the multiple recourses to "hum" shows a reflection that might have been instinctively felt, but never or rarely verbally expressed, as it is an identity to the past that is in the midst of being transformed. The same way WWI was used as a reference for the building of a national warrior culture, the war in Afghanistan has made huge steps in transforming Canadian war culture[17] and is often used as a point of reference for soldiers giving their own testimonies. WWI is often referenced as the only "real" war, and it played a particular role in the transformation of the Canadian identity. Soldiers distanced themselves from the empire, as the command was Canadian. However, the way WWI is represented does not always correspond to the way the soldiers of the First World War represented themselves. For today's military members, the *poilus* are now considered soldiers who experienced a "clean" war, where the enemy was clearly identifiable. By deduction, today's wars are dirty, because the enemy is undefeatable, being dressed as, and mimicking the lifestyle of, civilians. In that sense, WWI became the focal point, the horizon, the perfect war to which all other conflicts that came afterwards compare themselves.

WAR IS CHAOS: AFGHANISTAN

Canadian soldiers will make reference to WWI as the first time Canada distinguished itself on the international scene, in the same way that it is stipulated throughout the historiography. Since the First World War, soldiers have been perceived as "disciplined," "multitasked," and "courageous"[18] to a point that these representations of the Canadian soldiers became intertwined with the myth of the *coureur des bois*, the adventurous woodsman that left his mark in the North American collective imagination.[19] If this tradition of representing the warrior as a hero faded away after the Korean War, it regained its popularity in the dawn of the twentieth century with movies such as *A Few Good Men* and the more frequently quoted *Saving Private Ryan*. Many movies from the great wars borrow the same heroic imagery, but these wars are considered to be conventional, as opposed to the modern wars which are seen as asymmetrical.

> Chaos. War is chaos. Hum, war, war is different today because war – we, we have visions of war being something like *Saving Private Ryan* or World War I or all the movies. That's what I think people, even soldiers, have that impression until they, they go. But, hum, we don't fight conventional wars anymore. We, we fight force spectrum ops. We fight different. We fight, predominantly in foreign environments, optic [not clear], jungle and, and desert. So, we, we have a spectrum there so we have to be versatile in order to, to fight in those conditions. So, if a war like World War I, which involved all those, those, that full spectrum, you could drill it down to, "is a war being in the trenches for four years?" We don't do that anymore. Huh, "is a war, hum, a beach landing?" We don't do much of that anymore.[20]

Asymmetrical wars are often equated to chaos in war testimonies, and most of the time explained in reference to the great wars; the military training still has significant resonance with the trenches but they encompass much more. While for many the evocation of the great wars is tinted with nostalgia, for others it is seen as *passé*, as a world the modern military has outgrown for better or worse.

> No one likes the title "war" alright? But the Americans were taking – look at how many casualties the Americans took under, under not, under not the, the idea or the heading of war but a reoccupation or rehabilitation or whatever you want to call it. Hum, I'm sorry, if you're taking casualties on the numbers that they were taking everyday, just because it's not called "war," you're in war. Hum, and the whole thing with, with Canada, with the casualties that we were taking, hum, we were at war, we're still at war. We're, and, and the hard part is, is that in WWI, WWII, Korean War, hum, you could see your enemy. He wore a different uniform, he came from this direction. Hum, we're in, we're in the, we're fighting an idea. Huh, you can't look at somebody and say, "He's Taliban, he's an insurgent. He's going to stab me in the back, he's going to try and blow me up."[21]

This revered perception that WWI warfare was comprised of definitive battles with two identifiable opposing forces fighting for a visible gain of ground is recurrent in the testimonies of Afghanistan veterans. In Afghanistan, the enemy is a farmer, a local, a child, all unidentifiable from the civilians they are trying to protect. The battles in which they fight today do not provide the same visible gains and victories as the past.

> Hum, you're fighting an idea and, and that is so difficult and that is so, I mean, we, I mean the, the advantage for the insurgents is time. Because it's, how much does it cost to keep a Canadian soldier overseas. It costs huge dollars and, and there's the public opinion and, and, you know, huh, and all they have to do is wait. All they have to do is wait and they win because once the soldiers leave then they just go back to doing what they were doing. So, it's a very, it's very difficult – people want, people are results orientated. Huh, people are, we want instant gratification, we live in a disposable society where if it doesn't work, fix it, get a new one.[22]

If these soldiers consider a "real war" as only that which coincides with the trench warfare of WWI, then they have created a perception of their roles as soldiers that can never be attained through contemporary warfare. The soldiers realize that war is always changing, yet they continually return to the trenches of WWI to describe a "real war."

> War is just this amorphous thing that changes and it changes from engagement to engagement. So, we, we always, you know, we, we can train to fight in trenches but we're not going to do that. We could train to, to do [not clear] fine maneuvers like that, but sometimes we just don't do that. Afghanistan is not war. Huh, Afghanistan wasn't a war. The Gulf War was probably, or the Falklands War, was probably the nearest we had to troops fighting as conventional as we do with modern technology and the latest doctrine. So, regardless of all of that, war is chaos and we seek to make order out of chaos. We try to, to, huh, limit it, we try to find straight lines, we try to order it as best we can so that we can control it.[23]

Because of their own struggles with identifying their enemy and gaining advantage over the cause, the interviewed military members see conventional warfare as simplistic and organized – an ideal war to be sought after. The soldier quoted above describes war as chaos that needs to be given order, something that is difficult to do in asymmetric warfare. Comparably, in the quote below, he perceives a true war being something of order with straight lines, attacking a beach or a specific location and moving forward to maintain and gain ground.

> Because if war is beach landings, four years of fighting, trenches, blah, blah, then I guess that's war. Afghanistan, the Gulf War, Falklands, huh, Bosnia, I'm not sure they're wars. People, you know, people may say, "yeah it's a war," but it's, I think it's combat is what it is. I think it's combat. And you can say all of these were different forms of combat. The use of combat power to, hum, yeah to make, make a situation better.[24]

The soldier above provides an excellent and clear definition of the varying forms of warfare throughout history. He acknowledges that war is constantly changing, yet he fails to accept his own definition and explanations of warfare in relation to his own experiences. It is as if his own soldier identity is stuck on this historical image of a soldier in the trenches.

As illustrated above, testimonies are eclectic in nature, and the comparison of contemporary soldiers with the fighters of WWI does not always serve the same goal. On the contrary, soldiers experienced a range of different exposures to combat in Afghanistan. Some of their exposures were in peacekeeping missions, others in peacemaking missions, and still others in combat missions. Some saw their enemies and some never made contact with the enemy.[25] All of these environmental differences had a tremendous impact on the soldiers' perceptions of who they were, of how they were fighting, of what their exact role as a soldier was, and of how they identify themselves with soldiering. Although the vast majority (82 per cent) thought they were perceived as part of a professional army doing a great job, some actually thought they were not fighting a real war. Furthermore, they also thought they were not doing what they were trained to do, and, as such, compared their experience to the soldiers of WWI, or, at least, to how they perceived this experience.

> NO. 21: I wouldn't rule it out and it would be a lot more challenging. 'Cause we're, our army is very risk adverse so it'd be very interesting to see how things would change when you're actually dealing with a, a real army. Because the, they have the

> means to kick your ass and that kind of danger is increased. I think a lot of our, Afghanistan has made us kind of soft because we're, we sort of hide from casualties. Our military hides some casualties and we do everything we, we can to avoid because, but you know – strategically, the more we take casualties, the more likely the, you know, the pol, politics is gonna sway towards us from moving ourselves from the country, because our country is casualty adverse. So, if we run into a real war, like a real war, it'd be, huh, it'd be a whole new ball game.
> STÉPHANIE BÉLANGER: That's your reference for a real war?
> NO. 21: Yeah.
> STÉPHANIE BÉLANGER: But don't tell me you don't have the feeling you went to a real war?
> NO. 21: No, that wasn't a real war.
> STÉPHANIE BÉLANGER: Are you serious?
> NO. 21: Yeah, it was, I felt like I, like I was, huh, a sheriff, you know.[26]

This soldier's concept of a "real war" contributed significantly to his interpretation of his own experience in combat as being one of a sheriff rather than a soldier fighting an identifiable opposing force face-to-face, like in WWI. Although history makes a clear distinction between the great wars and the asymmetric wars, the soldiers themselves seem to have a very different perspective. Even soldiers who fought in the First World War, describing their experiences in testimonies or letters, struggled with identifying themselves as soldiers.

> So that was war! ... We had a whole other idea. What use were those nine months spent training to run on roads and in the fields if we were sentenced to immobility and rotting in the trenches to finally start our training over by learning how to become diggers.[27]

WAR IS CHAOS: TRENCHES

In many of the WWI soldiers' testimonies, their expectations and associated perceptions of real war were much different from what was experienced. The nature of trench warfare was not done fighting opposing troops in the field. The soldier below uses the same definition of war as the Afghanistan veteran who was speaking of WWI.

> [In battle] we barely are a human being. We are more like a small terrified animal who tries to hide like an ostrich and be forgotten by destiny. Nevertheless, we feel and suffer right in our gut every time we feel the ground shake under the shells ... As soon as the first shells fall we hear the injured soldiers' yells ... Under the cover of danger we work tirelessly to dig deeper even if we get in each other's way because of the narrowness of the hole ... We stop digging to bend down under the whistle of a shell before resuming our work. Everyone is hiding in a hole like us and no communication is possible anymore.[28]

The image presented by these WWI soldiers is much less heroic than those of modern nostalgic memories of the Great War.

> I lie down and I rest my head on a bag of dirt to sleep for an hour. Let me tell you that the bag was really the buttocks of a dead man. Killed the day before. I still slept. I positioned my machine guns and the six men required to man each machine. In the trench you can only hear cries and laments. You step on a body and you hear a painful yell. He is only injured. There are hundreds of them like that. A desolating sight.[29]

The disconnect between memories of WWI and the reality of the lived experiences seems to be a trend among Canadian soldiers throughout history. Even the soldiers of the Great War dreamed of a more heroic role, comparing their own experiences with distorted memories of the past. For this next veteran of WWI, as for so many of his comrades, the pinnacle of real wars were the Napoleonic Wars. This is the type of fighting he wishes he could have done.

> Their humblest holes or shelters, their most barren trenches told of the amount of physical work put into protecting themselves; they tell of the transformation of the standing soldier – as visible as could be – that fought in the 19th century into the crouched, invisible, humiliated fighter of the following century.[30]

The WWI soldiers felt inadequate in their role as compared to the glorious deaths of their counterparts from the Napoleonic Wars. The following quote from one of the soldiers interviewed by Jean Norton Cru reveals the soldiers' realization, through their own experience of war and death, that maybe his experiences in WWI truly were in line with those experienced by soldiers of the previous century.

> I used to picture this in the August's sun with the Marseillaise playing; killed in the line of duty. I used to picture it as a still pure, warm and green pasture only darkened by a single drop of blood. Maybe the Capitaine de La Tour d'Auvergne,[31] whose name lives for us like in an epic poem and who fell between ten others like our own company officers do. He might have died on a dark day in a skirmish without significance. His friends might have said: "Poor him! No luck! Re-enlisting to get killed like this at the other end of a German province." Oh the Napoleonic campaigns! And after we scrapped the mud of Vauquois from our caps and cleaned our shirts, here we are. In the wind of the bugles saluting the flag and between the bayonets hedges we hear the sounds waves of this 100 years old each day more legendary battle cry: "La Tour d'Auvergne ? – Killed in the line of duty!"[32]

Yet the nostalgia still provided the underlying tone to their description of what they lived. It is described as if the wars before were truer, and these soldiers can therefore never amount to anything as great or become legends like those of the past. However, history will tell us that they did become legends and that they became ideals for modern soldiers.

Today's soldiers, who choose the military as a career path even in the absence of any great war, struggle to define their own identity and purpose as soldiers. Especially within a military culture built on the premise of Canada's great involvement in trench warfare, these soldiers define their own roles in a conflict environment as being drastically different than it would have been in the past. As a result, there seems to be a reconstruction of the Great War, and it is based on this reconstruction, as opposed to the actual facts, that the soldiers define what a soldier should be.

CONCLUSION

Modern day soldiers tend to compare their own identity with a transformed, if not distorted, perception of soldiers of the past. WWI soldiers faced the same difficulties as today's soldiers, trying to accept that war is not dignifying, and never has been. The identities soldiers create and aspire towards in understanding and fulfilling their soldiering roles are based on glorified reconstructions of gruesome times. The organized war the Afghanistan veteran seeks, looking to the WWI soldiers of the past as examples of its success, is the same imagined war sought after by the WWI veterans themselves. The lived experience of war has less of an impact on how the soldier perceives his role as a soldier. Rather, it is based more on his own perception and understanding of that role through historical examples. His identity and perceived success as a soldier is based on how his lived experiences measure up to his pre-conceived notions of what a soldier should be, pre-conceived notions that are built on heroic images of soldiers in a world where war can be chaos-free – a world different from the one in which he lives.

NOTES

1 Cecil Anthony John (Tony), *Testimony: A Philosophical Study* (Oxford: Clarendon Press, 2006).

2 Jean Norton Cru, *Témoins* (Paris: Gallimard, 1929); Jean Norton Cru, *Du témoignage* (Paris: Allia, 1930).

3 Cru, *Témoins*, 52.

4 Frédéric Rousseau, "Comment écrire la guerre? L'affaire Norton Cru," in C. Dornier and R. Dulong (Dirs), *Esthétique du témoignage* (Paris: Éditions de la Maison des sciences de l'homme), 3–17; Rousseau, *Le procès des témoins de la Grande Guerre* (Paris: Seuil, 2003); Christophe Prochasson, "Les Mots pour le Dire : Jean-Norton Cru, du Témoignage à l'histoire," *Revue d'histoire moderne et contemporaine* 48, no. 4 (2001): 160–89.

5 Stéphanie Bélanger and Michelle Moore, "Public Opinion and Soldier Identity: Tensions and Resolutions," in *Beyond the Line: Military and Veteran Health Research*, edited by A. Aiken & Stéphanie Bélanger (Montreal: McGill-Queen's University Press, 2013), 103–13; Stéphanie Bélanger, "The Testimony of a War Amputee from Afghanistan: Discursive Myths and Realities," in *Shaping the Future: Military and Veteran Health Research*, edited by A. Aiken and Stéphanie Bélanger (Kingston, ON: Canadian Academy Press, 2011), 265–8.

6 The material we will be referring to is a collection of the greatest number (75; 63 hours; and 731,000 words) of testimonies of serving members that was never collected before. It covers two decades, from the

former Yugoslavia to Afghanistan, and it covers a wide range of operational experiences, from peace keeping to warfare. Stéphanie Bélanger, *Entrevues*, transcriptions by Laszewski S (collected October 2010–October 2011). These interviews are not available to the public. They are identified by their interview number (F20; F21; F49; etc).

7 Glen T. Howell and Martin Yelle, "Votre Opinion/Your-Say: Spring 2009 Core Section Results" (December 2011); Samantha Urban, "Your-Say: Spring 2007 Survey" (August 2008): 12; Samantha Urban, "Your-Say: Spring 2008 Results" (April 2010). This is an Internal DND Report.

8 R. Richardson, D. Verweij, and D. Winslow, "Moral Fitness for Peace Operations," *Journal of Political and Military Sociology* 32, (2004): 99–113; Walter Goldschmidt, "Inducement to Military Participation in Tribal Societies," in *The Anthropology of War and Peace: Perspectives on the Nuclear Age*, edited by Paul R. Turner and David C. Pitt (Granby, MA: Bergin & Garvey 1989), 15–31.

9 Annette Wieviorka, *L'ère du témoin* (Paris: Hachette, 1998), 186; T. Gomart, "Quel statut pour le témoignage oral en histoire contemporaine?," *Hypothèses* 1 (1999): 103–11; C.A.J. Coady, *Testimony: A Philosophical Study* (New York: Oxford University Press, 1995, 2002), 1002; H. Putnam, *Raison, vérité et histoire* (Paris: Les editions de Minuit 2005, 1981), 242.

10 Cru, *Témoins*, 727, 52.

11 Annette Wieviorka, *L'Ère du témoin* (Paris: Plon, 1998); Jay Winter, *Remembering War: The Great War between Memory and History in the Twentieth Century* (New Haven: Yale University Press, 2006); Dominick LaCapra, *Writing History, Writing Trauma* (Baltimore: Johns Hopkins University Press, 2001).

12 Kalí Tal, *Worlds of Hurt: Reading the Literatures of Trauma* (Cambridge: Cambridge University Press, 1996).

13 Winter, *Remembering War.*

14 Our translation from: "Assis, sur le bord de mon trou, je regardais mes camarades avec bravade, malgré que la rotule de l'un de mes genoux tremblait nerveusement, sans arrêt, même quand je l'empoignais solidement. Il n'y avait pas d'erreur, j'avais peur. Une peur viscérale qui me rivait les fesses pour m'empêcher de tout lâcher. J'avais peur. J'vais beau me raisonner, j'avais peur. Faire face à la mort lucidement est certainement la plus grande aventure de la vie et j'étais vraiment au royaume des claque-dents. Ici, toute vie intelligente suintait de peur, il n'y avait pas d'équivoque possible, je tremblais et ce n'était pas de

froid:" 101. Quoted from Maurice Juteau, *Ma drôle de guerre* (Farnham: Formulaires Ducharme Inc, 1980), 25 in, S. Vincent, *Ils ont écrit la guerre* (Montreal: VLB Éditeur, 2010), 309.

15 Bélanger, *Entrevues*, F60

16 Ibid., F19.

17 *Canadians' Views of the Canadian Forces and Its Elements – 2012*, Final Report, Submitted to Department of National Defence (Ekos Research Associates Inc, March 2012), 27; R.W. Murray and J. McCoy, "From Middle Power to Peacebuilder: The Use of the Canadian Forces in Modern Canadian Foreign Policy," *American Review of Canadian Studies* 40, no. 2 (2010): 177; D. Patrick, "5 Canadians Killed in Afghanistan, Roadside Bomb Hits Armoured Vehicle," *CBC News*, 30 December 2009; Gordon Smith, "Canada in Afghanistan: Is It Working?," *Canadian Defence & Foreign Affairs Institute* (Calgary: Canadian Defence and Foreign Affairs Institute, March 2007): 12.

18 Michael Goodspeed, "Le Canada et les nouveaux paradigmes de la guerre," *Revue militaire canadienne* 9, no. 1 (2009): 112–13; Colin Robertson, "The Past as Prologue: Sustaining Canadian Capacity for Defence, Diplomacy, and Development," *Journal of Military Strategic Studies* 12, no. 2 (2010).

19 Stéphanie Bélanger, "Regards canadiens sur la guerre d'Afghanistan,'" in *Expériences de guerres: Regards, témoignages, récits*, edited by Renée Dickason (Paris: Éditions Mare et Martin, 2012), 72–4.

20 Bélanger, *Entrevues*, F55.

21 Ibid., F64.

22 Ibid.

23 Ibid., F55.

24 Ibid.

25 A.B. Godefroy, ed., *Land Operations 2021 Adaptive Dispersed Operations, The Force Employment Concept for Canada's Army of Tomorrow* (Kingston: Directorate of Land Concepts and Design, 2007); Murray and McCoy, "From Middle Power to Peacebuilder," 171–7; L. Windsor, D. Charters, and B. Wilson, *Kandahar Tour: The Turning Point in Canada's Afghan Mission* (Mississauga, ON: Wiley & Sons, 2008), 265.

26 Bélanger, *Entrevues*, F21.

27 Claude Corneloup, 22nd battalion, 20 or 29 September 1915, 105 in Michel Litalien, *Écrire sa guerre. Témoignages de soldats canadiens-français (1914-1919)* (Montréal : Éditions Athéna, 2011), 305.

28 Our translation from: "[Au combat,] on reste à peine un être humain, on est plutôt un petit animal effrayé, qui se cache, comme l'autruche, pour être oublié d'un destin mauvais, mais meurtri brutalement en pleine chair, en pleines entrailles, par chaque éclatement proche dont le sol transmet les ondes en autant de vibrations douloureuses … Dès les premiers obus, on entend crier les blessés… Sous l'aiguillon du danger toujours renouvelé, nous travaillons d'arrache-pied pour approfondir notre trou; il est d'ailleurs si étroit que nous nous gênons les uns les autres … On s'arrête de pelleter pour courber le dos sous le souffle de l'obus, et puis on recommence. Chacun étant terré dans son trou comme nous le sommes nous-mêmes, aucune communication n'est plus possible." Jacques Meyer, "Les Journeaux Meyer", in Cru, *Témoins*, 208. Jacques Meyer arrives to the frontline as a sub-lieutenant and stays fourteen months (1915–16 plus a few months in 1918) at the age of twenty and twenty-one years.

29 Our translation from: "Je me couche et j'appuie la tête sur un sac de terre et je dors une heure. Laissez-moi vous dire en passant que ce sac de terre était les fesses d'un cadavre. Il avait été tué la journée précédente. J'ai dormi quand même. Je place mes mitrailleuses et les six hommes requis par machine. Dans la tranchée, ce n'est que plaintes et lamentations. On met le pied sur un cadavre et celui-ci lâche un cri de douleur, ce n'est qu'un blessé. Il y en a des centaines comme cela. C'est désolant." Honoré-Édouard Légaré, 22nd battalion, Hooge, Belgium, 6 May 1916 in Litalien, *Écrire sa guerre*, 305.

30 Our translation from: "Their humblest holes or shelters, their most barren trenches, told of the amount of physical work put into protecting themselves; they tell of the transformation of the standing soldier – as visible as could be – that fought in the 19th century into the crouched, invisible, humiliated fighter of the following century." Claude Châtillon, *Carnets de guerre* in Sébastien Vincent, *Ils ont écrit la guerre* (Montreal: VLB Éditeur, 2010), 309.

31 Théophile Malo de La Tour d'Auvergne-Corret was born 23 November 1743 in Carhaix, Brittany, and died 27 June 1800 at fifty-six years of age in Oberhausen, Bavaria. He was a French soldier, first grenadier, of the French armies under Napoleon.

32 Our translation from: "Jadis je voyais cela au grand soleil d'août au son de la Marseillaise; *mort au champ d'honneur*, je voyais cela dans une campagne verte et chaude, et pure encore, à part une tache de sang. Peut-être le capitaine La Tour d'Auvergne (Théophile Malo de La Tour d'Auvergne-Corret, né le 23 novembre 1743 à Carhaix en

Bretagne et mort le 27 juin 1800 (à 56 ans) à Oberhausen en Bavière, est un militaire français, 'premier grenadier' des armées françaises, sous Napoléon) dont le nom sonne pour nous comme un nom d'épopée, est tombé entre dix autres comme tombent nos officiers de compagnie; il sera mort un jour qu'il faisait gris, dans un petit combat sans intérêt; ses copains auront dit en passant: 'Pauvre vieux! Pas de veine! rempiler pour se faire tuer comme ça au fond d'une province allemande.' Ah! les campagnes napoléoniennes! Et quand nous avons raclé de nos capotes la boue de Vauquois, quand nous avons épouillé nos chemises, voici que nous autres, dans le vent des clairons véhéments qui saluent le drapeau, entre les haies de baïonnettes, nous écoutons se propager jusqu'à nous les ondes sonores de ce cri de plus en plus légendaire depuis cent ans passés: 'La Tour d'Auvergne? – Mort au champ d'honneur'!" André Pézard, "Les Journeaux," in Cru, *Témoins*, 229. André Pézard stayed twenty months at the front, from twenty-one to twenty-three years old, in the 10th division.

8

A Duty to Remember, a Duty to Forget: Examining Americans' Unequal Memories of the War on Armenians and the War on Jews

JEFFREY DEMSKY AND MELISSA KING

Americans maintain uneven memories of the twentieth-century genocides that targeted the Armenian and Jewish peoples. The war against Jews that came to be known as the Holocaust[1] is widely remembered in museums, monuments, cultural artifacts, and a standardized curriculum of lessons.[2] Although the US could have done more to help end the killings, Americans have worked tirelessly to uphold the victims' legacies. In contrast, there has been little enthusiasm to commemorate the war on Armenian Christians.[3] From 1915 to 1923, the years attributed to the killings, ordinary citizens and elected leaders had various opportunities to learn about Armenian suffering in the Ottoman Empire. That this information did not stir the US government to act is perhaps not surprising. What is notable, however, is that subsequent generations of citizens continue to maintain distance to these memories. The reasons for this abundance of concern for Jewish suffering, on the one hand, and the lack of interest for the suffering of Armenians, on the other hand, are not altogether clear. Discussing the imbalance is our paper's focus.[4]

Admittedly, each set of killings betrays unique characteristics, rendering a strict comparative framework problematic. However, there are thematic and narrative overlaps that suggest a dichotomous analysis could broaden knowledge about the ways Americans embrace or avoid genocide memories. The long-standing question of whether or not the Holocaust is comparable or should stand alone in commemorations is an important debate that rests somewhat outside this essay's focus.[5] Our interest involves studying the parallels and divergences, not necessarily in the chronology or consequences of the killings, but rather in their subsequent memorialization. This is a story about the ways that Americans reacted to news of European genocide, and how those reactions informed their broader thinking about victimization and survivorship.

We claim that a relationship exists between Americans' remembrances of the World Wars and their memories of the genocides that unfolded therein. The Armenian Catastrophe[6] coincided with the First World War, a conflict that Americans strenuously attempted to avoid. When the US eventually entered the fight, President Woodrow Wilson's administration struggled to explain what the nation was soldiering to achieve. Although some calls to "save the starving Armenians" permeated public and private discourse, the pleas did not influence policy decisions.[7] After the guns fell silent, the US began a hasty retreat from global affairs. In 1919, the US Senate rejected the Versailles Treaty. The next year, American diplomats withheld support for the Treaty of Sèvres that would have established an independent Armenia.[8] When the Soviet Federative Socialist Republic (later the Soviet Union) reclaimed eastern Armenia in 1920, more than just an ocean separated the US from Armenians.

Since the First World War's end, only one US president has formally acknowledged the Armenian genocide, in those words, during office.[9] The hush also pervades cultural discourse. Even within the Armenian-American community, contestations and ambiguities exist. Absent a clear commemorative context as part of the national narrative, the accounts of Armenian suffering reside outside of American memory. Linguistic challenges, requiring onlookers to read backward into the narrative with such terms as genocide, further complicate recollections. So, too, does the existence of a vigorous counter-narrative that rejects Armenians' claims.[10] Those Armenian Americans waging the "Struggle for Justice"[11] face a high threshold. Until they gain recognition of crimes perpetrated, the ambiguity surrounding this memory of genocide will continue to variably affect survivors' personal and collective identities.

These sorts of obstacles are not a challenge for Americans commemorating the Holocaust. It is true that during the 1930s and 1940s, the US did little to blunt the Nazis' war on Jews. However, beginning during the postwar decades and continuing today, successive generations of citizens have honoured the victims' memory.[12] This willingness to appropriate Holocaust lessons complements a wider process in which Americans have conflated their recollections of defeating Nazism with that of ending the war on Jews. Although fashioned, the memory exemplifies a pluralist mentality that saw in battling the Holocaust – and the racism it embodied – a metaphor for why the nation had fought.[13] In 1979, President Jimmy Carter speechified to this point: "Although the Holocaust took place in Europe," he explained, "the event is of fundamental significance to Americans ... It was American troops who liberated many death camps, and who helped to expose the horrible truth of what had been done there ... We are a humane people, concerned with the human rights of all peoples. We feel compelled to study the systematic destruction of the Jews so that we may seek to learn how to prevent such enormities from occurring in the future."[14] In this mindset, we see what might be called Americans' duty to remember the war on Jews. It exists in stark contrast to the ways Americans have avoided the legacy of one and a half million Armenians.[15]

Both sets of remembrances, however, confront shared challenges today. The twentieth century was an "Age of Genocide" where dehumanization led to intermittent mass murders. These abundant visible and known atrocities produce in memory landscapes what Judith Butler describes as a "differential distribution of grievability."[16] Ordinary people are now determining genocide values for themselves. This means that claims of exclusivity common to Holocaust discourse may come under fire. Armenians' lesser-known narratives may become dormant. The popularity of a fictionalized genocide genre also poses a dual challenge. Not only does memory misuse take hold, as people conflate historical and popular culture, but movies, novels, and television shows also contribute to a "de-territorialization" that can redirect the truth function of the accounts.[17] As third, fourth, and fifth generation witnesses construct cross-pollinated legacies, there exists a possibility that verifiable and accurate stories will disappear.[18] The reverse phenomenon, that over time challenges upon the canon reinforce its historical truthfulness, is also a possibility, and can end up producing greater orthodoxy of genocide memory than originally expressed by the survivor generation.[19]

What may determine continued memory is whether or not these episodes exist as simple narrative or can become useable past. Stewards of the Armenian Catastrophe continue to grapple with a century-long silence in the US. While the guardians of Holocaust memory are better positioned to teach from the tragedy, they face persistent contests from so-called deniers,[20] ill-educated citizens,[21] and the fact that remembering the past does not alter future behaviours.[22] In 1993, speaking during the US Holocaust Memorial Museum's opening, Elie Wiesel noted these limitations. From the rostrum, Wiesel exclaimed that "he could not sleep at night" because he knew that genocide was unfolding in Bosnia-Herzegovina.[23] He pleaded with President Bill Clinton, seated behind him, to stir the nation. Such comments highlight a kernel truth. It matters less to the contemporary nation if Americans dutifully honour victims' memories than it does that this guardianship affirms the idea that combating genocide bolsters the nation's values. Absent this commitment, ritualized remembrances may only end up highlighting, firstly, Americans' continued inability to stamp out the practice and, secondly, the unequal treatment of Americans who are descendants of survivors.

THE FIRST WORLD WAR: ACKNOWLEDGING ARMENIANS, FORGETTING THEIR GENOCIDE

In 1916, President Woodrow Wilson campaigned for his re-election by reminding Americans that he had "kept them out of war." Foreign policy neutrality was more than just American diplomatic tradition. Wilson feared that European events had the potential to sow domestic unrest.[24] Once the US entered the fighting, explaining the war effort was a primary challenge. Officials at the newly created Committee on Public Information used visual, textual, and auditory tools to mobilize enthusiasm.[25] Such efforts were not immediately successful. During the first six weeks following the war declaration, US government projections expected one million citizens to volunteer for military service. Fewer than 80,000 men joined up.[26] In 1917, Americans were only fifty years removed from the US Civil War. Its living memory discouraged young men from again taking up arms. Only after Congress passed the Selective Service Act – that in one year resulted in nearly ten million registrations – did the US possess the capacity to mobilize an overseas fighting force.[27]

The Committee on Public Information attempted to manufacture enthusiasm through a vigorous propaganda campaign. Central to this effort was the claim that German militarism was an ecumenical problem. People heard a lot about the sinking of the *Lusitania* and the Zimmerman Telegram; in public spaces they saw Germans dehumanized as rampaging gorillas and brutish Huns.[28] Similar themes dotted films of the period, including *Kaiser: Beast of Berlin* (1918), *Wolves of Kultur* (1918), *The Hun Within* (1918), and *To Hell with the Kaiser* (1918).[29] American newspapers also promoted this mindset, reporting stories of alleged German atrocities. A 1918 government poster, *Remember Belgium*, encapsulated these efforts. The image depicted the silhouette of a German soldier, set against the backdrop of raging fires, dragging a woman to implied instances of savagery.[30] Although such "Rape of Belgium" reports later proved to be more sensational than factual American opinion makers seized on the propaganda value.[31] This practice reinforced an emerging Anglo-American war narrative that cast the democratic nations as provoked from their neutrality by the aggressions of militant autocrats.

Interestingly, while trumpeting embellished reports, accurate stories describing mass-murdered Armenians attracted spotty attention. Perhaps this distance reflected Americans' focus on events in Western and Northern Europe, where many citizens envisioned the fight "Over There." American leaders were not wholly ignorant about the Armenians' plight, however, having known of such abuses within the Ottoman Empire since the 1890s.[32] It is here, in the ambiguity of acknowledgement and inaction, that America's untoward relationship to the Armenian genocide takes its form. No question exists as to the fact that prominent commentators in the English-speaking world frankly and persistently discussed the massacres.[33] The high death toll jarred many observers. America's wartime role as an associated power, with no formal connection to colonial matters, partially explains why the government did not stir. It does not, however, shed light on the broader question of why this information has persisted outside of national memory. In the absence of historical integration with the aims of the First World War in American discourse, it may well prove to be the case that no bridge of memory existed for Americans to approach the accounts. The degree to which this absence persists is manifest in contemporary struggles to build that bridge through the rewriting of curriculum and policy as well as through expressions of art and media.[34]

Credible evidence about the massacres was, and remains, hidden in plain sight. A *New York Times* headline from September 1915 proclaimed, "500,000 Armenians Said to Have Perished." The

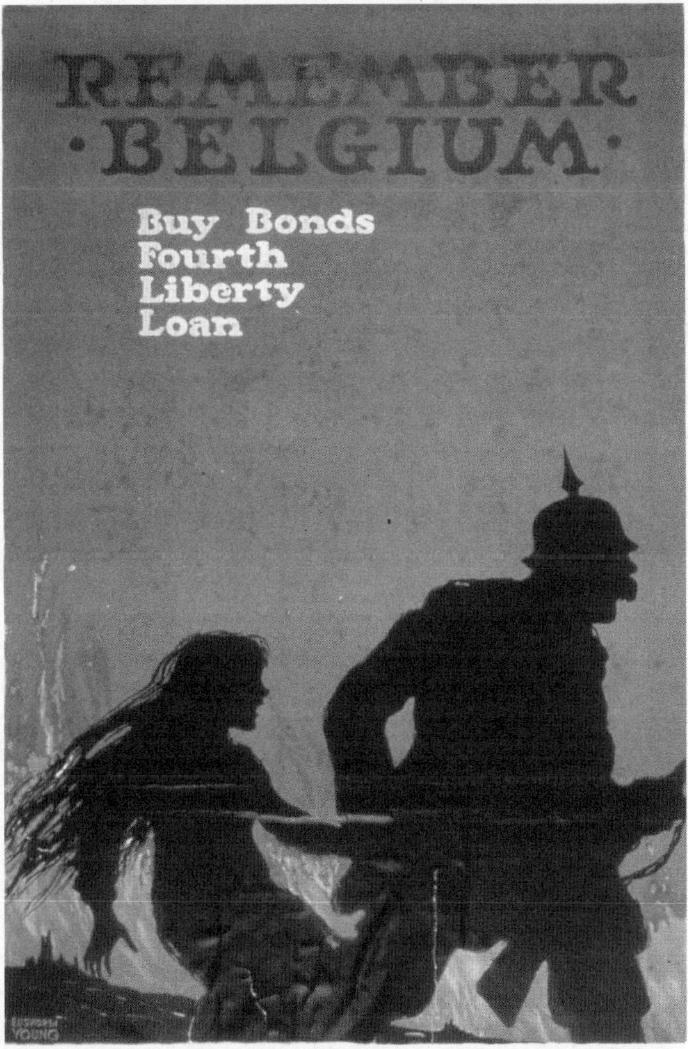

Figure 8.1 *Remember Belgium*, US government propaganda poster, 1918. This depiction of implied German savagery complemented an emerging American war narrative that its armed forces had stirred to end such barbarities. Image courtesy of the US Library of Congress.

subsequent story noted the "systematic murder of men … the women and children were turned out into the desert where thousands died of starvation."[35] This was not a fleeting report. Additional stories in the *New York Times* from 1915 – 145 published that year alone

– described the killings as "massacres," "slaughter," and "organized by the [Ottoman] government."[36] Writing decades before these terms became associated with the concept of genocide, the language offered both contemporary and subsequent onlookers a basis for classifying the deaths as extraordinary.

The issue also attracted attention within diplomatic circles. On 27 April 1915, only days after an event in Istanbul that has come to symbolically represent the genocide in Armenian memory, Secretary of State William Jennings Bryan cabled Henry Morgenthau Sr, US ambassador to the Ottoman Empire. His telegram stated:

> Russian ambassador has brought to our attention an appeal made by the Catholics [*sic*][37] of the Armenian Church that this government use its good offices with the Turkish government to prevent the massacre of non-combatant Armenians in Turkish territory. Will you please bring the matter to the attention of the [Ottoman] government, urging upon it the use of effective means for the protection of Armenians from violence at the hands of those other religions.[38]

This dispatch is one of many that set a basis for contemporary awareness within the government. It also established a wellspring for later memory. Although these acknowledgments of Armenian murders did not incite action, they possess value. Words matter because they cannot be undone. When there are enough of them, laying out cogent arguments, they challenge the members of subsequent generations to interrogate them for meaning.

Figures like Ambassador Morgenthau hastened this process, embedding the accounts into private and public discussions. As a result, knowledge of the massacres formed at the highest levels of government. On 15 July 1916, Morgenthau wrote to Secretary Bryan's successor, Robert Lansing. He informed the new secretary:

> Deportations of, and excesses against, peaceful Armenians are increasing. From harrowing reports of eyewitnesses, it appears that a campaign of race extermination is in progress under the pretext of reprisal against rebellion. Protests, as well as threats, are unavailing and probably incite the Ottoman government to more drastic measures, as they are determined to disclaim responsibility for their absolute disregard of capitulations.

I believe nothing short of actual force, which obviously the US are not in a position to exert, would adequately meet the situation.[39]

A year later, with the US military now mobilized, Ambassador Morgenthau raised the issue with President Wilson. He explained to Wilson that publicizing "the greatest crime of all ages, the horrible massacre of helpless Armenians and Syrians" could help define the war's message: "I feel positive such accounts will appeal to the mass of Americans in small towns and country districts as no other aspect of the war could, and convince them of the necessity of carrying the war to a victorious conclusion."[40] While the president did not act on this counsel, Morgenthau remained undeterred. In 1918, various domestic periodicals published excerpts of his accounts depicting Ottoman atrocities, as did *Red Cross* magazine.[41] That same year, Doubleday Publishers took up the cause with *Ambassador Morgenthau's Story*.[42] His narrative took clear aim at Ottoman culpability. "When the Turkish authorities gave the orders for these [Armenian] deportations," Morgenthau wrote, "they were merely giving the death warrant to a whole race; they understood this well, and in their conversations with me, they made no particular attempt to conceal the fact."[43]

Private domestic groups also publicized the Armenian cause. Members of such organizations as the Near East Relief, American Committee For Relief In The Near East, and National Armenian Relief Committee orchestrated public rallies and fundraisers.[44] As part of the campaign to call upon the US public, these groups commissioned poster art to educate and foster sympathy. *Lest We Perish*, an Ethel Franklin Betts painting,[45] depicts a young woman with palms opened and hands outstretched, clearly communicating that she needs help. Along with Betts's subtle depiction of a Western-looking young woman, such a gesture may have been meant to ask for charity or caretaking.

Douglas Volk[46] produced a similar print entitled *They Shall Not Perish*. His representation featured Columbia, her sword unsheathed, protecting a female child clutched to her legs. In the image, the American flag blankets the youngster, serving both as a practical and symbolic form of shelter.

These and other works represent the development of a marginalized discourse – this one centred on upholding Armenians' welfare – to the dominant anti-German war narrative.

Figure 8.2 *Lest We Perish*, private relief group fundraising poster, 1918. This depiction of a Near Eastern girl with arms outstretched communicates that she is asking for Americans' help in surviving Ottoman-imposed privations. Image courtesy of the Near East Relief Historical Society.

Humanitarian efforts did result, which had been oriented toward the Armenian cause since the 1890s. As a response to the Hamidian massacres,[47] interpreted as precursors to genocide, a host of humanitarian and relief organizations in the US together held a "Turkey Day." In accord with the Thanksgiving holiday, families across the country donated funds for "the starving Armenians."[48] This tradition

Figure 8.3 *They Shall Not Perish*, private relief group fundraising poster, 1918. This depiction of a child symbolizing the Near East, clinging to Colombia who symbolized America, reinforced wartime claims of righteousness. Image courtesy of US Library of Congress and the Near East Relief Historical Society.

persisted as reports of Ottoman violence continued to appear in American public discourse. In November 1916, the *New York Times* reported the "American Committee" was sending a "Christmas cargo of relief supplies to Armenian, Syrian, and Assyrian war sufferers."

This so-called "Christmas Ship," in fact the USS *Caesar*, was one of several arranged during the time.[49]

The British government also had knowledge of the troubling events in Anatolia; in fact, it might be observed they promulgated such knowledge in the English-speaking world.[50] In December 1916, following testimony proffered by Viscount James Bryce, Whitehall issued *The Treatment of Armenians in the Ottoman Empire, 1915–1916.*[51] This so-called "blue book" covered such topics as "Deportations: Antecedents and Procedures." It stated that 600,000 Armenian men, women, and children had been massacred.[52] In the mass of evidence, Bryce determined that displaced Armenians vulnerable to attacks, famine, disease, and the elements, numbered one million people. These claims soon found their way into American newspapers,[53] and also to Australian. For example, between 1915 and the early 1920s, the Commonwealth Button Fund of Australia collected monies in trams, buses, at railway stations, and at public rallies to purchase aid for Armenians.[54] In September 1922, a cargo of relief supplies – what newspapers reported to be Australian flour for "starving Armenian children" – arrived aboard a steamer from the Port of Melbourne."[55]

While these collective efforts did not end Armenians' misery, they set the groundwork for a shared memory, disparate from that of the First World War. However, that memory was less easily anchored in national history and became complicated by, and subjected to, a developing US practice of ambiguity.[56] As the centennial anniversary of the Armenian Catastrophe approaches, the silence mostly persists. Armenian-American students endure prescribed forgetting when their schools and universities forbid them to commemorate the genocide on the basis that it is not a recognized historical event.[57] Such cases point to the sway of dominant American memory, which does not contextualize accounts of the Armenian genocide, and as a result sometimes influences localized experiences akin to denial.

In 2009, during President Barack Obama's visit to Turkey, he referenced the *meds Yeghern*, an Armenian phrase that translates to the "great Crime." Speaking in a country where it is illegal to publicly refer to the "Armenian genocide," the president perhaps went as far as he could toward honouring memory of the event.[58] Despite such alacrity, however, patterns of support for the status quo of silence have held fast. In the US, reticence to legally commemorate the Armenian genocide can be traced to the Treaty of Lausanne (1923).[59] Although not a signatory, the US offered support for the treaty

Figure 8.4 Australian fundraising badge, 1918. Australians involved with raising monies to aid Near Eastern victims wore this artifact as a demonstration of the breadth of concern apparent across the English-speaking world. Image courtesy of Australian War Memorial.

and thereby to the Turkish provisional government, agreeing that a new Republic of Turkey would not inherit the legacies of the Ottoman state.[60] During this period, the US experienced a sea change in its view, prioritizing economic interests, with which an alliance with Turkey could prove useful, and further marginalizing the Wilsonian discourse of humanitarianism and assistance. The US and Turkey have maintained a strategic partnership from the 1920s to the present, with the effect of silencing memory of the Armenian genocide.[61]

These macro obstacles coexist with an additional challenge: the assimilation of Armenians into American society. During and shortly after the war, the largest wave of Armenian immigrants was welcomed into the US. The idea that Armenians were white Christians, who would easily assimilate into American society, complemented the interior narrative of helping brothers and sisters persecuted by

Muslim Orientals.[62] The legal conferring of whiteness, however, demanded that Armenian Americans downplay or omit the cultural differences important to their unique identity. This is to say that memories of Armenian suffering and genocide were institutionally displaced in the process of becoming white Americans.[63] If Armenian history was to be remembered, it was the history of European likeness melting into American society. Forgetfulness of Armenian distinction resulted in what some Armenian Americans term "white genocide,"[64] the assimilatory process that carries forward the intent of physical and historical genocide; that is, the annihilation of Armenian identity. Rejection of otherness and blindness to distinct experiences of suffering and survivorship, on which identity is constructed, informs both Armenian-American memory and American amnesia about the killings. Armenian memory in the US is often produced and expressed with the intent to remind that the elimination of memory is the last stage of genocide.[65]

Further, ambiguity reflected from the Armenian-American community towards the US contributes to forgetfulness. Multiple waves of Armenian immigration from dispersed communities, only some of which directly experienced genocide and its after-effects, have complicated remembrance. For example, Armenians who immigrated to the US from the Soviet Union have been described as a population with little to no memory of genocide, accused of downplaying Armenian history under the Ottomans to make sense of their struggles as an ethnic minority in the USSR.[66] The more recent visibility of Armenians who have come to the US with Arabic as a first language or with individual histories of military service in countries such as Iraq or Iran complicates efforts to link a racialized Armenian history to the narrative of the First World War. Increasing diversity in the Armenian-American community has led to various forms of antagonism from within and without, compromising the security and invisibility of whiteness earlier conferred.[67] Rather than finding that this visibility brings forth greater remembrances, the possibility exists that such misunderstandings of nuanced diversity may lead to further avoidance.

In 1981, during a Holocaust commemoration speech, President Ronald Reagan referenced the Armenian genocide.[68] This was a remarkable step that perhaps reflected the president's sensitivity to the large Armenian community that resided in his home state of California.

Reagan's intention, however, was to contextualize, or some may argue subordinate, memory of the Armenian genocide to that of the Jews who perished under Nazism. This lone statement of confirmation since 1914 typifies what we have termed an acknowledgment of Armenian suffering and a forgetting of their genocide. There are more than three-dozen monuments honouring Armenian victims across the US, but there is no national space of memory. Despite efforts to integrate these stories into American discourse, most of the nations' citizens remain disconnected. Whether this silence indexes denial, the influence of policy, or a genuine confusion about what to remember, such social forgetting lends itself to genocide invisibility, which carries with it the potential to damage the identities of all freedom-loving people.

WORLD WAR II: ABANDONING THE JEWS, AMERICANIZING THEIR GENOCIDE

In August 1942, representatives of the World Jewish Congress in Europe sent a communiqué to the US State Department. The so-called Riegner Cable outlined in detail the ongoing German genocide of European Jewry. Its author requested that diplomats share news of this message with Jewish American leaders. Instead of disseminating the information, officials suppressed the cable after determining that its contents were extraneous to "definite American interests."[69] Four months passed before President Franklin Roosevelt issued a public statement acknowledging the existence of a Nazi extermination program.[70] While candid, the president's proclamation was not a call to action. Fashioning a defense of Europe's Jews – explaining why helping Jews also helped America – was a challenge for private organizations to take up.

Groups such as Peter Bergson's Committee for a Jewish Army and Emergency Committee to Save the Jewish People in Europe led the way.[71] A primary tool they used to raise awareness levels was "advertising" how the Nazis' murdering of Jews violated American values laid out in the Four Freedoms (1941). On 16 February 1943, the "Bergson Boys" purchased a *New York Times* layout. In bold, capitalized letters, what appeared to be a banner headline reported: "For Sale to Humanity: Seventy Thousand Jews: Guaranteed Human Beings at Fifty Dollars a Piece." The accompanying text informed readers: "Rumania is tired of killing Jews. It has killed one hundred thousand of them in the last two years. Rumania will now give these Jews away for practically nothing."[72]

Also appearing on the page – and set at a diagonal angle to attract attention – was a typed business letter pointedly addressed to the "Four Freedoms." The short message read: "Dear United Nations' Leaders: I know that you are very busy, too busy perhaps to read the story on the left hand side of this page. For that reason, I am writing an ad. They are easier and quicker to read than stories."[73] Those who did read over the full-page message encountered a personal appeal about the Nazi war on Jews. "Join in this fight," the advertisement read, "to stop the wholesale slaughter of human beings … The force of your indignation and wrath can help save European Jewry."[74]

During 1943–45, Bergson's interest groups embedded these sorts of reminders in the *New York Times* and *Washington Post*. Although he and his supporters did not recognize it at the time,[75] such efforts to mediate genocide accounts foreshadowed what would become a wider postwar American embrace of Jewish memory.

The Emergency Committee also staged a theatrical pageant called *We Will Never Die* (1943).[76] This production, featuring some of the period's best-known actors, played to sold-out venues in cities from New York to Los Angeles. The pageant opened with narrators – Burgess Meredith, Paul Muni, and Edward G. Robinson – reading off a "roll call" of Jewish contributors to Western society.[77] Some of the names included Moses, Sigmund Freud, and Albert Einstein.[78] The second act, called "Jews in the War," retold stories of Jewish-American sacrifices in both the First and Second World Wars. Frank Sinatra appeared in the role of a young Jewish soldier. In the pageant's closing, the narrators explained – and this sentiment was also printed in the official program – the "massacre of Jews is not a Jewish situation. It is a problem that belongs to humanity … America is a dream of justice, a light held aloft to the sacred ways of humanity. Speak for us and give not only the Jews, but also mankind back its fair name."[79]

On 12 April 1943, *We Will Never Die* debuted in Washington, DC. The Constitution Hall audience included two hundred members of Congress, the entire cabinet, and the entire Supreme Court, as well as Mrs Roosevelt. The day following the performance, the *Washington Post* reported the event on its front page, and characterized the effort as a "gala."[80] However, despite this prominence, the event did not provoke greater levels of help. An Anglo-American conference

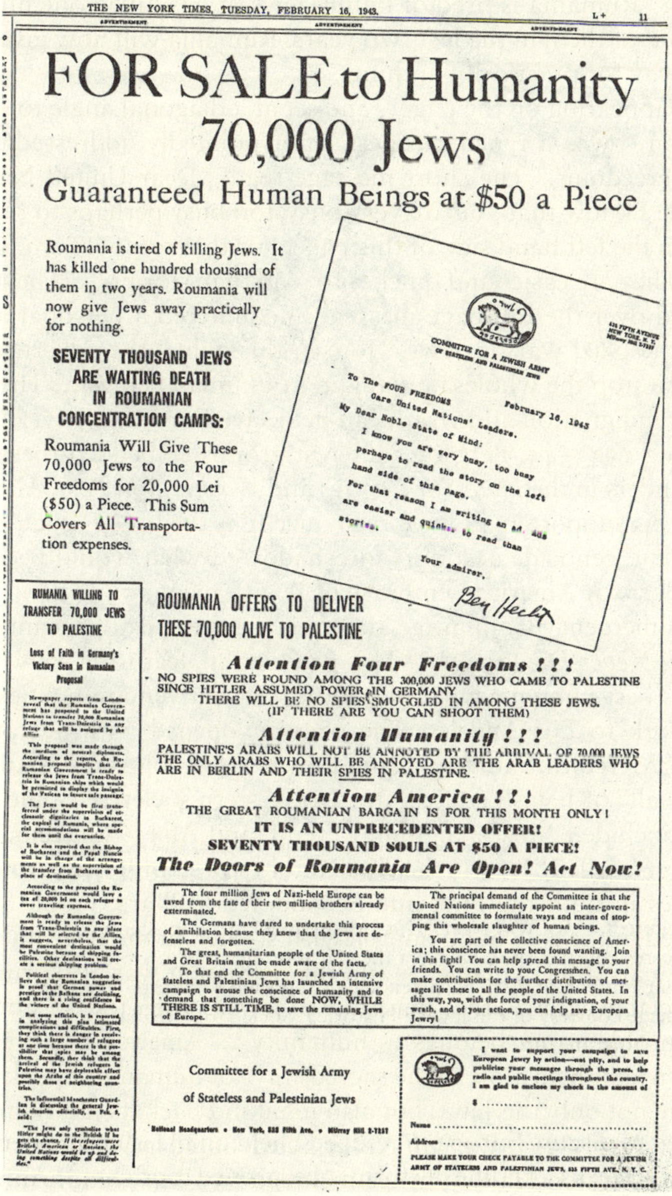

Figure 8.5 "For Sale to Humanity," private relief group advertisement, 1943. This *New York Times* advertisement on behalf of imperiled Rumanian Jews conflated the American "Four Freedoms" declaration with a defence of European Jewry. Image courtesy of David S. Wyman Institute for Holocaust Studies.

Figure 8.6 *We Will Never Die*, private relief group poster, 1943. This poster adorned the cover of a theatrical program whose plot held that combating the Jewish genocide supported American war aims. Image courtesy of the Jewish Historical Society of Greater Washington, DC.

arranged to discuss European refugees, held on the island of Bermuda only a few weeks after the performance, proved toothless.[81] American distance from the genocide also informed the War Department's later rejection of calls for air strikes against the Nazis' killing centres in Poland.[82]

Postwar scholars concluded this inaction constituted "abandonment."[83] Such judgments provided a contextual basis for layering

American memory about the Holocaust. They continue to influence thinking.[84] Whether the US could have, and should have, taken more steps to end the genocide is an important question.[85] However, our study asks how this perception – that not enough was done – has helped set the contours of American memorialization. Rather than rejecting the "failure to rescue" criticisms, the abandonment claims have contributed to a process in which Americans have come to remember the Holocaust as representative of what the US fought to end.

Rhetoric from the period supports this memory. Just because US government leaders took few steps to blunt the genocide does not mean they lacked caring. It is possible to remember lawmakers,[86] cabinet secretaries,[87] Supreme Court justices,[88] agency bureaucrats,[89] and even President Roosevelt as humanitarian but also practical about what could be done.[90] These leaders recognized that winning the Second World War posed the best opportunity to sculpt new ethno-racial norms. Publicly characterizing mass murder as abhorrent to American traditions was part of this potential reconfiguration. In March 1944, speaking as Hungarian Jews faced imminent deportation, President Roosevelt stated:

> In one of the blackest crimes of all history, the wholesale systematic murder of Europe's Jews goes on unabated. That these innocent people should perish, on the very eve of the triumph over the barbarism which their persecution symbolizes, would be a major tragedy ... These acts of savagery shall not go unpunished ... The United Nations has made it clear they will pursue the guilty. All who knowingly take part in the deportation of Jews to their death are equally guilty as the executioner. All who share the guilt shall share the punishment.[91]

These were not empty threats. Shortly after the fighting ended, the Allied International Military Tribunal arrested and indicted two dozen top Nazis. They were tried and convicted under new jurisprudence, "crimes against humanity," that imbued Jewish lives with a degree of value absent during a part of their lives.[92] This step also cleared a pathway for non-Jewish Americans to approach the accounts of European Jewish suffering in a structured context.

Postwar America notably welcomed increased Jewish visibility. During their tours of duty in Europe, American GIs had learned that persecuting minorities was abhorrent. Some had occasion to view firsthand what such bigoted practices had produced. Upon returning to their hometowns and cities, these former soldiers helped to promulgate a more inclusive mindset that stressed respect and tolerance.[93] In public leadership positions, as well as in private roles as the heads of new households, they constituted a new cohort that discouraged anti-Semitism. Charles Stember's *Jews in the Mind of America* (1966), funded by the Anti-Defamation League as part of a multipart series entitled "Patterns of American Intolerance," was the first study to aggregate data that demonstrated a decline in domestic anti-Semitism.[94] Stember examined the results of eighty-three polls that asked Christian Americans over 250 questions about their Jewish fellow citizens. He presented his findings in more than 120 tables, grouped in five subsections, covering attitudes toward Jews, associations with Jews, active hostility against Jews, and effects of the war on opinions toward Jews.

Striking declines in the number of bigoted sentiments recorded are apparent. For example, Stember found that in 1940, 63 per cent of respondents had affirmed the proposition that Jews had "objectionable traits." In 1962, however, the number of citizens expressing agreement with that statement had dropped by 40 percentage points.[95] In another table, Stember presented data related to the question of whether or not having a Jewish neighbour was objectionable. In 1938, one-quarter of Christian Americans found the possibility untoward; in 1962, however, only 3 per cent of respondents expressed reservations.[96] Such drops in recorded bigotry point to a marginalization of intolerant attitudes, in part owing to their association with discredited Nazi viewpoints. During the 1950s and 1960s, as Jews became "white,"[97] the Holocaust became a universalized tale compatible with influential Christian concerns.[98]

External events reinforced this process. In 1961, the Israelis' capture and trial of Adolf Eichmann taught second-generation Americans about the war on Jews. The event also provided a basis for explaining to later generations how America's defeat of Nazism had helped end such horrors.[99] A series of Arab-Israeli wars – depicted as an epilogue to the Holocaust – furthered this budding memory.[100] By the late 1970s, American support for what was characterized by some as the "Never Again" mentality appeared at the highest levels. In 1978, the US Congress established the Days of Remembrance ceremonies. That same year, President Jimmy Carter constituted a commission charged with developing plans to institutionalize the genocide's legacy.[101] In 1980, the United States Holocaust Memorial Council began the work of building a museum to honour those who perished. Since its 1993 opening, the US Holocaust Memorial Museum, constructed on land donated by the federal government, has shared commemorations with nearly forty million visitors.[102] Such breadth of contact encapsulates the scope of American commitment to remembering. Although such connections did not take hold during the early 1940s, when outlines of this conversation first appeared, postwar Americans recognized in the commemoration of Jewish suffering a lesson for humankind.

Cultural producers contributed to this attitude. Just a few months after Adolf Eichmann's war crimes trial, domestic television audiences had the opportunity to view a *Twilight Zone* episode entitled "Death's Head Revisited." The show explored social and ethical issues, in this case issues raised by the Eichmann trial with storylines relevant to Americans.[103] "Patterns of Force," a late 1960s *Star Trek* production, also rendered the dramatic realization of the Holocaust as an American moral paradigm.[104]

These episodic examples foreshadowed more comprehensive treatments. Films such as *The Sound of Music* (1965) won popular and critical praise across the English-speaking world. In 1978, the four-night miniseries *Holocaust* drew over 100 million American viewers. Interest in these stories – Anne Frank's tale[105] is another widely remembered account – points to what Alison Landsberg terms "prosthetic memory."[106] Observers with no first-hand connection to the survivors' experiences approximate intimacy to the trauma through internalization of second-hand, mass mediated, witnessing.[107]

Perhaps the most familiar example of an American cultural artifact bridging Holocaust memory is Steven Spielberg's motion picture *Schindler's List*. Its story tells of a Nazi factory owner who began to reject German racial laws and save Jewish lives. Such narratives tap into a familiar American messaging that depicts figures with negative pasts refashioning their behaviours in search of more positive futures. The progression from trauma and atrocity to healing, hope, and renewal is a plotline that warms the hearts of the audience that views it. Walter Reich has termed this practice the "Schindlerization" of Holocaust testimony.[108] Its appeal to Americans is clear. The film earned over $300 million and won seven Academy Awards. Overlaps connect Spielberg's actions and those of his film's protagonist. As Tim

Cole observed, Oskar Schindler was a capitalist who added value to items, including Jewish lives. Steven Spielberg earned profits sharing this story, and then added value to victims' memory by creating such organizations as the Survivors of the Shoah Visual History Foundation.[109]

Why Americans maintain this deep commitment to remembering the Jewish genocide puzzles some onlookers. Henryk Broder wonders:

> What is it with Americans and the Holocaust? They have two national Holocaust museums, with a third in the works, and almost every major city has its own Holocaust memorial ... from the fervor with which America commemorates the event, a naive observer might reasonably conclude that the Nazi Holocaust took place in the United States, and that Americans feel obliged to come to grips with this dark chapter of their history.[110]

Broder argues that what has come to be called the "Americanization of the Holocaust" has resulted in the proliferation of inauthentic renderings.[111] In one view, American dominance of the memory – and notably the ways that the English language[112] limits the capacity to imagine – not only fabricates false legacies but it also impedes nations with actual ties to the events from understanding their pasts.[113]

While Broder's observations are incisive, he has overlooked a more subtle process. The war on Jews did not directly impact Americans, but its memory has come to buoy wider aspects of their national identity. David MacDonald traces this impetus to the late 1970s and early 1980s, in the wake of the national traumas suffered during and after the Vietnam War. He argues that it was during this period Americans became increasingly tied to lore of its role as the antithesis of Nazi Germany.[114] Such perceptions cast the nation as a positive global agent, reminding citizens of past American rectitude and power. Although a memory construct, the glorification offered millions of people a framework for experiencing the sadness of Jewish suffering as well as the joy of American triumphs over such barbarism.

Such recollections, however, raise epistemological questions of whether or not people are remembering the Holocaust or are instead commemorating what American experts have come to say the genocide represented. It is possible the memory's current prominence is not necessarily rooted in recollections of its unique horror, but rather is the "hegemonic product of many years of strenuous intellectual labor by a handful of Jewish scholars and writers who have dedicated much if not all of their professional lives to the advancement of this exclusivist idea."[115] As Peter Novick notes:

> It is simply a fact – not less of a fact because anti-Semites turn it into a grievance – that Jews play an important and influential role in American cultural life. We are not just "the people of the book," but the people of the Hollywood film and the television mini-series, of the magazine article and the newspaper column, of the comic book and the academic symposium. The high visibility of the Holocaust in the US is a byproduct – to some extent an unintended byproduct – of American Jews' heightened concern with the Holocaust.[116]

The appearance of universality that surrounds Holocaust commemorations may cloak fault lines. Some Americans may be stumbling along into the future under the cover of convenient mystifications and complacently vague banalities about the imperative to "never forget."[117] This maxim, however, is not analogous to remembering. Despite the many books that are written about it, the many museums that are founded and devoted to perpetuating its memory, and the many films and plays that continue to draw large audiences, knowing about the Holocaust is not the same as upholding its lessons and legacies. Just because non-Jewish Americans currently join their Jewish neighbours in deploring the Holocaust may not simultaneously signal its shared memory.[118] Some people might venerate Holocaust accounts at the expense of confronting more localized tales of persecution, perhaps involving violence against African or Native Americans. Others may see in the legacy a metaphor for repentance, forgiveness, and ultimately closure. In this sense, Americans' long tradition of Holocaust commemorations may ultimately serve to teach later generations more about changing attitudes in the US than they do the Nazis' war on Jews.

CONCLUSION

In August 1939, on the eve of what would become the Nazis' war on Jews, Adolf Hitler spoke with his military commanders. Alluding to the so-called racial enemies he believed confronted Germany, he hearkened back to a discussion of events that took place during the First World War in the Ottoman Empire. “Who, after all,” Hitler is said to have asked, “speaks today of the annihilation of the Armenians?”[119] This quote points to the ambiguous memory of the Armenian genocide and reminds that what is remembered, along with what is forgotten, motivates and justifies particular courses of action.

As Henri Bergson noted a century ago, memories that survive do so because they are recognized as offering potential for action in the immediate.[120] In the quote above, Hitler is not attributed to asking about memory but about speech.[121] In contrast to a lack of historical knowledge, what may be referenced is a social forgetting,[122] intersecting ambiguous responsibility to others. With regard to the Armenian genocide, the ambiguity rests in a divergence between historical knowledge and social memory. This is not the case for the Jewish Holocaust, where social memory survives alongside an abundance of facts and narratives in service to US national identity. In this paper, we have claimed that unequal memories of these genocides are intertwined with memories of the larger wars surrounding them. While Americans do institutionally and to some degree popularly remember World War I, it tends to be remembered as an international affair into which the US was drawn and out of which Americans gained little in terms of an identity narrative. This is not the case with the Second World War, which transformed Americans’ understandings of their national identity and responsibilities to others.

Social forgetting or public silence can also be understood as the result of feelings of shame or guilt related to past complicity in the atrocities, including failures to blunt the killings. In the case of the Holocaust, in which abandonment of responsibility during the war has coincided with deep commemoration in later decades, it is possible that the remembrance of action enables Americans to re-imagine themselves. Perhaps in doing so, Americans employ Holocaust memory to deflect critical self-evaluation about their own twentieth-century attitudes toward eugenics, racism, and anti-Semitism. In the contrasting case of the Armenian genocide, visibility and humanitarian relief during the war years is associated with later forgetfulness. Here what might exist in the silence is an attitude which takes historical and contemporary issues to have been adequately resolved, with any remaining concerns on the part of the Armenian-American community taken as reflection of a minority issue rather than a national one.

In an age of postmemory,[123] it is a possibility that palimpsests of memory can be misused. Yet recent activisms in the US demonstrate that younger generations are able to "stand in the gap" between personal experience and national narratives.[124] Doing so can encourage a relation to memory distinct from that of ritualized remembrance, and one that might prioritize humanitarian over national value. At the same time, it draws on the national values embodied in memory that strives to "never forget," regardless of the (in)authenticity of the memory and perhaps also dissociated from the contexts of the two World Wars.

In October 2009, a group of Armenian Youth Federation members held a hunger strike in a Los Angeles public park.[125] As they felt pangs of hunger, they mentally associated them through imaginative processes with the hunger felt by their ancestors, real or symbolic, during Armenian deportations nearly a century ago. This enabled their intention to serve as witnesses to the American public and to past genocide. The intimate and embodied knowledge they produced can become a powerful motivation toward solidarity with others fighting genocide in the current moment. Another example may come from the organizations Jews Against Genocide and Jewish Voices for Peace, in which activists speak out in recognition of various genocides and promote practices of peace and tolerance on the basis of their personal and inherited survivorships. These perspectives reveal the possibilities that victims' memories could be equally honoured and that American commemorative efforts can be reinvigorated, linked to promoting humanitarian and global action against genocide. Such uses of memory are not primarily reflective of the dominant national narrative, but rather emanate from the particular communities where survivorship has always been about more than becoming American.

NOTES

1 Zev Garber and Bruce Zuckerman, "Why Do We Call the Holocaust 'The Holocaust?' An Inquiry into the Psychology of Labels," *Modern Judaism* 9, no. 2 (1989): 202.

2 Thomas Fallace, "The Origins of Holocaust Education in American Public Schools," *Holocaust and Genocide Studies* 20, no. 1 (2006): 80–102.

3 Peter Balakian, *The Burning Tigris: The Armenian Genocide and America's Response* (New York: Harper Collins, 2003), 390; Dennis Papazian, "The Changing American View of the Armenian Question: An Interpretation," *Armenian Review* 39, no. 4 (1986): 47–72; Ronald Grigor Suny, "Truth in Telling: Reconciling Realities in the Genocide of Ottoman Armenians," *American Historical Review* 114, no. 4 (2009): 930–46.

4 For discussion of the role of Holocaust memory in American imagination and in remembrance of other atrocities as genocide, see: Marc Nichanian, *The Historiographic Perversion* (New York: Columbia University Press, 2009), 26; Andreas Huyssen, "Present Pasts: Media, Politics, Amnesia," *Public Culture* 12, no. 1 (2000): 21–38; Gregory F. Goekjian, "Diaspora and Denial: The Holocaust and the 'Question' of the Armenian Genocide," *Diaspora* 7, no. 1 (1998): 3–24; Barbie Zelizer, *Remembering to Forget: Holocaust Memory Through the Camera's Eye* (Chicago: University of Chicago Press, 1998), 202.

5 Charles King, "Can There Be a Political Science of the Holocaust?," *Perspectives on Politics* 10, no. 2 (2012): 323; Christopher R. Friedrichs, "Teaching the Unteachable: A Canadian Perspective," *Annals of the American Academy of Political and Social Science* 548 (1996): 104; Dominick La Capra, *Representing the Holocaust: History, Theory, Trauma* (Ithaca: Cornell University Press, 1994), 20–1.

6 In Armenian history and memory, "Catastrophe," "great Crime," and "massacre" have been used to refer to what is today called "genocide." They continue to be used in Armenian and English. See David Kazanjian and Marc Nichanian, "Between Genocide and Catastrophe," in *Loss: The Politics Of Mourning*, edited by David Kazanjian and Marc Nichanian (Berkeley: University of California Press, 2003), 99, 125.

7 Merrill Peterson, "*Starving Armenians*": *America and the Armenian Genocide, 1915–1930 and After* (Charlottesville: University of Virginia Press, 2004), 85.

8 President Woodrow Wilson wished to see the creation of an independent Armenia. By 1920, however, owing in good part to his failing health, he was unable to help. See Justus Doenecke, *Nothing Less Than War: A New History of America's Entry into World War I* (Lexington: University Press of Kentucky, 2010), 127, 243; Balakian, *Burning*, 299–301.

9 In 1981, President Ronald Reagan used the phrase "Armenian genocide" in an executive order. See David L. Phillips, *Diplomatic History:*

The Turkey-Armenia Protocols (New York: Institute for the Study of Human Rights and Cambridge: Future of Diplomacy Project, Belfer Center for Science and International Affairs, Harvard Kennedy School, 2012), 5.

10 Ronald Grigor Suny and Fatma Müge Göçek, "Introduction," in *A Question of Genocide: Armenians and Turks at the End of the Ottoman Empire*, edited by Ronald Grigor Suny, Fatma Müge Göçek, and Norman Naimark (Oxford: Oxford University Press, 2011), 8–11; Nichanian, *Historiographic*, 59; Roger Smith, Eric Markusen, and Robert Jay Lifton, "Professional Ethics and the Denial of the Armenian Genocide," *Holocaust and Genocide Studies* 9, no. 1 (1995): 2.

11 The phrase "struggle for justice" refers to support of the Armenian cause, seeking legal and official recognition of the Armenian genocide and sometimes including calls for recompense. For an example of activist discourse using the phrase see "AYF Western US Urges Withdrawal from Protocol Process," 10 September 2009, http://asbarez.com/70200/ayf-western-us-urges-withdrawal-from-protocol-process/(accessed 30 September 2014).

12 Hasia Diner, *We Remember with Reverence and Love: American Jews and the Myth of Silence after the Holocaust, 1945–1962* (New York: New York University Press, 2009), 15; Lawrence Baron, "The Holocaust and American Public Memory, 1945–1960," *Holocaust Genocide Studies* 17, no. 1 (2003): 62–88; Deborah Lipstadt, "America and the Memory of the Holocaust, 1950–1965," *Modern Judaism* 16, no. 3 (1996): 200.

13 Deborah Dash Moore, *GI Jew: How World War II Changed a Generation* (Cambridge: Belknap Press of Harvard University Press, 2004), 10; Joseph Bendersky, "Dissension in the Face of the Holocaust: The 1941 American Debate over Anti-Semitism," *Holocaust and Genocide Studies* 24, no. 1 (2010): 85–116.

14 As quoted in James Young, "America's Holocaust: Memory and Politics of Identity," in *The Americanization of the Holocaust*, edited by Hilene Flanzbaum (Baltimore: Johns Hopkins University Press, 1999), 72–3.

15 Taner Akçam, *The Young Turks' Crime Against Humanity: The Armenian Genocide and Ethnic Cleansing in the Ottoman Empire* (Princeton: Princeton University Press, 2012), 253–63; Fuat Dündar, *Crime of Numbers: The Role of Statistics in the Armenian Question (1878–1918)* (New Brunswick, NJ: Transaction Publishers, 2010), esp. chapter 3; Ben Kiernan, *Blood and Soil: A World History of Genocide*

and Extermination from Sparta to Darfur (New Haven: Yale University Press, 2007), 415.

16 Judith Butler, *Frames of War: When Is Life Grievable?* (London: Verso, 2009), 24.

17 Daniel Levy and Natan Sznaider, *The Holocaust and Memory in the Global Age* (Philadelphia: Temple University Press, 2006), 108, 188; Arlene Stein, "Whose Memories? Whose Victimhood? Contests for the Holocaust Frame in Recent Social Movement Discourse," *Sociological Perspectives* 41, no. 3 (1998): 520.

18 Alvin Rosenfeld has concluded the term Holocaust has become so "plastic in its application as to make it sometimes meaningless as an historical referent." See Rosenfeld, *The End of the Holocaust* (Bloomington: Indiana University Press, 2011), 50, 269.

19 Cihan Tugal, "Memories of Violence, Memories of Nation: The 1915 Massacres and the Construction of Armenian Identity," in *The Politics of Public Memory in Turkey*, edited by Esra Özyürek (Syracuse: Syracuse University Press, 2007), 149–52; Federico Finchelstein, "The Holocaust Canon: Rereading Raul Hilberg," *New German Critique* 96 (2005): 7; Anny Bakalian, *Armenian-Americans: From Being to Feeling Armenian* (New Brunswick, NJ: Transaction Publishers, 1994), 3, 358.

20 Deborah Lipstadt, *Denying the Holocaust: The Growing Assault on Truth and Memory* (New York: Free Press, 1993).

21 Veronica Rocha, "Rialto School Officials Apologize for Holocaust Assignment," *Los Angeles Times*, 7 May 2014, http://www.latimes.com/local/la-me-holocaust-rialto-20140508-story.html (accessed 28 September 2014).

22 Alan E. Steinweis, "The Auschwitz Analogy: Holocaust Memory and American Debates over Intervention in Bosnia and Kosovo in the 1990s," *Holocaust and Genocide Studies* 19, no. 2 (2005): 276–89.

23 As quoted in Young, "America's," in Flanzbaum, ed., *Americanization*, 82.

24 Robert Zieger, *America's Great War: World War I and the American Experience* (Lanham: Rowman & Littlefield Publishers, 2000), 207.

25 Stephen Vaughn, *Holding Fast the Inner Lines: Democracy, Nationalism, and the Committee on Public Information* (Chapel Hill: University of North Carolina Press, 1980), 83, 98, 116.

26 David Woodward, *The American Army in the First World War* (London: Cambridge University Press, 2014), 49.

27 Gerald Shenk, *"Work or Fight!" Race, Gender, and the Draft in World War One* (New York: Palgrave Macmillan, 2005), 5.

28 Celia Malone Kingsbury, *For Home and Country: World War I Propaganda on the Home Front* (Lincoln: University of Nebraska Press, 2010), 169, 218.

29 Jeffrey Demsky, "Four Freedoms, For All: American Information Agencies and the Effort to Publicize Nazi Crimes against Humanity," *Revue LISA/LISA e-journal* 10, (2012), http://lisa.revues.org/4869 (accessed 30 September 2014).

30 Kimberly Jensen, *Mobilizing Minerva: American Women in the First World War* (Urbana: University of Illinois Press, 2008), 30.

31 David R. Spencer, *The Yellow Journalism: The Press and America's Emergence as a World Power* (Evanston, IL: Northwestern University Press, 2007), 199; Gregory Pfitzer, *Picturing the Past: Illustrated Histories and the American Imagination, 1840–1900* (Washington, DC: Smithsonian Institution Press, 2002), 187.

32 In the late nineteenth century, under Sultan Abdul Hamid II, Armenians in the Ottoman Empire endured abuses ranging to from double taxation to pogroms. See Taner Akçam, *A Shameful Act: The Armenian Genocide and the Question of Turkish Responsibility* (New York: Holt, 2006), 40–3.

33 Marc Nichanian, "Testimony: From Document to Monument," in *The Armenian Genocide: Cultural and Ethical Legacies*, edited by Richard Hovannisian (New Brunswick, NJ: Transaction Publishers, 2007), 45–7; Balakian, *Burning*, 219, 251.

34 Nicole E. Vartanian, "'No Mandate Left Behind'? Genocide Education in the Era of High-Stakes Testing," in Hovannisian, ed., *Armenian*, 177, 229.

35 "500,000 Armenians," *New York Times*, 24 September 1915.

36 Samantha Power, *A Problem from Hell: America and the Age of Genocide*, 2nd ed. (New York: Basic Books, 2013), 9.

37 Secretary Bryan's cable should have read "Catholicos," the head of the Armenian Apostolic Church. His imprecision perhaps reflected a wider lack of institutional knowledge about the region and its peoples.

38 Document included as part of online exhibit, "The First Refugee and the Last Defense: The Armenian Church, Etchmiadzin, and the Armenian Genocide," presented by the Armenian National Institute, Washington, DC, Mother See of Holy Etchmiadzin, Armenian Genocide Museum-Institute, Tsitsernakaberd, and Republic of

Armenia National Archives, http://www.armenian-genocide.org/files/first_refuge.pdf (accessed 19 August 2014).

39 Document included as part of online exhibit, "Teaching the Armenian Genocide," presented by the University of Minnesota Center for Holocaust and Genocide Studies, Minneapolis, Minnesota, http://chgs.umn.edu/museum/exhibitions/homememories/teaching.html (accessed 26 August 2014).

40 As quoted in Rouben Paul Adalian, "American Diplomatic Correspondences in the Age of Mass Murder: The Armenian Genocide in the U.S. Archives," in *America and the Armenian Genocide of 1915*, edited by Jay Winter (New York: Cambridge University Press, 2003), 113–14.

41 Henry Morgenthau, "The Greatest Horror in History," *Red Cross Magazine* (March 1918): 7–16.

42 Henry Morgenthau, *Ambassador Morgenthau's Story* (Garden City: Doubleday, 1918), 36.

43 As quoted in John Kifner, "Armenian Genocide of 1915: An Overview," *New York Times*, 7 December 2007, http://www.nytimes.com/ref/timestopics/topics_armeniangenocide.html (accessed 19 August 2014).

44 Balakian, *Burning*, 279, 317, 359; Papazian, "Changing," 45. For focused discussion of particular efforts of the Near East Relief, see Leshu Torchin, "'*Ravished Armenia*': Visual Media, Humanitarian Advocacy, and The Formation of Witnessing Publics," *American Anthropologist* 108, no. 1 (2006): 214–20.

45 Betts was a well-known children's book illustrator. Some of her most popular drawings from the period appeared in *The Complete Mother Goose* (New York: Frederick A. Stokes Company, 1909) and in Frances Hodgson Burnett, *A Little Princess* (New York: Charles Scribner's Sons, 1909).

46 Volk was a well-known American landscape artist who studied under J.L. Gérôme at the École des Beaux Arts in Paris. In 1919, he was selected by the American National Art Committee to create a pictorial record of decision makers during World War One. Volk contributed the portraits of King Albert of Belgium, British Prime Minister David Lloyd George, and American General John J. Pershing, http://www.thefamousartists.com/douglas-volk (accessed 6 September 2014).

47 Named after Sultan Abdul Hamid II and his military irregulars known as the Hamidiye, the Hamidian massacres typified Ottoman brutality toward Armenians during the 1890s. See Stephan Astourian, "The

Silence of the Land: Agrarian Relations, Ethnicity, and Power," in Suny et al., eds. *Question*, 65; Akçam, *Shameful*, 40–6.

48 Notably, such humanitarianism addressed only the symptom – starving Armenians – rather than the unchecked Ottoman violence that caused their suffering. See Peterson, "*Starving*," 6; Balakian, *Burning*, 75–80.

49 "Send Ship," *New York Times*, 26 November 1916.

50 Both British and French diplomats saw the potential for gain in Ottoman lands. In 1916, they signed the Sykes-Picot Agreement partitioning large swaths of the Empire. Publicizing Ottoman crimes perhaps lent credibility to these aggrandizements, http://avalon.law.yale.edu/20th_century/sykes.asp (accessed 1 October 2014).

51 Bryce, *Treatment*, http://net.lib.byu.edu/~rdh7/wwi/1915/bryce/. Evidence of high-level British concern with Ottoman brutality against a passive people cropped up well before the Armenian tragedy. In 1876, William Gladstone published *Bulgarian Horrors and the Question of the East* (London: J. Murray, 1876). Chapters such as "Sketch of the Turkish Race and Government" and "Discovery of Bulgarian Horrors" foreshadow many of the themes later associated with the Armenian killings.

52 Bryce, *Treatment*. The book's front cover was royal blue.

53 Power, *Problem*, 9.

54 In total, Australians donated over seven thousand pounds. Australia War Memorial. http://www.awm.gov.au/collection/REL39129/ (accessed 7 July 2014).

55 "Armenian Fund Relief Gift," http://www.armeniangenocide.com.au/australiaresponse (accessed 27 September 2014).

56 Phillips, *Diplomatic*, 5; Keith David Watenpaugh, "The Origins of Armenian Genocide Denial and League of Nations' Humanitarianism 1920–1922," *Armenian Review* 52 (2010): 45–63; Aida Alayarian, *Consequences of Denial: The Armenian Genocide* (London: Karnac Books, 2008), 32; Philip H. Gordon, "The United States and Turkey: A View from the Obama Administration," http://turkey.usembassy.gov/statement_031710.html (accessed 31 Jan 2013); Richard Hovannisian, "Denial of the Armenian Genocide in Comparison with Holocaust Denial," in *Remembrance and Denial: The Case of the Armenian Genocide*, edited by Richard Hovannisian (Detroit: Wayne State University Press, 1999), 202, 230.

57 Personal communications and interviews conducted by co-author (King) during 2009–10 through the University of California, Riverside.

58 Mentioning the Armenian "genocide" violates the "public denigration" clause of the Turkish penal code. See Belinda Cooper and Taner Akçam, "Turks, Armenians, and the G-Word," *World Policy Journal* 22, no. 3 (2005): 84–6.

59 Notably, there have been some French commemorative efforts. See: Scott Sayare, "French Council Strikes Down Bill on Armenian Genocide Denial," *The New York Times*, 28 February 2012, http://www.nytimes.com/2012/02/29/world/europe/french-bill-on-armenian-genocide-is-struck-down.html?_r=0 (accessed 20 September 2014); F. Stephen Larrabee and Ian O. Lesser, *Turkish Foreign Policy in an Age of Uncertainty* (Santa Monica: RAND, 2003), 106.

60 Ronald Grigor Suny, "Writing Genocide," 21; Razmik Panossian, *The Armenians: From Kings and Priests to Merchants and Commissars* (New York: Columbia University Press, 2006), 234–6; Simon Payaslian, "The United States Response to the Armenian Genocide," in *Looking Backward, Moving Forward: Confronting the Armenian Genocide*, edited by Richard Hovannisian (New Brunswick, NJ Transaction Publishers, 2003), 137–8.

61 Gordon, "United"; Smith et al., "Professional," 3.

62 Two American court cases, in 1909 and 1925, defined Armenians as racially white. See John Tehranian, *Whitewashed: America's Invisible Middle Eastern Minority* (New York: New York University Press, 2009), 50; Janice Okoomian, "Becoming White: Contested History, Armenian American Women, and Racialized Bodies," *MELUS* 27, 1(2002): 218–20.

63 Okoomian, "Becoming," 214.

64 Personal communications and interviews conducted by co-author (King) during 2009–10 through the University of California, Riverside.

65 Jean Baudrillard, *Simulacra and Simulation*, 2nd ed. (Ann Arbor: University of Michigan Press, 2010), 49–51; Richard Hovannisian, "Denial," in Hovannisian ed., *Remembrance*, 202; Smith et al., "Professional," 13–14.

66 Rubina Peroomian states this case forcefully in "Historical Memory," in Hovannisian ed., *Armenian*, 97.

67 Sarah Mekdjian, "Tension entre centralité et fragmentation: les quartiers arméniens à Los Angeles," *Diversité urbaine* 8, 1 (2008): 45–61; Razmik Panossian, "The Armenians: Conflicting Identities and the Politics of Division," in *Nations Abroad: Diaspora Politics and International Relations in the Former Soviet Union*, edited by Charles King and Neil J. Melvin (Boulder: Westview Press, 1994), 79–103. For

anti-Armenian discrimination in Los Angeles, CA, see Stephanie O'Neill, "Racist Incidents Spark Debate on City Image," *The Los Angeles Times*, 26 November 1987, http://articles.latimes.com/1987-11-26/news/gl-24929_1_city-officials (accessed 29 September 2014); Veronica Rocha, "Three Armenian Police Claim Discrimination by Glendale Police Department," *L.A. Now*, 8 March 2012, http://latimesblogs.latimes.com/lanow/2012/03/3-armenian-police-claim-discrimination-by-glendale-department-.html (accessed 30 January 2013).

68 Ronald Reagan, Proclamation 4838, 22 April 1981, Armenian National Institute US Presidential Statements, http://www.armenian-genocide.org/Affirmation.63/current_category.4/affirmation_detail.html (accessed 20 September 2014); see also Vigen Guroian, "Post-Holocaust Political Morality: The Litmus of Bitberg and the Armenian Genocide Resolution," *Genocide and Holocaust Studies* 3, no. 3 (1988): 305.

69 Gerhart Riegner, *Never Despair: Sixty Years in the Service of the Jewish People and the Cause of Human Rights* (Chicago: Ivan R. Dee, 2006), 59–60.

70 Jeffrey Demsky, "Immigration and the Nazi Era," in *The Making of Modern Immigration*, vol. 1, edited by Patrick Hayes (Santa Barbara: ABC CLIO, 2012), 373.

71 Monty Noam Penkower, "Vladimir (Ze'ev) Jabotinsky, Hillel Kook-Peter Bergson, and the Campaign for a Jewish Army," *Modern Judaism* 31, no. 3 (2011): 332–74; Samuel Merlin and Rafael Medoff, *Millions of Jews to the Rescue: Bergson Group Leader's Account of the Campaign to Save Jews from the Holocaust* (Washington, DC: David S. Wyman Institute for Holocaust Studies, 2011), 54; Judith Tydor Baumel-Schwartz, *The "Bergson Boys" and the Origins Of Contemporary Zionist Militancy* (Syracuse: Syracuse University Press, 2005), 81, 136; David Wyman and Rafael Medoff, *A Race against Death: Peter Bergson, America and the Holocaust* (New York: Free Press, 2002), 19–24; Louis Rapoport, *Shake Heaven and Earth: Peter Bergson and the Struggle to Rescue the Jews of Europe* (New York: Gefen, 1999), 78.

72 "Advertisement," *New York Times*, 16 February 1943.

73 Ibid.

74 Ibid.

75 During his postwar life, Bergson expressed what he termed a sense of "failure" owing to the fact that his advocacy did not instigate a broad rescue. See Wyman and Medoff, *Race*, 162–5.

76 Stephen Whitfield, "The Politics of Pageantry, 1936–1946," *American Jewish History* 84, no. 3 (1996): 221; Monty Penkower, "In Dramatic Dissent: The Bergson Boys," *American Jewish History* 70, no. 3 (1981): 286.

77 Robert Rosen, *Saving the Jews: FDR and the Holocaust* (New York: Thunder's Mouth, 2006), 327.

78 Whitfield, "Politics," 240.

79 *Palestine Statehood Committee Papers, 1939–1949*, edited by Katherine Morton (Wilmington: Scholarly Resources, 1982), reel 8: 0264.

80 "Official Washington Attends Gala," *Washington Post*, 13 April 1943.

81 Robert Shogun, *Prelude to Catastrophe: FDR's Jews and the Menace of Nazism* (Chicago: Ivan R. Dee, 2010), 196; Louise London, *Whitehall and the Jews, 1933–1948: British Immigration Policy, Jewish Refugees, and the Holocaust* (New York: Cambridge University Press, 2000), 191.

82 Richard Overy, *The Bombers and the Bombed: Allied Air War over Europe, 1940–1945* (New York: Viking, 2013), 402–3; Michael Neufeld and Michael Berenbaum, eds., *The Bombing of Auschwitz: Should the Allies Have Attempted It?* (New York: St Martin's, 2000); Rafael Medoff, "'A Foolish Encroachment upon the Allied High Command'? American Jewish Perspectives on Requesting U.S. Military Intervention against the Holocaust," *Modern Judaism* 20, no. 3 (2000): 306.

83 David Wyman, *The Abandonment of the Jews: America and the Holocaust, 1942–1945* (New York: Pantheon, 1984). See also John Roth, *Holocaust Politics* (Louisville: Westminster John Knox Press, 2001), 217; Henry Feingold, *Bearing Witness: How America and Its Jews Responded to the Holocaust* (Syracuse: Syracuse University Press, 1995), 113, 144; Deborah Lipstadt, "America and the Holocaust," *Modern Judaism* 10, no. 3 (1990): 387; Herbert Druks, *Failure to Rescue* (New York: R. Speller, 1977), 94.

84 C. Paul Vincent, "The Voyage of the St. Louis Revisited," *Holocaust and Genocide Studies* 25, no. 2 (2011): 252–89; Melissa Jane Taylor, "Bureaucratic Response to Human Tragedy: American Consuls and the Jewish Plight in Vienna, 1938–1941," *Holocaust and Genocide Studies* 21, no. 2 (2007): 243–67; Max Paul Friedman, "The U.S. State Department and the Failure to Rescue: New Evidence on the Missed Opportunity at Bergen-Belsen," *Holocaust and Genocide Studies* 19, no. 1 (2005): 26–50.

85 William Rubenstein, *The Myth of Rescue: Why the Democracies Could Not Have Saved More Jews from the Nazis*, 2nd ed. (New York: Routledge, 2002), 206.

86 Rafael Medoff, *Blowing the Whistle on Genocide: Josiah E. Dubois, Jr. and the Struggle for a U.S. Response to the Holocaust* (West Lafayette: Purdue University Press, 2009), 6.

87 Of particular note were Interior Secretary Harold Ickes and Treasury Secretary Henry Morgenthau Jr, whose father had played a leading role in raising awareness levels about Armenian suffering a generation earlier. See Sarah Peck, "The Campaign for an American Response to the Nazi Holocaust, 1943–1945," *Journal of Contemporary History* 15, no. 2 (1980): 376, 386.

88 Associate Justice Frank Murphy formed the National Committee Against Nazi Persecution and Extermination of the Jews. This private organization included Vice President Henry Wallace, Wendell Willkie, and numerous officers from the Protestant Episcopal Church. See "New Group Set Up to Protect Jews," *New York Times*, 31 January 1944.

89 Gregory Wallance, *America's Soul in the Balance: The Holocaust, FDR's State Department, and the Moral Disgrace of an American Aristocracy* (Austin: Greenleaf Press, 2012), 151–2.

90 Richard Breitman and Allan Lichtman, *FDR and the Jews* (Cambridge: The Belknap Press of Harvard University Press, 2013), 59.

91 *Department of State Bulletin* 10 (1944): 277–8.

92 Leila Nadya Sadat, "Crimes against Humanity in the Modern Age," *American Journal of International Law* 107, no. 2 (2013): 337; Vivian Grosswald Curran, "Gobalization, Legal Transnationalization and Crimes against Humanity: The Lipietz Case," *American Journal of Comparative Law* 56, no. 2 (2008): 364–5; Margaret McAuliffe deGuzman, "The Road from Rome: The Developing Law of Crimes against Humanity," *Human Rights Quarterly* 22, no. 2 (2000): 338.

93 Michelle Mart, "The 'Christianization' of Israel and Jews in 1950s America," *Religion and American Culture: A Journal of Interpretation* 14, no. 1 (2004): 114; Deborah Dash Moore, "Jewish GIs and the Creation of the Judeo-Christian Tradition," *Religion and American Culture* 8, no. 1 (1998): 31–53.

94 Charles Stember et al., *Jews in the Minds of America* (New York: Free Press, 1966), x.

95 As quoted in Spencer Blakeslee, *The Death of American Anti-Semitism* (Westport: Praeger, 2002), 44.

96 Ibid. Interpreting the polls can be an imperfect exercise. Melvin Tumin has observed that status-seeking bigots, as well as rural citizens who moved to urban areas seeking employment, might suppress their anti-Semitism publicly, even for a lifetime. See Tumin, *An Inventory and Appraisal of Research on American Anti-Semitism* (New York: Freedom Books, 1961), 45.

97 Eric Goldstein, *The Price of Whiteness: Jews, Race, and American Identity* (Princeton: Princeton University Press, 2006), 189, 209; Karen Brodkin, *How Jews Became White Folks and What That Says about Race in America* (New Brunswick, NJ: Rutgers University Press, 1998), 138.

98 Caitlin Carenen, "The American Christian Palestine Committee, the Holocaust, and Mainstream Protestant Zionism, 1938–1948," *Holocaust and Genocide Studies* 24, no. 2 (2010): 273; Tom Lawson, "Shaping the Holocaust: The Influence of Christian Discourse on Perceptions of the European Jewish Tragedy," *Holocaust and Genocide Studies* 21, no. 3 (2007): 404; Theodore Y. Blumoff, "The Holocaust and Public Discourse," *Journal of Law and Religion* 11, no. 2 (1994–95): 595. For a counterexample, depicting continued anti-Semitism among Catholic Church leaders, see Suzanne Brown-Fleming, 'The Worst Enemies of a Better Germany': Postwar Anti-Semitism among Catholic Clergy and U.S. Occupation Forces," *Holocaust and Genocide Studies* 18, no. 3 (2004): 379–401.

99 A. Dirk Moses,"Das römische Gespräch in a New Key: Hannah Arendt, Genocide, and the Defense of Republican Civilization," *Journal of Modern History* 85, no. 4 (2013): 877; Dalia Ofer, "We Israelis Remember, but How? The Memory of the Holocaust and the Israeli Experience," *Israel Studies* 18, no. 2 (2013): 76; Charles Turner, "The Motivating Text: Assigning Hannah Arendt's *Eichmann in Jerusalem*," *PS: Political Science and Politics* 38, no. 1 (2005): 68.

100 Rachel Fish, "Bi-Nationalist Visions for the Construction and Dissolution of the State of Israel," *Israel Studies* 19, no. 2 (2014): 21; Rosenfeld, *End*, 273; Michael Oren, *Six Days of War: June 1967 and the Making Of the Modern Middle East* (Oxford: Oxford University Press, 2002), 97.

101 In 1979, the US government created the Office of Special Investigations. This bureau's mission centred on deporting former Nazis that had been granted American citizenship. Despite these efforts, some erstwhile Nazis living in the US received years of governmental benefits. See Adam Chandler, "The Ex-Nazi Collecting Social Security,"

The Atlantic, 20 October 2014, http://www.theatlantic.com/international/archive/2014/10/the-ex-nazis-collecting-social-security/381672/(accessed 30 October 2014).

102 "About the Museum," http://www.ushmm.org/information/about-the-museum (accessed 15 September 2014).

103 Jeffrey Shandler, "Aliens in the Wasteland: American Encounters with the Holocaust on 1960s Science Fiction Television," in Flanzbaum ed., *Americanization*, 36.

104 Ibid., 39.

105 Rosenfeld, *End*, 50; Robert Sackett, "Memory by Way of Anne Frank: Enlightenment and Denial among West Germans, circa 1960," *Holocaust and Genocide Studies* 16, no. 2 (2002): 243–65.

106 Alison Landsberg, "America, the Holocaust, and the Mass Culture of Memory: Toward a Radical Politics of Empathy," *New German Critique* 71 (1997): 63–6. See also Alan Berger, "The Holocaust, Second-Generation Witness, and the Voluntary Covenant in American Judaism," *Religion and American Culture: A Journal of Interpretation* 5, no. 1 (1995): 24–5.

107 Harriet Parmet has argued that figures such as Sylvia Plath were tormented by an inability to close off distance to Holocaust trauma. In this interpretation, the "denial" of authentic suffering served as a muse in Plath's writings. See Parmet, *The Terror of Our Days: Four American Poets Respond to the Holocaust* (Bethlehem: Lehigh University Press, 2001), 73.

108 Walter Reich, "Unwelcome Narratives: Listening to Suppressed Themes in American Holocaust Testimonies," *Poetics Today* 27, no. 2 (2006): 466. For a related discussion, see Janet Ward, "Holocaust Film in the Post-9/11 Era: New Directions in Staging and Emplotment," *Pacific Coast Philology* 39 (2004): 38.

109 Tim Cole, *Selling the Holocaust: From Auschwitz to Schindler: How History Is Bought, Packaged, and Sold* (New York: Routledge, 1999), 81.

110 Henryk Broder, "We Invented the Holocaust!," *Transition* 89 (2001): 74.

111 Sarah Pinnock concludes Americanization makes the Holocaust relevant to new generations, "ensuring that it is remembered at all." See Pinnock, "Atrocity and Ambiguity: Recent Developments in Christian Holocaust Responses," *Journal of the American Academy of Religion* 75, no. 3 (2007): 516. Pól Ó. Dochartaigh, however, wonders if remembering historical fiction is of any real use. He

laments the process, typified in the film *U-571*, which falsely depicts Americans breaking the Germans' secret "Enigma" code. See "Americanizing the Holocaust: The Case of 'Jakob the Liar,'" *Modern Language Review* 101, no. 2 (2006): 459.

112 Eric Sundquist, "Witness without End?" *American Literary History* 19 (2007): 66; Lawrence Langer, "Hearing the Holocaust," *Poetics Today* 27, no. 2 (2006): 300; Alan Rosen, *Sounds of Defiance: The Holocaust, Multilingualism, and the Problem of English* (Lincoln: University of Nebraska Press, 2005), 36.

113 Broder, "We," 90.

114 David MacDonald, "First Nations, Residential Schools, and the Americanization of the Holocaust: Rewriting Indigenous History in the United States and Canada," *Canadian Journal of Political Science* 40, no. 4 (2007): 997.

115 David Stannard, "Uniqueness as Denial: The Politics of Genocide Scholarship," in *Is The Holocaust Unique? Perspectives In Comparative Genocide*, edited by Alan S. Rosenbaum (Boulder: Westview Press, 1996), 167.

116 Peter Novick, "The American National Narrative of the Holocaust: There Isn't Any," *New German Critique* 90 (2003): 32.

117 Alan Mintz, *Popular Culture and the Shaping of Holocaust Memory in America* (Seattle: University of Washington Press, 2001), 174.

118 Novick, "American," 33.

119 Richard Breitman, *The Architect of Genocide: Himmler and the Final Solution* (New York: Knopf, 1991), 47; Kevork Bardakjian, *Hitler and the Armenian Genocide* (Cambridge: Zoryan Institute, 1985), 1. Significant debate centres on the question of whether or not Adolf Hitler actually uttered this statement. As historical consultant Peter Black noted to co-author (Demsky) in a written correspondence, Hitler rarely mentioned the Armenians in either his writings or ramblings. Moreover, the harsh language associated with the popular quote appears only in a questioned version of the speech, one provided to Louis P. Lochner, the chief of the Associated Press Bureau in Berlin, by a "German youth leader." While questions about the authenticity of the Lochner version surfaced immediately after the war, the rendition has nevertheless taken hold in popular and academic memory. The only unquestioned reference that Hitler made to the mass killings in Eastern Anatolia lies in an opinion piece, approved by Hitler and published in the Nazi Party newspaper, *Illustrierte Beobachter*, dated 24 May, 1930. The article is

reproduced in Christian Hartmann, ed., *Hitler: Reden, Schriften, Anordnungen*, vol. 3 Zwischen den Reichstagswahlen: July 1928–September 1930, January 1930–September 1930 (Munich, Saur: 1995), 202–6.

120 Henri Bergson, *Matter and Memory*, trans. by Mary Margaret Paul and W. Scott Palmer (Hong Kong: Forgotten Books, 2012 [1911]), 70–80, 87, 105–6.

121 Wolf Gruner, "What Would Germans in the Third Reich Know about the Armenian Genocide?," paper presented at *Looking Backward, Moving Forward*, a symposium, Glendale Library Central Branch, Glendale, CA, 18 April 2010.

122 Rosalind Shaw, "Displacing Violence: Making Pentecostal Memory in Postwar Sierra Leone," *Cultural Anthropology* 22, no. 1 (2007): 66–93.

123 The term references the transmitted and (re)produced memories of generations after the experiential moment. Marianne Hirsch, "The Generation of Postmemory," *Poetics Today* 29, no. 1 (2008): 103–28.

124 Carol Kidron, "Embracing the Lived Memory of Genocide: Holocaust Survivor and Descendant Renegade Memory Work at the House of Being," *American Ethnologist* 37, no. 3 (2010): 429–51.

125 Personal communications and interviews conducted by co-author (King) during 2009–10 through the University of California, Riverside.

9

Representing My Lai: Duty of Memory or Memory of Duty?

RAPHAËL RICAUD

On 16 March 1968, American soldiers from the Americal Division, officially known as United States Army C Company, 1st Battalion, 20th Infantry Regiment, 11th Brigade, 23rd Infantry Division, marched into a tiny hamlet in the Gulf of Tonkin. For the sake of convenience, I shall refer to this hamlet as My Lai. Though the US troops found no Viet Cong there, the soldiers brutalized and put to death hundreds of unarmed villagers (mainly old men, women, children, and even infants). This episode came to be a turning point in what is usually referred to as "the Vietnam media war." Indeed, a year and a half later, freelance investigative journalist Seymour Hersh's pieces[1] in the US media came as a shock to the American public. Additionally, the impact of the colour photographs taken by army photographer Ron Haeberle cannot be overestimated.[2] My Lai is now part of the obligatory Vietnam War narrative,[3] and the massacre is declined under different names, different spellings, and different pronunciations including: Pinkville,[4] My Son,[5] Song My,[6] Son My, My Lai 4,[7] or Thuan Yen, Tu Cung, Binh Tay, Bin Dong, Trung Hoa, Co Luy, and My Khe.[8] Could this plural identity reflect fragmented memories? On the one hand, there is the memory of duty: army recollections of professional obligations in wartime. On the other, journalists and historians alike make it their duty is to unearth memories, no matter how unpleasant. How did the memory of duty coexist with the duty of memory then? Can the two be reconciled with time? This chapter will address the issue by tapping into the fragmented memories of soldiers, journalists, public figures, and artists.

A SUMMARY OF THE EVENTS

To begin, it is necessary to open with a brief, factual summary of the events as they took place on 16 March 1968. It would be pointless to claim that such a summary can be value-neutral. I shall nonetheless try to encompass the viewpoints of the concerned parties.

Initial reports of the My Lai massacre appeared in the form of military records, dated 16 March 1968. A written report provided by the task force command testified to the existence of a search-and-destroy operation on that day,[9] in which 128 Viet Cong were killed.[10] This piece of information was relayed in the "Five O'Clock Follies," which relied essentially on body counts[11] to inform Western journalists on the American Army's progress. The figures were also included in *Stars & Stripes* magazine, an official US Army publication. Given the high number of casualties in the Vietnamese camp, Company C was praised by General Westmoreland. Indeed, the type of guerrilla warfare conducted by the Viet Cong rarely gave American troops the opportunity to meet the enemy face to face.[12] In Vietnam, direct confrontations were the exception, not the rule. Consequently, clear-cut American victories were rare.

The first army report eventually disappeared[13] and the massacre was not reported above the division level. The soldier who was in charge of archives at the time remembers two distinct moments when his superiors asked for the report. The first time, some cosmetic changes were made to the report before it was returned to him, and the second time the report was simply not returned.[14]

With the original written report nowhere to be found, one might think that there would have been no mention of My Lai at all. However, many soldiers could not keep what they had witnessed to themselves.[15] Hugh Thompson, a helicopter pilot, realized from the air that what had taken place was a massacre of civilians[16] and not an operation against the Viet Cong.[17] After having helped repatriate a dozen Vietnamese civilians, he reported on what he had seen to his superior[18] and to his chaplain;[19] neither one nor the other relayed the information. Ron Haeberle, an army photographer, wanted to talk about what he had seen and photographed, but convinced that the negatives of the photos he had taken would be destroyed, he did not officially report the incident. As for Private Michael Bernhardt, who had refused to take part in the massacre,[20] he was instructed by his superior, Captain Medina, not to do anything stupid like write to his congressman. Last but not least, the soldiers who took part in the operation were asked not to discuss My Lai among themselves or with others.

THREE CAN KEEP A SECRET IF TWA BE AWA

Soldiers now even claim they were sent on unnecessarily dangerous missions after My Lai. Some died during such missions. This was one way to be sure they would never speak about My Lai. According to Joe Grimes, then squad leader: "I truly believe that we were sent there to never return; that we were never gonna make it out of there. And that just stuck in my mind, why are they doing this, why are they sending us out at night? You know to get rid of these twelve people here? And then the next night they send another twelve and get them?"[21]

All this made the massacre a secret, and just like any secret, what made it valuable was the ability to share it with a selected audience. Thus, Ron Ridenhour, a sub-machine gun operator who joined the C Company after the events, heard of the massacre inadvertently. When the experienced troopers tried to impress younger ones with their war stories over a beer, they would mention My Lai:

> Hey man did you hear what we did at Pinkville?
> So what did you do at Pinkville?
> Oh, man, we massacred this whole village.
> What?
> Yeah, we massacred this whole village. We just lined them up and killed them.
> What do you mean?
> Men, women and kids, everybody, we killed them all.
> Well, how many was that?
> Oh, I don't know, three or four hundred I guess, at least. A lot, everybody we could find.
> We didn't leave anybody alive, at least we didn't intend to.[22]

Ridenhour inquired with other soldiers for confirmation of this massacre. Not only did the other soldiers confirm, but they fleshed out the story with sickening details. They mentioned the rapes, the children used as target practice, and those thrown into an irrigation ditch before being methodically machine-gunned. Ridenhour made contact with Michael Bernhardt, the private who had refused to take part in the massacre, but who had nevertheless witnessed the entire operation. Together, they decided to keep things quiet until they were discharged, and then tell the world. Ridenhour wrote to his congressman in March 1969. Morris K. Udall, an Arizona representative, took note of the letter and asked for an investigation by the Pentagon.[23] This was what led to the Peers Commission. Another investigation, the Hébert Committee, was ordered by Richard Nixon around the same time. The two commissions differed in many ways, but described similar facts, namely that the troops' psychological discomfort, their fatigue, irresponsible command, and the trivialization of violence led to the massacre. The reasonings of the two commisions, however, were different.[24]

The Peers Commission denounced the killing of civilians. The Hébert Committee, on the other hand, was particularly interested in the disciplinary dysfunction of the army in its own ranks. In both reports, the dysfunction was depicted as being the fault of individuals. Even if the army was portrayed as disorganized, it was not questioned as an entity. In the end, only one person came to bear responsibility for the massacre (termed an *incident* and *tragedy on a large scale* by the army): Lieutenant Calley. As such, My Lai is represented as an accidental event that would never have happened if the usual procedure through official channels had been observed.

START SPREADING THE NEWS

In 1969, the media started paying attention. Ridenhour's letter aroused the interest of Seymour Hersh, who undertook a thorough investigation. Articles in the American press as well as the pictures taken by Haeberle (published in the *Cleveland Plain Dealer* in black and white and in colour in *Life*) revealed the scale of the massacre.[25] The combination of text and images crudely showed the horror perpetrated by US troops. This shocked the entire American nation. Some tried to find excuses,[26] claiming the frustration of fighting an invisible enemy was bound to lead to something like this (Kelman and Hamilton, 15).[27] Soldiers themselves testified to this. According to then radio operator Fred Widmer: "We started pulling regular patrols end of January, beginning of February. Once we started down in the Pinkville area, we started losing people. They were being picked off one by one. This is when we got our initiation into the realities of Vietnam with booby traps, mines, snipers."[28]

Writer Philip Caputo recalls that they even felt the ground itself had become the enemy: "The infantryman lives on the ground. He walks on the ground, he sleeps on the ground, he eats on the ground. When you've got booby traps and land mines all of a sudden the earth becomes the enemy in a way, because you don't know what it may conceal."[29] Tim O'Brien felt very much the same: "Where do you sit, and where do you put your feet, there or there? And that choice is life or death."[30] Yet others felt that "the frustrations of guerrilla warfare do not adequately explain My Lai,"[31] but still saw it as an accident.

As opposition to the war in Vietnam grew in the US, My Lai was depicted by some as a deliberate army technique aimed at terrorizing the Vietnamese people. In other words, they thought of it not as an accident, but as a deliberate act of terror. This is what some media intellectuals have called state terrorism.[32] Thus My Lai is not to be viewed as a singular, isolated incident, but rather as part of a broader set of tactics. Noam Chomsky for instance believes that massacres such as the one in My Lai are nothing compared to carpet bombings in Vietnam, Cambodia, and Laos, which have produced far more deaths and injuries among civilians.[33]

At this point in time, My Lai became a political argument. The terms of the debate changed. People wondered if such a massacre was a moral fault, unlike America and unworthy of her? Or was it its underbelly? In the words of theologian Reinhold Niebuhr, speaking of and to America, "This is a moment of truth when we realize we are not a virtuous nation."[34] In its 22 November 1969 editorial, the *New York Times* reflected the mood of the time when pondering the moral consequences and impact of the tragedy: "The United States public must know – and face – the long-suppressed facts about what may turn out to have been one of this nation's most ignoble hours."[35] In this soul-searching process, if My Lai came to be seen as an integral part of the history of the nation, then it could be equated to the earlier treatment of another people: Native Americans.

A (MOVING) PICTURE IS WORTH A THOUSAND WORDS

Enter the realm of entertainment. A number of movies have directly or indirectly dealt with My Lai. Some of these movies can clearly be labelled as belonging to the Western genre, among them is *Soldier*

Blue (1970). Although very few remember this film today, it must be claimed that such movies mattered: the Western mythology played itself out in Vietnam, and vice versa.[36] The most striking element in this movie is the graphic violence. Scenes of killing, beheading, and rape were so explicit that no less than twenty minutes of the movie were cut when it was shown on TV. Because of the reversal of roles, *Soldier Blue* can be seen as a *revisionist* Western. The cavalry, which by way of analogy is the US military in Vietnam,[37] traditionally embodies order, discipline, and merit. But in *Soldier Blue*, soldiers are beastly brutes. They rape and kill in the name of the US nation. The level of violence was beyond the threshold of what was deemed acceptable at the time. The images on screen, shocking in themselves, are even more shocking when one realizes that soldiers in uniform were supposed to embody law and order. In theory, the movie is about the Sand Creek Massacre. In 1970, however, cowboys and Indians were a thing of the past and it was understood that the film was an allusion to Vietnam.[38] During the final assault, horses trample the American flag. The symbol may be heavy-handed but speaks volumes: the founding values of America are flouted to a point of no return.

Yet the Western was not the only genre that tackled the issue of the My Lai massacre. In yet another not-so-memorable movie[39] called *The Trial of Billy Jack* (1974), the issue at stake was whether America still had a moral compass. In the film, Billy Jack is a US Army veteran on trial. He answers the questions that are put to him.[40] When the My Lai massacre is mentioned, Billy Jack replies that he was an eyewitness of a similar massacre which took place seven months before My Lai. He claims he refused to take part. This massacre is then shown on screen in a flashback. We see civilians forced into a pit and then machine-gunned to death. Babies' cries are heard. A child is then seen running for his life, before being shot in the back by a US soldier. These atrocities are echoes of My Lai.

The excerpt from the movie suggests that the My Lai massacre is not an isolated incident. At the same time, it shows one brave soldier who refuses to obey orders. In the movie, America has lost its moral compass, and so have those who follow criminal orders. But the few heroic figures that are strong enough to challenge these orders, no matter what the cost, have a clear conscience.[41] This stand-alone act of bravery would be a recurring *motif* in the 1970s. In Oliver Stone's *Platoon* (1986), there are explicit references to My Lai. US soldiers use their lighters to set fire to Vietnamese huts. Some try to rape two teenage girls before Private Chris Taylor (played on screen by actor Charlie Sheen) comes to their rescue. There is nonetheless a major difference with My Lai. Not only did the rape not happen, but more generally, civilian lives were spared. It is as if the movie had the power to erase the massacre from the American collective memory through the intervention of a brave soldier.

In the 1980s, the concept of organized terror decided by high-ranking state officials was no longer part of the public discourse. Conscience was no longer the problem of America as a collective entity. It became a personal matter. The questions seemed to be: What would I have done as an individual? What choices would I have personally made if faced with a similar situation?

MEMORY IS THE SPACE IN WHICH A THING HAPPENS FOR A SECOND TIME[42]

One may wonder what remains of My Lai for those who have not directly experienced it, either as actors or spectators. In other words, what representation of My Lai for the next generation? The 1990s and 2000s constituted a form of amnesia. US textbooks mentioned the incident in passing but rarely made an explicit account of it.[43] According to Rajiv Evan Rajan and Lacy Mitchell, who conducted a study of textbooks accounts of My Lai, "All textbooks contain substantial chapters on the Vietnam War, and some mentioned damage caused to the Vietnamese countryside or the unintentional bombing of civilians. Nevertheless, the majority of textbooks avoid any explicit reference to the My Lai massacre."[44] Consequently, when asked, most American high-school and college students were unable to identify the term My Lai. This saddened writer Tim O'Brien, who wanted to share his experience of the war with the younger generation, but could not. "Now, more than 25 years later, the villainy of that Saturday morning in 1968 has been pushed off to the margins of memory. In the colleges and high schools I sometimes visit, the mention of My Lai brings on null stares, a sort of puzzlement, disbelief mixed with utter ignorance."[45] This was why O'Brien decided it was important to fight the "erasure of history."[46] When he was talking to a class of students about the importance of literature, or about his own work, he always took the time to mention and explain My Lai. He believed it was his duty to keep the memory of the massacre alive just as a generation of Americans believed it had been their duty to serve in Vietnam. These conflicting logics are encapsulated in his pieces and still haunt him.

It must be said that O'Brien joined the unit after the massacre and therefore took no part in it. Yet he could sense that something was wrong every time he and his company walked into the hamlet of My Lai or its immediate surroundings: "The hostility of the eyes of the surviving kids and the women, and the few men who were still left, a mixture of incredible fear, coming out of those black eyeballs as they stared at us as we walked into the villages, with hatred: the two combined. It's an emotion that's hard to describe until you actually see it in somebody's eyeballs. And you can feel it when it's on you."[47]

Paradoxically, it was the unsaid anger of the surviving victims that prompted O'Brien to write about My Lai. Or to be more specific, it made him feel the urge to express the ricochet consequences and impact of My Lai, as his involvement in the event was only indirect. O'Brien was compelled to write about something which nearly happened to him, could have happened to him, but in the end did not – strictly speaking – happen to him. It happened to those around him, but created a lasting impression. The magnitude of the shockwaves, however, can entirely be felt in his prose. To that extent, he became involved in the My Lai massacre just as much as the protagonists themselves. And so did its readers. Through its conversion in celebrated literature, My Lai leaves the immediate sphere of the media and that of the personal and instead becomes universal.

O'Brien's tales of Vietnam prompted a new generation of Americans who had only indirectly experienced My Lai to go on a pilgrimage. As Vietnam's frontiers gradually opened up in the 1990s, tourism expanded. A growing number of Americans backpackers included My Lai in their trip. Consequently, tourist guidebooks and travel literature[48] included My Lai as a place one must see, a sure sign of the renewed – albeit marginal – interest it generated.

CONSTRUCTING IDENTITY THROUGH FRAGMENTED MEMORIES

Today, the fragmentary resurfacing of My Lai in the media and in American culture gives it a jigsaw puzzle quality. One can assemble the pieces to try to make sense of it. Depending on the era's political orientation, though, the meaning changes.

Thus, William Calley is in turn executioner and American hero. In 1969, when the papers claimed he coldly executed women and children in the hamlet of My Lai, he was the villain. However, the executioner was soon to become a hero for American conservatives. The argument went as follows: because he was a soldier, he defended the honour of his country. He obeyed orders.[49] War is not without collateral damage. There have always been casualties among civilians, and Vietnam is no exception to the rule. When sentenced to prison, Calley was presented as a scapegoat by supporters of the "Free Calley movement." Following demonstrations in Washington, Calley's sentence was reduced first to twenty years, then eventually to ten. Calley served three years before being released. He was granted parole on 10 September 1975.[50]

Today, documentaries explain the actions of Calley through a psychological bias:[51] Calley, in search of a father figure, wanted to please his captain, Ernest Medina.[52] Medina was the one who gave the orders to kill civilians. According to former team leader Thomas Turner, "My first impression of Lieutenant Calley was he was always trying to please Captain Medina. He'd go out of his way to do things that were not called for and trying to please Captain Medina and that, to me it made, in my mind, it made Captain Medina resent him even more."[53] It was not until 2009 that Calley publicly expressed remorse.[54] However, he insisted that although he was sorry, he was only obeying orders.[55] Calley went from executioner to hero in the 1970s. He is now presented as a victim, and perceived as such.

However, the most dramatic turnaround is the treatment of Hugh Thompson, the helicopter pilot. Thompson threatened to open fire on his own troops if they tried to impede his air rescue of civilians. In the Peers Commission, and all the more in the Hébert Committee,[56] this act was portrayed as unpatriotic. In the 1980s, Thompson was regarded as the "voice of sanity."[57] Today, Hugh Thompson is depicted as the only real hero of My Lai.[58] His heroism lies in the fact that he was able to make a moral choice by listening to what his conscience was dictating. This scenario is worthy of a Hollywood movie. Would Oliver Stone have filmed it this way if he had had the chance to produce *Pinkville*? Nobody knows.[59] However, documentaries (for instance Frontline's *Remember My Lai*, *60 Minutes*, *Interviews With My Lai Veterans*, and those on PBS: American Experience's *My Lai*) never fail to salute Thompson's courage. For instance, in Frontline's *My Lai*, Lawrence Colburn – Thompson's gunner – recalls: "Mr. Thompson calculated they had less than thirty seconds to live. He told us, 'I'm going over to the bunker and get these people out myself. And if these American soldiers fire on these people or me when I'm getting them out of the bunker, shoot them.'"[60]

What had been depicted as treachery during the Peels and Hébert hearings has now become heroism. Thompson's act of bravery thus fully turns around the contemporary narrative. His Wikipedia page, for example, indicates that it was he who ended the massacre at My Lai, nothing less. It is as if this exceptional event held pride of place in the My Lai episode. The massacre itself then becomes the background or the setting of a heroic action. The original situation has thus been reversed.

CONCLUSION

To be sure, in almost half a century, the My Lai massacre as narrative has undergone several changes. Originally, My Lai was depicted as a military blunder. The radical left took it as an example of organized terror decided at the highest level of the US government. Once publicized, My Lai was instrumentalized for political purposes.[61] The military involvement of the US in Vietnam was questioned. Moreover, the existence of such a massacre came to disturb the conscience of the US during the 1970s. In the 1980s, the massacre was largely a matter of personal identity, and the question seemed to be: what would I have done had I been a soldier? In the 1990s, My Lai – as narrative – almost came to be erased from American history. Today, memory fragmentation and contextualization erect the executioners of yesterday into victims. Such an inversion does not leave much room for Vietnamese civilians and their families. Recognition of their existence and their suffering is nevertheless essential to the duty of memory, as much as it is to the memory of duty. A symbolic gesture, such as the construction of a memorial, could start the healing process.

In Vietnam, one of the principal massacre sites was indeed turned into a memorial.[62] To the American mind, a black plaque listing the names of My Lai's victims[63] immediately conjures up the Vietnam Memorial in Washington, DC. But the American memorial is about the Vietnam War, not about My Lai. The memorial in Vietnam is about the sadness and horror of a massacre. The shame and contrition will not go away by itself, as My Lai is still "an open wound in the American psyche."[64] Or, in the words of writer Tim O'Brien, still in shock after all those years, "You don't have to be in Nam to be in Nam."[65] My Lai will always haunt the American conscience, just as much as it is a trauma for the families of the victims in Vietnam. A dual recognition of the massacre, however, could be part of the healing process for all parties concerned. Such a recognition has been considered in the not-so-distant past.[66] The time may have come to consider it again.

NOTES

1 Seymour Hersh, "Lieutenant Accused of Murdering 109 Civilians," *St. Louis Post-Dispatch*, 13 November 1969; Seymour Hersh, "Hamlet Attack Called 'Point-Blank Murder,'" *St. Louis Post-Dispatch*, 20 November 1969; Seymour Hersh, "Ex-GI Tells of Killing Civilians at Pinkville," *St. Louis Post-Dispatch*, 25 November 1969.

2 William M. Hammond, *Public Affairs: The Military and the Media, 1968–1973* (Washington, DC: Government Printing Office, 1996), 224.

3 Tim Larimer, "Echoes of My Lai," *Time International*, 16 March 1998.

4 Walter Goodman, "My Lai: Hard to Forget, Hard to Remember," *New York Times*, 23 May 1989.

5 David Margolick, "To Hanoi by Train, a Journey of 1,000 Miles," *New York Times*, 9 November 1997.

6 Hersh, "Hamlet Attack Called 'Point-Blank Murder.'"

7 Herbert Kelman and V. Lee Hamilton, "The My Lai Massacre: A Military Crime of Obedience," in *Sociology: Exploring the Architecture of Everyday Life/Readings*, edited by David M. Newman and Jodi O'Brien (Los Angeles: Sage, 2013), 14.

8 William R. Peers, *Report of the Department of the Army Review of the Preliminary Investigations Into the My Lai Incident, Volume I, the Report of the Investigation* (Washington, DC: United States Government Printing Office, 14 March 1970), 1–16.

9 According to French Historian Romain Huret, the Americal News Sheet was the first army print media to provide a report (albeit a misleading one) on My Lai. Romain Huret, "La rumeur de Pinkville. Les commissions d'enquête sur le massacre de My Lai (1969–1970)," *Le Mouvement Social* (2008): 222.

10 Kendrick Oliver, *The My Lai Massacre in American History and Memory* (Manchester: Manchester University Press, 2006), 31–2.

11 "The principal measure of military success was the 'body count' – the number of enemy soldiers killed – and any Vietnamese killed by the US military was commonly defined as a 'Viet Cong.'" Kelman and Hamilton, "The My Lai Massacre," 23.

12 Writer Tim O'Brien captures the essence of it best when interviewing a former Viet Cong: "Mr Tan speaks genially of military tactics while we make the bumpy ride out toward the Batangan. 'US troops not hard to see, not hard to fight,' he says. 'Much noise, much equipment. Big columns. Nice green uniforms.' Sitting ducks, in other words, though Mr Tan is too polite to express it this way." Tim O'Brien, "The Vietnam in Me," *New York Times*, 2 October 1994.

13 Oliver, *The My Lai Massacre*, 34.

14 Seymour Hersh, *Cover-Up: The Army's Secret Investigation of the Massacre at My Lai 4* (New York: Random House, 1972), 222–5.

15 Hersh, "Lieutenant Accused of Murdering 109 Civilians."

16 F. Edward Hébert, House Committee on Armed Services, *Armed Services Investigating Subcommittee, Investigation of the My Lai Incident: Hearings of the Armed Services Investigating Subcommittee of the Committee on Armed Services*, 91st Congress, 2nd session (Washington, DC: Government Printing Office, 1970), 234.

17 Kelman and Hamilton, "The My Lai Massacre," 18.

18 Barack Goodman, "My Lai," *American Experience*, PBS, 2010.

19 Myra MacPherson, *Long Time Passing: Vietnam and the Haunted Generation* (Bloomington: Indiana University Press, 2009), 494.

20 Hersh, "Hamlet Attack Called 'Point-Blank Murder.'"

21 B. Goodman, "My Lai."

22 Ron Ridenhour, untitled article, *Digital History*, accessed 30 June 2015, http://www.digitalhistory.uh.edu/active_learning/explorations/vietnam/r_ridenhour.cfm.

23 Peers, *Report of the Department of the Army Review*, 1–7.

24 Huret, "La rumeur de Pinkville."

25 Hébert, *Armed Services Investigating Subcommittee*, 249–85.

26 "Even at the time, most Americans seemed to shrug it off as a cruel, nasty, inevitable consequence of war. There were numerous excuses, numerous rationalizations." O'Brien, "The Vietnam in Me."

27 Kelman and Hamilton, "The My Lai Massacre," 15.

28 B. Goodman, "My Lai."

29 Ibid.

30 Ibid.

31 "My Lai: An American Tragedy," *Time* (5 December 1969): 23–4.

32 See the preface by Richard A. Falk in Noam Chomsky and Edward S. Herman, *Counter-Revolutionary Violence: Bloodbaths in Fact & Propaganda* (Andover, Massachussetts: Warner Modular Publication, 1973).

33 Amy Goodman, "The Life and Times of Noam Chomsky," *Democracy Now*, 26 November 2004.

34 Robert D. McFadden, "Calley Verdict Brings Home the Anguish of Home to Public," *New York Times*, 4 April 1971, quoted in Oliver, *The My Lai Massacre in American History and Memory*, 3.

35 "An American Nightmare," *New York Times*, 22 November 1969.

36 J. Horbeman, "How the Western Was Lost Tracking the Decline of an American Genre: From Appomattox to Vietnam to Disney World," *Voice* (27 August 1991): 49–54. Likewise, Coppola had this to say about *Apocalypse Now*: "My film is not a movie; it's not about Vietnam … It *is* Vietnam." Sean McCann, "Therapy for a Wounded Nation," *The Common Review* 4, no. 3 (2006): 32.

37 Vietnam was hinted at in Cowboy and Indian movies just as Western metaphors were used on the field: "Meanwhile, in the real Vietnam, dangerous areas were known as Indian country, Vietnamese scouts were termed 'Kit Carsons,' and more than a few grunts echoed the notorious slogan coined by General Phil Sheridan a century before, painting THE ONLY GOOD GOOK IS A DEAD GOOK on their helmets or flak jackets. Lieutenant William Calley [convicted of killing women and children at My Lai] complained that the Vietnamese laughingly called him and his men 'cowboys.'" Horbeman, "How the Western Was Lost," 49–54.

38 Rick Newby, *The Rocky Mountain Region* (Westport, CT: Greenwood Publishing Group, 2004), 176.

39 Harry Medved and Randy Dreyfuss, *The Fifty Worst Films of All Time (And How They Got That Way)* (New York: Warner Books, 1978).

40 In hindsight, the fictional scene is very much like the real-life Peers and Hébert commissions. The soldiers who were being tried made a moral decision and questioned the authority of an almighty entity.

41 Private Bernhardt, in Hersh's early pieces, is depicted as having made such a courageous moral choice: "Bernhardt told the interviewer … 'there are some orders that I have to personally decide whether to obey; I have my own conscience to consider.'" Hersh, "Hamlet Attack Called 'Point-Blank Murder.'"

42 Paul Auster, *The Invention of Solitude* (London: Penguin Books, 1988), 87.

43 Rajiv Evan Rajan and Lacy Mitchell, "Constructing and Remembering the My Lai Massacre," in *American Memories: Atrocities and the Law*, edited by Joachim J. Savelsberg and Ryan D. King (New York: Russel Sage Foundation, 2011), 43.

44 Ibid.

45 O'Brien, "The Vietnam in Me."

46 Brad Buchholdz, "Novelist Tim O'Brien Wants Us to Remember My Lai," *Statesman.com*, 29 May 2010.

47 Ibid.

48 Margolick, "To Hanoi by Train."

49 "'They're using this as a Goddamned example,' one officer complained. 'He's a good soldier. He followed orders.'" Hersh, "Lieutenant Accused of Murdering 109 Civilians."

50 Kelman and Hamilton, "The My Lai Massacre," 17, 22. See also W. Goodman, "My Lai." "Lieut. William L. Calley Jr, the only member of Charlie Company to be convicted, was sentenced to life imprisonment and was paroled after three years."

51 "Soldiers from Charlie Company, some of whom had never spoken publicly about the events of 16 March 1968 ... appear to be more interested in seeking understanding than in expressing remorse." Mike Hale, "A Dark Day That Still Resonates," *New York Times*, 26 April 2010.

52 Kelman and Hamilton, "The My Lai Massacre," 15.

53 B. Goodman, "My Lai."

54 "Calley expresses remorse for role in My Lai massacre in Vietnam," *Los Angeles Times*, 22 August 2009.

55 B. Goodman, "My Lai."

56 Hébert, *Armed Services Investigating Subcommittee*, 228–34.

57 W. Goodman, "My Lai."

58 Hale, "A Dark Day That Still Resonates."

59 According to official sources, "'Pinkville,' the Oliver Stone project about the My Lai massacre in Vietnam, was supposed to have begun filming in Thailand in early December, 2007 and United Artists announced ... that it had pulled the project because of problems with the script." David M. Halbfinger, "For Film Companies, A State of Flux," *New York Times*, 24 November 2007. Nonetheless, other voices claim that more tangible and political factors brought the project to a halt.

60 B. Goodman, "My Lai."

61 McCann, "Therapy for a Wounded Nation," 32.

62 Margolick, “To Hanoi by Train.”
63 Kelman and Hamilton, “The My Lai Massacre,” 16.
64 Hale, “A Dark Day That Still Resonates.”
65 O’Brien, “The Vietnam in Me.”
66 Larimer, “Echoes of My Lai.”

10

Zimbabwean Liberation War Memories: Two Perspectives – *Harvest of Thorns* (Shimmer Chinodya) and *Echoing Silences* (Alexander Kanengoni)

ANNIE GAGIANO

War in its devastation appears to compel profound creative efforts in the literatures of many lands in its aftermath. The war-plagued continent of Africa[1] is no exception: writers strive to "tell the human tale" despite the "caterpillar" of war appearing to have "devoured" (in Wallace Stevens's words) "great Africa."[2] Amina Said writes that the continent's poet-historians ("griots") "hasten/to rebuild our legends/with their wounded words."[3] The task of disentangling war's political, moral, and social complexities and the individual and familial impact of a war is not undertaken by all who write of it with equal "emotional truth," a rare quality described as "different from honesty and more resilient than fact" by Chimamanda Ngozi Adichie.[4] War memories get conscripted by states to serve ideological causes; the multiple sacrifices and range of suffering it took to fight or to win the war are homogenized and dissenting voices are suppressed, often violently. This has been particularly evident in Zimbabwe, where a leading historian has coined the expression "patriotic history" to refer to officially sanctioned accounts of the 1964–80 Liberation War silencing the exposure of atrocities and internal dissent.[5]

While all wars affect and involve whole societies and are never restricted in their effects and methods to actual combatants, guerrilla wars are probably those in which supposed civilians are most directly drawn into battles, punished for support to the enemy side or becoming incidental victims to combatants' armed encounters. Moreover, ruthless erasures of rural settlements and "burnt earth" strategies are used to cow civilian populations. During the Zimbabwean war of liberation, the cities remained relatively isolated from the military confrontations, to some extent because the guerrillas fought on foot without aerial support, partly because the racially segregated urban populations remained closely monitored and policed, and probably also because the guerrilla bases were outside the Rhodesian borders, in neighbouring countries.

The archive of war memories functions in three distinct articulations. The first, historiography, occurs in texts where the presentation of war as fact, record, or information is discernibly impartial or balanced, compliant with international academic standards. While historiography can never be entirely accurate, such writing does not serve ideological purposes. Eschewing the affective, written history is often seen as "dry" – detached from the very knowledge it seeks to communicate in lucidly explicating how a war came about, what its key events and most significant results were, and judiciously weighing the gains and losses of this momentous process. Zimbabwe has produced and attracted a number of fine historians and scholarly commentators whose books[6] and numerous articles are worth consulting.

The second central function to which war memory is assigned is to serve as a society's foundation myth, taking the role of the originating event in a nation's history. Unashamedly partisan or ideological, this appropriation requires tailoring aspects of war memory to fit a political purpose. Such representation nevertheless claims complete validity in the (re)construction of viable nationhood. Inevitably exclusionary of several sectors of society – in the case of Zimbabwe, of particular ethnicities, roles, genders, and public figures – it glorifies and centralizes others; in Zimbabwe, these are the Shona people, ZANU/PF (the dominant political party) and its wartime predecessor the Zimbabwean African National Liberation Front (ZANLA), as well as the romanticized figure of the powerful, victorious, male guerrilla fighter. History writing of this kind is that which has been labelled "patriotic history."[7]

The third manifestation of war memory can be called the personal, even though it enters the public domain when textualized. Personal war memory centres on war as experience(d), generally allowing affective expression. Memoirs, auto/biographies, interviews, novels, and other types of narrative fiction, plays, and poetry as well as films and musical lyrics relating to the war are plentiful in Zimbabwe and occur in the three main languages: Shona, Ndebele, and English. Some of these are clearly intended to promote official nationalism, while others attempt factuality or try to be emotionally true to personal perceptions and events. Partly because the language is internationally accessible, but mainly because they are major literary achievements, the novels *Bones* by Chenjerai Hove, *Harvest of Thorns* by Shimmer Chinodya, writings by Dambudzo Marechera such as his collection *Scrapiron Blues*, *Echoing Silences* by Alexander Kanengoni, and *The Stone Virgins* by Yvonne Vera[8] are the most resonant and compelling among Zimbabwean works of fiction embodying war memories. According to Itai Muwati and D. E. Mutasa, "By being more inward looking than Shona authors who search for violators from without the guerrilla circles, [Zimbabwean] English fiction writers place the history of violence in perspective, establish its origins and even comment on its development."[9]

HISTORICAL AND LITERARY CONTEXTS

The Great Zimbabwe Ruins are evidence of Shona domination in the area during the thirteenth and fourteenth centuries and of powerful and prosperous indigenous rule in ancient times. During the nineteenth century came an incursion from a breakaway group of South African Zulus (the warlike Ndebele) who in 1840 established their rule over the southwestern region now named Matabeleland. After his British South Africa Company had started mining and farming in the region, super-colonist Cecil John Rhodes in 1893 found a pretext for war against the Ndebele ruler Lobengula, easily subduing the Ndebele and Shona resistance (known as the First *Chimurenga* of 1896–97) by means of superior weaponry. The area was named Southern Rhodesia, becoming a British crown colony in 1923. During the early 1960s Shona and Ndebele volunteers took up arms and guerrilla warfare began as settler repression intensified. In 1965 Prime Minister Ian Smith (whose minority settler government and intransigent racial attitudes strongly resembled those of apartheid South Africa) unilaterally declared Rhodesia independent of Britain. After fourteen years of warfare, known locally as the Second *Chimurenga*, Zimbabwe became an independent country under indigenous rule; the Shona party ZANU/PF under Robert Mugabe took power after the 1980 elections. Tensions between the Shona

ZANLA and the Ndebele ZIPRA forces re-erupted in the immediate aftermath of independence when Ndebele veterans were accused of hoarding weaponry to launch an uprising against ZANU/PF. The notorious Korean trained Shona Fifth Brigade was sent into Matabeleland during 1983 and 1984 on a punitive expedition. Close to 20,000 people (mostly civilians) were killed in the course of this operation that took on near-genocidal proportions, but knowledge of it was repressed by the government.

Invocation of a supposedly ongoing Third *Chimurenga* in contemporary state discourse,[10] despite the absence of actual war in post-liberation Zimbabwe, was introduced as a rallying cry to resist international, mainly Western, condemnation of the government policy of invasion of white-owned farmland, validated as a process undertaken by and for the war veterans who had previously resented the lack of tangible rewards for their sacrifices. Third *Chimurenga* rhetoric is vehemently anti-British, anti-colonial, and anti-Western; it glorifies the ruling elite, war veterans, traditional patriarchy, and rural life. Kizito Muchemwa and Robert Muponde refer to "the strategies of domination employed by hegemonic masculinity," seeing "war masculinity" as "the major source" of "the contemporary crisis of manhood" in Zimbabwe.[11] Historical and literary contexts are strongly intertwined in Zimbabwe;[12] according to Robert Muponde, "The literature of Zimbabwe is inextricably bound to the violence of the land that engendered it." In his assessment, "[Chenjerai] Hove's novel [*Bones*] colludes with the basic rhetoric of the nationalists" while he also believes that "Shimmer Chinodya, in his *Harvest of Thorns*, [was] writing within the complex cache of metaphors that launched the 'third Chimurenga,' namely, the lack of recognition of war veterans in post-war Zimbabwe, and the subsequent sense of entitlement nurtured by the war veterans in national politics."[13]

Harvest of Thorns and *Echoing Silences* have garnered far more appreciative responses from most other commentators, particularly for not merely endorsing state rhetoric in their conception or execution. Itai Muwati and Davie Mutasa write that the "vision of history" of the novelists in English "[achieves] the dual objective of telling the truth and undermining the legitimacy of the official nationalist narrative as an instrument of hegemony."[14] Alexander Kanengoni's *Echoing Silences* has been described as "the most intense expression of horror and disillusionment with the war yet published in Zimbabwe."[15] Ironically, he has more recently become a beneficiary of the land redistribution policy and has written favourably of Robert Mugabe, the very leader whom he implicitly excoriates in the final part of this novel. The paradox is highlighted by Stephen Chan, who states that "What Kanengoni has not done is to offer sustained intellectual apologia for Mugabe and his policies," seeing Kanengoni's text as permeated with "regret for war's atrocities and that war restarted in Matabeleland after liberation."[16] Whatever the truth of his present-day political opinions, Kanengoni's novel stands as a refusal to obscure the horrors of the Liberation War, the legitimacy and inevitability of which are nevertheless understood and recognized.

Book-length monographs on Zimbabwean literary history include those of Flora Veit-Wild and Ranka Primorac.[17] A noteworthy collection of literary analyses was assembled by Robert Muponde and Ranka Primorac.[18] Particularly relevant to the present essay is a chapter by Kizito Muchemwa in which he writes that "both written colonial history and the black oral tradition are often involved in similarly stressing a monolithic past and memories that either reduce to subsidiary roles or consign to oblivion the pasts of women, children, and those who are not indigenes." He stresses the importance of literary texts in which "ways of remembering and forgetting the past are probed" and which uncover "the skeletons in the nation's cupboard" instead of presenting "patriotic packag[ing] of the past."[19] The particular moral courage of novelists working in a fraught environment as the Zimbabweans do, whose writing proves the extent to which they are willing to risk resisting political pressure in producing texts that do not endorse the officially sanctioned type of war memory, must be noted and commended. Comments by Liz Gunner, published in 1991, remain true for the contemporary Zimbabwean situation: "Fiction ... has the potential to interrogate, subvert, redefine events and periods, and if necessary work against the grain of a complacent nationalist discourse eager to mythologize key events of the past. Thus novels written a while after an important event are sufficiently distant from it to be reflective rather than celebratory, but they can also attempt to reproduce the earlier period and through fiction put it back anew at the centre of the reader's consciousness, making at the same time a commentary on the present."[20]

JUXTAPOSITION: CONVERGENCES AND DIVERGENCES

Very different as the two texts are, there are remarkable similarities in their accounts of the Second *Chimurenga*. Both Benjamin and Munashe join the Liberation War for primarily idealistic reasons; both are disappointed by the outcome and convey some sense of betrayal of their sacrifices. Both authors convey awareness of the more sordid, brutal, and ignominious aspects of the war, on both sides. The titles respectively indicate failed hopes and eerie emptiness, though in both texts the full impression created is far more complex and nuanced. Both texts are very moving, primarily because neither protagonist is so brutalized that he loses his humanity. While both novelists depict the war from the ZANU/ZANLA/Shona side, neither text is ethnically partisan, rabidly anti-white or an anti-colonial diatribe, although the moral validity of an uprising against colonial domination, exploitation, and racial injustice is never in doubt.

Evocations of war memory in Zimbabwe are often tailored to suit specific political ends, used to exclude criticism or opposition, or simply declared irritating and irrelevant.[21] Yet, as Zimbabwean publisher Irene Staunton has stated, "Our writers have become our truth commission."[22] Particularly important is the emotional effort expended by Chinodya and Kanengoni in bringing women's roles,[23] civilians' (especially rural dwellers'), and children's presence and participation in the war to the fore, and their complete avoidance of the "swaggering soldier" stance in the depiction of their respective protagonists. Remarkably, the crucial event in both narratives is the protagonist's beating to death of a woman, on military orders. This may be the iconic image of the Liberation War in both texts, even though the two experiences differ in that Benjamin accepts the justice of the summary execution, whereas Munashe cannot so consider the killing of the woman and her baby. The iconic image speaks powerfully against militarism, male power, and the viability of war as a moral rescue effort.

There are distinct structural differences between the two texts. Chinodya casts a novelistic net over a longer historical sequence than does Kanengoni, telling a familial, social, and national history over two generations. His novel is a *bildungsroman* of a special kind; in the first part, the focus is on the protagonist's mother's move from her "country-humble"[24] background to her married life in the city where she and Benjamin's father, a clerk in the colonial administration, achieve a degree of prosperity and join a rigidly disciplinarian Christian group. In the second part, the eldest son Benjamin grows from a cowed teenager into a confident and politically assertive young Zimbabwean, toughened by war. The society grows from a colony into self-government, still hamstrung by the poverty of the majority. Kanengoni's structure is temporally more complex, using a shorter timeframe but a non-linear narrative set largely in the troubled mind of the traumatized war veteran Munashe, whose war memories interrupt his postwar life with flashbacks and flashbacks within those, sometimes evoked mid-sentence, creating the sense of an individual (and a society) haunted by "echoing,"[25] phantasmagoric recurrences. Whereas the feel of Chinodya's narrative is compassionate, with an authorial tenderness towards his characters occasionally embodying humorous perspectives, he articulates awareness of the dreadful and shameful aspects of the war as well as of the disappointing consequences. In Kanengoni's text, the dominant feeling is that of horror and a moral fierceness of perspective. Both authors see the Liberation War's central importance and necessity in the development of their society, while remaining aware of its ambiguities and the atrocities involved.

SHIMMER CHINODYA: *HARVEST OF THORNS* (1989)

Chinodya's protagonist Benjamin joins the guerrillas as a youngster of seventeen years after his arrest for participation in a protest march when the settler government announces its intention of extending the military call-up to black youths. He first experiences war when the camp across the Mozambican border where he is receiving training – containing mainly black Rhodesian war refugees – is attacked at dawn by Rhodesian forces.

> In the lull he heard voices shouting, yelling, screaming, feet crashing through the foliage … New sounds converged from the sky – the chugging of helicopters. A ring of helicopters swept over the camp, closing the fugitives in.
>
> An arc of people turned back and ran the way they had come, back to the centre. Bodies were mowed down by the guns in the helicopters.

> He scurried through the frantic herd turning back towards the centre. Leaves rained down on him, bullets stitched the rocks on either side of him.
>
> He saw children ahead of him, scattering into the grass. A naked woman passed him, charging through the bushes, arms flailing, her big flabby breasts whipping around her, and, ahead of him, two combatants were swinging an anti-aircraft gun out of the foliage.
>
> The helicopters plunged over the rim of trees ahead, where he was going … sweeping the people back in. The children turned back to the centre. Ahead of him the big naked woman rocked in the air and plunged. Still he chugged on, past her, over a string of small bodies, away from the camp.[26]

When he gets back, he searches frantically for Ropa the camp teacher, "this girl with lines on her forehead" as Benjamin describes her, a young woman with whom he had exchanged his first kiss, but discovers only her body, "sprawled face down … clutching a child in each arm." He finds that "suddenly he too was running, screaming at the sky with upraised fists 'Bastards! Bastards!'" [27]

The ruthlessness of war is underlined by the deaths of the children and by the deeply felt loss of the young woman who had made their care her priority, as it is in the sight of the older woman's "flailing breasts" and by the image of fleeing, "easy" victims in the running refugees, reduced to a "herd" hunted down from the sky. Benjamin is electrified into fury by these horrors; this is the true moment of his enlistment and Chinodya's demonstration of the validity of the Liberation War effort. It is, at the same time, a viscerally vivid and poignant passage because Ropa, the dead eighteen-year-old teacher, had been made "real" to us by evoking Benjamin's admiration and love for her gentle, caring, and courageous nature.

Much later, when Benjamin has taken the *nom de guerre* Pasi NemaSellout, meaning "down with traitors," he is ordered, along with another of the small guerrilla group of young soldiers in their fighting unit, to beat to death a woman who had attempted to poison one of their comrades and betrayed their group's position to the Rhodesian forces so that they came under deadly aerial attack. The beating is done at night in the village at a community gathering or *pungwe*; what horrifies Benjamin is that, even as he recognizes the justice or even necessity of the execution, he is made to participate bodily in her death. Aspects of the woman's appearance trigger vivid childhood memories of his mother, from whom he is estranged. Attempting to clarify his horror and dismay, Benjamin mentally composes a letter to his mother. In it, he refers back to Ropa's death – "*there was that girl under the trees with the children and I thought I'd be used to it*" – and to the more recent death of his young comrade who was killed in the attack: "*It was brown rocks and black soil where we put him and we had to dig it with our bayonets and I didn't think it would be like that, him there with the roots brushing his pimples, lying there where his mother didn't know, without a blanket ... I didn't think it would be like that.*"[28] This brings home Benjamin's (and his comrade's) youth and emotional vulnerability, his experience of war as an "unhomed" and exiled condition and how the rallying cry to be/come a "son of the soil" has come terribly true for them.

When the rainy season relentlessly sinks through their resolve, the war drags on and on and their supplies are depleted. "When the rain came, bringing with it flu and malaria, it soaked through their clothes and skins to their bones, washing the patience out of them, exposing their brittle longings."[29] Benjamin observes that the combat group has no real unity: "Each comrade was really on his own ... it was futile, if not foolish, to expect friendship."[30] Chinodya evokes the bleakness of inactivity during war, the loss of resolve and the depletion of purpose as well as the terrible isolation and existential loneliness. The men turn on each other and feelings of desperation lead to rule-breaking, even acts of rape.

Late in the war, in a razed and burnt-out village, Benjamin encounters a terrified girl searching frantically for her parents; she is Nkazana, the young woman to whom he will get married. Later they will discover her parents' corpses in the river, both with their throats cut, but as he tells her to wait in hiding, he senses an enemy soldier's presence. Benjamin pursues and fatally wounds this man, finding the dying soldier in the village church. He can only stare at the man, who begs him, "in a perfect, white man's English" to "finish [him] off." Benjamin does not do this, but when the man dies, he covers the body with the altar cloth. This is the only face-to-face combat death of an enemy soldier that Benjamin is shown witnessing, but there is no triumphalism in him; feeling "tired and empty," he returns to Nkazana and there he "let her cry and hold on to him."[31] Benjamin's need to give and be given comfort confirms his innate gentleness.

At the end of Chinodya's novel, having seen how little has changed in the lives of ordinary black Zimbabweans, Benjamin tells his brother-in-law that the "real battle ... may never even begin." What embitters him is "not being given the chance to catch up" with those who sat out the war in the cities, whereas "those who went out to fight will carry the scars for the rest of their lives." A village girl like Nkazana, too, he notes, witnessed horrors of which city dwellers have no inkling. Even a sell-out like his father now "carries a [party] card and is a comrade."[32] With neither a school-leaving certificate nor demobilisation papers, Benjamin is not even assured of a place in the post-liberation army. He had walked out of the assembly point without an official discharge, tired of "British and Canadian troopies politely bossing us around" and furious that Rhodesian soldiers were walking about freely "while we were herded into the points like prisoners of war."[33]

Chinodya nevertheless ends the narrative on a note of muted hope as Benjamin tenderly observes the "little hill of a nose, a pink line of pursed lips and two brown leaves for ears" of his tiny, newborn son, promising himself that "he'll do all he can to raise the little bundle in the cot ... though all he has is a pair of chapped hands."[34] Disappointments, anger, and anxieties loom large, but Benjamin, the bullied boy burdened with guilt by what he calls his "exaggerated Christian family"[35] and by the pre-war taunts of the politically radicalized, has survived the war without being broken; he has discovered his courage and worth but not become brutal, retaining a life-cherishing capacity for tenderness. In his portrait of Benjamin and of the circumstances from and within which he grows to maturity, Chinodya pays tribute to the reservoir of deep humanity on which his society drew to take on the terrible duties of the Liberation War. In this, there is hope.

ALEXANDER KANENGONI: *ECHOING SILENCES* (1997)

In Kanengoni's novel, the first enemy contact is also a Rhodesian dawn attack on a village in which most of the protagonist Munashe's small fighting unit is killed. When he returns from the cave where he had taken shelter with a fellow guerrilla whose festering wound took days to kill him, he is told that one other comrade survived the attack, while the bodies of three others were flown over the village, "dangled beneath the belly of the helicopter." The villagers spare him the information that "fifteen of their fellow tribesmen had been killed" and "headman Kajese's village ... burnt to the ground."[36] The worst horrors of Munashe's war experience invariably happen at the behest of brutal commanders, however. Returning to base after a gruelling march, Munashe is ordered to guard a woman digging a grave. Although he has no idea of the circumstances, their relentless, crazed security officer has sentenced her to death for having been married to one of the leaders of a ZANLA rebellion against perceived corruption in the top command. When the grave is sufficiently deep, Munashe is ordered to beat her – and the baby on her back – to death. He screams and begs to be spared, but is forced at gunpoint to execute the atrocity, a deed causing a rupture in his psyche not to be healed in his lifetime. Life becomes nightmarish; he sees the war as "an insatiable incinerator that would burn them all up."[37] He can no longer regard the war as just; it has lost all social meaning and become demonic, an unnatural, man-made disaster.

There is a recurrent focus on the deaths of children in Kanengoni's text. When he is ordered to an exterminated refugee camp, "a young woman holding a torn blood-smudged baby shawl, booties and napkin," unable to speak, can only point "a trembling hand at the hill behind which" the camp had been. Munashe sees "whole bodies of little boys and girls, young men and women, old men and old women" among headless corpses, "crushed skulls, shattered faces, missing limbs and shredded stomachs," even "the tiny abandoned bodies of suckling babies." Horribly, "swarms of heavy, green flies hovered over the bodies" and a "small girl with a gaping wound," sitting calmly in a donga, asks him, "Am I going to die, comrade?"[38] Almost unbearable as this is to read, the evocation of the indiscriminate slaughter wrought by the bombing of a refugee camp is necessary to place on record and it is filtered through Munashe's mourning, empathetic gaze. He cannot answer the little girl, only weep in the arms of a woman whom he has come to love, a fellow recruit. In this moment of shared, deep feeling, she tells him of her sexual enslavement by a brutish commander; after three abortions, she is experiencing "menopause at twenty."[39]

The protagonist bears witness to brutalities on both sides of this socially embedded war. He will later come across the corpse of the woman he had loved, the victim of a gang rape by enemy soldiers. After the war Munashe tells his wife that he "died" early in it;

"[w]hat survived through the war was [his] ghost,"[40] he says. Before the war he thought it important to volunteer because "[s]omething had to be done to change" the squalor of blacks' lives, but during the war Munashe becomes appalled by "the internal mass arrests, the torture, the detention and even the executions." He forms "the shameless resolution" to continue fighting only to avenge the deaths of the raped woman and the one he was forced to beat to death. His war experience "atomizes" or "de-socialises" him. Munashe never escapes from the war's grip; he is haunted by the spirit of the woman with the baby on her back to the extent that it erodes his sanity. This accords with the Shona belief system that unredeemed killing will bring an *ngozi* or avenging spirit to life. Munashe tries to return to Mozambique where the atrocity occurred, but his plans are thwarted. Another spirit, that of Kudzai, the woman he had loved during the war, gives him comfort. He delays for a long time informing her family of her death as promised, because she is still alive to him, someone who shared his wartime sufferings.

At Kudzai's family home, Munashe finds that her younger sister resembles Kudzai. Slowly, he learns to trust and love her and they marry. He finds employment and his life seems to steady out after the years of postwar wandering, during which his younger brother cruelly taunted him as insane, foolish, and useless. But the stability begins to crumble when his war nightmares start eating into his waking life. Kanengoni movingly evokes the agony in his mind as a talented, decent man is wrecked by war memories. The last part of the novel depicts the Shona exorcism ritual which Munashe's family belatedly undertakes. The ritual focuses on wartime suffering with an especial focus on the women Munashe encountered in the course of the war. Eventually his family takes him to the faraway village of the woman he had beaten to death with her baby. Munashe's body and soul are taken over by the dead woman; he croons a lullaby, rocks, and "suckles" the imaginary baby. Her mother laments at the pitiful sight: "Is this you, Rudo my daughter? Is this how you have decided to come back to me? Is this the grandchild you promised you would bear for me?"[41]

The harrowing scene ends as Munashe rushes out into the night; the next morning, his body is found in the mountains. One small redemptive note is struck when we hear that, in the village of the woman he beat to death, Munashe "would always be remembered as the guerrilla fighter who brought two distant villages together to mourn."[42] The text ends with a scene in the afterworld where the woman he killed forgives Munashe, and he is reunited with Kudzai. At a "spirit rally," the assassinated ZANU/PF leader Herbert Chitepo then exhorts Zimbabweans to destroy nepotism, tribalism, regionalism, and corruption.[43] Chitepo's speech echoes Kanengoni's title: "What I fear most is that we will not leave anything to our children except lies and silence ... It all began with silence ... because some of us felt that we would compromise our power ... [Hence] when we came to tell the history of our country and the history of the struggle, our silences distorted the story and made it defective [and] translated itself into fear ... against imaginary enemies." In the same speech Chitepo expresses detestation of the "high-sounding words" with which politicians silence criticism, stating that, "the struggle continues," in an allusion to the need to articulate truthful war memories, and to revive the ideals for which the war was originally undertaken.[44]

CONCLUDING REMARKS

The meaning of war can never lie in the war itself. It must be sought in the anguish of war memories, in truthful recall and in continuing the battle against the evils which caused war and those it causes in its turn. Texts like the two discussed here powerfully evoke the war for liberation from colonial rule in Rhodesia / Zimbabwe in its complexity. The most serious question they raise is whether the war's exacerbation of internal divisions could fatally undermine the gain of political self-rule. The novels thus engage us in the task they set themselves, of deepening social and historical understanding of the Second *Chimurenga* – its ironies, its achievements, and its horrors – recalling *and* interrogating it. The novels explore the roots of war and its reverberations afterwards; they articulate the affective *weight* of war.[45]

Each novelist's evocation (in his protagonist) of a character[46] with whom we make an emotional connection and whose judgment we trust renders achievable the difficult attempt to understand what is at stake in a war. It is as if the war becomes apprehensible through the recounted experience of the protagonist and the associated experience of a people, transmuted into the vicarious experience of emotionally open reading of texts in which African, Zimbabwean, and individual sorrows, sufferings, challenges, and achievements become imaginatively accessible.

Zimbabwe's best Liberation War fiction serves a purpose resembling the postwar exorcism ritual which Munashe undergoes, recalling Benjamin's lengthy outpouring of his thoughts about the war to his brother-in-law at the end of their respective narratives. In these sessions, an accounting as much as a recounting occurs. As Kizito Muchemwa writes, "The spirits of the dead haunt individuals, families and communities [in Zimbabwe] ... demand[ing] remembrance, recognition, and re-incorporation into cultural memory ... No one meaning is allowed to be dominant ... [in these] suppressed discourses ... contain[ing] memory and history. To allow these discourses to be rehabilitated is to allow memory and history pushed to the periphery to be relocated to the centre."[47]

Wars are deep matters and, even if considered justifiable, invariably bring about new forms and instances of oppression. Facing this is not easy and never popular, but writing of it with the gravitas of Chinodya and Kanengoni and other authors like them is the great social task of the finest war fiction.

NOTES

1 "War and the threat of war is one thing the huge continent shares without a quibble," writes Chimalum Nwankwo in "The Muted Index of War in African Literature & Society," *[War in] African Literature Today* 26 (2008): 11.

2 American poet Wallace Stevens uses world-wide images to indicate disasters of great magnitude in his poem "Puella Parvula." Stevens, *The Collected Poems* (New York: Vintage Books, 1990), 456.

3 Amina Said, "The Africa of the Statue," in *The Heinemann Book of African Women's Poetry* (London: Heinemann, 1995), 35.

4 Adichie uses the expression to explain her admiration for Shimmer Chinodya's *Harvest of Thorns* (Harare: Baobab Books, 1989), a novel she refers to as one of her models for the writing of her own "war novel," *Half of a Yellow Sun* (New York: Knopf, 2006). http://www.guardian.co.uk/books/2006/sep/16/fiction.society (accessed 2 May 2010).

5 Terence Ranger, "Rule by Historiography: The Struggle over the Past in Contemporary Zimbabwe," in *Versions of Zimbabwe: New Approaches to Literature and Culture*, edited by Robert Muponde and Ranka Primorac (Harare: Weaver Press, 2005), 217–43. Compare Kizito Muchemwa, "Some Thoughts on History, Memory, and Writing

in Zimbabwe," in *Versions of Zimbabwe: New Approaches to Literature and Culture*, edited by Robert Muponde and Ranka Primorac (Harare: Weaver Press, 2005), 195–202.

6 Ngwabi Bhebe and Terence Ranger, eds., *Soldiers in Zimbabwe's Liberation War* (London: James Currey, 1996); Stephen Chan and Ranka Primorac, eds., *Zimbabwe in Crisis: The International Response and the Space of Silence* (London: Routledge, 2007); Brian Raftopoulos and Alois Mlambo, eds., *Becoming Zimbabwe: A History from the Pre-Colonial Period to 2008* (Harare: Weaver Press, 2009); Sabelo Ndlovu-Gatsheni, *Do 'Zimbabweans' Exist? Trajectories of Nationalism, National Identity Formation and Crisis in a Postcolonial State* (Oxford: Peter Lang, 2012); Alois S. Mlambo, *A History of Zimbabwe* (Cambridge: Cambridge University Press, 2014).

7 Ranger, "Rule by Historiography: The Struggle over the Past in Contemporary Zimbabwe," in *Versions of Zimbabwe*, 231.

8 Chenjerai Hove, *Bones* (Harare: Baobab Books, 1988); Chinodya, *Harvest*; Dambudzo Marechera, *Scrapiron Blues* (Harare: Baobab Books, 1994); Alexander Kanengoni, *Echoing Silences* (Oxford: Heinemann, 1997); Yvonne Vera, *The Stone Virgins* (Harare: Weaver Press, 2002). These have all attracted scholarly commentary, several articles comparing two or more of the listed texts. Ranka Primorac is to my knowledge the only other commentator to have compared *Harvest of Thorns* and *Echoing Silences*, but she does so from rather different perspectives from my own in Primorac, *The Place of Tears: The Novel and Politics in Modern Zimbabwe* (London: Tauris, 2006). I have written previously on the texts by Hove, Marechera, and Vera in individual articles.

9 Itai Muwati and Davie E. Mutasa, "Representations of the Body as Contested Terrain: The Zimbabwean Liberation War Novel and the Politics of Nation and Nationalism," *South African Journal of African Languages* 31, no. 2 (2011): 199.

10 See Ranka Primorac and Robert Muponde, "Introduction: Writing against Blindness," in *Versions of Zimbabwe*, xiii.

11 Muchemwa, Kizito and Robert Muponde, "Introduction: Manning the Nation," in *Manning the Nation: Father Figures in Zimbabwean Literature and Society*, edited by Kizito Muchemwa and Robert Muponde (Harare: Weaver Press, 2007), xv, xix.

12 The British but Zimbabwe-focused historian Terence Ranger succinctly explicates the historical background and Liberation War

references in *Echoing Silences* in his useful Introduction to Kanengoni's novel, *Silences*, v–viii.

13 Robert Muponde, "Land as the Text of Zimbabwean History," interview by the Nordic Africa Institute, http://www.nai.uu.se/research/areas/cultural_images_in_and_of_zimbabwe/literature/muponde (accessed 5 February 2010).

14 Muwati and Mutasa, "Representations," 199–200.

15 Terence Ranger, "The Fruits of the Baobab: Irene Staunton and the Zimbabwean Novel," *Journal of Southern African Studies* 25, no. 4 (1999): 696.

16 Stephen Chan, "The Memory of Violence: Trauma in the Writings of Alexander Kanengoni and Yvonne Vera and the Idea of Unreconciled Citizenship in Zimbabwe," *Third World Quarterly* 26, no. 2 (2005): 373.

17 Flora Veit-Wild, *Teachers, Preachers, Non-Believers: A Social History of Zimbabwean Literature* (Oxford: Hans Zell, 1992); Primorac, *Place of Tears*.

18 Muponde and Primorac, *Versions of Zimbabwe*.

19 Kizito Muchemwa, "Some Thoughts on History, Memory, and Writing in Zimbabwe," in *Versions of Zimbabwe*, 197.

20 Liz Gunner, "Power, Popular Consciousness, and the Fictions of War: Hove's *Bones* and Chinodya's *Harvest of Thorns*," *African Languages and Cultures* 4, no. 1 (1991): 77–85.

21 One respondent to a questionnaire wrote that "Younger writers … are exploring different kinds of communities" and have little to no interest in the war: "We didn't ask the old ones to go to the struggle. We don't want to hear about that." P. Alden, "*Dies Irae*: Days of Wrath, Days of Crisis: A Report on the Current Situation in Zimbabwean Creative Writing," Nordiska Afrikainstitutet/The Nordic Africa Institute, http://www.nai.uu.se/research/finalized projects/cultural images in and of/zimbabwe/patricia-alden-on-creativ (accessed 15 October 2014); "Patricia Alden on Creative Writing 2007," http://www.nai.uu.se/research/finalized_projects/cultural_images_in_and_of/zimbabwe/patricia-alden-on-creativ (accessed 15 October 2014).

22 I. Staunton, "Postcolonial African Literature: The Experience of Zimbabwe (1): The Seventeen-Year Civil War and Its Immediate Literary Aftermath," 10, http://www.postcolonialweb.org/zimbabwe/miscauthors/staunton1.html (accessed 3 October 2014).

23 Compare to: "The struggle of female ex-combatants has only just begun. It offers a story that has not been told publicly in Zimbabwe"

in Tanya Lyons, "The Forgotten Soldiers: Women in Zimbabwe's Liberation War," *Southern Africa Report* 12, no. 2 (1997): 12, http://www.africafiles.org/article.asp?ID=3850. Subsequently, *some* of these "women's [hi]stories" have been published or filmed.

24 Chinodya, *Harvest*, 27.

25 Kanengoni, *Echoing*.

26 Chinodya, *Harvest*, 145.

27 Ibid., 145, 146, 147.

28 Ibid., 217, original italics.

29 Ibid., 219.

30 Ibid., 234.

31 Ibid., 255.

32 Ibid., 273.

33 Ibid., 273–4.

34 Ibid., 276–7.

35 Ibid., 272.

36 Kanengoni, *Silences*, 20.

37 Ibid., 30.

38 Ibid., 83.

39 Ibid., 85.

40 Ibid., 97.

41 Ibid., 127.

42 Ibid., 133.

43 Earlier, Munashe had been horrified to see Shona troops going off to quell political opposition in Matabeleland at the start of what became the Matabeleland massacre, asking in an appalled voice, over and over: "Another war?" Ibid., 93–7.

44 Ibid., 132.

45 Compare the words of Wallace Stevens: "The soldier is poor without the poet's lines" in the 1942 poem, "Notes toward a Supreme Fiction." Stevens, *The Collected Poems of Wallace Stevens* (New York: Vintage, 1990), 407.

46 Compare the following: "The character is not the fruit of a more or less minute and precise observation, but the form taken by moral judgement," a statement by Alberto Moravia. Moravia, *Man as an End*, trans. by Bernard Wall (New York: Farrar, Strauss, and Giraux, 1965), 67.

47 Muchemwa, "Some Thoughts on History, Memory, and Writing" in *Versions of Zimbabwe*, 198.

11

"What does it matter to us?" War and the Masculine Ideal in Louisa May Alcott's *Little Women* and L.M. Montgomery's *Rilla of Ingleside*

LAURA M. ROBINSON

Miss Cornelia asks the question "What does it matter to us?" at the beginning of L.M. Montgomery's *Rilla of Ingleside* (1921) in response to the local newspaper's story about an archduke being murdered. It matters deeply, of course, as this assassination sparks the First World War. As the boys and men of Glen St Mary, Prince Edward Island, troop dutifully off to war, the women are left at home to occupy themselves as best they can. While Montgomery's *Rilla* explores in detail Canada's role in the war in Europe, Louisa May Alcott's *Little Women* (1868–69), set as it is during the American Civil War, does not explore the politics and details of the various battles. Both novels set the coming-of-age stories of their feisty heroines during wartime, thus presenting the politics of the home front while the men are at a war that will come to shape the nation. While Judith Fetterley argues that Alcott's civil war is "an obvious metaphor for internal conflict,"[1] the war is also literal as it is in *Rilla*. Both Alcott and Montgomery offer a critique of the masculine values that their novels ostensibly endorse by exploiting the war theme to marginalize the men, a tactic that Jan Susina laments in *Little Women*. Susina argues that male readers do not identify with Alcott's girls' story because Alcott "relegates males to the margins."[2] In both novels, boys and men are variously too young, too old, wounded, traumatized, killed, or absent because of the war. The circumstance of war enlarges and thus reveals the pernicious masculine ideal that men are literally compelled to follow. Ultimately, Montgomery's and Alcott's war fictions document and commemorate not only the women who stepped outside of their gender roles but also the men who could not.

BOYS AND MEN IN GIRLS' STORIES

Both novels constitute or follow in the tradition of girls' stories and, as such, highlight the construction of girlhood. In *Secret Gardens*, Humphrey Carpenter indicates that *Little Women* is one of the first such books which gave rise to many others; Montgomery's *Anne of Green Gables* is one of several that Carpenter cites.[3] Similarly, Sarah A. Wadsworth argues that Alcott "was instrumental in defining, shaping, reinforcing, and revising the qualities, interests, and aspirations of the girls who comprised that [juvenile] market."[4] Moreover, Wadsworth underscores Alcott's strategies by suggesting that she "simultaneously resisted and revised traditional models of femininity while mediating her readers' desire for conventional female plots."[5] Montgomery's iconic *Anne of Green Gables* and the books that follow, such as *Rilla*, fall within the tradition begun by Alcott, as Carpenter notes, a tradition that carries forward a similar strategy. Mary Rubio identifies Montgomery's dominant approach, clearly echoing Alcott scholars. Montgomery, she writes, "both works within the traditional literary genre of domestic romance and yet circumvents its restrictive conventions when she critiques her society."[6]

Neither writer challenges gender roles in an openly rebellious fashion in her fiction; however, they both create a world in which boys and men exist on the periphery of very busy and interesting girls' and women's lives. Eve Kornfeld and Susan Jackson label girls books such as *Little Women* and *Anne of Green Gables* as "fictional female utopias" in part because of the dearth of men.[7] Carolyn Heilbrun writes that *Little Women* is "a memorable dream of sisterhood, perhaps the one fictional world where young women, complete unto themselves, are watched with envy by a lonely boy."[8] Like Rilla's brother Walter wishing he was a girl in order to avoid the battleground, the Marches' neighbour Laurie longs to be part of the sisterhood he sees next door. Showing the male figures on the outside desiring to be part of the feminine domestic world does more than foreground and celebrate the girls' daily lives; it indicates the constructed and rigidly enforced, but ultimately mutable, nature of gender roles. Boys and men, too, can wish for the domestic, and not only because the alternative, in this case war, is not attractive. Looking at Montgomery's *Rilla of Ingleside* alongside *Little Women* highlights the wartime setting of each and demonstrates how damaging the masculine ideal is.

A WORLD AT WAR

Both *Little Women* and *Rilla of Ingleside* interrogate traditional gender roles, and I suggest that they do so, in part, because of the wartime setting. Volume one of *Little Women* is a Christian tale about four sisters who learn to fight temptation on their path to becoming proper little women while their father is away at the American Civil War. Montgomery's novel, the final installment in the Anne of Green Gables books, tells the story of fourteen-year-old Rilla, Anne's daughter. While Rilla adopts a war baby and starts a Junior Red Cross League to raise money and stitch items for the soldiers, her only real ambition is to marry Kenneth Ford, a young man off at war.

While the tales thus appear to be rather traditional and conservative, both novels trouble straightforward gender roles. The gender-bending of *Little Women* has been discussed by many critics, notably by Karin Quimby in her exploration of Jo's tomboy identity. By arguing that Jo is a queer figure, Quimby also shows how the male characters are sidelined: "Even though *Little Women* brings its tomboy heroine to the expected end of marriage, this conclusion is so unsatisfying and incoherent that most readers reject it in favor of the far more queer middle of Jo's plot,"[9] which centres on the sisters and not on potential romantic interests, Laurie or Professor Bhaer. Some examples of Alcott's gender play are the following: the blurring of gender roles between Laurie and Jo; Jo's irrepressible tomboyishness; her cropping her hair to raise money for her father, physically and metaphorically emphasizing her boyish character; and the sisters playing gentlemen in their Pickwick Club which further complicates gender when they do not want Laurie, a boy, to join their "ladies' club" in which they all sport male monikers.

Critics have not been so quick to identify the gender-bending in *Rilla*, and yet the novel demonstrates a similar disquiet toward gender roles. I have argued elsewhere, in an article about femininity in *Rilla*, how several characters, such as Walter, Faith, Gertrude, and

Susan, disrupt a clearly defined gender categorization, as Laurie and Jo do in *Little Women*, by desiring to be or by being described as akin to another gender. In her depiction of the family cats, the story of which opens the novel, Montgomery sets the stage for troubling gender. While I have discussed this in "L.M. Montgomery's Great War: The Home as Battlefield," it is worth reiterating here as the family cats clearly stand as symbols of gender fluidity. When Jack Frost, the household tomcat, surprises everyone by giving birth, the Blythes continue to refer to the feline as male: "The Blythes had been so accustomed to regard Jack Frost as a member of the male sex that they could not get out of the habit. So they continually used the masculine pronoun, although the result was ludicrous."[10] The narrator cites an example of family members telling the kitten to go to his mother and get *him* to bathe him. Montgomery is not necessarily challenging rigid gender roles by this bi-gendered cat, although at first glance this construction is quite remarkable. However, because it has a split personality, Jack Frost's kitten is named after the monstrous hero of a dark Victorian novel: Dr Jekyll / Mr Hyde. Dr Jekyll is the sleepy, affectionate facet, whereas Mr Hyde has a "tread as heavy as a man's" and a "savage snarl."[11] The language used to describe him, particularly "as a man's," characterizes the monstrous and mean aspect of the animal as masculine. From its outset, Montgomery's novel thus opens up traditional gender roles to scrutiny, but does so in a subtle manner by embedding the gender trouble in a humorous depiction of household pets.

Thus, both novels invite a reconsideration of gender roles, largely because of the wartime setting. Scholars who examine gender roles during wartime generally agree that war forces necessary change on gender expectations. Susan Grayzel states that, "Regardless of where it took place, wartime mobilization upset traditional gender arrangements."[12] More specifically, Billie Melman points out that historians generally argue that the concept of war is intertwined with gender because "the war ... was experienced and conceived as a project of remasculinization (or disillusionment with remasculinization)."[13] Leo Braudy likewise suggests that wartime enforces a "more single-minded and more traditional" masculinity than does peacetime.[14] However, Michael Roper's examination of post–First World War memoirs challenges the idea that war emphasizes a heroic ideal. He argues that a code of manliness was undermined by the war and that the memoirs "moved away from the belief in a singular, hegemonic notion of manliness and toward a more differentiated perception of masculine subjectivity."[15] Paul Fussell's conclusion to his cultural study of the First World War might best describe the underpinnings of what happens with gender during wartime. Fussell does not discuss gender directly, but he does state that "every war is ironic because every war is worse than expected,"[16] and he shows how this irony manifests in all of the literature about the war. Perhaps Fussell's analysis can be linked to these other critics' gender analyses by suggesting that wartime masculinity is inherently ironic as well, which is what both Alcott and Montgomery highlight by showing the impossibility of fulfilling a masculine ideal, particularly in wartime.

Both Alcott's and Montgomery's novels at once assert an idealized wartime masculinity and decidedly undercut it. In *Little Women*, male sacrifice is godly and good. Meg explains how she feels about her father being in the war: "I think it was so splendid in Father to go as a chaplain when he was too old to be drafted, and not strong enough for a soldier."[17] Men also provide. The elderly and lame Mr Lawrence gives the girls a lavish Christmas breakfast when they sacrifice theirs to the starving Hummels; he purchases a fish for a hungry woman willing to work for food; he presents Beth with a piano. Clearly, however, these representations of male valour and provision are double-edged, suggesting that Alcott's novel also questions this masculinity. Meg damns her father with faint praise, commenting, underhandedly, on his age and lack of strength. Mr Lawrence can provide because he, too, is aged and infirm, thus he stays at home.

Rilla similarly constructs and dismantles a masculine ideal centred on war. Schoolteacher Gertrude Oliver responds with awe to a story Rilla's brother Jem tells about a hero from the Balkan War. Gertrude regards the man's behaviour as "godlike."[18] Jem's hero is a doctor, not a soldier, who, even though both of his legs were "smashed to pulp," dragged himself to all the wounded, saving others' lives.[19] This representation of heroic masculinity is not stereotypical, as the man is sacrificial by ministering to others to his own detriment rather than conquering. Jem relates this tale moments before war is declared in the novel, setting the reader up for a revised masculine ideal. That Jem's hero ultimately dies, however, demonstrates how unviable this, or any, heroic ideal is.

In addition to seemingly supporting, but actually revising, masculine values, each novel depicts its respective war variously as hardship and as game, showing the mixed messages given to prospective soldiers. In *Little Women*, where the fighting is introduced on the opening page of the novel, Jo longs to partake in the adventure of war. When the English visitors, the Vaughns, play croquet with the Americans (Laurie and the girls), the game unfolds like the American Revolution: "The English played well, but the Americans played better, and contested every inch of the ground as strongly as if the spirit of '76 inspired them."[20] When Laurie is upset with his grandfather, he and Jo dream of escaping to the war. Jo imagines "the novel charms of camps and hospitals, liberty and fun."[21] However, Alcott's novel also points out that wartime requires sacrifices – the sisters cannot have presents for Christmas, for example. Beth acknowledges that her father will not be having a very merry Christmas at the front.[22] Marmee relates a story so that the sisters reassess their small sacrifices. She explains how she met a man and asked him whether he has sons in the army: "Yes, ma'am. I had four, but two were killed, one is a prisoner, and I'm going to the other, who is very sick in a Washington hospital."[23]

In *Rilla*, there is a similar spirit of adventure and sacrifice, but Montgomery clearly traces the changing attitude to the war as it progresses. First, almost every chapter begins with a detailed update on the war. Jem and Kenneth regard the war as an adventure and as a "Great Game."[24] Walter provides a counterbalance to this perspective in surprisingly modernist language: "War was a hellish, horrible, hideous thing – too horrible and hideous to happen in the twentieth century between civilized nations. The mere thought of it was hideous, and made Walter unhappy in its threat to the beauty of life."[25] When the boys, Jem and Jerry, write their letters home, their experience of war has not been one of great adventure. They discuss picking cooties and killing rats, mud and trenches, and their comrades dying next to them. When Rilla's youngest brother, Shirley, enlists, the passage describing his leaving demonstrates clearly the shifting perspectives on war and heroism: "So Shirley went – not radiantly, as to a high adventure, like Jem, not in a white flame of sacrifice, like Walter, but in a cool, business-like mood, as of one doing something, rather dirty and disagreeable, that had just got to be done."[26]

EMPOWERING WOMEN

In the absence of the men, the female characters must take on more duties; these new tasks are justified by a parallel to the men on the front lines. This irony – comparing domestic life to the battlefield – empowers the women at home by demonstrating how difficult some of their trials are. Jo feels that "keeping her temper at home was a much harder task than facing a rebel or two down South."[27] Walter teases Rilla for adopting a war baby: "It took more courage for you to tackle that five pounds of new infant, Rilla-my-Rilla, than it would be for Jem to face a mile of Germans."[28] Suffering pain and yet carrying on with her chores, the housekeeper, Susan, states that "Rheumatism is bad enough but I realize, and none better, that it is not to be compared to being gassed by the Huns."[29] The irony of the comparisons between daily domesticity and the atrocities of war at once encourages female submission to their circumstances and exposes how onerous and sacrificial women's daily life can be. Thus, both Alcott and Montgomery use this irony to revise an understanding of heroism to include women's domestic lives.

While scholars are divided on whether war, particularly the First World War, has empowered women, as Melman points out,[30] both Alcott and Montgomery's novels underscore girls' expanded powers once the men are at war. Most obviously, Jo becomes the "man of the family" with her father away,[31] a role that remarkably does not diminish upon his return. Each sister contributes to the family and the community. Both Jo and Meg work to pay the bills. Amy and Beth labour within the home. Marmee works for various charities having to do with the war. As Kornfeld and Jackson argue, Alcott seems to present a female utopia where men are almost unnecessary. Alcott emphasizes women's independence throughout the first volume. When the English visitor, Miss Kate, expresses shock that Meg is a governess, Mr Brooke is quick to defend not only Meg but American girlhood: "Young ladies in America love independence as much as their ancestors did, and are admired and respected for supporting themselves."[32] Alcott's girls and women are just as responsible for attaining independence as the soldiers of the American Revolution were. Jo certainly symbolizes the spirit of independence. For example, she weeps over her first published story "for to be independent and earn the praise of those she loved were the dearest wishes of her heart."[33]

Montgomery scholars have been unified in their position that Montgomery's war novel depicts a world of empowered and feisty girls and women. The housekeeper Susan, in particular, is described as being akin to the Canadian soldiers who fought at Vimy Ridge: "The spirit that animated her gaunt arms was the self-same one that captured Vimy Ridge and held the German legions from Verdun."[34] Andrea McKenzie identifies both Susan and Rilla as heroic figures representing the nation, and Amy Tector argues that "Montgomery's portrayal of home-front sacrifice empowers her female characters."[35] While many of the girls and women's tasks are quite traditional in nature – sewing, knitting, getting up concerts – Rilla thinks that she "must take the boys' place" by bringing her mother the first mayflowers of the year, as each boy did before leaving for war.[36] While she ultimately does not need to, as young Bruce remembers to pick the flowers for the matron Anne, the language itself indicates that the girls need to fill the roles left empty by the boys and men.

DISEMPOWERING MEN?

In Alcott's and Montgomery's novels, war is empowering to the girls and women, and both texts expand the notions of heroism to validate and valorize the home front. What, then, does war mean for the men? Elizabeth Young argues that Alcott uses the Civil War setting to reimagine gender roles by privileging "female self-mastery as a metaphorical model for male development and fantasi[zing] a reconstructed nation in which men become little women."[37] Young's argument is compelling, yet in her vigorous analysis of Alcott's revisioning of the nation's body politic, she overlooks the fact that many of Alcott's men are somehow disabled or ineffective. Rather than empowering, then, her argument that Alcott presents a feminized ideal for men suggests that impaired men are equivalent to little women. In *Little Women*, many of the male characters are lame, ill, and ineffectual, and they are thus characterized regardless of the war. Mr March lost the family money through an unwise investment in a friend. Uncle March has died. The King family's brother somehow disgraces the family. Mr Lawrence is old and infirm, needing to rely on a cane. The editor Mr Dashwood, Laurie's peer Ned Moffat, and young Mr Tudor all boast dubious characters. Professor Bhaer is older and poor and ill-groomed. Ironically, then, men are still very necessary for women's survival. The Hummels are poor and starving, for example, because they have no father to provide for them. It is interesting to note here that the March mother and girls are the ones who provide for the Hummels, an act that leads, ultimately, to Beth's death, suggesting the type of outcome one can expect if one steps too far outside of traditional gender roles.

Moreover, the war affects boys and men by emphasizing society's expectations of men's valour. When young Laurie is ready for college, his tutor Brooke is left without a job. He explains to Meg: "As soon as [Laurie] is off, I shall turn soldier. I am needed." Meg's response addresses the implicit pressure on men to join the fight: "I am glad of that! … I should think every young man would want to go."[38] Even when Mr March goes off to war as a chaplain, his profession is not at heroic as it should be, which is evident when Mrs Moffat embellishes Mr March's role in the war to a guest at her party: "Daisy March – father a colonel in the army – one of first families, but reverses of fortune, you know."[39]

In *Rilla*, the men have little choice but to join up, unless they are previously wounded like Rilla's beau, Kenneth. When Kenneth's football injury heals, he is off to war. Walter thinks he may be able to avoid battle due to his bout of typhoid. The past illness cannot keep him out of the line of fire, however. Walter's battle to avoid joining up suggests Montgomery's criticism of war, as Tector has argued. She writes: "Walter is the emblem of masculine sacrifice in *Rilla*."[40] Critics such as Benjamin Lefebvre have argued that Walter is the most unmasculine character: a romantic poet who wishes he was a girl to avoid the war. Lefebvre explains that "Montgomery is expanding the notion of manhood" through the character of Walter.[41] Walter feels he cannot volunteer because war is brutal and ugly, and he cannot imagine "thrusting a bayonet through another man."[42] However, he faces enormous societal pressure to join the war effort. In addition to an anonymous malicious letter he receives,[43] he also gets an envelope containing a white feather, a symbol of cowardice.[44] Irene Howard, one of Rilla's friends, tells Rilla an insult she heard directed towards Walter. Rilla cannot even write it in her diary.[45] He explains the pressure on him: "A perfectly fit fellow, of military age, who doesn't join up is looked upon as a shirker and treated accordingly."[46] While Rilla begs him not to enlist, she is relieved when he does: "Amid all her pain she was conscious of an odd feeling of relief in some hidden part of her soul, where a little dull, unacknowledged soreness had been lurking all winter. No one – *no one* could ever call Walter a slacker now."[47] Men must fight, if they are to be considered men at all.

The devastation war causes the male characters indicates that both authors are commenting on the impossibility of fulfilling the masculine ideal. Marmee volunteers for Soldiers' Aid Societies, demonstrating a need to help the men who have been in battle. Some men return, as Mr March does, with chronic illness, which leads to another example of gender-bending within the novel. The narrator describes the mother and sisters around the father "like bees swarming after their queen."[48] At the beginning of volume two, the narrator explains that even with the war over, "The hospitals and homes [are] still full of wounded 'boys' and soldiers' widows."[49] The boys and men of *Rilla of Ingleside* are all deeply scarred by the war, both emotionally and physically. Carl Meredith is blinded in one eye; Walter dies on the battlefield. The narrator writes of the boys who had previously been dancing lightheartedly at Four Winds Point: "Two of them were sleeping under the Flanders poppies … Others were wounded in the hospital."[50] Indeed, the narrator later discusses the men returning from war after armistice: "None of them came back just as they went away, not even those who had been so fortunate as to escape any injury."[51]

What is striking, however, is the effect of wartime masculinity on the boys and men. Some, like the gender-ambiguous, college-bound Laurie in *Little Women*, seem completely oblivious to the war, except as far as it offers escape from domestic constraints. On the other hand, Mr Brooke "did his duty manfully for a year, got wounded, was sent home, and not allowed to return. He received no stars or bars, but he deserved them."[52] Later, however, the narrative calls kind-hearted Brooke into question when newly wedded Meg must deal with his temper. Meg's mother says, "He has a temper, not like ours, – one flash, and then all over – but the white still anger that is seldom stirred, but once kindled, is hard to quench. Be careful, very careful, not to wake this anger against yourself."[53] While the narrative does not directly connect this temper to his war experience, the disturbing admonition to her daughter to avoid eliciting his anger suggests that his character is not or is no longer ideal. A parallel with war injury emerges when Beth asks the English visitor, Frank Vaughn about his experiences hunting. He ruefully explains that his present disability – he is lame with a crutch – resulted from a hunting injury.[54] While not an example of war exactly, the use of weapons and violence mirrors that of war and leads to disabling injury.

Frank Vaughn's debilitation as a result of attempting to kill an animal is strangely echoed in *Rilla*. Young Bruce Meredith attempts to sacrifice something he loves to save Jem, who is wounded and missing in action. In a misguided bargain with God, Bruce drowns his beloved kitten, Stripey, in order to bring Jem back. This is what boys must learn in the world of Montgomery's war: to suffocate their emotions and destroy life. In doing so, they themselves are wounded, physically or emotionally. In their texts that commemorate women's heroism and valour, then, Alcott and Montgomery expose a clear conundrum: while men have little choice but to enlist in the war effort and behave in specific masculine ways, the pursuit of this masculinity leads to injury, wounds, trauma, and death. The most contradictory character in *Rilla* is Walter, whom Owen Dudley Edwards and Jennifer H. Litster describe as "both the idealized Canadian war bard dying among his countrymen ... and the sensitive artist in a crass, conformist, crusading climate."[55] Walter shows his refusal to relinquish his emotions in a letter to Rilla:

> The boys of my year are going – going. Every day two or three of them join up. Some days I almost make up my mind to do it – and then I see myself thrusting a bayonet through another man – some woman's husband or sweetheart or son – perhaps the father of little children – I see myself lying alone torn and mangled, burning with thirst on a cold, wet field, surrounded by dead and dying men – and I know I never can.[56]

But he does. And he dies. Through his death, Montgomery's novel exposes the unviability of his type of compassionate or feminized masculinity in wartime.

So, alongside the depiction of the daily heroism of women that emerges in wartime, Alcott and Montgomery decry the pressure on men to live up to an untenable and damaging masculine ideal. Most fascinating, when the armistice is declared in the novel, the kitten of the gender-ambiguous Jack Frost, now the full-grown Dr Jekyll–Mr Hyde who embodies the extreme of both masculine and feminine traits, disappears for good. Perhaps Montgomery's novel, like Alcott's before hers, is thus expressing hope that the gender expectations of docility for women and savagery for men might not exist in the postwar world.

NOTES

1 Judith Fetterley, "Little Women: Alcott's Civil War," *Feminist Studies* 5, no. 2 (Summer 1979): 370.

2 Jan Susina, "Men and *Little Women*: Notes of a Resisting (Male) Reader," in *Little Women and the Feminist Imagination*, edited by Janice M. Alberghene and Beverly Lyon Clark (New York: Garland Publishing, 1999), 163.

3 Humphrey Carpenter, *Secret Gardens: A Study of the Golden Age of Children's Literature* (London: George Allen & Unwin, 1985): 93–4, 98, 227n77.

4 Sarah A. Wadsworth, "Louisa May Alcott, William T. Adams, and the Rise of the Gender-Specific Series Book," *The Lion and the Unicorn* 25, no. 1 (2001): 19.

5 Ibid., 18.

6 Mary Rubio, "Subverting the Trite: L.M. Montgomery's 'Room of Her Own,'" *Canadian Children's Literature* 65 (1992): 8.

7 Eve Kornfeld and Susan Jackson, "The Female *Bildungsroman* in Nineteenth Century America: Parameters of a Vision," *Journal of American Culture* 10, no. 4 (Winter 1987): 70.

8 Carolyn G. Heilbrun, "Louisa May Alcott: The Influence of *Little Women*," in *Women, the Arts, and the 1920s in Paris and New York*, edited by Kenneth W. Wheeler and Virginia Lee Lussier (New Brunswick, NJ Transaction Books, 1982), 25.

9 Karin Quimby, "The Story of Jo: Literary Tomboys, Little Women, and the Sexual-Textual Politics of Narrative Desire," *GLQ: A Journal of Lesbian and Gay Studies* 10, no. 1 (2003): 4.

10 L.M. Montgomery, *Rilla of Ingleside* (Toronto: Seal Books, 1989), 3.

11 Ibid., 4.

12 Susan R. Grayzel, *Women and the First World War* (London: Routledge, 2002), 77.

13 Billie Melman, "Introduction," in *Borderlines: Genders and Identities in War and Peace, 1870–1930* (New York: Routledge, 1998): 4.

14 Leo Braudy, *From Chivalry to Terrorism: War and the Changing Nature of Masculinity* (New York: Vintage, 2005), xvi.

15 Michael Roper, "Between Manliness and Masculinity: The 'War Generation' and the Psychology of Fear in Britain, 1914–1950," *Journal of British Studies* 44 (2005): 356.

16 Paul Fussell, *The Great War and Modern Memory* (Oxford: Oxford University Press, 2000), 7.

17 Louisa May Alcott, *Little Women* (New York: Penguin, 1989), 9.

18 Montgomery, *Rilla of Ingleside*, 25.

19 Ibid., 25.

20 Alcott, *Little Women*, 117.

21 Ibid., 199.
22 Ibid., 22.
23 Ibid., 41.
24 Montgomery, *Rilla of Ingleside,* 35.
25 Ibid., 20.
26 Ibid., 207.
27 Alcott, *Little Women*, 10.
28 Montgomery, *Rilla of Ingleside*, 68.
29 Ibid., 103.
30 Melman, "Introduction," in *Borderlines*, 5.
31 Alcott, *Little Women*, 6.
32 Ibid., 124.
33 Ibid., 147.
34 Montgomery, *Rilla of Ingleside*, 217.
35 Andrea McKenzie, "Women at War: L.M. Montgomery, The Great War, and Canadian Cultural Memory," in *Storm and Dissonance: L.M. Montgomery and Conflict*, edited by Jean Mitchell (Newcastle: Cambridge Scholars Publishing, 2008), 83–108; Amy Tector, "A Righteous War? L.M. Montgomery's Depiction of the First World War in *Rilla of Ingleside*," *Canadian Literature* 179 (2003): 80.
36 Montgomery, *Rilla of Ingleside*, 209.
37 Elizabeth Young, "A Wound of One's Own: Louisa May Alcott's Civil War Fiction," *American Quarterly* 48, no. 3 (1996): 441.
38 Alcott, *Little Women*, 126.
39 Ibid., 86.
40 Tector, "A Righteous War?," 76.
41 Benjamin Lefebvre, "Walter's Closet," *Canadian Children's Literature* 94 (Summer 1999): 15.
42 Montgomery, *Rilla of Ingleside,* 47.
43 Ibid., 90.
44 Ibid., 81.
45 Ibid., 87.
46 Ibid., 90.
47 Ibid., 119.
48 Alcott, *Little Women*, 211.
49 Ibid., 224.
50 Montgomery, *Rilla of Ingleside*, 185.
51 Ibid., 272–3.
52 Alcott, *Little Women*, 224.
53 Ibid., 279.

54 Ibid., 127.
55 Edwards, Owen Dudley, and Jennifer H. Litster, "The End of Canadian Innocence: L.M. Montgomery and the First World War," in *L.M. Montgomery and Canadian Culture*, edited by Irene Gammel and Elizabeth Epperly (Toronto: University of Toronto Press, 1999), 36.
56 Montgomery, *Rilla of Ingleside*, 81.

PART THREE

Collective War Memories in Art and Popular Fictions

PART THREE

Collective War Memories in Art and Popular Fictions

12

(Re)Telling World War II in British Comic-Land from the 1940s to the 1960s

RENÉE DICKASON

Each country has its own way of reflecting on its performance in wartime and the UK was no exception, with official and unofficial sources offering a particularly British account of the Second World War both during the hostilities and after they had ended. For the British, World War II was a unique experience in a number of ways. Unlike its predecessors, this was no conflict taking place in foreign countries or on distant oceans involving only army and navy personnel, but one in which the country felt itself under immediate threat of foreign invasion and found itself without military allies from outside the Empire and Commonwealth until the start of the German invasion of the USSR in June 1941. Well beyond this date, British towns and cities were targets for aerial bombardment which caused huge structural damage and killed some 60,000 civilians, the menace persisting into the spring of 1945 with attacks by frightening new weapons, first V1 flying bombs and then V2 rockets. Moreover, the privations and constraints of war were the lot of almost everyone: household goods as well as food were rationed or simply unobtainable, military conscription and compulsory war work were imposed on large swathes of the population, and children (with or often without their mothers) were evacuated to unfamiliar parts of the country from towns and cities considered most at risk from attack. Finally, World War II was also the "war of words,"[1] not just for Britain, of course, as citizens in all countries engaged in the Second World War were force-fed a diet of "information"[2] devised by rulers, occupiers, dictators, collaborators, or defenders to condition both behaviour and thought. The methods and strategies employed were influenced by the national priorities of the moment and evolved with the different stages of the conflict. They also varied according to the degree of constraint that accompanied them and the willingness of the target audience to play the game and suspend its disbelief at some of the less plausible claims and assertions that were made. This takes us to the role of comics in the battle for hearts and minds.

The following examination of the (re)telling of World War II is based on comics intended for a juvenile audience produced and published in Great Britain during WWII and in a period of some twenty-five years after the restoration of peace. The approach to comic-land in this paper is deliberately wide-ranging, for the term "comics" escapes clear critical definition, a task comparable to, as Paul Gravett asserted, "*nailing jelly.*"[3] Gravett's own *Great British Comics*[4] makes substantial reference to strip cartoons in publications for adults as well as to material from humorous magazines intended for children, more generally known by the term "funnies." On the other hand, Adam Riches's *When the Comics Went to War* makes only sparing references to this genre, concentrating principally on "adventure comics" which are also known as "boys' weeklies" (Orwell) or "boys' story papers" (Gravett and Stanbury).[5] Denis Gifford's *International Book of Comics* and Mike Conroy's *War Comics: A Graphic History*[6] cover both adventure papers and funnies, but with a preference for the former. On balance, the differences between the two, at the beginning of the period covered by this chapter at least, lay in the subject matter, the degree and type of humour employed, and in the funnies' preference for the comic strip format (with its brevity, visual input, and speech bubbles attractive to a younger audience). Adventure comics favoured full-length text-based stories with illustrations. That said, the two forms were relatively age unspecific, for older children, teenagers and, in secret, some adults could enjoy the funnies. From the 1960s onwards, text-based war stories were in rapid decline, being largely superseded by longer comic strips. The first part of this study is dedicated to the telling of the war in real time (i.e. during the conflict), and primarily devoted to the funnies, the content of which sometimes echoed the official version of the patriotic behaviour expected from civilians. The second section, on the other hand, explores how adventure stories published after the war used mostly fictional narratives to give due emphasis to the British role in achieving a successful outcome. As some of these stories featured heroes who had already appeared in wartime numbers of adventure comics, the chronological distinction between the two sections can only be approximate.

TELLING HISTORY IN THE MAKING OR EVERYDAY HEROES

In general terms, the comics produced during the Second World War can be seen as the blueprint for all future representations of the conflict in the medium. By transmitting the ideas prevalent at the time, and apparently recounting the stresses of daily life "as it happened," comic-land constructed an immediate image of what war was like. It reinforced the messages conveyed in other media (radio, film newsreels, photographs, newspaper cartoons, and comic strips),[7] thereby complementing the posters and exhortations of the Ministry of Information (MOI). Slogans like "KEEP CALM AND CARRY ON" and "YOUR COURAGE, YOUR CHEERFULNESS, YOUR RESOLUTION WILL BRING US VICTORY" were the watchwords for good citizenship and participation in the war effort on the home front, including for youngsters who found similar sentiments in the pages of their favourite reads. The 1930s had been the golden age of British comics with publishers offering adventure story papers for girls as well as boys, with a substantial number of well-established humorous papers, and with the birth of D.C. Thomson's *The Beano* and *The Dandy*, an innovative model which used bright colours and quality printing, and abolished written text in favour of speech bubbles that broke the mould for funnies. These two publications were to dominate the market during the war and long after. The advent of war was to bring harder times: shortage of paper meant that several titles were lost and those that remained were reduced to fortnightly publication, sometimes sharing stories and characters. All of this did little to dampen readers' enthusiasm. It was important that youngsters should see the established heroes or heroines of their funnies setting the example in wartime situations. But this theme was not overdone, for many of their adventures were not war-related, and the humour and entertainment were all the more enjoyable for being typical and predictable.

DOING DOWN THE DICTATORS

One of the more simplistic humorous techniques exploited in wartime funnies was the derision for enemy leaders who were obvious targets. Belittling or ridiculing them was a way of proving British superiority and led to expectations of a successful outcome to the war. This method was far from original, as visual and verbal denigration of the enemy had been a standard device in British print cartoons at least since the Napoleonic Wars. Anticipating the Second World War from 1938 onwards, Basil and Bert, the "very private detectives" in *The Jester*, found themselves dealing with a "nasty dictator" called Ateful Adolf in a country called Dictatorland, which he ruled with the aid of a certain General Snoring and their cronies Dr Gobbles and Herr von Drippingtop. Needless to say, the detectives always came out on top, for the premise of the humour was obvious: the enemy were inferior, their very names were funny, and the idea they might be dangerous was simply ridiculous. Hitler and Goering, aka Addie and Hermy the "nasty Nazis,"[8] were also the butts of humour in the *Dandy*. In December 1940, these caricatural figures, notable for their poor command of English and their gluttony rather than their intelligence, found themselves on a boat heading for Istanbul when all they wanted was to acquire a turkey for their Christmas dinner. A later adventure showed them in pursuit of a tin of bully beef which had been taken to the local rubbish dump. Once there, they found themselves thwarted as they were unable to get their hands on the food, all tin openers and knives having been requisitioned to make iron crosses. Trying to make the best of a bad job, they offered to swap their booty for a sandwich being eaten by a passing boxer who was training for a fight. Again, the outcome was not what the two had hoped for: the can proved to be a dummy used only for shop window displays, and the enraged pugilist took his revenge by using the two Nazis as punch balls.

Explaining this intricate story shows just how much improbable but not always anodyne detail could be crammed into the nine small frames and speech balloons that made up a comic strip. The reference to the iron crosses served comically both to diminish the status of Germany's highest military honour, of which Hitler had been a recipient in the Great War, and to suggest the mismanagement of the country during the Third Reich. The punishments exacted on comic-land's Nazis were typical of those normally inflicted on schoolchildren, thus both making them appear more vulnerable and diminishing their status. Hitler and his acolytes were at times punched, sometimes violently, as when the *Dandy*'s Desperate Dan sends the Führer flying back to Germany with a single blow, or at other times they were kicked in the pants. But, like disobedient children, they fail to learn their lesson and keep coming back for more.

The ridiculing of Hitler in the media was far from being limited to the funnies, nor was the treatment he received without potential topical relevance. An MOI poster from December 1941 with the caption "Just a Good Afternoon's Work" showed him being slapped in the face by a woman who had just volunteered for war work following new legislation. Moreover, caricaturing him was a particularly easy task, his moustache and plastered-down hair and his wearing of clothes adorned with the swastika were unmistakable. Two covers from the story paper *Adventure* in June and July 1940 illustrate the point clearly. In addition to his other physical attributes, Hitler has the staring eyes and drawn features of someone enduring mental torment as he sits tied to a chair (11 June 1940) or with his hands over his ears (13 July 1940) to block out the accusations and threats of vengeance apparently uttered against him ("traitor!" "Hitler must go!" "I'll get you yet!" "your doom is sealed!" "your time is coming!"). The immediate cause of his distress is not apparent, but the first cover has one obvious additional purpose: using the picture to attract readers who may win war savings certificates if they purchase the comic ("War savings certificates offered free to readers"). Such savings were a way for ordinary citizens to help finance the war. Presumably, Hitler's anxiety is related to the entirely imaginary activities of the Slippery Slink, a band of clever British actors and musicians operating as secret agents within Germany, detailed in this number of the paper. There may perhaps also be a passing reference to the successful evacuation of British troops from Dunkirk, after which further bad news for the Führer cannot be ruled out and even Lord Haw-Haw may prove unable to explain away, hence the question emblazoned across Hitler's uniform: "What will Lord Haw-Haw say about this?"[9] The second cover, whose threats are related to a story beginning in this number of the comic, "The Man who haunted Hitler," may also suggest that the failure to destroy the British army could cost Germany dear.

Hitler was not the only dictator on the receiving end of barbs in the funnies. Mussolini, aka "Musso the Wop … A Big-A-Da-Flop," was regularly lampooned in *Beano* and *Dandy* illustrations by Sam Fair, who also drew Addie and Hermy, but had already received critical attention from David Low in the *Evening Standard* in a cartoon dated 6 April 1940 showing him as a non-belligerent sitting on a fence between British and German armies, refusing to commit himself.[10] With vanity and arrogance to complement his lack of intelligence and common sense, and nothing to compensate for his poor command of English, the Duce was, if anything, even more ridiculous than his German counterpart. Striding boastfully to deliver the news, sporting a wig made from a horse's tail, or failing to distinguish between real and exploding cigars have their inevitable consequences: the revenge of the broadcaster who sabotages his microphone, a rapid exit pursued by the offended horse, and an explosion that nearly blows his head off when he tries to light up. But perhaps the ultimate indignity is receiving a suggested variety of cures for insomnia sent to him by *Beano* readers in October 1941: a hammer to hit himself on the head, rat poison, and an old sock to "stuff in [his] big mouth."[11]

In fact, as this example suggests, in this Manicheistic genre the nation's enemies who tangle with the readers or their comic strip heroes always come off second best. Hitler is outwitted in the pages of the *Skipper* by child magician Wuzzy Wishbone, who has just joined the army and steals important military plans from under his nose while the carrier pigeons intended by a German spy to take secret information to the fatherland are shot down in the gardens of his stately home, Bunkerton Castle, by Lord Snooty and his friends. In a later *Beano* adventure (August 1942), Hitler himself tries to lead the invasion of England at the time of Bunkerton Garden Fete, only to fall into a trap set by the same Lord Snooty and his pals, who are rewarded with mammoth takings for the war effort. They receive a commendation from Churchill himself bearing the citation, "Never was so much collected, so quickly by so few," a transparent reference to a sentence from the prime minister's famous parliamentary speech made at the height of the Battle of Britain some two years before.[12]

FIGHTING THE GOOD (PATRIOTIC) FIGHT

The fact that such purely fictional exploits as Lord Snooty's or Wuzzy Wishbone's were clearly in the realm of children's fantasies did not limit their value, for even such hypothetical small victories were likely to remain in young readers' minds and to sustain morale. These were objectives not only of government information campaigns but also of the editors of funnies and story papers who were equally anxious to blend fact and fiction in order to encourage active participation in real war efforts. Their favourite comic human or animal heroes and heroines set the example for real youngsters to follow. A *Dandy* front page of August 1940 was a good example: Korky the cat was seen wearing the armband of the Local Defence Volunteers, putting to flight a band of Nazi parachute mice wearing helmets marked with swastikas.[13] In the same comic, Desperate Dan performed inspiring feats of enormous strength such as using his peashooter to bring down German aircraft and sink U-boats.

Ordinary readers could do none of these things, of course, but funnics and story papers were as anxious as the government to show them the smaller things they could do to participate in the war effort. In 1940, the editor of *Adventure* offered a full illustrated page of advice entitled "How a Boy Can Help to Win the War" (although the suggestions presumably applied to girls as well). These proposals for good citizenship included reporting anything or anybody suspicious to the police or military, not spreading rumours and discouraging others from doing so, collecting waste paper and metal, buying savings certificates to finance the war effort, calmly taking refuge in air raid shelters in the case of alerts, avoiding distracting soldiers on guard duty, and offering to carry messages after air raids. The fight against waste was a regular theme of government instructions to the population and featured fully in all media, but comics gave their own particular slants to the campaign. The 1940 *Dandy* and *Beano* shared a common advertisement frame urging children to collect waste paper which would be "used in the making of shells, bullets, depth charges, and even important parts of tanks." Entitled "Paper Helps to Make Hitler Bite the Dust," the advertisement featured smiling children carrying waste paper, dragging Hitler attached to a dog's lead behind them along the pavement. Captions for other similar advertisements with Hitler as target included "Paste Him with Paper" and "Hit Back at Hitler with Paper."

Story papers used a somewhat more elaborate register. For instance, an *Adventure* insert from January 1943 reminded its readers that even comics could be recycled for the war effort ("Any old magazine will help to fill his magazine. Our snipers will take care of the Huns if you take care of waste paper."). Desperate Dan reinforced the same message. In another 1940 *Dandy* vignette, adopting the posture of Kitchener's "Your Country Needs YOU" poster in 1914 and Churchill's recent "Deserve Victory!" Dan was shown, finger pointing straight at the reader, exclaiming "YOU can help Britain by collecting waste-paper." In a nod towards ongoing MOI campaigns, Pansy Potter, the *Beano*'s strongman's daughter, transformed herself into a sandwich girl to encourage readers to put their money into war savings. But this small frame insert had more than one target: a poster on the wall behind her bore the message "Kill Him with

War Savings" and contained a picture of the Squander Bug, an evil creature frequently found in MOI posters. The Squander Bug's true allegiance was indicated by the swastikas covering its body, and its purpose was always depicted as tricking the unwary into making unnecessary, wasteful purchases at a time when money could be much better spent, for instance on war savings, and when scarce space on cargo ships could be better occupied by more useful items. This single example therefore shows, once more, how efficient the visually based format used in funnies could be. Young readers were presented with two messages simultaneously in the same illustration by a familiar character, in some ways like themselves, which reminded them of other advice or warnings they had seen elsewhere and might want, as good citizens, to point out to others.

BATTLING THROUGH: TELLING "WARTIME" EVENTS DURING THE WAR

It would be misleading to suggest that the war was the only preoccupation of funnies and story papers in comic-land, for readers of both genres were anxious to continue to enjoy the adventures, tricks, and jokes which they had been accustomed to in peace time, and which helped editors both to retain their customers and to sustain morale and good humour as the government wished. Nevertheless, the task facing the two types of comics was different. As much of the material for the funnies was taken from the realms of fiction and fantasy suited to the younger readership, there was no need for explicit references to the war. Indeed, anything too specific could have upset the delicate balance of the real and the unreal on which the publications' success depended. For adventure story papers, however, there was a potential problem. Ongoing events could only be treated through the prism of fiction, as censorship severely restricted the supply of information, reliable or otherwise. But there was a risk that too great a dose of fantasy might clash with the other content of the papers and the expectations of their readers. In the event, the publications chose to favour the imaginative over the factual. As Adam Riches wrote about D.C. Thomson's "Big Five"[14] adventure papers, "Many of the characters in the comics had superhero qualities, and the stories often had a strong element of either science fiction or the supernatural – or both."[15]

To counter this danger, one method adopted by publishers both during and after the war to give added credibility to their work was recourse to familiarity by recycling stories in different comics and by creating new adventures for established characters with whom the reader was well acquainted. When the 1930s began, the mixture in boys' story papers[16] was the familiar diet of cowboy, spy, crime, school, adventure, and sports. The few war stories they contained were from the Great War, but as the threat of a new conflict and aerial invasion grew, there emerged spy and science fiction adventures, themes that were to form the backbone of wartime stories.[17] Meanwhile, 1938 and 1939 saw the birth of new heroes, Rockfist Rogan (*Champion*), and the secret air fighters of Q Squadron (*Hotspur*), along with the rediscovery of W.E. Johns's Biggles (*Modern Boy/Boy's Own Paper*), all of whom lived to fight another day in postwar comics.

A few wartime episodes had more than a ring of truth, or at least of plausibility, about them. Pupils at the *Hotspur*'s Red Circle School found themselves invaded in October 1939 by new arrivals from "a big town," a transparent reference to evacuation, and in January 1943 they had to share their accommodation with American troops in Britain preparing for the future reconquest of mainland Europe. An almost simultaneous cover of *Adventure* praised the exploits of heroes who escaped the Nazis (a British airman shot down in Norway, a French adjutant who flew across the English Channel in an ancient monoplane, five French boys who crossed the same water by canoe, a Scottish seaman who jumped from a prison train in France, an English governess employed in Poland, and a Belgian newspaper editor aided by a French Scarlet Pimpernel). But such details remained few and far between, and readers expecting firm news or even vaguely realistic accounts from the battlefronts were to be disappointed. Those who could believe in new wonder weapons could take satisfaction from reading of the airmen of Q Squadron deploying the Flyer Crusher (*Hotspur*, July 1943) to destroy German E-boats, even if the war ended before they could deploy the rocket-launching Flying Smasher (October 1945). In any case, by this time revolutionary technology had already come to the skies above Britain in the form of the V1s and V2s, and far worse was being planned by the Tube Alloys and Manhattan projects, which culminated in the making of the first atom bomb.

In hindsight, two other stories seem to touch on matters of great historical interest. "Seven Iron Crosses," set in Berlin and carried by *Adventure* in 1943, ended with the British getting their hands on the German Panzer Code, admittedly a much more exciting tale than the painstaking wartime work of the scientists at Bletchley Park, whose breaking of the German Enigma Code gave Britain and its allies a big advantage over the enemy. "The Ghost Voice Speaks" (*Rover*, March 1943) recounted the activities of a mystery man, known only by his code name Nemo, who had the technological equipment to interrupt broadcasts by Joseph Goebbels to the German nation and substitute them with his own subversive messages. This story recognizes the important role played by wartime propaganda, and is not without echoes of the "black propaganda" transmitted to German troops by the British Political Warfare Executive from a false German source, *Soldatensender Calais* (Soldiers' Radio Calais), from October 1943 onwards.

One other wartime story that stands out is "V for Vengeance" (*Wizard*, 1942), the first adventure of the "Deathless Men," escapees from concentration camps who had sworn to avenge themselves by killing leading Nazis. The first of their victims, Otto Leben, head of the Gestapo in Paris, is assassinated in this story. The exploits of the Deathless Men were (re)published in *Wizard* from 1959 onwards and in comic strip format in *Hornet* six years later, an example of the potential longevity of some adventures. The name Otto Leben is fictional, although other Nazis to be eliminated included Joseph Goebbels, Hermann Goering, Heinrich Himmler, and Adolf Hitler. If one leaves aside the improbability of anyone actually escaping from a concentration camp, the plot was notable for the suggestion that opposition to Nazism existed in Germany and occupied Europe, a substantial morale booster for British readers. Story papers may not have been able to tell the events of war as they happened, but what they did achieve, apart from vastly entertaining their readers, was, deliberately or inadvertently, to evoke hidden aspects of the war, some of which only came to public attention after the end of hostilities.

RETELLING NATIONAL HEROICS

For a number of reasons indicated above, recounting the events of the Second World War in real time was an impossible task for comicland, and the (re)telling the key events in the nation's overseas military participation could only really be done once the conflict was over. By this time, the interest of the war for the funnies had all but disappeared and this narration was left to the story papers, which nevertheless had a number of factors to bear in mind. Competition had arrived in the form of imported American comics which had been banned in 1939, while the amount of space available in any weekly number had to be shared between war stories and the other items the papers usually carried. Moreover, a balance had to be struck between fact and fiction, the credible and the implausible, in publications intended as entertainment rather than newspapers of record. This dilemma was heightened both by the fact that the need to sustain public morale and maintain the war effort no longer existed and that the end of censorship and the stories told by returning servicemen and servicewomen meant that there was a growing awareness of what the war had really been like. Last but not least, Britain's role in the conflict was not to be undervalued. It was necessary to stress the nation's contribution to victory by presenting the courage of its armed forces, through the valour of its real or fictional heroes, especially in view of the nation's lack of military success at least in the early part of the war, when the country was mostly on the defensive. The few small naval victories – the Battle of the River Plate (December 1939), the Battle of Taranto (November 1940), and the sinking of the *Bismarck* (May 1941) – were more than outweighed by the sinking of HMS *Hood* in May 1941. In addition, the disastrous loss of Singapore in 1942, after which some 100,000 Australian, British, and Indian POWs were to endure the horrors of Japanese captivity, was the worst disaster and largest capitulation in British military history.

The miraculous escape of most of the British Expeditionary Force from Dunkirk in June 1940 was seen as a happy and widely publicized omen for the future, but this was no military triumph for, as Churchill was quick to point out, "Wars are not won by evacuations."[18] The Battle of Britain that followed was an obvious success, with the prime minister and the nation paying tribute to the "few," the small number of (mostly young British) RAF pilots[19] who staved off assaults by the Luftwaffe that could have paved the way for an airborne or maritime German invasion. The tide finally turned with the British army's first major victory at the Battle of El Alamein in October-November 1942, which marked "the end of the beginning" of the war. British forces thereafter played their full part in the war in Italy, the successful D-Day landings, and subsequent fighting which led to the liberation of occupied Europe. These later successes were part of engagements so massive that they were initially beyond the scope of adventure story papers.

"SUPERHEROES" AND SMALL-SCALE VICTORIES

War comics were obliged to treat their subject with a degree of delicacy in the years immediately following the war. In order to show the British military in a positive light, some careful selection of material was required. Reflecting the Royal Air Force's high reputation earned in the Battle of Britain, the first major heroes were airmen. Battler Britain, Rockfist Rogan and Matt Braddock, VC and bar, may not have had the aura of American superheroes, but, as their names suggest, they were nonetheless remarkable characters, each with his own typically British eccentricities, who were to enjoy long careers stretching over several publications. Wing Commander Robert "Battler" Britton was a gentleman, as befitted a senior RAF officer, but loved killing and went into battle with a cry of tally-ho. Flight Lieutenant Rogan, a fearsome boxer as well as an ace flyer, had taken to the air as early as 1938 in *Champion*. The highly decorated Pilot Sergeant Braddock chose to remain a non-commissioned officer and was not afraid to contradict his superiors when he thought they were in the wrong, as they usually were in arguments with him. Such incidents evoked echoes of Kipling's famous line "the backbone of the Army is the Non-commissioned Man!"[20] which suggested that it was the NCOs, sergeants, and corporals, rather than the officers, who really knew how the military was run. In another typically British reference, Braddock's adventures were narrated by his admiring navigator George Bourne in Sherlock Homes/Doctor Watson fashion.

All three of these aces carried out their fictional heroics in the context of actual airborne missions, which added a (false) touch of reality to their adventures. As fighter pilots, Britton and Rogan fought in the Battle of Britain, while Braddock from Bomber Command participated in the attacks on the V2 rocket establishment in Peenemünde and the first thousand-bomber raid on Cologne. Some of the other comic-land stories from the 1940s and 1950s had a similar ring of truth about them. The exploits of British POWs tunnelling their way out of Calitz Camp (*Lion*, 1953) echoed, in name at least, the real break-out from Colditz, while pole-vault escapers featured in a 1957 number of *Tiger* recalled a successful escape by prisoners using a wooden vaulting horse to conceal both themselves and their equipment.[21] These were, however, no more than symbolic victories over the enemy. On the other hand, although isolated incidents, the activities of the Lone Commandos (*Lion*, 1952) and of the Lost Pals of Platoon 9 (*Lion*, 1953, 1956), operating respectively in occupied France and behind enemy lines in Italy, could be imagined as having had greater military significance. Moreover, they could not simply be dismissed as pure fiction, as they were similar to possible comparable secret missions in wartime. Though small-scale and conducted by elite troops rather than ordinary soldiers, these British victories left readers in no doubt about the competence and determination of the British military.

THE EAGLE'S MISSION, OR (RE)TELLING THE WHOLE TRUTH?

Only a month after VE Day, the June edition of *Boy's Own Paper* carried an article outlining the main events of the war, entitled "The Way We Came Through." This account was predictably too brief and too tinged with relief at the outcome to offer more than an outline of what the conflict had really been like. Even with increasingly greater distance from events, other story papers, concentrating on often imagined individual heroics or specific events, made no attempt to offer a fuller narrative. It fell to Rev. Marcus Morris, the founder and editor of *Eagle*, a relatively expensive but high-quality comic, to provide a full definitive British re-telling of the war. Morris, an Anglican clergyman from Lancashire, was a man with a mission, which he explained in the foreword to the *Best of Eagle*, published several years after the comic's demise. He wrote:

> The phenomenal rise and rule of the comic in America, plus a study of the papers and publications that children were reading in this country, seemed to point to an obvious moral – and hence came the idea of Eagle. Many American comics were most skilfully and vividly drawn, but often their content was deplorable, nastily over-violent and obscene, often with undue emphasis on the supernatural and magical as a way of solving problems. But it was clear to me that the strip cartoon was capable of development in a way not yet seen in England except in one or two of the daily and Sunday newspapers and that it was a new and

> important medium of communication, with its own laws and limitations. Here, surely, was a form which could be used to convey to the child the right kind of standards, values and attitudes, combined with the necessary amount of excitement and adventure.[22]

Eagle was not a war paper; its emphasis was on adventure and fantasy, as suggested by its iconic cover character, Dan Dare, "Pilot of the Future," but editor Marcus Morris regularly included true-life features in back-page serial strip cartoons. In 1957 and 1958, one such was devoted to the life of Winston Churchill, the "Happy Warrior." This serial hagiography made substantial use of exact references and quotations included in speech bubbles, and short scenes capturing the former prime minister's courage and thirst for action. It was made all the more attractive and dynamic by Frank Bellamy's striking and original illustrations of Clifford Makins's text. By alternating, in photographic fashion, between close-up and medium and distance views, using frames of different sizes and sometimes irregular shapes, highlighting key moments in vignettes distinct from the other pictures, and with illustrations in vivid or darker colours appropriate to the content, Bellamy was able to associate the qualities of "documentary" images and the rapid pace of battle.[23] The Second World War, Churchill's finest hour as well as the nation's, was given pride of place, with the truthful, albeit highly selective, coverage reinforcing what was already in popular memory and in the minds of the comic's young readers. All the key elements of what had become the official British version of events were included: the declaration of war; the phoney war; the parliamentary debate on the failed Norway campaign, after which Churchill replaced Neville Chamberlain as prime minister; the evacuation of Dunkirk and the Battle of Britain, both accompanied by extracts from Churchill's speeches in parliament and on BBC radio; the thwarted German invasion; the Blitz;[24] the battle of El-Alamein; the invasion of Italy; D-Day (dubbed "the greatest invasion in history"); and the progress on the Western Front, culminating in the announcement of victory in Europe, rapidly followed by Churchill's acknowledgement that he had been defeated in the general election and could no longer remain prime minister. *The Eagle*'s retelling of the war was faithful to Morris's intentions. Its tone was dignified, its approach was apparently unbiased, and, from the reader's point of view, it was exciting, educative, and informative. It was also to leave a mark in other ways on future stories relating war events for young people: it showed that real facts, adventure, and entertainment could coexist; it demonstrated the appropriateness of the comic strip technique for war adventures; and it reinforced the message that longer stories could be included provided an appropriate format was used.

"DIGESTING" WAR

Even before the "Happy Warrior," editors in comic-land had begun to realize that major stories or events could be covered in their publications. As early as 1951, Amalgamated Press (AP) had launched the *Thriller Picture Library*, introducing a new form of digest publication with each number containing a single comic strip story extending over sixty-four small pages. One such adventure in 1956 concerned "Battler" Britton, an RAF hero familiar to readers of the *Sun* acquired by AP in 1949. The company rapidly recognized it had discovered a winning formula to meet the demand for war stories and launched the dedicated *War Picture Library*, under its new name of Fleetway Publications, in September 1958. The first story, "Fight Back to Dunkirk," covered just the sort of conflict that adventure comics had previously felt themselves unable to handle: a long narrative of a campaign that had, despite all the British heroism depicted, what could only be an inconclusive outcome rather than a military triumph, since readers had more than a passing acquaintance of what had happened at Dunkirk. The success of the new venture was such that the new publication was joined within three years by the *Combat Picture Library*, Fleetway's *Battle Picture Library*, and D.C. Thomson's *Commando*, which survives to this day, albeit having left World War II behind to deal with more recent conflicts.

For readers, these new digests had a number of attractions over their predecessors: their more substantial and therefore more interesting story lines, and their ability to link fictional stories into an already familiar factual context. Major combats where the British military was heavily involved, such as the Battle of Britain or D-Day, could be included in more detail than in previous adventure stories. In short, as Mike Conroy puts it, "There was a reality to the stories lacking in the heroics of weekly comics; the heroes may have been larger than life but their exploits were no more outrageous than the tales the readers might have heard from their fathers and grandfathers. Death was also part of the contract."[25] In the early years too, writers based their stories on their own experiences, as they had seen combat themselves. Moreover, these digests focused exclusively on war stories and therefore aimed at a more specific target audience. Readers' expectations were met more readily and they could feel that the publications treated them with more respect, for "these books [could] be considered the first attempt to raise the age level of comics in Britain" as they were "produced for a higher age group than the comic weeklies, teenagers and up."[26] For writers and editors, of course, there was no reason why the same war context could not be used for several stories with the same heroes, thereby allowing more character development and cross publicity between publications from the same stable.

Faced with this competition and the changing expectations of readers, older-style adventure papers had to adapt. The newcomers of the early 1960s – *Victor* (1961), *Valiant* (1962), *Hornet* (1963), and *Hurricane* (1964) – all came in comic strip rather than text form. In the final years before it was absorbed into *Rover* in 1963, *Wizard* gave pride of place to war stories, carrying reruns of the adventures of the Deathless Men, the Nazi killers who had first appeared in 1942. It also included factual advice in 1959 to would-be soldiers on how to be good infantrymen, and revealed some of the tricks of the trade of a sniper, thereby allowing readers to appreciate the finer details of the stories they read, and perhaps to prepare for National Service, which was only finally abolished in 1963. *Victor* also added authenticity by including actual wartime events, thereby helping to fix them in collective memory. A number from August 1964 retold the scuttling of the German battleship *Graf Spee* after the Battle of the River Plate (1939), the event already having been made into a film in 1956, and the paper added real-life stories from the Second World War and earlier. This feature, notable for beginning on the front cover and finishing on the back cover of each number, recounted, for instance: the Zeebrugge Raid in 1918; the heroism of Captain Ervine-Andrews, who won the Second World War's first VC, awarded for his valour during the retreat to Dunkirk; the courage of the crew of HMS *Pangbourne* and the Gloucestershire Regiment, also at Dunkirk; and of Sergeants East and Mitchell of the Royal Marines.

The postwar evolution of war story papers may be said to have concluded with the creation of two more specialist publications, the highly popular *Warlord* (D.C. Thomson, 1974) and *Battle Picture*

Weekly (Fleetwood, 1975), which offered new perspectives on the representation of the war for younger readers. Both had their own recurrent, idiosyncratic (anti-)heroes. Lord Peter Flint and Union Jack Jackson in *Warlord*, and Major Eazy and the Rat Pack in *Battle*, were all unconventional: Jackson, a British commando fighting for the US Marines, attracted the ire of his fellow soldiers by the patriotic Union Jack he had drawn on his helmet; the Rat Pack (all ex-convicts) hated their CO more than they did the enemy; Major Eazy was so laid-back as to be the antithesis of a military officer; and Lord Peter was an upper-class conscientious objector, except when performing his day job as Warlord, a top secret agent. The papers offered a new, obviously fictional, take on wartime British heroism, but were innovative in other ways. *Warlord* invited readers to send in letters recounting their fathers' and grandfathers' personal memories of war experiences, or proposed they should relive the war vicariously by joining the Warlord Secret Agent Club. Additionally, the two papers even went so far as to suggest, however hesitantly, that the grievances of World War II might be allowed to disappear into the more distant past by running stories of good German soldiers obliged to fight on the Russian Front. *Battle*'s Panzer G-Man, Kurt Slinger, was accused of cowardice, and, as punishment, was forced to fight as a Panzer Grenadier alongside tanks while *Warlord*'s Major Heinz Falken was sent to a punishment battalion for failing to carry out atrocities during the 1940 Blitzkrieg as ordered by his commander. Mike Conroy argues,[27] perhaps tongue in cheek, that this device prevented war comics from having to show British troops being killed, but he also quotes *Warlord* editor Bill Graham who stresses that writers wanted to put an end to the jingoism prevailing until the 1970s and to "tell stories about all the fighting men in the major conflicts in a more realistic fashion."[28]

Wherever the truth in the argument lies, thirty years of peace in Western Europe had left their mark, while the Cold War continued, something for readers like editors to ponder. One later story included in *Battle* (1979) is worthy of particular mention for the light it casts on the retelling of war: *Charley's War*, written by Pat Mills and drawn by Joe Colquhoun. Carried away on a wave of patriotic fervour, young Charley lies about his age and enlists in the army, only to find himself at the age of sixteen a terrified participant in the horrors of the Battle of the Somme. He survives this engagement, and, with the support of his fellow soldiers, recovers sufficiently from the experience to continue fighting, although his best friend is killed and other mates are injured. Against all odds, Charley survives, thinking he has done his duty, only to be conscripted in 1939, and once more sent to France, evacuated from Dunkirk and left wondering why he became a soldier in the first place. This is where the story ends, although Mills had planned to finish it with Charley on the dole in 1933, hearing of Hitler's rise to power. Charley's story could be considered as tragic, and if it is not anti-military, it is at least anti-jingoistic and in line with the caveats that some of the later comic stories were, albeit timidly, suggesting to their readers about how war was portrayed.

CONCLUSION

Unlike press cartoons, whose primary target was not specifically British youth and which, by their very nature, mostly followed the ongoing political events that fuelled the day-to-day news and affected the understanding of immediate history and its potential repercussions, comics, broadly speaking, encompassed more global notions designed to condition (young) readers and to make them realize some of the implications of the wartime period, as well as indicating the proper behaviour to adopt as good British citizens. The aim was not to frighten or traumatize the young souls but rather to let them know that the country was living through an exceptional crisis which would undoubtedly be overcome by a heroic nation peopled by faithful and proud British patriots, embodying all the aspirations of "Rule Britannia." Conformity to the guiding values of the United Kingdom was central to the messages conveyed in the stories and adapted to the age(s) of the unquestioningly patriotic and un-rebellious readers. The lesson to be drawn was that they would one day be proud to prove their loyalty by fighting for their country because, in order to remain strong and powerful, any nation needs the stamina, courage, and determination of the new generations. In wartime, when being a winner is a prerequisite, being a hero is a must.

This theme underlies the stories conceived in the funnies for younger readers which concentrated on acts of imagined heroism but also emphasized the duty of all to play a full part in the everyday battles on the home front. The funnies were a good medium both to entertain and to educate children, demonstrating that respect for British values was a major key to success. For this young, captive readership, awareness of real facts about military campaigns or decisions taken by the politicians involved in the meanders of a war was not essential. The ongoing events of war could only be fictionalized; censorship prevented anything like reliable or complete information from being available and, in any case, credibility was not a key objective. Indeed, fiction was surely the most efficient way to narrate the unspeakable and helped to build hope and nurture the seeds of victory as, inevitably in times of worldwide conflicts, one has to be economical with the truth in the interest of state security.

Nevertheless, the representation of WWII in comics was true to itself and respectful of the country's well-being and of the young readers' sensitivities and emotions. After the war, there seemed to be a need to perpetuate and preserve collective memory and national heritage, as WWII was integrated into adventure and action stories. These plots for older youngsters were more elaborate: they emphasized risks and danger; they magnified the deeds and exploits of the combatants; and they retold and highlighted events, some of which were in the public domain while others had been deliberately kept secret or indulged in the fantasy of fiction weaving together imagination, testimonies, and real facts as narrated in British history books. Through all this, of course, the heroes were British, though it is noticeable that as the war became more remote in time, the assessment of former enemies became less hostile. Memories of WWII resurface whenever the nation is involved in other conflicts (like the Falklands War) or when British mobilisation and patriotism are required. The Second World War has remained the yardstick by which the country's wartime determination and sacrifice are judged and the telling and retelling of this conflict in comic-land (funnies and adventure papers) has helped to set the criteria by which later military engagements have been assessed.

NOTES

1 To quote the title of volume 3 of Asa Briggs's monumental *History of Broadcasting in the United Kingdom* (Oxford: Oxford University Press, 1970).

2 British and American governments both used this euphemism for their organisations designed to influence public opinion (Ministry of Information and Office of War Information). Nazi Germany included

both Propaganda and Popular Enlightenment (*Volksaufklärung*) in the title of the ministry run by Joseph Goebbels.

3 See http://www.paulgravett.com/articles/article/encarta (accessed April 2015). Contrary to what might be expected, a comic is not necessarily humorous and in this paper the word is used generically and may apply, according to the context, either to funnies or to adventure/story/boys papers; the sub-genres are distinguished where necessary.

4 Paul Gravett and Peter Stanbury, *Great British Comics* (London: Aurum, 2006).

5 Adam Riches, Tim Parker, and Rober Frankland, *When the Comics Went to War* (Edinburgh: Mainstream, 2009); G. Orwell, "Boys' Weeklies," in *Horizon,* No. 3 (London: Victor Gollancz, 1940); Gravett and Stanbury, *Great British Comics.*

6 Denis Gifford, *International Book of Comics* (London: Hamlyn, 1984); Mike Conroy, *War Comics: A Graphic History* (Lewes: Ilex, 2009).

7 The *Daily Express* continued to publish Rupert Bear cartoons throughout WWII even when shortage of newsprint limited the paper to a single double page. Polite, well educated, and proudly British, Rupert was a role model for his young readers. On the other hand, the *Daily Mirror*'s comic strip adventures of the glamorous Jane, who shed more and more clothes as the war developed, did much to sustain the morale of troops serving at home and abroad.

8 The assonance and alliteration are obviously deliberate, but more significant perhaps is the linguistic register suited to children. The term has connotations of the repugnant, unpleasant, spiteful, and unwelcome, but not the evil or the frightful, which seems entirely appropriate to the desired emotional reaction of young readers. Additionally, the portrayal of the two leading Nazis evokes memories of W.K. Haselden's dismissive cartoons of Big and Little Willie, his names for the Kaiser and his son, which appeared in the *Daily Mirror* during the Great War.

9 Lord Haw-Haw was the nickname given to William Joyce, an Irishman who broadcast to Britain over the airwaves of the German official radio station *Reichssender Hamburg* between 1939 and 1945. During the Phoney War, before hostilities started in earnest, Haw-Haw attracted a considerable audience.

10 To great British displeasure, Fascist Italy delayed entering the war, on the German side, until the defeat of France in 1940 was almost complete.

11 As quoted in the cartoon: "stuff in your big mouth."

12 Winston Churchill, "Never in the field of human conflict was so much owed by so many to so few," speech to the House of Commons, 20 August 1940.

13 Behind the fantasy of the story lies solid historical fact. The Local Defence Volunteers (later renamed the Home Guard) had been founded in May 1940 on the initiative of Anthony Eden, Secretary of State for War. The volunteers, men too old or unfit for military service, were deployed in their home areas prepared to defend the country against airborne or maritime invasion. In August 1940, like Korky, they were still awaiting their uniforms.

14 Thomson's Big Five were *Adventure* (1921–), *Wizard* (1921–), *Rover* (1922–), *Skipper* (1930–) and *Hotspur* (1933–). All survived the war except *Skipper*, which ceased publication in 1941. Riches's comments could equally apply to Thomson's rival, Amalgamated Press (AP, subsequently to become Fleetway and later IPC), whose *Gem*, *Magnet*, and *Triumph* were withdrawn in 1940, leaving the publisher with only *Champion* (1922–) and *Knockout*, acquired from J.B. Allen in 1939 and renamed *Knockout Comic and Magnet* in 1940. The only other surviving wartime story paper was the venerable *Boys Own Paper* founded in 1879.

15 Riches, Parker, and Frankland, *When the Comics Went to War*, 98.

16 Girl readers also enjoyed some of the material in boys' papers even though there were publications such as *Crystal*, the *Girl's Friend*, and *Schoolgirl* with stories specially written for them. Only *Crystal* was still in print at the end of the war. These publications are beyond the scope of this chapter.

17 The story of Huncher Newman, a British secret agent installed at Belwood School and working on a secret electric ray that could bring down enemy aircraft, was carried by *Hotspur* throughout 1939, providing continuity between pre-war and wartime numbers.

18 Speech to the House of Commons, 4 June 1940.

19 Twenty per cent of the pilots were from outside the UK. The largest foreign contingent was Poles. Kelly Bell, "The Forgotten Few: Polish Airmen Fought during the Battle of Britain," March 2007 (originally published in *Aviation History* magazine). http://www.historynet.com/the-forgotten-few-polish-airmen-fought-during-the-battle-of-britain.htm.

20 In "The 'Eathen," a poem written in 1896 by Rudyard Kipling and published in the collection *The Seven Seas*.

21 These exploits were already in the public domain at the time of the adventure story publications. Pat Reid's autobiographical account of the *Colditz Story* first appeared in 1952, while the story of the *Wooden Horse* had been filmed in 1950.

22 M. Morris, *The Best of the Eagle* (London: Ebury Press, 1977).

23 The visual quality of *Eagle*'s account of the war must not be underestimated. There are striking similarities between some of the frames and vignettes of the "Happy Warrior" and panels in the Overlord Embroidery in the D-Day Museum in Portsmouth, UK.

24 The standard term for the bombing of British cities, a misuse of the name of the successful German military technique on mainland Europe, *Blitzkrieg* or "lightning war."

25 Conroy, *War Comics*, 108.

26 Gifford, *The International Book of Comics*, 147.

27 Conroy, *War Comics*, 120.

28 Bill Graham, *Warlord*, quoted in Conroy, *War Comics*, 120.

13

War Memory in British Soldier Songs of the First World War

JOHN MULLEN

In what is no doubt the biggest wave of commemoration events in British history, the myriad activities organized for the centenary of the outbreak of the Great War have made it clear to more people than ever that "remembering" is not simply recalling the past, but seeing the past, in the words of Paul Fussell, "remembered, conventionalized, and mythologized."[1] In this contribution I would like to look at how one particular cultural object – the soldiers' song – has been used over the last century to revive a memory of the war, for particular and varying objectives.

THE MAJOR CHARACTERISTICS OF SOLDIERS' SONGS

Soldiers' songs are generally anonymous, invented by troops to sing in groups, whether on the march or at rest behind the lines. They are sometimes referred to as "trench songs," though in front-line trenches they may not have been much used. They were not written to be sold, and so are distinct from commercial music-hall songs performed at theatres such as "It's a Long Way to Tipperary" or "Oh, What a Lovely War!" They are normally only a few lines long, and are set to well-known tunes, since their inventors were rarely trained musicians. The tunes come from music hall hits or from hymns, and the songs often exist in a series of variants, since each group of singers might add or change a verse or two.

Soldiers' songs have existed since well before 1914,[2] but the fact that First World War armies were exceptionally large, and immobile for long periods, made for a much richer production. There was even, during the war, a certain popularization of some soldiers' songs among civilians via the music hall; a few singers, such as male impersonator Hetty King, produced on-stage medleys of "songs the soldiers sing."

The First World War soldier songs are available to us because of collections published either at the time, often by officers (since they had more access to publishing),[3] or by veterans after the war, who collected them through associations such as the British Legion, or through appeals in the press.[4] Sometimes collections of "songs the soldiers sang" do not distinguish between music hall songs and soldiers' songs.[5] This is unfortunate, because the filters the two genres needed to pass through to become popular were quite different.

I have previously worked on a corpus of 160 soldiers' songs. Most of these were in published collections, although some were quoted in the press during the war or appeared in personal diaries. The repertoire for such an ephemeral type of singing was varied and unstable. A local newspaper, *The Burnley News*, declared in 1919:

> Nearly every unit in the British army has songs in its repertoire that are their own peculiar treasure and are not sung by anyone else. These are usually composed by the company "funny man" ... These songs however, have often only quite a short reign of popularity and are soon discarded and never sung again.[6]

The British soldiers' song repertoire is widely recognized as dissenting in character, making them very different from commercial music hall songs.[7] Dissenting music hall songs were rare because of the centrality of sing-along to the music hall experience. The singer was expected to persuade almost the whole of the audience to sing along with the chorus. If half refused to sing, the turn would be deemed a failure, and the singer might well find himself/herself without further bookings. Thus anti-war songs were not sung, since they would neither achieve consensus among the audience nor be favoured by generally conservative theatre managers anxious to gain valued respectability by showcasing their patriotism.[8]

The soldiers' songs, if they were to catch on, had also to be consensual, but within a much more restricted social group: the lower ranks of the army, solidly made up of working class men. Superior officers were likely to be absent during the singing, or "turning a deaf ear." It is very significant, then, that the soldiers' songs are uncompromisingly dissenting and reject warmongering, hatred of Germans, and glory of war discourses. They almost never go so far, however, as to be pacifistic or mutinous for the same reason: the need to achieve consensus within the immediate groups who are being expected to sing along.

It is essential to remember that the soldier songs do not represent the only group-singing activity of the lower ranks. They also sang, in unison, music hall hits and religious hymns. The soldiers' songs constitute in fact a supplementary repertoire, used to express sentiments which are not provided for by the other repertoires. Thus, none of the soldiers' songs are love songs because recruits' knowledge of music hall songs was sufficient to provide any love song required – there was no need to invent any. Similarly, the sentiment of trusting resignation in God or destiny, well-provided for in popular hymns, is not found in the soldiers' songs. The two main types of sentiment not provided by other repertoires are the vulgar and the dissenting, as briefly illustrated by these two extracts from songs:

1 Do your balls hang low
Do they dangle to and fro
Can you tie them in a knot
Can you tie them in a bow?
Can you sling them on your shoulder
Like a lousy fucking soldier
Do your balls hang low?[9]

2 Greeting to the Sergeant
You've got a kind face you old bastard
You ought to be bloody well shot
You ought to be tied to a gun wheel
And left there to bloody well rot[10]

"PATRIOTIC" WAR MEMORY AND THE SOLDIERS' SONGS

The repertoire of soldier songs becomes, after the war, a part of war memory which can be either forgotten or (selectively) revived and used for different ideological purposes. There had been collections of soldiers' songs published while the war was still going on, but two ex-soldiers decided in 1930 they wanted a more comprehensive collection. This was the now classic publication edited by John Brophy and Eric Partridge entitled *The Long Trail: What the British Soldier Sang and Said in 1914–1918*. At fourteen years old, Brophy had joined the army as an underage volunteer, and later in his life became a journalist on the *Daily Telegraph*. Partridge, who was somewhat older, had been a schoolteacher before the Great War, served in the Australian army, and would later become known as a writer, producing, in particular, a series of dictionaries of slang. Indeed, in addition to a few dozen songs, the 1930 volume contained a dictionary of soldier slang and a substantial explanatory introduction. The songs were sorted into categories including: "Songs Sung on the March," "Songs Sung Either on the March or in the Billets," and "Songs Rarely If Ever Sung on the March." The categorization shows the almost anthropological interest of the editors in transmitting some of the texture of the ordinary frontline soldiers' lives. It also suggests the nostalgic revival that was part of the writers' objective.

Sadly, it is not the case that a dozen different ex-soldiers collected songs and published their views about the meanings of the songs. Rather, we have just the one book with just one viewpoint. It is valuable and interesting, but we must take into account that an ex-soldier who becomes a journalist with the *Daily Telegraph*, a British newspaper with a very precise political orientation, may well not be representative. The question of why only one such book should appear is likely to be linked to the fact that before the Second World War, publishing interest in the First World War focused on general questions of strategy and battle tactics, or on diplomatic and political analyses. The experience of the ordinary soldier was thought an unsuitable subject for study. It is also well documented that a large proportion of ordinary soldiers preferred not to discuss their war experience, often not even with close family members.

Brophy and Partridge's book was well received, and the work was republished in 1930, 1931, 1965, 1969, 1972, and 2008. The collection not only circulated the memory of the songs, but also a discourse on the nature of the repertoire. This discourse insisted firstly on the authenticity of these "grass roots" songs, representing the war memory of the ordinary soldier, very distant from either official anthems or high culture musical productions such as Benjamin Britten's *War*

Requiem or Ravel's *La Valse*. As the *Evening Telegraph* declared, these pieces "come from the ranks, especially from the private soldiers without ambition to bear office or special responsibility."[11] Brophy's introduction to a later edition also stressed authenticity:

> They are the songs of homeless men, evoked by exceptional and distressing circumstances; the songs of an itinerant community, continually altering itself under the incidence of death and mutilation.[12]

Secondly, the dissenting tone of much of the repertoire was underlined:

> One of the major themes of the soldiers' songs was the theme of satire, on the war, and on all kind of mock heroics. They blatantly denied the sugary patriotism, the "let me like a soldier fall" attitude, and brought out all the bitterness, the disillusionment, in a spirit of jocular irony.[13]

Indeed, sentiments such as the following are quite typical:

> What did you join the Army for?
> Why did you join the Army?
> What did you join the Army for?
> You must have been bloody well barmy!

On the song "I Want to Go Home,"[14] the 1930 reviewer commented:

> I think there is infinite pathos in that song. It marks the first disillusionment of the volunteer when he discovered that war is not romantic, and that the Germans were not subhuman.[15]

Establishment commentators have regularly seemed ill at ease with the dissenting content, and attempted to find ways to reduce its impact. A Scottish journalist in September 1939 (no doubt a time when the eventuality of cynical soldiers was a sensitive subject) insisted:

> Tommy loved "safety valve" songs. Anyone unaccustomed to the workings of the British mind might have thought melancholy

> ditties were an indication of a weakening morale. But it was only the British way of keeping ourselves cheery by exercising our traditional right to grumble.[16]

This term "grumbling" will be heard right up to the present day from those who wish to insist that the dissenting content of soldier songs is not to be taken seriously. The term, however, is problematic: to grumble is, according to the *New Oxford Dictionary*,[17] "to complain or protest about something in a bad-tempered but typically muted way." Can the bitter and even murderous tone of some of these songs[18] really be reduced to being "bad-tempered," a question of individual mood? And is public group singing a "muted" form of protest? This definition of soldiers' songs as "grumbling" is an example of the conventionalizing and mythologizing of which Fussel speaks. The tremendous postwar popularity of a song like "Pop Goes the Major," a 1920s music hall song whose subject is the joy of finding one's superior officer from wartime and burning him alive,[19] suggests a more solid content to the dissent in soldiers' songs, as does the tremendous force within war memories of a "lions led by donkeys" view of hierarchical relations inside the army.

Along with dismissal as "grumbling," a more sophisticated opinion frequently encountered is that which sees dissenting singing as a deliberate way of exorcising one's own cynicism and demoralization. This is suggested already in the 1930 review:

> But, although [the soldier song repertoire] expresses the soldiers' war weariness, it also conquers it with ridicule, and that was how they kept going … Messrs Brophy and Partridge have produced a most unusual book that brings back the spirit of the war, and the spirit that won the war.[20]

Malcolm Brown, author of a dozen titles on the First World War, writes in the introduction to the 2000 edition of Brophy and Partridge's collection a similar view:

> Oh yes, there's anger and cynicism, and a world-weary longing for the whole damned thing to be over, and couldn't we all go back to dear old Blighty? But there's also a strong sense that by slagging off the war, and finding ways of laughing, even jeering, at it, the men deputed to fight it could find a courage that gave them the determination to win through.[21]

John Brophy, in his own introduction to the 1965 edition, seems to go even further:

> When the romantic conception of war proved false, out of date, useless, the man in the line was helped in his daily endurances if he could ridicule all heroics and sing, with apparent shamelessness "I Don't Want to Be a Soldier" or "Far Far from Ypres I Long to Be." These songs satirized more than war: they poked fun at the soldier's own desire for peace and rest, and so prevented it from overwhelming his will to go on doing his duty. They were not symptoms of defeatism, but strong bulwarks against it.[22]

So the memory of war presented in these largely dissenting songs is reinterpreted in a way that the traditional narrative of determined troops who do not doubt can be maintained. Brophy's rhetoric seems effective, and allows conservative opinion to embrace the soldiers' songs in war memory. It is notable that the newspaper that in 2008 republished the Brophy and Partridge collection was the *Daily Telegraph*, generally recognized as the most conservative of the serious daily newspapers. It was not the *Guardian* or the *Independent*, which might be expected to be more open to antimilitarist sentiment.

Although it is obviously true that the songs helped the soldiers survive, it by no means follows that their main effect was to increase the determination of the troops to fight. As Tony Ashworth's work comprehensively shows,[23] soldiers frequently had other priorities, such as working out how to avoid fighting without being caught by superior officers. Even if, as ex-soldiers themselves, Brophy and Partridge deserve their voice to be heard, does this discourse not represent a case of dominant ideology reinterpreting the voice of the dominated? Through their songs, the soldiers seem to be showing their hatred of their superior officers and their cynicism about official patriotism, but we are told that this only appears to be the case. Popular grassroots expression is reduced by post hoc cultural revisionism to a simple means of psychological relief aiming to reinforce fighting spirit.

My analysis does not of course imply that the dissenting tone of the British soldier songs shows a structured pacifist ideology or a reasoned political opposition to the Empire's war aims. In a situation where practically all the available political leadership – union leaders, feminist leaders, and influential intellectuals – campaign in favour of the war, a politicized opposition was simply not available to most rank and file soldiers.

"ANTIMILITARIST" WAR MEMORY AND THE SOLDIERS' SONGS

After this patriotic/nostalgic configuration, the second major way in which these songs have been used to revive and create memories is by antimilitarist groups, singers, and writers. By far the most important example of this has been a series of artistic productions, of which the stage musical *Oh What a Lovely War!*, first produced in 1963, is the best known.[24] This production was inspired by a radio documentary, *The Long, Long Trail.* Its creator, Charles Chilton,[25] whose father had died at the age of nineteen in the First World War, wished to find more information about his father's experience. He said he was looking for "the true songs of the trenches" which would show, he believed, an authentic expression of grassroots experience. The resulting programme was broadcast on the BBC in 1961, and contained a mix of historical information, music hall songs, and soldiers' songs. The tone was one of disgust with the war.[26]

After hearing *The Long, Long Trail*, Joan Littlewood and her theatre workshop collaborated with Chilton and others to produce their innovative musical production. Littlewood was an influential experimental theatre director, best known for her productions of Brecht's plays and *A Taste of Honey* by Shelagh Delaney. In *Oh What a Lovely War!*, the Great War is presented as an Edwardian end-of-the-pier Pierrot show. In the first act the audience is encouraged to sing along with jingoistic music hall songs from the first few months of the conflict, such as "We Don't Want to Lose You, but We Think You Ought to Go." In the second act, they sing along mostly with the soldiers' songs, which represent the disillusion and anger of the ordinary soldiers crushed by a military machine serving elite interests. The bitterly sarcastic presentation of the war as a Pierrot show is intended to echo the tone of the dissenting soldiers' songs, though unlike the soldier song repertoire, the show communicates a coherent political critique of the war as the result of a society divided between ordinary people only good for cannon fodder, and an extremely rich elite who profit from the division and re-division of the world between competing empires.

From the point of view of war memory, it is important to note that Littlewood not only proposes to audiences a particular discourse on the war, presenting soldier songs as particularly suitable vehicles to transmit a truth she considers hidden by official discourses, but she also proposes a war memory activity: that of sing-along. Singing in unison has been defined by musicologist Philip Tagg as "a rather obvious aural icon of individuals sharing (supposedly or actually) a common cause, or identity, or set of values and beliefs."[27] That is to say that, as the soldiers' songs were in their original contexts, the songs of *Oh What a Lovely War!* are proposed in the theatre for group singing. In each situation, the attempt to build a public emotional expression of anti-war consensus is the aim.

The theatre production, which was a tremendous critical success, soon moved to the West End.[28] Littlewood was keen that the anti-war message should be the most prominent element: a scoreboard on stage showed the rising death toll throughout the war. On the US stage it was replaced by a count of US citizens who became millionaires by selling arms during the war, an addition that caused frequent walkouts from the more expensive seats.[29] In the French production in Paris in 1963, the Chanson de Craonne, a well-known antimilitarist song from 1917, was sung on stage, although at the time the song was still banned.

Those who have the dough, they'll be coming back,
'Cause it's for them that we're dying.
But it's all over now, 'cause all of the grunts
Are going to go on strike.
It'll be your turn, all you rich and powerful gentlemen,
To go up onto the plateau.
And if you want to make war,
Then pay for it with your own skins.

There is conventionalizing and mythologizing in *Oh What a Lovely War!* too, of course, notably in the presentation of the soldiers' songs as a relatively pure authentic voice of the lower ranks to be contrasted with the jingoistic music hall. In fact, a mix of music hall songs and soldier songs is used. The title song "Oh What a Lovely War" is not a soldier song, but a music hall hit, and its existence underlines the fact that the dichotomy of music hall songs/soldier songs has been much exaggerated. If there are practically no jingoistic soldier songs, there is significant dissent expressed in the music hall repertoire.[30]

Despite Littlewood's determination that the radical message not be lost, not all antimilitarists were happy with the production. Some were very conscious of the complexity of presenting an anti-war message through sing-along: Littlewood's husband, communist singer and actor Ewan MacColl, accused the show of leaving audiences "feeling nice and comfy, in a rosy glow of nostalgia."[31] Littlewood, for her part, comments on the effects of her presentation of war memory:

> *Oh What a Lovely War* awakened race memory in our audiences. At the end of each performance people would come on stage bringing memories and mementoes, even lines of dialogue which sometimes turned up in the show.[32]

Littlewood's claim is that her production revived and revealed important truths about the war at this time when veterans were still common. Recently, this claim has been vigorously contested by important commentators, such as the British Education Secretary Michael Gove, who claimed in 2014:

> The conflict has, for many, been seen through the fictional prism of dramas such as *Oh! What a Lovely War*, *The Monocled Mutineer and Blackadder*, as a misbegotten shambles – a series of catastrophic mistakes perpetrated by an out-of-touch elite. Even to this day there are Left-wing academics all too happy to feed those myths.[33]

Mr Gove is not alone: the play has become a frequent target for historians who have chosen the label "revisionist" and who wish to defend different aspects of Empire policy from 1914 to 1918. In his 2002 book, Brian Bond writes, "For a new generation in the 1960s the play and film of *Oh What a Lovely War* had a dramatic effect … Until … recently, historians had either reinforced the myths, or had failed to counter them."[34] Others go further: "Who will not have seen the scurrilous 1960s film *Oh What a Lovely War!* or the equally reprehensible and more recent BBC production *Blackadder*,"[35] writes Frank Davies, while Wolfson history prize winner Andrew Roberts, in his *A History of the English-Speaking Peoples since 1900*, also denounces its "outrageous lampooning."[36]

The stage show was succeeded by a film version, directed by Richard Attenborough and starring Susannah York, John Gielgud, Laurence Olivier, Vanessa Redgrave, and Dirk Bogarde. Attenborough was able to get the funding to produce the film by impressing the financiers with a star-studded cast. The film was the sixteenth most popular movie at the UK box office in 1969.[37]

Given the fact that the film's box office results were not those of a smash hit, that the theatre show was not shown professionally in the theatre for over twenty years, and the first DVD release of the film was in 2006, ten years after DVD film formats became common,[38] it seems highly unlikely that the musical had the decisive effect on popular views of the war which some have claimed. Its lasting influence in some circles, though, is attested by its prominent presence in 2014 on the BBC History website.[39]

THE SONGS IN THE TWENTY-FIRST CENTURY AND TENSIONS WITHIN DISCOURSES

We have seen, then, the soldiers' songs used by two politically dissimilar traditions. The question of why this is possible will be dealt with in the conclusion, but first I would like to present some very recent uses of the songs, which sometimes reveal tensions inside the two discourses.

The development of the internet and particularly of YouTube has made visible uses of the soldiers' songs in local or marginal events which would previously have been invisible. I have collected a few examples, which involve some of the most well known of these songs. The one most frequently sung is "Hanging on the Old Barbed Wire," one of the most bitter of the pieces, which includes the following lyrics:

If you want to find the Sergeant
I know where he is (x3)
He's lying on the canteen floor
I saw him, I saw him
Lying on the canteen floor I saw him,
Lying on the Canteen floor

The brass hats … Drinking claret at Brigade HQ.
The general: pinning another medal on his chest.
The politicians … Drinking brandy at the House of Commons bar.

If you want the old battalion
I know where they are (x3)

They're hanging on the old barbed wire.
I saw them, I saw them
Hanging on the old barbed wire I saw them
Hanging on the old barbed wire.[40]

Cover versions of such songs constitute a commemorative activity, and in most cases it is part of an antimilitarist and anti-establishment activist discourse. The highly successful Leeds rock group Chumbawumba included the song in 2008 on their album *English Rebel Songs 1381–1914* alongside songs about the fourteenth-century Peasants' Revolt, radical Diggers during the English Civil War, and the Chartist Movement of the mid-nineteenth century.[41]

The songs fit most readily into musical genres which have been constituted as dissenting, in particular folk genres and punk rock. In 2007, Frank McConnell produced a folk version (few instruments, regional accent) of "Hanging on the Old Barbed Wire" accompanied by two other, somewhat suggestive, soldiers' songs: "That's the Wrong Way to Tickle Marie" and "Mademoiselle from Armentiers."[42] The CD also contains readings of a series of war poems of which the dominant theme is antimilitarist. In 2007, Peter Rothstein produced a theatre show entitled *All is Calm – the Christmas Truce of 1914*, a recounting of the 1914 truce, with several soldiers' songs including "We're Here Because We're Here," "I Want to Go Home," and "Hanging on the Old Barbed Wire," as well as a series of carols and quotations from interviews with soldiers. The show went on stage in the United States between 2007 and 2014, and was also produced for the radio. In the United Kingdom, Folk at the Oak, a series of local folk concerts in Crick Northamptonshire, used both "Hanging on the Old Barbed Wire" and "I Don't Want to Be a Soldier."[43] In a 2011 concert, David Olney, a folk singer, sang an *a capella* version of "Hanging on the Old Barbed Wire." The US punk group Sucker Punched by Christ produces an accelerated version with prominent drums and angry punk voicing, the singer stripped to the waist, a style perhaps particularly suited to the bitter tone of the song.[44]

Not all uses of the soldiers' songs in recent years are in antimilitarist or anti-establishment contexts, however. The version by The Spinning Jennys,[45] whose band name evokes "the olden days" and who sing dressed in Edwardian clothing with a Union Jack draped on their piano, is followed by singing of music hall songs such as "A Long Way to Tipperary" and "Pack Up Your Troubles." The general tone of the concert seems to be nostalgia, so the cynical soldiers' song might seem out of place.

More distant still from antimilitarism is the case of the Military Wives Choir. This singing group is a pro-military initiative aimed at raising public support for British soldiers and ex-soldiers, particularly in the context of the first ten years of the twenty-first century when mass public opposition to British military interventions, actual or potential, in Iraq, Afghanistan, Iran, and Syria has been so vocal.[46] The choir sang the following soldiers' song at a number of their concerts:

The Bells of Hell go ting-a-ling-a-ling
For you but not for me:
For me the angels sing-a-ling-a-ling,
They've got the goods for me.
Oh! Death, where is thy sting-a-ling-a-ling?
Oh! Grave, thy victory?
The Bells of Hell go ting-a-ling-a-ling
For you but not for me.

This soldiers' song, initially reported as being sung sardonically by soldiers leaving the trenches to their replacement regiments, was part of the Military Wives Choir concert in York in October 2013.[47] The singers sang in evening dress, in a traditional choral style accompanied by a grand piano, and the song was inserted into a medley with "The Bells Are Ringing for Me and My Gal," a 1917 wedding song used in the 1942 musical comedy of the same name.

Another use of a soldiers' song by institutions close to the military establishment is contained in the poetry reading organized in April 2014 by the Royal United Services Institute (RUSI) conflict war and culture event, in partnership with the Josephine Hart Poetry Foundation. The Royal United Services Institute presents itself as "an independent think tank engaged in cutting edge defence and security research. A unique institution, founded in 1831 by the Duke of Wellington."[48] Other recent RUSI events include "General Stanley McChrystal on Operational Leadership," the "Chief of Defence Staff Lecture," and "Anders Fogh Rasmussen on NATO and Missile Defence." At their cultural event, top British actor Rupert Evans read "I Don't Want to Be a Soldier" in formal poetry reading style, complete with cravat and leather-backed chair.

I don't want a bayonet up my arsehole
I don't want my bollocks shot away
I'd rather stay in England
In merry merry England
And fuck my bloody life away.

These examples bring up the question of appropriation, to whom the soldiers' songs might be seen to belong. As a number of commentators have pointed out, military policy in contemporary society requires ideological campaigns at home. Lindsay German of the Stop the War Campaign writes that, "Given that wars tend to be unpopular, the government and military try to recast appeals for war as support for individual troops."[49] The use of soldiers' songs to showcase concern for the lives of individual soldiers can be part of attempts to defend British military policies. For antimilitarists, on the contrary, First World War soldier songs are presented as belonging to the tradition of opposing elite plans which are against the interests of the mass of the people.

Tensions in antimilitarist uses of the soldiers' songs can appear. In Derby, for the centenary of the outbreak of the First World War, the musical play *Oh What a Lovely War!* was produced. This might appear to be a clearly antimilitarist choice. Nevertheless, one sees the following note: "Tickets are priced £6, with £1 from each sale being donated between The British Legion and Help for Heroes." The choice of charities, in particular Help for Heroes, participated in the opposite discourse, since a "hero" is necessarily someone wounded or killed in a worthwhile cause (brave serial killers are not called heroes). The Help for Heroes website is clearly not antimilitarist, as the founder makes it clear that "I loved my time in the army."[50] The choice of these charities is likely to be a response to common opinions of which tradition the songs should belong to, and the naming of two charities is probably a sign that there was some disagreement involved. In late 2014, another production of the show announced that profits would be given to a hospital for military veterans.[51]

CONCLUSION

One of the reasons these songs speak to us today is because of what they say about human beings faced with extreme, life-threatening situations. This is, perhaps, just one more aspect of a more general characteristic of cultural production: the preference of cinema, television, and even visual art for extreme situations – murders, kidnappings, catastrophes – is well known. For creating and communicating war memories, we have shown that soldiers' songs are highly flexible objects. French historian Nicolas Offenstadt categorized discourses on war memory as made up of three major strands: genealogical or family discourses, local pride discourses, and activist discourses.[52] Soldiers' songs can be seen as belonging to two separate activist discourses. Antimilitarists who stage or support the 2014 production of the musical comedy *Oh What a Lovely War!* are hoping it will encourage anti-war feeling and activism, which in the Britain of the last fifteen years has been at its highest point for several decades. For the Military Wives Choir or the *Daily Telegraph*, the celebration of these songs of "modest heroes" fits with campaigns of solidarity with "our soldiers" in these twenty-first-century wars. This celebration is part of a right wing populist discourse which takes for granted the general correctness of the military policy of the British state, and campaigns for more recognition of the cost to ordinary soldiers; such discourses also hope to mute opposition to British foreign policy.

How can many of the same songs be used in such radically different ways? In fact, the anti-militarists and the military populists have some things in common. Both share, along with a large section of the population, a desire to explore close-up the texture and feelings of life in the trenches. This experiential approach to the war has been dominant in the centenary, as witnessed by the new galleries at the Imperial War Museum, or their campaign "Lives of World War One."[53] Both groups want to privilege the voice of the ordinary soldier. For the military populists, the heroes who fought for the Empire deserve listening to and having their life in wartime vividly recounted, despite the dissenting tone of much of the soldier song repertoire. At the end of the day, these soldiers won, and clear victories for Britain have been much rarer these last decades, leading to an increased concentration in conservative circles on past glories. The fact that the dissenting tone of the songs had often been toned down even in the trenches in order to please a mixed group of other ranks makes this process of re-appropriation easier.

For the anti-militarists, the victims of a bloodbath which in no way served their interests deserve to have their voices heard, in particular in order to underline the huge gap between their viewpoint and that of the military authorities. The fact that the soldiers sing about suffering and sometimes about dying, but not about killing, facilitates both the initial popularity of the songs among frontline soldiers and the incorporation of the songs into each of these two discourses.

The importance of popular song in war memories, I think, will bear further exploration, which to be fruitful needs to keep in mind that popular music must be analyzed as a mass activity and not just as a corpus of texts and melodies. For a particular repertoire, such as the soldier songs, understanding the songs also means understanding the selection mechanisms which allow a song to join the repertoire. There is also a need for further research on the "nostalgia" aspect of the use of these songs. Nostalgia was considered a danger for some of the team producing *Oh, What a Lovely War!* and is often a sentiment difficult to identify and analyze. A number of researchers have worked on nostalgia and popular music, and the application of some of their conclusions to the case of soldiers' songs would certainly be productive.[54]

NOTES

1 Paul Fussell, *The Great War and Modern Memory* (Oxford: Oxford University Press, 2000; first published 1975), ix.

2 See for example Roy Palmer and Lyn Macdonald, *What a Lovely War: British Soldiers' Songs* (London: Michael Joseph, 1990).

3 Frederick Thomas Nettleingham, *Tommy's Tunes* (London: Erskine Macdonald, 1917); Nettleingham, *More Tommy's Tunes* (London: Erskine Macdonald, 1918).

4 John Brophy and Eric Partridge, *The Long Trail: What the British Soldier Sang and Said in the Great War of 1914–1918* (London: André Deutsch, 1965).

5 See for example: Max Arthur, *When This Bloody War Is Over: Soldiers' Songs of the First World War* (London: Piatkus, 2001); Martin Pegler, *Soldiers' Songs and Slang of the Great War* (Oxford: Osprey, 2014).

6 *Burnley News*, 20 September 1919.

7 Also, indeed, different from German or French soldiers'songs, but this cannot be covered here. A full analysis of British soldiers' songs can be found in chapter 6 of John Mullen, *The Show Must Go On! Popular Song in Britain in the First World War* (Farnham: Ashgate, 2015).

8 Similarly, music hall songs about the glory of war, or calling for men to volunteer, almost completely disappear after the first few months of the war.
9 Arthur, *When This Bloody War is Over,* 89.
10 Brophy and Partridge, *The Long Trail*, 67.
11 *Evening Telegraph*, 2 July 1930.
12 From Brophy's introduction to Brophy and Partridge, *The Long Trail*, 4.
13 *Evening Telegraph*, 2 July 1930.
14 "I want to go home. I want to go home/I don't want to go in the trenches no more/Where whizzbangs and shrapnel, They whistle and roar./Take me over the sea/Where the Alleyman can't get at me/Oh my! I don't want to die./I want to go home."
15 Ibid.
16 *Dundee Courier*, 12 September 1939.
17 *New Oxford Dictionary* (Oxford: Oxford University Press, 2001).
18 The song about General Shute comes to mind, which ends "A shit would be shot without mourners/if someone shot that shit Shute."
19 Bob Adams and Robert Hargreaves, *Pop Goes the Major! I've Found My Sergeant Major* (London: Francis, Day & Hunter, 1920).
20 *Evening Telegraph*, 2 July 1930.
21 John Brophy and Eric Partridge, *Daily Telegraph Dictionary of Tommies' Songs and Slang 1914–18* (London: Frontline, 2008), viii.
22 Brophy and Partridge, *Daily Telegraph Dictionary of Tommies' Songs and Slang*, 18.
23 Tony Ashworth, *Trench Warfare 1914–1918: The Live and Let Live System* (London: Pan, 1980).
24 Joan Littlewood and Theatre Workshop, *Oh What a Lovely War* (London: Methuen, 1967).
25 Chilton had already made radio documentaries on other subjects, including the American Civil War and the Salvation Army, in each case using songs from the subject periods to bring his documentaries to life.
26 In January 2014, a BBC radio documentary about Charles Chilton's original show was broadcast.
27 Philip Tagg, *Music's Meanings* (New York: Mass Media Scholars' Press, 2012), 451.
28 Howard Goorney, *The Theatre Workshop Story* (London: Eyre Methuen, 1981), 127.
29 M. Sweet, "Oh What a Lovely War – Why the Battle Still Rages," *Daily Telegraph*, 1 February 2014.

30 *Textes et Contextes*, no. 6 (2011), https://revuesshs.ubourgogne.fr/textes&contextes/sommaire.php?id=1309/.

31 Goorney, *The Theatre Workshop Story*, 128.

32 J. Littlewood, *Joan's Book* (London: Methuen, 1994), 694.

33 *Daily Mail*, 2 January 2014.

34 Brian Bond, *The Unquiet Western Front: Britain's Role in Literature and History*, (Cambridge: Cambridge University Press, 2002), i.

35 Frank Davies and Graham Maddocks, *Bloody Red Tabs: General Officer Casualties of the Great War 1914–1918* (London: Leo Cooper, 1995), 2.

36 Andrew Roberts, *A History of the English-Speaking Peoples since 1900* (London: Harper Perennial, 2008), 57.

37 *Sunday Times,* 27 September 1970.

38 Barbara Newman, "Another Opening, Another Show: Kat and the Kings and Oh What a Lovely War!," *Dancing Times* (May 1998): 725, 727.

39 http://www.bbc.co.uk/guides/zws9xnb.

40 All the examples which are quoted here were easily found on YouTube in November 2014.

41 https://www.youtube.com/watch?v=_K1BdDVvV9Q (accessed 29 November 2014).

42 Arthur, *When This Bloody War Is Over*, 76.

43 https://www.youtube.com/watch?v=yL2NqXZITLY (accessed 29 November 2014).

44 https://www.youtube.com/watch?v=wfbnKwB19So (accessed 29 November 2014).

45 Not to be confused with the Swedish rock group the Spinning Jennies.

46 The anti-war demonstration in London on 15 February 2003 was estimated by organizers to count two million people, while police estimated 750,000. http://www.dailymail.co.uk/news/article-161546/Anti-war-protest-Britains-biggest-demo.html (accessed 10 October 2014).

47 https://www.youtube.com/watch?v=gSjeEcv-IHY.

48 www.rusi.org (accessed 20 June 2016).

49 *The Independent*, 23 October 2014.

50 http://www.helpforheroes.org.uk/news/(accessed 14 October 2014).

51 http://www.walterpaulproductions.co.uk/page_3019948.html.

52 Nicolas Offenstadt, *14–18 Aujourd'hui: La Grande Guerre dans la France contemporaine* (Paris: O. Jacob, 2010), 11.

53 http://www.iwm.org.uk/exhibitions/iwm-london/first-world-war-galleries (accessed 26 October 2014).

54 See for example Frederick S. Barrett, Kevin J. Grimm, Richard W. Robins, Tim Wildschut, and Constantine Sedekides, "Music-Evoked Nostalgia: Affect, Memory, and Personality," *Emotion* 10, no. 3 (2010): 390–403.

14

Stanley Spencer: A Very Private Memorial

LILIANE LOUVEL

Stanley Spencer (1892–1959) is one of the most famous figurative painters of the first half of the twentieth century in England, whereas he is quite unknown in France. His quaint paintings are often found repulsive or bizarre but always interesting. He is more particularly famous for his paintings in the Tate Gallery: *The Resurrection, Cookham* (1924); *Swan Upping at Cookham* (started before he left for the war in 1916 and finished when he came back); and *Apple Gatherers*. Although one can see some of his paintings here and there in England (in Hull for instance at the Ferens Gallery, where his famous *Onions* but also one of Patricia Preece's portraits as well as the *Portrait of Major O.E. Kay* can be seen, together with *Gathering at the Terrace at* 47, a painting by Richard Carline representing a brooding Stanley standing apart from a group of friends including Hilda, R. Carline's sister and Spencer's first wife[1]), they are not always easily accessible. We can note only one major exhibition in London at the Royal Academy, *Stanley Spencer, R.A.* in 1980, and only one catalogue of his entire work published in 1992. There have been a number of exhibitions in Britain (either solo or with other painters) over the years, most of them in Cookham, a few in the US like *Stanley Spencer: An English Vision* 1997 in Washington, DC, and in Beaubourg the *Les réalismes 1919–1939* exhibition in 1980.

Stanley Spencer has always been closely identified with Cookham, the small Berkshire village which he called his heaven, going so far as signing his letters "Cookham," a nickname used for his friends.[2] This was where he was born and where he spent most of his life. It ranks first and foremost in his paintings; the Cookham War Memorial bears the name of his brother Sydney too. Spencer went to the Slade School and made friends there: the Carline family, Henry Lamb, Nevinson, Nach, and Gertler.[3] During his time at the Beaufort Hospital in 1916, he also fell under the influence of Desmond Chute, who introduced him to Saint Augustine's *Confessions*, and in particular to the notion of "replenishment": "Ever busy, yet never at rest. Gathering yet never needing, bearing, filling, guarding, creating, nourishing, perfecting, seeking though thou hast no lack."[4] According to Keith Bell, this led Spencer to believe that "There is something wonderful in hospital life. I think doing dressings when you are allowed to do things in peace and quiet is quite inspiring. The act of doing things … is wonderful"[5] – something we will find in his very domestic pictures of a hell of war.

The Spencer boys paid a heavy tribute to the war: Sydney the eldest brother was killed in 1918; Horace suffered from bouts of malaria leading to his eventual collapse; Percy served in France and was wounded when his headquarters was bombed; Gilbert, who was also a painter, emerged relatively unscathed; and Stanley chose to enrol in 1915 as an ambulance man. He was first sent to the Beaufort Hospital, a grim former lunatic's asylum near Bristol, where he served as an orderly taking care of the wounded arriving from the front. Then, after training at Tweseldown camp, he was sent to Macedonia in August 1916 at the time of the Somme offensive. Macedonia was then considered a sideshow of the front in France and Belgium. British troops were engaged alongside French troops on the Greek front fighting the Bulgarians in the Balkan War. In October 1917, he asked to be transferred to the Royal Berkshires, his home regiment. His experience was first-hand, for he served under a triple commission: as orderly, then ambulance man, then ending up as a private soldier, not to mention as a patient too.

Stanley Spencer's paintings devoted to the First World War include *Travoys Arriving with Wounded at a Dressing Station at Smol, Macedonia, September 1916*, which is at the IWM, and the commemorative *Unveiling Cookham War Memorial* (1921–22). *The Resurrection*, *Cookham* (1924) indirectly refers to the war, which one can understand when cognizant of the context. They are preludes to the Burghclere Memorial and the fascinating series it depicts, thus creating a pictorial narrative and an emotionally charged one. As a true pictorial commemoration it was also a way to come to terms with trauma.

Although these paintings, especially *Travoys*, are strikingly and unusually beautiful, I will concentrate on the famous cycle Spencer produced for the Burghclere Memorial. I was lucky enough to be able to make it to Somerset House in January 2014 where the paintings, at least those executed on canvas, were exhibited while the Memorial was undergoing repair. The title of the exhibition is a phrase by Spencer, "A Heaven in a Hell of War," which captures the paradox of Spencer's own relationship to his experience during the war and his way of coping with its sequels. This will be the thread running though this paper. It will first concentrate on the context of the production of the fresco cycle of these war paintings. Then it will move on to the paradox at the heart of this visual panorama: the way war seems to be standing in the wings. It will conclude with Spencer's unfailing trust in the power of a spiritual good and his optimistic view of life in Christ.

THE CONTEXT IN WHICH HE PAINTED THE MEMORIAL: WORLD WAR I AND AFTER

Stanley Spencer was commissioned by the War Office in July 1918 (a bit late in the day) to do work related to the conflict. All through his army years, he made sketches which unfortunately were left behind when his battalion had to leave their encampment to engage in battle against the Bulgarians. Most of the sketches were never retrieved, but some of those that were rescued helped in the elaboration of *Travoys* and of the Burghclere Memorial. The intention of the ministry was to create archives, to build memorials all over the country to celebrate the common man, including an art collection.[6] This was intended as a Hall of Remembrance. Nationwide there were a lot of fierce discussions and heated arguments about how best to commemorate the dead soldiers and how best to bury the fallen, particularly the thousands and thousands left on the battlefields in France and Belgium. How should they choose an unknown soldier? There was a lot of arguing nationwide about the shape of the commemoration and the choice of a proper cenotaph. Should crosses, memorials, or simple headstones be chosen to mark the place of the fallen buried abroad? The latter were eventually chosen. The scale of the desolation was huge, as was the number of the fallen in the devastated landscapes, the bare no man's land, evoked by a few figures and objective measurements given by Paul Gough: 80,000 dwellings were destroyed or damaged as well as 17,466 schools, public buildings, and churches. "The populations of the regions diminished by nearly 60 per cent."[7] The places were desolate, wasted places of death, mere boneyards. Nothing was left standing in some places.

"During the war, Spencer had intimate, often grisly, experience of death, although he mentions little in his letters or post-war reminiscences of his regular duty on burial parties."[8] By 1920, 4,000 men were searching for human remains. Even in 1930, up to forty bodies were being handed over each week to the French authorities according to Gough following historians' reports. As late as May 2014 shells were retrieved from a field in Northern France.

This emotional commemorative context explains the Burghclere Memorial scheme; not only a personal commemoration, it was also a kind of personal redemption for the Berhend family. Mrs Berhend's brother, Lieutenant Henry Willoughby Sandham, served in Macedonia like Spencer, and came back from the war badly damaged. He contracted malaria, the scourge of the troops posted there, and, like Spencer, was very ill from an enlarged spleen. During one of his crises, Mary Berhend tried to help him, and gave him brandy while waiting for an ambulance. She always thought this was what eventually killed him.

Some time later, in 1923, the Berhend family saw some of Spencer's paintings (they already owned *Swan Upping at Cookham*) and, knowing he had served in Macedonia like Lieutenant Sandham, asked the painter to make a project for a memorial in Hampshire. This was an encounter of a kind, for the Berhend family's desire for atonement and reparation in mourning met Spencer's expectations. Indeed, he had already started making projects for war compositions. He wrote to Hilda, his first wife:

> Since I have been here [at Lamb's House in Poole Dorset], I have hardly been out at all. I have been so much moved by a scheme of war pictures that I have been making compositions for, that all my time here has been on this. I have drawn a whole architectural scheme of the pictures. The end wall is to be a tall circular topped picture of that idea I told you about – the resurrection of the soldiers in Salonica … This idea, as far as what it appears like, is at present the vaguest, and yet it will, I know, be the best. The frame around this picture is broad and is composed of, on either side, four pictures, quite small, of incidents occurring

> outside tent doors ... a man lacing up a tent door for the night, a man pinning handkerchiefs on the tent to dry.[9]

The project was already firmly composed in his mind, even in architectural terms as the quotation reveals, following the strong impression left by his experience at the front and the possibility of the generous offer by the Berhend family. Nevertheless, it took him several years to complete, starting with the building of the chapel and two almshouses on either side. Spencer only started on the paintings in 1927, having elaborated the whole scheme before altering it as it went along. The ensemble was completed in 1932 with the impressive end wall. The paintings were oil on canvas, for the English climate would not allow the technique of the fresco to last because of the dampness. The larger ones (the top tier) were realized in oil on canvas glued to the walls.

The chapel gave Spencer the opportunity not only to celebrate and pay homage to one of his favourite Italian painters, Giotto, whose arena chapel in Padua Spencer revered, but it also offered him a way to write his own particular narrative, remembering his war years. For the structure of a series of frescoes or paintings disposed spatially in a chapel, as in galleries of old in the big house for instance, makes up a kind of apparatus (see Agamben after Foucault). Thus the series spread along the walls constrains the viewer or spectator and makes him/her live a particular experience: walking along the gallery, the spectator looks at (rather than reads) the paintings in a sequence of time (and not only space), and reconstructs a narrative as he/she walks along and peruses the walls. Ultimately, it is in the spectator's head, in the viewing process, that the whole story has been told and the experience (re)lived. The narrative is told on three levels or registers. It may be seen as a compound of a fresco cycle and of a polyptich, often a triptych (when one excepts the end wall paintings and *The Crucifixion,* for instance). It follows the rules of composition of an altarpiece or retable.

The lower level unfolds a series of four panels on either side making up the predella of the whole project. They are devoted to life at the Beaufort Hospital, which Spencer thought of as a kind of hell. On top of these panels, four lunettes of greater size are aligned under an arched top. All but one are devoted to life on the Macedonian and Bulgarian fronts, which he saw as making a heaven in a hell of war. On top of those eight panels, all realized in oil on canvas (which could thus be deposed and exhibited at Somerset House), two long panels painted on and glued to the walls (not exhibited then) describe two scenes: one, the *Riverbed at Todorov*; the other, a *Camp at Karasuli*. At the far end of the chapel, on the end wall under an arch, is deployed the monumental (21 feet by 17.5 feet) *Resurrection of the Soldiers*, which itself unfolds on three levels, but could not be removed from the wall. It plays the role of a pala of altar. He encompassed the entire project under what he called his "Holy Box."

A PARADOXICAL ENTERPRISE: MAKING "ONE'S HEAVEN IN A HELL OF WAR"

Spencer's paintings of the war strike one as being very different from the other paintings of the same experience. They hold nothing that could be expected as in works by Bomberg, Lamb, Nash, or Nevinson, some of which are also exhibited in the same Tate Gallery room as Spencer's *Resurrection*. The contrast is striking. The latter seems to have nothing to do with the war. But as we will see, the contrary is the case.

In Spencer's paintings, there are no exploding shells or grim depictions of life in the trenches with mud, rats, and haggard men in drab colours. *Dug-Out*, which is set in a trench, offers a totally different pictorial rendering. In a paradoxical way, it is a sort of combination of Armistice Day and Resurrection, according to Gough. Yet some traits may be found in common with famous war paintings like John Singer Sargent's *Gassed*.

Sargent's *Gassed* was commissioned in July 1918 to make the central piece of the Hall of Remembrance. At the age of sixty-two, Sargent went to the front, together with Tonks, Spencer's teacher at the Slade. He was deeply shocked by what he witnessed. The painting was finished in March 1919 (IWM). It offers an instance of poignant narrative realism: displayed on two horizontal levels (as in Greek frieze), men are lying on the ground, victims of an attack of mustard gas, and in-between, on a duckboard, along another horizontal line, nine blind men are being led by two orderlies (Spencer was an ambulance man) towards a dressing station, the guide ropes of which are visible on the right (something Spencer represented too in *Making a Firebelt*). As in Breughel's *Parable of the Blind*, they are holding onto their neighbours' shoulders, but they may be led to a kind of redemption and not to a fall. The setting mustard-like sun dimly shines in the background where another detail of troops is approaching the dressing station from the back. To the rear, a football match with very fit players is going on, hinting at the proximity of life and death, of games and war often linked by the spirit of a battle.

Henry Lamb's picture *Irish Troops in the Judean Hills Surprised by Turkish Bombardment* (1919)[10] is very different from Spencer's *Travoys* (1919), although they display some common traits including the same high vantage point, the same proportions, the depiction of a camp with soldiers, and similar tents. As Gough suggests, they might have been meant as a tandem for the "ambitious Hall of Remembrance" planned by the ministry. Lamb's painting represents an encampment under a bombardment where all hell breaks loose in its direst forms. Destruction is at work, with heavy clouds of smoke, men with their heads in their hands, soldiers carrying their wounded comrades away from the field, collapsed bodies, and other men trying to find shelter against the violence of the surprise attack. One man is depicted trying to escape it all by going out of the frame. On the contrary, in *Travoys*, Spencer chose not to show destruction but reparation of a camp unit, a field surgery where the wounded were taken after a battle. The religious allusion, and the pictorial reference to the nativity and the adorations of the magis or shepherds, is clear in the composition of the painting and the interplay between brilliantly lighted zones and zones left in darkness. This is another way of showing one's hope and belief in a possible kind of resurrection of the bodies, something Spencer repeatedly goes back to as befits a traumatic state. A fine instance of denegation maybe: refusing to see so as to better see what lies beyond and eventually survive the catastrophe.

What Spencer offers is a rendition of his very private way of coping by displaying the very homeliness and privacy of his experience and the prevalance of his inner world. What we get in the Burghclere Memorial is quiet everyday life scenes, even domestic ones, and not the dramatic explosions of war on the front. In the lower register of the predellas we can see a lot of what was going on at the Beaufort Hospital (a hellish world according to Spencer), where wounded soldiers were brought in to recuperate: orderly sorting of bags on arrival, filling tea urns, having tea in hospital, making beds, sorting the laundry, and, above all, cleaning (bodies, rooms, pieces of furniture, utensils) and replenishing bodies and dishes or containers.

In the lunettes too (except one), the visions of his time in Salonica show soldiers at rest, sent on quiet errands or busy doing jobs linked to their life in the tents: getting water, resting, making a fire, cleaning the camp, and displaying their kits for inspection. The top shows two camps in Bulgaria. The end wall is dedicated to the great *Resurrection of the Soldiers*, a calm almost serene mixture of the mundane and the holy, of everyday life in afterlife.

As an orderly first, and then as an ambulance man for most of the war, Spencer was on the side of reparation, of taking care of wounded soldiers, of trying to bring them back to life (often for them to go back to the front), and of curing them. He stood between the front and the rear. He was there to help mend the soldiers' bodies and to help them to recover from trauma. As Gough suggests, apropos of *Travoys*:

> The wounded figures in *Travoys* are caught in that indeterminate zone between life and death, balanced in a state of transubstantiation that would be explained more fully in the walls of the Oratory. They belonged to "a different world than those tending them," suggested Stanley, "in it" but not "of it."[11]

No wonder then to see that he depicted more mundane occupations from his own standpoint deep in his self-absorption. When posted to Macedonia and then on the Bulgarian front, he experienced war at closer range but still privileged the individual quieter spiritual vision, the private world he tried to save at all costs in the midst of a very violent collective catastrophe. He did not aim at rendering heroic actions, but showed the humble conditions of the common man when waiting to be called up to the front.

Thus, in Spencer's rendition, the war appears in its consequences, not in the brutal confrontation with death and lethal weapons but in the result of the blows it inflicted to all. Without showing the direct experience of shock and horror, it still looms large in the background and imparts the paintings with an eerie, even *unheimlich* (un-homely within the homely) atmosphere, something to which Spencer's pictorial choices of composition, perspective, colour, interplay between light and darkness, and deformations contribute. In the predellas, the damage has been done; in the lunettes, it is being done or on the brink of being done. The times are clearly separated, and impending doom is reserved for the lunettes.

WAR THERE AND ITS CONSEQUENCES

The war is stalking men in the wings, and its presence has to be decoded to be "seen" and felt, like the return of the repressed element, as a non-visible "event" always on the brink of breaking out with its dire consequences, a terrible threat which is going to strike out, or has already done so nearby. The soldiers seem to be engrossed in their everyday life occupations, but the distant roar of death can be heard (and Spencer was very sensitive to sounds so that he would "always associate the 'clanging' sound of metal on stone, 'as if bars of steel coming together' with the anticipation of the cumbersome mule-drawn sledges and their bearer escorts"[12]). As Gough suggests, this is similar to Breughel's famous *Fall of Icarus*, where the ploughman keeps at his task with bent head while the nearing catastrophe (that of the fallen Icarus only visible thanks to the detail of his flailing legs) has already taken place. Spencer took great care over details and was dedicated to rendering objects as accurately as possible. We could also find a formal similarity between some of Breughel's paintings involving crowds like *The Sermon* (National Gallery, Budapest) or *The Triumph of Death* (Prado), where the rendition of people's backs and heads, their tightly packed crowdedness, is close to some periods in Spencer's career. He also shared with Breughel a taste for domestic scenes with people busy serving other people and carrying food and drink, as in *Peasant Wedding* (Kunsthistorisches Museum), and for a high vantage point, as in *The Adoration of the Magi* in the National Gallery (including distorted bodies and twisted faces as well).

If war is visible in its consequences, the much longed-for peace also figures there, like a muffled sound one might hear if attentive enough (see the figure to the right in *Stand-To* or *Dug-Out*). A paradoxical mixture of what one has to confront (danger) and what one is longing for (peace). Spencer was trying to recreate the feelings of inner domestic bliss (Gough 165) he longed for so much.

In the following, I propose a brief survey of the paintings and the narrative they unfold in the visitor's mind, which would deserve much more care and comment as Gough's book, among others, testifies.

Arriving at the hospital is the only lunette in which an episode from the Beaufort Hospital is "described" – they usually figure in the predellas. As befits the opening of the series, this is an arrival: the wounded are reaching the gates of another hell, after that of the war. The gatekeeper looks more like a prison warden than like St Peter, although he is holding similar keys. It is the only episode, together with *Map Reading,* in which flowers (rhododendron bushes) appear, bringing in a variation in colour and design.

The predellas. According to Renaissance altarpieces or retables, or to the different registers of a fresco cycle as in Padua, the smaller sized lower tier depicts mundane episodes of life on earth, that of a saint for instance.[13] The middle level classically depicts Christ, the Virgin, and the saints, and the upper level is reserved for God (or the Ascension or Assumption).

In *Frostbite,* a kind of tunnel protects the injured lower limbs of a soldier. An orderly is looking after the injured feet. This scene is interesting for it is also a painter's painting. It quotes several influences on Spencer. The orderly arriving with buckets actually looks like an angel with two round wings. In the background, a nurse is framed by a door as in Dutch painting, a picture within a picture, a domestic scene spied from another room like a series of Chinese boxes. In the foreground, pieces of a jigsaw puzzle, similar in design and colour to the carpet nearby, seem to indicate that as in *Tea at the Hospital* – in which a reflecting figure is sitting to the left of the picture in the foreground – thinking and pondering over the puzzling experience of war is a major issue.

The Lunettes

Ablutions depicts washing and cleaning wounds by orderlies. We note a Spencer figure (the only one in uniform) to the right that will reappear in several compositions, sometimes in the same location.

Kit Inspection shows soldiers getting ready with army issues. The brown colour and the separate blankets on which kits are displayed gave Spencer the occasion to achieve a pictorial feat of great impact. At the same time he shows how order was maintained in a highly disordered context.

Dug-Out depicts Spencer's very particular view of a dug-out, a kind of protective hole dug in the sides of the trenches to offer refuge. The painting was also called *Stand-To*, the moment when soldiers have to stand at the ready. There is nothing grim and frightening there; the officer looks like an angel, with his wing-like foliage and the grenades, which make him look like Saint Sebastian. The coils of barbed wire at the top balance the composition but are also reminiscent of an incident in Spencer's life as a private, when he got entangled in a coil of barbed wire which had to be cut through to free him. Barbed wire coils figure in several paintings of the scheme and in the *Resurrection*. To the right, a soldier seems to be listening to something coming from the right-hand side; Spencer suggested it might be the announcement of the much longed for armistice. At the same time, the soldier is looking in the direction of the *Crucifixion of the Soldiers* nearby. An attitude symmetrically is echoed by the three soldiers leaning towards the scene in the tent in *Reveille,* which stands on the other side of *The Crucifixion*, the three of them making a triptych when considered together and apart within the overall cycle.

In *Reveille*, soldiers are shown getting up in a tent. They are struggling with the fine mesh of mosquito nets rendered necessary by the insects, the scourge of the troops in Macedonia, infecting them with malaria, which Spencer suffered from twice. It was fatal to Mary Berhend's brother. The three men to the right look like onlookers flying in or angels heralding the end of the war, which is consistent with the fact that this lunette is coupled with the *Frostbite* predella depicting a scene in which patients are being looked after, which also contains allusions to the old masters as we saw previously.

Filling Water-bottles depicts another common chore of army life. But again its composition, its tones, and the theme of replenishment (echoed by *Tea in the Hospital Ward* in the predella beneath) hold connotations of satisfaction more than feelings of loss and despair. Once more, the figures of the three soldiers, whose macintoshes are flying off their shoulders, look like three angels gathered at a fountain. A companion piece of *Filling Tea Urns*, it also depicts the separation between the former inmates of the hospital, the "lunatics" to the rear, and the orderlies.

Map Reading, in its turn, shows soldiers at rest while an officer (the only one to have access to such important documents as maps) is trying to find his way in a dangerous alien country. The map shows all the places Spencer had been to in Macedonia. The composition of the scene – the spread out bodies lying prone on either side of the officer mounted on his horse, the triangular composition (like a mandorla), with the soldiers at the top picking up bilberries in flowering bushes – looks more like a scene in some Garden of Eden than at war. Yet the very still lying figures are reminiscent of other shapes lying on the battlefield never to rise again. A trivial but important detail in the foreground is a soldier (another Spencer-like figure?) making sure the horse has its share of food.

This lunette is coupled with *Bedmaking* in which the comfort of a hot-water bottle, of being in bed, is countered by the fact that the wounded or sick were hit by the war. On the wall, one can see family photographs (many of which are Spencer's: his father, Hilda his first wife, his brother) and the figure lying swaddled in his bed may represent Spencer undergoing a bout of malaria, for if the scene may be located at the Beaufort Hospital it may also be in a room in Macedonia.

In *Firebelt*, the soldiers are building protection against the enemy. Once more this complex picture shows a non-dangerous activity: soldiers are using pieces of a Bulgarian newspaper to build their firebelt. All around the tents, the grass has been scorched black, making up a protective belt. The tents are depicted in details with all the ropes and pegs. A Spencer-like figure is busy with a pole to the right and echoes other similar figures of himself depicted in the camp at Karasali, in the frescoes on the wall in the upper tier, or in *Ablutions*. In these, he is the only fully clad figure dealing with a huge pole.

This busy lunette is coupled with the predella dealing with *Cleaning Lockers*, where a lot of activity is going on too. The two elements, fire and water, are associated. But in the predella the danger is not looming in the background. In *Firebelt, Map Reading, Filling Waterbottles, Reveille*, *Dug-Out,* and *Kit Inspection,* the war is surrounding the soldiers, whose actions are rendered necessary by the presence of the unseen enemy and whose lives are at stake, which is the theme taken up by *The Resurrection of the Soldiers*.

MEMENTO MORI AND THE TRIUMPH OVER DEATH

In this great painting on the end wall of the chapel, death has taken place. The time is the past there. Logically, as this was painted after the war, the action takes into account the result of the Great War with its millions of dead young men. But contrary to what one might expect, this striking great end wall painting does not carry gloomy ideas or melancholy. On the contrary, it shows the joy and relief of resurrecting. It is not a frightening Judgment Day, as in Giotto's fresco in arena, but a true sharing of life after death in Christ.

If *Reveille* may be seen as a *memento mori* or as a vanity – the mosquitoes dancing on top of the nets are reminders of danger and of impending threats like malaria and other even more dangerous ways of losing one's life – *The Resurrection of the Soldiers* goes beyond death and the many dead soldiers of the war. It depicts the hope of a coming back to life, hope in a resurrection, a resurrection as a way of coming back to life for the lucky ones who will come back to their families, and a resurrection in Christ for the fallen ones. It is also a resurrection in people's minds with the celebration of the dead soldiers, who will not be forgotten. It is an act of rememoration and of remembrance/re-member-ance (i.e. assembling the different severed (blown up) parts of a body, of a family, of a nation). This was no fortuitous act after a war during which many soldiers saw their comrades blown to pieces, disappearing into thin air, one minute there, the next, gone.

The resurrection was one of Spencer's favourite themes, which he dealt with in no less than six variations over the years. In this extraordinary painting, the everyday life of the soldiers is hinted at. But here, they are rising from the ground. This also echoes his own experience of coming out of the dug-outs hollowed in the trenches, and seeing an apparently deserted battlefield, empty under the sky, all of a sudden full of soldiers coming up from the trenches to launch an attack. Seemingly buried alive they all came back to life to wreak havoc and kill the enemy. This very strong picture of soldiers rising from the ground, sometimes still half engaged in it, impressed itself so hard on his mind that it also figured in one of his letters in which he describes and draws corpses buried in a graveyard coming up and walking through the wall of his room, to his great delight.

This picture represents a true triumph *over* death and not a *danse macabre*, not a triumph *of* death as in medieval paintings or in Breughel's as we saw earlier or later, during the Second World War, with the despair of Nussbaum's *Triumph of Death*. For Spencer's resurrection is imbued with happiness and a quite stupendous life-in-death quality. It could have been gruesome, but it is so full of energy and life that it goes beyond the usual despairing kind of dark war pictures. It also corresponds to a general feeling after the war of the desire of families to be reunited with their dead soldiers, the belief that so many dead could not be just that – dead. An Australian painter, Will Longstaff, painted a striking *Menin Gate at Midnight* in 1927, showing the ghosts of soldiers marching in front of a memorial at Ypres. But the soldiers there are represented in a spectral diaphanous mode whereas Spencer's are very similar to living people.

In *The Resurrection of the Soldiers*, all the figures are put on the same level. Christ is standing in the upper part but is no bigger than the other soldiers. The composition of the painting is clever: it is distributed according to three tiers, as in classical religious paintings, devoted to mundane life, then to a scene around Christ painted like a workman, and above, the realm of God and angels, in this instance more dead soldiers and landscape. The middle soldier leads the eye to Christ and to the upper part. The two mules and their turned necks draw two arabesques. The standing figure to the right is echoed by one to the left. The light colour of the ruined wall of the village finds its equivalent in the light colour of the river to the left.

The crosses, of course, are powerful elements of the structure. They may have been inspired by something similar to a photograph of the dead soldiers lying under white crosses, reproduced in Clough's book. During his time in Macedonia and in the Berkshire regiment, Spencer had to bury numerous soldiers. As he told a reporter in 1927: "I had buried so many people and saw so many dead bodies that I felt that it could not be the end of everything."[14]

> I had hoped to convey in a series of "waves" receding upwards & backwards, the first few varied degrees of states of consciousness & feeling & its influence on their behaviour, that the fact of having resurrected would occasion. This shaking hands & awareness state is followed by a feeling of gratitude & a desire to express it to something, & they remember the cross; their last piece of earthly impediments or equipment. This cross was placed on the graves or whatever men fell was placed there, as a symbol of hope for their ultimate resurrection & redemption & was looked upon & thought of as such.[15]

The white crosses strike one by their colour and the very strong structural role they play in the picture. When one first approaches it, one is confronted with an outstanding apparent confusion of white crosses going in all directions, which is wrong for they all answer a particular purpose. At the bottom they serve as frames to individual portraits of soldiers. The cross in the middle points to the turned round neck of the mule and thus leads the eye towards the top of the picture, towards the soldier lying prone on one of them, deep in thought (a Spencer-like figure reminiscent of the reflecting figure in *Tea in the Hospital Ward*). Christ (a diminutive figure like in Breughel's *Baptism*) stands right over him with crosses, as if magnetically attracted by him, and more crosses lead to a calvary-looking mountain with a line of poplar trees in the background like so many cypresses in Golgotha paintings. But here there is no skull at the bottom of the crosses – Adam's skull usually figured there symbolizing the original sin Christ died in redemption for a sin Spencer did not believe in – but a bush flowering to the left of the altar at the bottom of it all, a symbol of nature's renewal and yearly resurrection, most appropriate at Easter time (itself being the combination of the Fall and of its redemption with the Annunciation and the Crucifixion).

Animals figure prominently, in particular the mules, often pink ones that Spencer liked so much and that were so present on the war scene like horses. They were indispensable to pull carriages and cannons, to carry food, victuals, equipment, and wounded soldiers as we can see in *Travoys*. Spencer enjoyed their presence so much that he represented four of them in this *Resurrection*, with two privates cosily coiled between them. He even went as far as writing that they deserved a "Mons star sort of thing."[16]

Other animals like rabbits and tortoises (a common animal in these parts with which soldiers liked to play) often appear in the pictures. This is a fact also acknowledged in many war accounts and fictional testimonies such as T. Findley's *The Wars*, for instance, where one of the soldiers keeps a sketch book in which he draws all kinds of animals they could keep in the trenches including a toad, a mouse, and a hedgehog, as if the presence of animals had a soothing effect and enabled the soldiers to give vent to their affectivity bruised by the inhuman war.

This all corresponded to Spencer's very deep belief and spiritual aspiration which probably helped him survive during his war years. He strove to carry his home and familiar world (like dear Cookham) within himself like a precious reliquary containing holy relics from home. This is something we can see with the pictures represented in *Bedmaking*, but also in his letters, in which he asks or thanks his friends for small art books of Italian painters (Gowans and Gray publications) he used to carry with him. His own private guarded sanctuary of the beloved heaven of Cookham and his family helped him to survive the experience, and also explains the paradoxical quality of his singular representation of the war, for he strove to find "God in the real bare things."[17]

Spencer's testimony is invaluable, although he was not on the terrible French and Belgium fronts; it is marginal perhaps, as in the wings, when he was kept in the rear as an ambulance man. But at first-hand anyhow especially when billeted on the Bulgarian front where he had to deal with the battles and their consequences by picking up the wounded and the dead, and bringing them back to the camp to be healed or buried. When depicting his experience in Bulgaria, his paintings turn darker, as on the wall between the lunettes devoted to the camps at Karasuli or Todorovo, once again portraying soldiers washing clothes and digging while two laden mules are quietly passing in front of them. *Building a Riverbed at Todorovo* shows soldiers engrossed in a kind of puzzle-making activity, designing a sort of pavement with a frieze and mosaic-like drawings of black cobblestones. The frieze may be viewed as a comment on what Spencer himself was busy doing in the chapel, where the predelles looked like as many friezes to the main arched subjects. At least it was a way of making sense of the puzzle of war, trying to make order out of the chaos of the world. Let us listen to him once more:

> There was something so unreal about no man's land & still more about Bulgars land; I began to imagine that they were not real or rather that they belonged to a different kind of realness. Hearing that cart in the road was like listening to people talking in Hades. All my thoughts about the Bulgars led me into the night, there was a "day" in my Bulgarian world, but it was at the other end of night in a remote sense that our "tomorrow" is; their "day" semed to me a prolongation of our night. Our midnight comes at 12 o'clock, but their midnight never comes, they are always going towards it.[18]

This is a fantastic piece of writing about the loss of landmarks and the conscience of time when one finds oneself stranded in foreign parts under terrible conditions. A process of dematerialization results from a voyage into an eerie dehumanizing no man's land. Then one had to remember the experience and fit little pieces of memory-like cobblestones into the wider puzzle of a picture, be it in the bed of a Bulgarian river.

Spencer's amazing "fresco" shows by its very size and the variety of the scenes depicted in it the intense reaction to his experience on the war front. It took him six years to complete, six years also to come to terms with the trauma of this excruciating time far from heaven-like Cookham. The fact that Spencer triumphed over melancholy, despair, and despondency may have been a comfort to people in distress who had lost their beloved ones, and first and foremost to the Berhend family, without whom he could not have carried out his project. Although strongly affected by the death of his brother Sydney, Spencer maintained a life-loving attitude grounded in a strong inner spiritual life and the teachings of St Augustine as relayed by Desmond Chute. In the midst of despair, menial work is a comfort against the pit of suffering: we remember the importance of the notion of "replenishment." But over the years, after almost a hundred years now, when most of us in Europe and beyond still remember vivid tales and testimonies of the "Great War" transmitted in our families by grandparents, such paintings are also testimonies of what it takes to be a human being in the face of an inhuman war (is there such a thing as a human war?), which was only the prelude to even more unheard-of horrors: resilience, the belief in beauty, the trust in one's own very private vision, hope, and the comfort of animals. In *Riverbed at Todorovo*, one of the mosaics displays a striped dog-like figure (reminiscent of a Roman *cave canem*?) and the other one a target like red cross (the Red Cross? St George's?)

Painting figures is definitely a way to reach out to the other, the viewer, to think in material forms as Delacroix pointed out in his diary. A visual kind of thought, a statement, which is also the overall *impression* left on our minds by the paintings of Spencer on the walls of the Burghclere Private Memorial to Captain Sandham.

NOTES

1 See http://www.bbc.co.uk/arts/yourpaintings/galleries/locations/ferens-art-gallery-3518.

2 See the letters, in particular those to the Raverats, in Adrian Glew, ed., *Stanley Spencer: Letters and Writings* (London: Tate Publishing, 2001).
3 See on this subject, *A Crisis of Brilliance*, book and exhibition at the Dulwich Gallery, 2013.
4 TAM, Letter to Richard Carline, 5 July 1928, quoted by Keith Bell, *Stanley Spencer: A Complex Catalogue of the Paintings* (London: Phaidon Press, 1992), 79; Paul Gough, *Stanley Spencer, Journey to Burghclere* (Bristol: Samson and Company, 2006). See also: Richard Carline, *Stanley Spencer at War* (London: Faber and Faber, 1978); Glew, ed., *Stanley Spencer*; Kitty Hauser, *Stanley Spencer* (London: Tate Publishing, 2001); Kenneth Pople, *Stanley Spencer: A Biography* (London: Collins, 1991); Gilbert Spencer, *Stanley Spencer by His Brother Gilbert* (London: Gollancz, 1961, reprinted, Redcliffe Press, 1991); David Haycock, *A Crisis of Brilliance, Five Young British Artists and the Great War* (Old Street Publishing, 2010); and also an exhibition at the Dulwich Gallery 2013.
5 Stanley Spencer, *Letter to Richard Carline*, quoted in Bell, *Stanley Spencer*, 79.
6 Gough, *Stanley Spencer*, 157.
7 Ibid., 157.
8 Ibid., 156.
9 Letter to Hilda, 31 May 1923 quoted by Gough, *Stanley Spencer*, 99.
10 Reproduced in Gough, *Stanley Spencer*, 88.
11 Ibid., 87.
12 Stanley Spencer, *Notebooks*, 1945–47, TGA 733.3.86, quoted in Gough, *Stanley Spencer*, 93n93.
13 See André Chastel, *Histoire du rétable italien* (Paris: Liana Levi, 2005).
14 Gough, *Stanley Spencer*, 152.
15 Stanley Spencer, *Notebooks*, 6 December 1947, TGA 733.3.86, quoted in Gough, *Stanley Spencer*, 166, 179n60.
16 Gough, *Stanley Spencer*, 165n57.
17 Stanley Spencer to Desmond Chute, 3 June 1918, Spencer Gallery, Cookham, quoted by Gough, *Stanley Spencer*, 156.
18 Stanley Spencer to Sir Michael Sadler, 30 November 1922, TGA 8221.2.173, quoted by Gough, *Stanley Spencer*, 87.

15

Shining Faces: Terrence Malick's *The Thin Red Line* in the Light of Levinas

GILLES CHAMEROIS

"Levinas and war: at first, the subject seems incongruous."[1] These are the first words in Stéphane Mosès's study of the paradoxical relations between war and a philosophy usually associated with alterity, hospitality, and God's injunction "Thou shalt not kill." What I intend to do is to parallel this paradox with the paradox offered by Terrence Malick's film *The Thin Red Line*. The film is unmistakably a war film, following Charlie Company in the turmoil of the Battle of Guadalcanal, but it also offers contemplative episodes and, memorably, numerous metaphysical and religious meditations in its pervasive voice-overs. My own meditation will thus attempt to bring together two paradoxical relations: the relation which unites the representation of war and metaphysical reflection in the film, and the relation which leads from hostility to hospitality in Levinas.[2] To begin, it is necessary to follow the movement of Levinas's demonstration in *Totality and Infinity*.

There are three stages in the relation to war in *Totality and Infinity*. The book starts by acknowledging the reality of war, which is indeed the whole basis for the book's endeavour, and is the topic of most of the important preface. Stéphane Mosès and François-David Sebbah insist on the contrast between the customary view of the philosopher of love and peace and the grounding of his whole argument in the fact that "each being is war."[3] War is often an equivalent for history, and for the deadening force of totality, itself the main object of the book: "The visage of being that shows itself in war is fixed in the concept of totality, which dominates Western philosophy. Individuals are reduced to being bearers of forces that command them unbeknown to themselves."[4] The second stage in the relation to war unfolds in the key chapters centred on the face; paradoxically, war is also an experience that can break totality and open to infinity. "Only beings capable of war can rise to peace. War like peace presupposes beings structured otherwise than as parts of a totality."[5] Perhaps a way to sketch a quick representation of this paradox is through replacing "Totality" and "Infinity" by two terms equally pervasive in Levinas: "the Same" and "the Other." A society where everybody is the same would have no reason to experience war, but would choke in its totalizing sameness. On the contrary, war acknowledges the Other as Other:

> War presupposes the transcendence of the antagonist; it is waged against man. It is surrounded with honors and pays the last honors; it aims at a presence that comes always from elsewhere, a being that appears in a face. It is neither the hunt nor struggle with an element. The possibility, retained by the adversary, of thwarting the best laid calculations expresses the separation, the breach of totality, across which the adversaries approach one another.[6]

The book closes on a third stage in its relation to war. The title of the last chapter is "Being as Goodness – the I – Pluralism – Peace." Jacques Derrida concentrates on this last stage in *Adieu: To Emmanuel Levinas*. War presupposes peace, hostility presupposes hospitality:

> Whereas for Kant the institution of an eternal peace, of a cosmopolitical law, and of a universal hospitality, retains the trace of a natural hostility, whether present or threatening, real or virtual, for Levinas the contrary would be so: war itself retains the testimonial trace of a pacific welcoming of the face.[7]

This peace is not the "bourgeois peace of the man who, at home behind closed doors, rejects what negates him outside, it is not the peace conforming to *the unity of the One*, which is disturbed by any alterity."[8] On the contrary, it is a peace that is hospitable to alterity. And this peace comes before war, not after, or rather it is anachronistic.[9]

In my study of *The Thin Red Line*, I will mostly concentrate on the experience of alterity in war, so on the second of the stages just delineated in Levinas. However my conclusion will attempt to show that the film follows a movement parallel to that of *Totality and Infinity*, from the acknowledgment of war to war seen as an opening onto the infinite to, finally, a preexisting, originary, or rather anachronistic peace. This movement can best be expressed by the contrast between the images of nature that open and close the film. At the beginning a crocodile threateningly advances into water, at the end a party of children rowing together, then a couple of budgerigars, then a single coconut sprouting a green leaf offer an image of reconciled men, and of reconciled nature, although "re-conciled" is a bad choice of words, as nature's peace is anachronistic.[10]

The question however is not to "explain" the film, to give its "message," even less the "message" of its numerous monologues. This would indeed be one of the "hermeneutical banana skins"[11] that Simon Critchley warns us against, in reference mainly to Heidegger, the philosopher most often associated with Malick. I believe Levinas himself would have agreed on the very impossibility of philosophical thought totally to account for the aesthetic experience insofar as it offers an "experience in the fullest sense of the word" – as I believe Malick's film does – an experience which "precisely means a relation with the absolutely other, that is, with what always overflows thought." Indeed, "infinity overflows the thought that thinks it. Its very *infinition* is produced precisely in this overflowing."[12] In short, my explication cannot be the application of a philosophical discourse onto an artistic one which necessarily escapes totalization. Rather, it should be the "interimplication"[13] of the two discourses: the confrontation and dialogue between the two discourses might uncover "elective affinities" as it attempts "to fold onto each other two texts that have similar diagrams and thus to open up a field of intricate resonances."[14] It might then be an opening rather than a closure, and it might in particular open a space for discussion – for future discussion as I will make no such attempt here, although I will point out a few places where it might prove profitable – on how Malick's film resonates differently with Levinas and with Heidegger, as Levinas's work is often in confrontational dialogue with that of Heidegger.

I will first see how the very structure of the film can be thought alongside Levinas's reflection on the time separating us from death, as the film opens and closes on memories of such moments. I will also deal with the paradoxes entailed in a visual medium's relation to a thought which, no less than Heidegger's, is critical of the predominance of the visual. I will then focus on the numerous voice-overs, concentrating more on their status as monologue than on their actual content, so in Levinas's terms concentrating more on the "Saying" than on the "Said." This distinction will also guide me in my analysis of dialogue. Dialogue is of course central both to Levinas's philosophy of alterity and to the film's meditation, structured around key dialogue scenes. Monologue must make way for dialogue, and dialogue must be real dialogue, in the Levinassian sense, face to face. It must be an opening to the Other, and especially to the very paradigm of the Other, to the enemy, and I will study in that light the scenes involving Japanese prisoners. I will conclude on the words that close the film, or rather, again, on the particular circumstances of their uttering more than on the words themselves.

TIME AND VISION

In its very structure, the film is articulated around the time separating man from death. The film closes on the death of its main character, Witt, or rather on the memory of Witt's death amongst the men of Charlie Company. The film also opens on Witt and on his memory of his mother's death: "I just hope I can meet it the same way she did. With the same … calm. Because that's where it's hidden – the immortality I hadn't seen." Witt does indeed meet death with the same calm that he admired in his mother, and the suspension of time before death can be felt to be at the core of the film, as Simon Critchley writes: "It is this pause between 'same' and 'calm' that I want to focus on, this breathing space for a last breath. For I think this calm is the key to the film and, more widely, to Malick's art."[15] Critchley analyzes how this calm is evoked for the spectator at the moment of Witt's death. I will only add that the whole film can be seen as an expansion of this moment of suspension. The echo between the memory of the death of Witt's mother at the beginning of the film and his own death and its memory in Charlie Company at the end makes of the whole film a suspension of the time before death. Witt's status as an AWOL on an island at the beginning of the film can then be seen as a symbol of this suspension. In war, any place is an island amidst surrounding death, any time is time stolen from death. War, for Levinas, leads first and foremost to this realization:

> Time is precisely the fact that the whole existence of the mortal being – exposed to violence – is not [Heideggerian] being for death, but the "not yet" which is a way of being against death, a retreat before death in the very midst of its inexorable approach. In war death is brought to what is moving back, to what for the moment exists completely. Thus in war the reality of the time that separates a being from its death, the reality of a being taking up a position with regard to death, that is, the reality of a conscious being and its interiority, is recognized.[16]

Thus, in the recognition of this suspended death, war paradoxically opens a space of freedom, of freedom against totality, in the form of interiority. Of course, the particular form this interiority takes in *The Thin Red Line* is the voice-over. The role of the voice-over in the film could be described in Levinas's words as the apology for one's own interiority, this interiority's use of monologue to resist totalization. We will study the monologues in that light, and as well see their limits, and how they must make way for dialogue, but we first need to think of the voice-overs in the film in their antagonistic relation to images.

Levinas indeed insists on the fact that vision is on the side of totality, on the side of history – that is, of war – inasmuch as its leaves no space for individual freedom, and in particular for the expression of interiority in the form of apology:

> The judgment of history is set forth in the visible. Historical events are the visible par excellence; their truth is produced in evidence. The visible forms, or tends to form, a totality. It excludes the apology, which undoes the totality in inserting into it, at each instant, the unsurpassable, unencompassable present of its very subjectivity.[17]

It might seem paradoxical to apply such comments on the visible to a visual medium,[18] but they do resonate with the uneasy relationship between voices-over and images in the film, and also with the oppressive ubiquitousness of the camera. This point has been acutely pointed out by Michel Chion in his excellent book on the film, which I will refer to extensively: "The camera angles and movements in *The Thin Red Line* emphasize that the characters can be seen from any point in space. The world of the film is 360 degrees open."[19] Chion mentions the fact that characters themselves reflect on this: one soldier exclaims, "There's always someone watching," someone who's higher in rank and, seemingly, higher in his ability to exert surveillance. "There's no place to hide," says another soldier. The camera, with its extensive use of the Steadicam and the Akela crane, seems to be hovering around each and every character. But as Chion notes, the camera never offers us an all-encompassing view from above. The use of the Akela crane is symptomatic: it is one of the highest cranes available, and yet the only motivation for its use was that it would not ruin the grass. John Toll, the cinematographer, explains:

> One of the tougher challenges we faced was preserving the look of this waist-high grass. You couldn't walk through the grass more than a couple of times without leaving these huge paths … I began thinking about using the Akela crane, which has an extremely long, 72' arm that would allow us to get the camera into places where we couldn't walk or lay dolly track.[20]

In other words, with the Akela crane, the camera becomes pure vision, with no interaction with the world other than visual. The crane is used as the equivalent of a dolly with no material impact on the ground, and it does not adopt a point of view from above.[21] Only nature is allowed such a point of view in the film, in two different forms. Firstly, sometimes birds look at human beings on the ground, because they are interested in their flesh, like the vultures circling around the Japanese casualties, or with a more quizzical gaze, like the owl observing the patrol up river. Secondly, light seems to be able to reach the innermost recesses. Chion gives one paradigmatic example in *Days of Heaven*:

> The valuable glass lost by Richard Gere, resting underwater on the river bed at night. What makes this such a magical image is that we have the impression that a ray of light from the full moon (which we saw in a previous shot) is striking the glass even at the bottom of the river. Nothing can be hidden.[22]

It is specifically in that light, under that light should I say, that human beings seem to be given no chance to meet each other, if we follow Levinas in his developments on light and vision:

> Vision is not a transcendence. It ascribes a signification by the relation it makes possible. It opens nothing that, beyond the same, would be absolutely other, that is, in itself. Light conditions the relations between data; it makes possible the signification of objects that border one another. It does not enable one to approach them face to face … To see is hence always to see on the [Heideggerian] horizon. The vision that apprehends on the horizon does not encounter a being out of what is beyond all being.[23]

The first problem facing the soldiers on the island is not even to approach objects face to face, but to hide from the panoramic view, whose most striking images take the form of light illuminating shadows, accessing the darkest recesses of the rainforest, even piercing through the individual leaves, and piercing through the clouds in one memorable shot during the battle.[24]

How is it possible to escape from this panoramic vision and this panoramic presence of light? The answer is the same in Levinas and in Malick's film: through the apology. In using the word to denote the "plane of the inner life"[25] and its discourse, Levinas of course plays on the etymology of the word: only discourse, *logos*, can separate; *apo-* can break totality in the defense of its own subjectivity, its own interiority. In the film as well, interiority is the first element to be opposed to vision and pervasive light, and it takes the form of monologues in voice-over.

MONOLOGUE

These monologues are never more noticeable in the film than when they occur in the midst of a battle, for it is most logically then that the soldiers need monologues to resist engulfing totality. Levinas explains that this is the aim of thought or "psychism," and his analysis can also be a way to approach the metaphysical dimension of these monologues:

> The original role of the psychism does not, in fact, consist in only reflecting being [à la Heidegger]; it is already a way of being [une manière d'être], resistance to the totality. Thought or the psychism opens the dimension this way requires. The dimension of the psychism opens under the force of the resistance a being

> opposes to its totalization; it is the feat of radical separation. The cogito, we said, evinces separation. The being infinitely surpassing its own idea in us – God in the Cartesian terminology – subtends the evidence of the cogito, according to the third Meditation.[26]

If we follow Levinas, it is thus only natural that in the midst of battle, the individual turns to the idea of the infinite, "the idea of the infinite is us," which is so often alluded to in *Totality and Infinity*. My aim however is not to concentrate on the content of these monologues, nor is it to defend them from accusations of being "metaphysical hoaxes;"[27] I do not think they need that. Nor do I intend to follow their much more interesting study as exemplars of "vernacular metaphysics."[28] In Levinassian terms, I want to focus on their "Saying" rather than on their "Said," on the conditions of their utterance rather than on what is actually being said. This "Saying" is "antecedent to the verbal signs it conjugates, to the linguistic systems and the semantic glimmerings, a foreword preceding languages."[29]

There are several factors that lead the spectator to ponder on the conditions of the utterance by unsettling the meaning of the words, their "Said," by making it to some extent contingent upon these conditions. First, the meaning of the words is often suspended because their relation to images is constantly questioned. Again, Chion offers the best examples:

> When there is a flashback, the image seldom follows the voice. Nor is the inner voice in the action; it provides a free, often atemporal commentary. It seldom reacts to what is happening or has just happened.[30]

Chion notes specific discrepancies between words and images, and remarks that from this point of view *The Thin Red Line* follows Malick's preceding work, *Days of Heaven*, but takes an opposite course: "This 'under-verbalized' film [*Days of Heaven*] is followed by one that is over-verbalized: everything is described in words after being shown. As a result, we continue to detect a lack of balance, an unease between words and actions."[31]

Also, as Chion and others[32] have remarked, quite a few voice-overs share the same Southern accent, which makes their attribution difficult, and informs their meaning to a great extent. This in itself is a proof if need be of the fact that meaning does not lie alone in the words but in their utterance by a given individual, in their Saying as much as in their Said. We are denied any stable meaning to ascribe to the words themselves, and can only grapple with them, and recognize variations of "the idea of the infinite in us," but the meaning of the words remains suspended on their possible attribution or misattribution to a character. In particular, the final voice-over has been given different attributions by different critics, thus greatly informing the meaning each gives to the words. I will come back to this in my closing remarks but, in fact, what will guide my reflection until then is that the monologues must run the risk of incomprehension to turn into dialogues with the spectator. So the criticism denouncing "metaphysical hoaxes," utterly missing the point as it is, could be valuable after all inasmuch as it proves beyond question the possibility of misunderstanding that is essential to the dialogue between film and spectator. There can be no misunderstanding in monologue, quite obviously, and monologue, if it represents a first step in the attempted escape from totality, must open onto dialogue, and onto real dialogue in the Levinassian sense, that is dialogue face to face.

One way to begin to think about this necessary opening might be the fate of Private Jack Bell. He escapes, often in the midst of battle, into the memory of his fusion with his wife, and in imaginary dialogue with her, exclaiming for example, "Flow together, like water, till I can't tell you from me." Towards the end of the film, after the main battle, he receives a letter in which she announces that she has found another man. The failure of Bell's dream could be read as an indictment; his dream of fusion did not allow him to meet the other, it only recreated a totality of two beings, and amounted to the same, to Ego: "If to love is to love the love the Beloved bears me, to love is also to love oneself in love, and thus to return to oneself. Love does not transcend unequivocably – it is complacent, it is pleasure and dual egoism."[33]

The whole thrust of Stéphane Mosès's analysis of Levinas's relation to war is that no such "return to oneself" can be the appropriate answer to war, but that the only escape from war lies in the "idea of the infinite in us." For Mosès, Levinas follows on Franz Rosenzweig's efforts to meditate the consequences of war – in the case of Rosenzweig World War I – and on his efforts to find an escape from the reign of totality that war seems to herald, but with a complete shift as to the sort of place which might provide escape:

> For Rosenzweig, as we have seen, this extra-territorial place is the Ego, the subject anchored into the affirmation of his irreducible singularity. And it is precisely this attempt at starting philosophy once more from the perspective of the pure experience of the Ego that Levinas refuses ... This explains his radical shift of perspective in relation to Rosenzweig: there is no place for anything outside the system of Totality, save for exteriority itself ... Levinas, taking inspiration from a famous passage in Descartes's Meditations, calls this exteriority the idea of the infinite.[34]

But, as Mosès points out, the idea of the infinite in us is not something which can be grasped and thematized, but something that can only be shown through

> a lived experience, that of the revelation of the Other's exteriority. The other man, in his radical alterity, imposes himself as non-integrable, as one who cannot be reduced to an element among others in the totality of which I myself am a part. The place external to the system of Being, from which the very notion of Totality loses its meaning, is not the Ego, but the Other.[35]

Thus, if quite obviously Bell's imaginary dialogue with his wife, which is but an imaginary amalgamation with the other half of his couple, cannot be a viable escape from war, the monologues which meditate the "idea of the infinite in us" will not suffice either. The idea of the infinite in us must be met in the face of the other, and in the dialogue with the other, and mostly with the enemy, who constitutes the very paradigm of the Other.

DIALOGUE

Unsurprisingly, Levinas insists on the importance of dialogue as a possible way out of totality, and specifically the totalizing form of history, which is never so acute as in war:

> Though of myself I am not exterior to history, I do find in the Other a point that is absolute with regard to history – not by amalgamating with the Other, but in speaking with him. History is worked over by the ruptures of history, in which a judgment is

> borne upon it. When man truly approaches the Other he is uprooted from history.[36]

The Thin Red Line is structured around three important dialogues between Welsh, the cynic or the almost-cynic-but-not-quite, and Witt, the Christic figure. However, these dialogues are marked by radical incomprehension. Chion remarks on these dialogues and on other dialogues in the film that they are not much more than monologues, as is often the case with Malick: "Many dialogues in Malick's films are in fact thus monologues, allowing the words to resonate in the silence of the 'interlocutor' – and echoing the intermittent interventions of the narrative voice or inner monologue."[37] Of the three dialogues between Welsh and Witt that define the trajectory of these essential characters, and thus the trajectory of the whole film, this is especially true of the one that takes place in the middle of the film, in a grass field just before the final assault on the Japanese bunker. In fact Welsh does most of the talking, and Witt offers his face. But this face is an answer, and Levinas's words seem strikingly fitting to Witt's dazed and dazzling face especially:

> The face is a living presence; it is expression … The face speaks. The manifestation of the face is already discourse. He who manifests himself comes, according to Plato's expression, to his own assistance. He at each instant undoes the form he presents.
>
> This way of undoing the form adequate to the Same so as to present oneself as other is to signify or to have a meaning. To present oneself by signifying is to speak. This presence, affirmed in the presence of the image as the focus of the gaze that is fixed on you, is said.[38]

The first exchange between Welsh and Witt had taken place at the beginning of the film, when history, in the form of a patrol boat, had caught up with Witt, AWOL with another soldier in a Melanesian village. Then Witt had answered Welsh's affirmation that there was "no world but this one" with the counter-affirmation that he thought he had "seen another world." His silent face during the second dialogue is a much more potent affirmation that there is something beyond totality, that there is a way of being "otherwise than being," precisely because the silent face eschews words, which always run the risk of pretending to totality. Dialogue does not only amount to words, it is first and foremost a way of accepting the face of the other. Again war is the best way to make this dimension sensible, and most particularly the relation to Japanese prisoners after the battle, in some of the most harrowing scenes in the film. As an introduction to their analysis, I will recall Levinas's well-known insistence on the ethical dimension of the defenseless face:

> Infinity, stronger than murder, already resists us in [the face of the Other], is his face, is the primordial expression, is the first word: "you shall not commit murder." The infinite paralyses power by its infinite resistance to murder, which, firm and insurmountable, gleams in the face of the Other, in the total nudity of his defenceless eyes, in the nudity of the absolute openness of the Transcendent. There is here a relation not with a very great resistance, but with something absolutely other: the resistance of what has no resistance – the ethical resistance. The epiphany of the face brings forth the possibility of gauging the infinity of the temptation to murder, not only as a temptation to total destruction, but also as the purely ethical impossibility of this temptation and attempt.[39]

Malick presents us with the most graphic and the most effective way of showing the importance of the Biblical interdict in staging the actual murder of a number of defenseless Japanese soldiers who are attempting to surrender or who have surrendered.[40] Levinas reminds us that the interdict does not preclude the possibility of murder, but nevertheless claims antecedence:

> For the Other cannot present himself as Other outside of my conscience, and his face expresses my moral impossibility of annihilating. This interdiction is to be sure not equivalent to pure and simple impossibility, and even presupposes the possibility which precisely it forbids – but in fact the interdiction already dwells in this very possibility rather than presupposing it; it is not added to it after the event, but looks at me from the very depths of the eyes I want to extinguish, looks at me as the eye that in the tomb shall look at Cain.[41]

Films, like dreams, present possibilities in the form of images, and there cannot be any image more strongly expressive of the possibility of murder than actual murders. These murders give meaning to the fact that a certain number of soldiers do refuse to murder. In the same way, the insistence on nudity, misery, and hunger in Levinas seems to be given literal expression in the scenes involving Japanese prisoners:

> The nakedness of [the face of the stranger] extends into the nakedness of the body that is cold and that is ashamed of its nakedness. Existence is, in the world, a destitution. There is here a relation between me and the other beyond rhetoric. This gaze that supplicates and demands, that can supplicate only because it demands, deprived of everything because entitled to everything, and which one recognizes in giving … – this gaze is precisely the epiphany of the face as a face. The nakedness of the face is destituteness [*la nudité du visage est dénument*]. To recognize the Other is to recognize a hunger.[42]

The nakedness, hunger, shame of the Japanese prisoners is an injunction to sanctity. It is also a "Saying" that, without any words being said, demands that, "Prior to the said, saying uncovers the one that speaks, not as an object disclosed by theory, but in the sense that one discloses oneself by neglecting one's defenses, leaving a shelter, exposing oneself to outrage, to insults and wounding."[43] There is nothing surprising in the fact that Witt, the Christic figure, responds to this demand, once again offering his face, or more prosaically chewing gum, as a token of care. But again the injunction, the demand of the destitute face is given a graphic expression in the actual profanation which the face seems to forbid. One of the soldiers, in horrible images,[44] desecrates faces by literally plunging into them with his hands and with pliers to collect golden teeth. In a chilling sequence, this soldier will remember his desecration and the words of a Japanese soldier he cruelly teased, and will burst into tears. Chion comments on the importance of the sequence:

> Strangely, western commentators have shown no interest in what the Japanese are saying. I have asked a student to translate it. When Dale sadistically tells the Japanese prisoner he is going to die, the prisoner repeats over and over that the American too will die one day. Neither expects to be understood by the other. It is this speech that will remain, these phonemes incomprehensible

> to Dale (Kisamawa shinundayo) that – as revealed in a brief flashback – he keeps within him without having understood them, embedded in him like a blade, a dagger, a wound to the quick, which is for him a chance to live again as a human being, no longer dehumanised by the war. His tears, in which none of his companions join or sympathise with him, are the sign of his return to humanity.[45]

In Levinas's terms, it could be said that although the American soldier did not understand the "Said" of the Japanese's discourse, he finally understood his "Saying." In fact, his double misunderstanding, as the words are the words that the kamikazes utter when they are just about to die and bring death to their enemy, has turned into a deeper understanding. The very possibility for misunderstanding is at the basis of a dialogue that does not amount to the same, that really opens one to the other, that does not bring back to totality but opens to the infinite. What has been finally understood by the soldier, even though he did not understand the words themselves, and even though the meaning with which the Japanese uttered them, their "Said," was much different, is the fact that human beings share their common mortality, and share the time before they die, the "not yet" of time before death.[46] And this realization is a redemption, and a redemption of time itself. We saw that the film itself is the expansion in memory of two instants that precede death, that of Witt's mother and that of Witt. In a parallel manner, in the sequence under consideration, the realization in retrospect, by a soldier guilty of one of the most infamous deeds in the film, of the shared humanity of the face in the form of tears is an instant that transcends time and opens to the infinite, and recalls Levinas's words on tears:

> The identity of the present splits up into an inexhaustible multiplicity of possibles that suspend the instant. And this gives meaning to initiative, which nothing definitive paralyses, and to consolation – for how could one sole tear, though it be effaced, be forgotten, how could reparation have the least value, if it did not correct the instant itself, if it did not let it escape in its being, if the pain that glints in the tear did not exist "pending," if it did not exist with a still provisional being, if the present were consummated?[47]

And the spectator himself shares the misunderstanding of the words if he is not Japanese, and the understanding of the tears, most probably through his own.

CONCLUSION

I would like to conclude on a misunderstanding of my own, one that in fact I remain faithful to, hoping unashamedly that in great films as "in great books all our misreadings result in beauty."[48] The misreading is symptomatic of the way in which the monologues seem to await possible attribution and thus possible interpretation, and open in their very indecision a dialogue with the spectator. "Maybe these voices, erring on the surface of the screen, are where the force of cinema itself comes into its own."[49] And maybe erring in their attribution is only accepting that interpretation should be floating and open too. Here is the text of the final monologue, but again I will not deal with the words themselves, beautiful as they are, so much as with the circumstances of their Saying:

> Darkness from light. Strife from love. Are they the workings of one mind? The features of the same face? Oh, my soul, let me be in you now. Look out through my eyes. Look out at the things you made. All things shining.

Most critics attribute the words to Witt, who has just died and been buried and mourned by the company, and would then be speaking from beyond his grave. But Robert Pippin is right in correcting them:

> So now we come to one of the most startling facts about the film. Unless one has an extremely sensitive ear, it is almost impossible to realize that this voice we hear at the very beginning – by far the most frequent voice we will continually hear sound the most general reflections and questions about the meaning of war, killing, death, and the place of such violence in nature, and which will voice the last reflection we hear ("All things shining") – belongs not to Witt, an almost inescapable attribution on first hearing, but to a character we have barely caught a glimpse of: one Private Edward B. Train, played by John Dee Smith … He is an unlikely candidate to be the one raising the large questions he does, to say the least.[50]

Quite a radical shift in attribution and interpretation; quite a radical unsettling of attribution and interpretation. On first seeing the film, one of my most moving experiences in the cinema in a long time, I had attributed the words to Welsh, which is obviously not the case. While obviously owning to my mistake, I do continue to cling to that particular misreading, however. I see in it the spark that Witt saw in Welsh during their final dialogue when he exclaimed: "I still see a spark in you." "Where is your spark, now?" were Welsh's words in front of Witt's grave after his death, seeming to imply that it had been lost. In speaking the final words Welsh would accept as his own the spark that he thought lost when he was looking at Witt's grave. Certainly this misreading is in keeping with Welsh's last authentic words in monologue, words addressed to God, "If I never meet you in this life, let me feel the lack," if we accept the negative theology of, for example, French poet Roger Munier, "God's absence is, as absence, theophanic."[51] And Levinas reminds us that "faith purged of myths, the monotheist faith, itself implies metaphysical atheism. Revelation is discourse; in order to welcome revelation, a being apt for this role of interlocutor, a separated being, is required. Atheism conditions a veritable relationship with a true God."[52]

The recognition of God's absence, then, would be for Welsh a necessary step towards his final acceptance of Witt's spark. This misinterpretation, more importantly for the meditation at hand, is in keeping with the general movement of *Totality and Infinity*. Welsh has evolved from declared cynicism to dialogue with Witt to, finally, acceptance of Witt's spark after his death. *Totality and Infinity* starts with the lucid but potentially disabused acknowledgement of war, and then goes on to recognize in the midst of war, and sometimes because of war, the idea of the infinite in us, and finally embraces this idea in the form of goodness and peace.

A misreading is indeed a fragile basis to claim that "two texts … have similar diagrams" – to use Hanjo Berressem's words again – and to endeavour "to fold [them] onto each other." I hope however to have managed to some extent "to open up a field of intricate resonances." In the two texts, the time before death, its recognition, and its memory are of paramount importance. The two texts are an indictment of the totalizing role of vision, quite paradoxically in the case of the film. To totalizing vision, and totalizing history in the form of war, the two texts oppose the separating force of the apology. This apology, by necessity a monologue, must however make way to dialogue. This dialogue must be real dialogue, face to face. It entails the possibility of misunderstanding, but can lead to acknowledge what lies beyond words, "exposure without reserve to the other, which is saying."[53]

NOTES

1 Stéphane Mosès, *Au-delà de la guerre : trois études sur Levinas* (Paris: Éditions de l'Éclat, 2004), 7. All translations of sources given in French are mine. One of the two articles by François-David Sebbah that also helped me in my reflection opens on the same paradox is François-David Sebbah, "C'est la guerre," *Cités* 25 (*Emmanuel Levinas: une philosophie de l'évasion*, 2006): 41–54.

2 The complex relation between the two words is unravelled by Jacques Derrida in *Adieu: to Emmanuel Levinas*, translated by Pascale-Anne Brault and Michael Naas (Stanford: Stanford University Press, 1999), 49–50, 85–90.

3 Sebbah, "C'est la guerre," 43. This assertion is the object of an entire article by François-David Sebbah. "Décrire l'être comme guerre," in *Emmanuel Levinas et les territoires de la pensée*, edited by Danielle Cohen-Levinas and Bruno Clément (Paris: Presses universitaires de France 2007), 139–55.

4 Emmanuel Levinas, *Totality and Infinity: An Essay on Exteriority*, translated by Alphonso Lingis (Pittsburgh: Duquesne University Press, 1969), 21, quoted in Sebbah, "C'est la guerre," 43.

5 Levinas, *Totality and Infinity*, 204.

6 Ibid., 222–3.

7 Derrida, *Adieu*, 88.

8 Emmanuel Levinas, "Paix et proximité," *Les Cahiers de La nuit surveillée* 3 (*Emmanuel Lévinas*), edited by Jacques Rolland (Lagrasse: Verdier, 1984), 339–46, 342. In all quotes the emphasis is the author's.

9 See Derrida, *Adieu*, 90.

10 See the analysis of these final shots in Michel Chion, *The Thin Red Line* (London: British Film Institute, BFI Modern Classics, 2004), 72. Robert Pippin also studies the succession of these final images in "Vernacular Metaphysics: On Terrence Malick's *The Thin Red Line*," *Critical Inquiry* 39 (Winter 2013): 247–75, 275.

11 Simon Critchley, "Calm: On Terrence Malick's *The Thin Red Line*," *Film-Philosophy* 6, no. 48 (27 October 2014). Critchley questions the

notion of "Heideggerian Cinema," taking the expression from Marc Fursteneau and Leslie MacEvoy, "Terrence Malick's Heideggerian Cinema: War and the Question of Being in *The Thin Red Line*," *The Cinema of Terrence Malick: Poetic Visions of America*, edited by Hannah Patterson (London: Wallflower Press, 2003), 173–85. A middle ground is offered by Robert Sinnerbrink in "A Heideggerian Cinema? On Terrence Malick's *The Thin Red Line*," *Film-Philosophy* 10, no. 3 (December 2006).

12 Levinas, *Totality and Infinity*, 25.

13 Richard Pedot, "Tout s'explique : deux mots de la fin célèbres," *Ranam* 37 (*Expliquer*, 2004): 61–8. Pedot borrows the term to Shoshona Felman's study of Lacan's approach of literary texts in Felman, *Jacques Lacan and the Adventure of Insight: Psychoanalysis in Contemporary Culture* (Cambridge, MA: Harvard University Press, 1987).

14 Hanjo Berressem, "Serres Reads Pynchon/Pynchon Reads Serres," *Postmodern Culture* 11, no. 3 (May 2001).

15 Critchley, "Calm."

16 Levinas, *Totality and Infinity*, 224, translation slightly modified.

17 Ibid., 243.

18 A similar paradox has been noted by critics using Heidegger, a philosopher equally wary of vision. Fursteneau and MacEvoy state rather curiously that "cinema seems a strange choice for poiesis," as if what was under scrutiny was Malick's use of cinema to illustrate Heidegger, rather than the critics' use of Heidegger – or Levinas – to explain Malick. Fursteneau and MacEvoy, "Terrence Malick's Heideggerian Cinema," 185. The paradox is also the starting point of Bradford Vivian, "The Question of the Cinema," *The Journal of Speculative Philosophy* 19, no. 3 (2005): 250–66.

19 Chion, *The Thin Red Line*, 37.

20 John Toll, "The War Within," interview with Stephen Pizzello, *American Cinematographer* 80, no. 2 (February 1999): 42–58, quoted throughout in the web pagination (accessed 27 October 2014), 1–4.

21 Much to the disagreement of the crane's technicians: "Our expert technicians, Michael Gough and Mark Willard, kept wanting to show off how high it would go, but I kept hammering them with my mantra: 'It's a dolly, not a crane.'" Toll, "The War Within," 2.

22 Chion, *The Thin Red Line*, 37.

23 Levinas, *Totality and Infinity*, 191. Vision and knowledge are constantly paralleled in *Totality and Infinity*, and are constantly said to offer no escape from totality, quite on the contrary. Jacques Derrida

probes the limits of this paradoxical bringing to light of the totalizing role of light in "Violence and Metaphysics: An Essay on the Thought of Emmanuel Levinas," *Writing and Difference*, translated by Alan Bass (London: Routledge, 1978), 67–192. See Sean Gaston's discussion in *Derrida, Literature and War: Absence and the Chance of Meeting* (London: Continuum, 2009), 38.

24 John Toll confirms that the effect was willed: "We had some days when the light changes happened so quickly that we just shot through them ... We didn't fight the conditions; we just tried to make them part of the story. In fact, for one Akela shot of the soldiers climbing up the hills, we waited specifically for a light change to happen. The scene starts out in heavy cloud cover, but the sun comes out and reveals these guys sneaking through the grass. That particular light change worked well for us." Toll, "The War Within," 3.

25 Levinas, *Totality and Infinity*, 240.

26 Ibid., 54.

27 Tom Whalen, "'Maybe all men got one big soul': The Hoax within the Metaphysics of Terrence Malick's *The Thin Red Line*," in *It's What We Do Best: Essays on War Films by Godard, Malick, and Carpenter* (Black River Falls, WI: Obscure Publications, 2009), 20–31.

28 Pippin, "Vernacular Metaphysics."

29 Emmanuel Levinas, *Otherwise than Being, or Beyond Essence*, translated by Alphonso Lingis (Pittsburgh, PA: Duquesne University Press, 1981), 5, 41–9.

30 Chion, *The Thin Red Line*, 56.

31 Ibid., 65.

32 See for example Pippin, "Vernacular Metaphysics," 251–2.

33 Levinas, *Totality and Infinity*, 266.

34 Mosès, *Au-delà de la guerre*, 42–4.

35 Ibid., 44–5.

36 Levinas, *Totality and Infinity*, 52.

37 Chion, *The Thin Red Line*, 60.

38 Levinas, *Totality and Infinity*, 66.

39 Ibid., 199.

40 This staging of the murdering of prisoners is one of the common points between *The Thin Red Line* and *Saving Private Ryan*. The two films, shot at the same moment, are often compared, and the difference of treatment of these episodes is probably the most patent example of the abyss separating the two films.

41 Levinas, *Totality and Infinity*, 232–3. Derrida comments on this passage in *Adieu*, 17, 31n.

42 Levinas, *Totality and Infinity*, 75.
43 Levinas, *Otherwise than Being*, 49. In my own use of the words "Said" and "Saying," I keep the capitals present in the French version – "Dit" and "Dire" – but they are absent from the translation and thus from the quotes.
44 Although what makes them horrible is their symbolic power and not the graphic exactness of the shots or of the makeup, as in *Saving Private Ryan*. See the comments by John Toll, whose wife was chief makeup artist on *Saving Private Ryan*, shooting at exactly the same time as *The Thin Red Line*: "I had been trying to get Terry to do more graphic combat right from the beginning, but he didn't see the picture that way. After talking to my wife [on the phone], I'd tell him, 'Hey, Lois is doing all of this graphic blood stuff on *Private Ryan*.' And he'd reply, 'Oh, really? I don't think I want to do anything like that.'" Toll, "The War Within," 4.
45 Chion, *The Thin Red Line*, 60.
46 Levinas, *Totality and Infinity*, 224.
47 Ibid., 238. One of the most beautiful texts on tears in the face of death is Jacques Derrida's homage to Jean-Marie Benoist, "The Taste of Tears," in *The Work of Mourning*, translated by Pascale-Anne Brault and Michael Naas (Chicago: Chicago University Press, 2001), 105–10.
48 Proust's words in *Contre Sainte Beuve* are quoted in Gilles Deleuze and Claire Parnet, *Dialogues* (Paris: Flammarion, 1996), 11. Deleuze comments: "This is a good way to read: all misreadings are good – always provided that they do not consist in interpretations, but relate to the use of the book, that they multiply its use."
49 Michel Chion on voices-over in general, in *La voix au cinéma* (Paris: Cahiers du Cinéma/Éditions de l'Étoile, 1982), 15.
50 Pippin, "Vernacular Metaphysics," 257–8.
51 Roger Munier, *Pour un psaume* (Orbey: Artfuyen, 2007), 73. The sentence is followed by these words: "As absence of everything, covering everything, space and time, past and future, everything except the present, in its elusiveness touching eternity." The recognition of God's absence as theophanic is as redeeming of time itself as tears are according to Levinas.
52 Levinas, *Totality and Infinity*, 77. See Levinas's discussion of this passage in "L'assymétrie du visage," interview with France Guwy, *Cités* 25 (*Emmanuel Levinas : une philosophie de l'évasion*, 2006): 122–3.
53 Levinas, *Totality and Infinity*, 168.

16

Our War (BBC3) – The War in Afghanistan as Filmed by British Soldiers: From Capturing the Real to Building a Narrative and a Discourse

DAVID HAIGRON

Since the beginning of British intervention in Afghanistan in 2001, many accounts of the war (blogs, books, etc.) written by participants in the conflict have already been published.[1] In addition, soldiers on the frontline have made extensive use of digital cameras, camcorders, and mobile phones to record their daily experiences and share those images with fellow combatants or with friends and family back home. This includes sequences filmed at their base but also scenes of confrontation with the Taliban ("contact situations" in military parlance). This rather new phenomenon has been made possible by the use of GoPro video cameras attached to the soldiers' helmets, the recorded footage from which offers the viewers an immersive experience of what being caught in the enemy's fire actually means. In 2011, ten years after the beginning of the war, the BBC was granted permission by the Ministry of Defence (MOD), which had so far exerted censorship over it, to use that footage. These videos constitute the raw material on which the BBC3 documentary series *Our War* is based.

Our War aims at showing "the war in Afghanistan as seen through the eyes of the young soldiers on the frontline."[2] The first season (three one-hour episodes broadcast in June 2011) covers a period stretching from April 2007 to September 2010, while the second (aired in August 2012) focuses on more recent events.[3] The series won a British Academy Television Award in May 2012 in the "factual series" category. Initially entitled *Your War*, the BBC's collaborative project with the MOD started in 2010, when all the military involved in Operation Herrick[4] were invited to send their videos to a dedicated URL. All the files however had first to go through their unit's press officer, as the MOD wanted to keep control over the footage, some of which had already been posted on YouTube by soldiers despite the ministry's recommendations. The MOD had no editorial rights as such but retained a say should it deem that information given in the series might put the lives of soldiers at risk. The idea was to provide frontline soldiers with a platform to share their vision of the war and to reflect in a most authentic, unbiased way the reality of their day-to-day experience in Afghanistan.[5] In this regard, their accounts and their videos constitute "testimonies" that shed unique light on the ongoing conflict. The selected videos are commented upon by a voice-over providing detail on the context, and are intercut with interviews conducted in the UK with the protagonists of the scenes (and sometimes with the parents of those who died in the shown sequences).[6]

Though the approach chosen is described by the executive producer as "the purest form of observational documentary making,"[7] this does not mean that the series remains neutral, that it does not comment on its own content, or that it does not offer a "discourse." The word "discourse" implies, first, that the programme adopts or reflects a point of view, and therefore suggests an interpretation, and second, that it addresses a target audience to whom it conveys information (cognitive function) while aiming at triggering a reaction, be it better understanding, agreement, or emotion (conative function). In this regard, the documentary might contribute to shaping the general public's perception of the war, and in the long run might influence how the conflict will be remembered. Yet, because of the structure of the programme (interviews of soldiers mixed with excerpts from raw footage commented upon in voice-over), its discourse may be polyphonic and consequently ambiguous. Finally, in addition to the aforesaid cognitive and conative functions, the producers also had to take communicational considerations into account and to conceive the series in terms of storylines and characters. This process of "emplotment"[8] tends however to emphasize the spectacular and graphic aspects of war with soldiers being turned into the characters of a seemingly scripted narrative (an impression reinforced by the editing and the use of slow-motion effects, music, etc.).

This article examines how the aforementioned discourse is constructed, and questions the objective that it serves by analyzing the representation of the Afghan conflict offered in the TV documentary series *Our War*. It rests on microanalyses (study of the production techniques, commented scenes, quotations from the soldiers' accounts), interviews of producer Colin Barr in which he details his project, and essays on the narrativisation of history, so as to explore how oral and video "testimonies" are "emploted" in order to build a "discourse" on unfolding events, or, in other words, how the history of the present is being written. This, in the end, raises the question of the extent to which today's interpretation of the present fashions people's future collective memory of the war.

CAPTURING THE REAL: REPRESENTATION BASED ON VIDEO TESTIMONIES

Following the 9/11 attacks, the United States and the United Kingdom launched Operation Enduring Freedom in Afghanistan on 7 October 2001 with a view to removing the Taliban from power and capturing Osama bin Laden, the alleged head of the terrorist organisation al-Qaeda that had claimed responsibility for the attacks.[9] The International Security Assistance Force (ISAF) was only officially set up in December 2001 in accordance with the Bonn Conference to provide legal framework to the allied intervention and help the newly created Afghan Transitional Authority reconstruct the country after the Taliban had been ousted from Kabul.[10] In this regard, the British troops' primary mission was to maintain peace and display "courageous restraint" so as to win the local population's "hearts and minds" over to the new government.[11] Many high-ranking officers were also of the opinion that it might help the army restore the credibility it had lost in Iraq.[12] In April 2006, the British took command of military operations in the southern province of Helmand (*UK Joint Helmand Plan*).

This provides the context in which all the videos used in the documentary series *Our War* were made. Sequences of daily routine and bawdy camaraderie filmed at the COP (combat outpost) alternate with scenes of patrols and confrontations with the Taliban. In the latter instances, the footage recorded by helmet cameras offers a first-person perspective on the events and allows the viewers to "live" them as though they were in the soldier's head.[13] The restricted field of vision, the jerky frame, the sounds of gunfire, accelerated breathing and shouting, the sense of chaos as everyone runs for shelter, the fact that the enemy remains unseen, the fear of seeing one of the soldiers – or the "cameraman" himself – being hit by a bullet all creates a strong "reality effect."[14] All the commentaries published in the press about the series insist on that dimension:

> On October 7, 2001, Britain went to war in Afghanistan. Last night that conflict entered our living rooms in the most direct and visceral way … Every time the programme cut to a standard talking head, it was like being pulled physically from the action; every time it returned to the desperate struggle to save Private Gray's life – there were scenes of him tumbling repeatedly from a lightweight stretcher – it was like being placed back in it. It became clear that we were watching a "death in action." Despite the efforts of the medics sent to evacuate him, Gray was pronounced dead in the helicopter that had come to save him.[15]

> Hearts and minds stuff it wasn't, and what we saw was a gripping hour-long film of the confusion and terror involved in fighting an enemy that you seldom see and are only aware of when you hear the sound of gunfire or an IED explodes. "I was shittin' meself," said one squaddie. Me too, and I was thousands of miles away in London.[16]

Colin Barr, the executive producer of the series, points out that his intention was not to say or show everything, contrary to some soldiers and their families' expectations:

> My job as an executive producer is to make sure we don't sanitise war unnecessarily, especially if you're trying to make a series of films that are as close to the reality of it as you can get. But, at the same time, my job is to make sure that people don't just turn off because it's just too much.[17]

The series therefore does not include footage of British combatants stepping on IEDs (improvised explosive devices), nor does it show maimed soldiers, though the devastating effects – both physical and psychological – of home-made landmines are dealt with at length. Attacks and explosions are announced by the voice-over before they actually happen so as to defuse the shock they may cause, and the most serious casualties are only described orally.

British soldiers are both actors and victims in the conflict. They also are witnesses. The videos that they record and, to a lesser extent, the accounts that they give in the interviews are "testimonies."[18] In historiographical terms, a testimony is "an autobiographically certified narrative of a past event"[19] that is collected so as to support historical facts and constitute "documentary proof" that is then "placed into an archive."[20]

In the present case, the testimonies take the form of videos whose content echoes the oral accounts given by the interviewees. This device questions the suspicion usually attached to oral testimonies. In his work on memory and history, French philosopher Paul Ricœur writes that "Suspicion unfolds itself all along the chain of operations that begin at the level of the perception of an experienced scene, continuing on to that of the retention of its memory, to come to focus in the declarative and narrative phase of the restitution of the features of the event,"[21] and posits that this suspicion can be cleared by "the indisputable trustworthiness of the camera's eye."[22] In the videos recorded by the soldiers, the three operations (perception, retention, and restitution) rely on digital cameras and memory cards. These films may therefore capture something that the soldier wearing the camcorder has missed, record a scene that his memory has not retained, or, when played back, enable diverging recollections of a scene to be reconciled. Considering the conditions in which most footage was recorded, interpreting it may however be problematic. On the one hand, the images testify that what the interviewees talk about did happen the way they report it. But, on the other, it is often difficult to make sense of the raw footage if it is not contextualized and put into perspective. The images become inseparable from the interviews and the commentary in voice-over. Only the editing process, therefore, gathers together the "essential features of the fact of testifying": "the assertion of the factual reality of the reported event," "the fact that [this] assertion of reality is inseparable from its being paired with the self-designation of the testifying subject" ("I was there"), "a dialogical situation" in which the witness "is in the position of a third-person observer with regard to all the protagonists of the action" and the convergence of all the testimonies on a similar event so as to dispel suspicion about their accuracy.[23]

These testimonies document the history of the war in Afghanistan and, at the same time, tell individual stories: the protagonists are identified, their names are given, they talk about their own experiences and speak about all the other people who were involved in the scene. In other words, they tell stories about themselves, to themselves, but also to the audience of the documentary series. In doing so, they become the characters of a narrative.

MAKING SENSE: TURNING THE REAL INTO A NARRATIVE

Imposing a storyline structure on a sequence of sometimes loosely related events denotes an attempt to make sense of these events by establishing a causal link between them. In other words, it signals a bid to order the real. The process of "emplotment" implies that events deemed significant and individuals deemed salient be selected so as to create a cohesive and coherent story that unfolds in time (with a beginning, a middle, and an end) and follows its own logic. This approach is fully endorsed by the producer whose job was to select and edit the soldiers' videos. Colin Barr explains that "the kind of unmediated experience this footage offers the viewer is undeniably a powerful story-telling device,"[24] and describes his method as follows:

> You'd be looking for exactly the same things you'd look for any documentary. You're looking for a good, strong cast of characters that you can engage with, beginnings and middles and ends. And then, what we would do when we'd found that sort of material, we'd go back, speak to the person who had shot it, speak to all the people who had featured within it, and then retrospectively build the story around the footage so you then have multiple perspectives on a kind of single layer of footage.[25]

Although each episode focuses on different individual portraits, recurring "characters" feature throughout the series: the young recruit who finds in the army a place that society has always denied him; the one who wanted to escape a dull life, see the world or prove himself; the one who remembers his time in Afghanistan as the best period in his life; the one who confesses the adrenaline rush that being shot at gives him; the veteran who has been discharged from the army and suffers from PTSD (post-traumatic stress disorder); the tough, down-to-earth, experienced sergeant leading his platoon with authority; the benevolent, caring officer (lieutenant, captain, major, etc.) acting as a paternal figure; the devoted medic; and others.[26] The country itself – dubbed "Afghan" by the soldiers – constitutes a character distinguished by its topography and its population.

In production terms, storytelling implies the use of technical devices. Barr explains:

> *Our War* is an attempt to try and tell the story of the conflict in Afghanistan using the words and pictures of the soldiers themselves. So what we try and do is as far as possible to produce it so that it feels unmediated and raw, and like this is close to the experiences as it's possible to get, really. But as you can imagine, it takes a huge amount of effort, a huge amount of editing, a huge amount of production techniques to try and make it feel like it's entirely been told through their eyes.[27]

This also involves scoring a music theme for the series or using slow-motion sequences. Emotion is seen as a gateway to understanding:

> That has to work on an emotional level. If it's not, it becomes a war porn thing. And YouTube does that. You know you can go on YouTube and type in "IED blast" and you'll get reams of raw footage of just horrible stuff. What we do, as documentary makers, is making it emotional, is making you care and that's what those interviews are about.[28]

He points out in conclusion that the voice-over commentary was meant to provide information about the context but was not intended to talk viewers into a certain interpretation. One may therefore deduce that the scenes that apparently lacked "direction" (in production terms and in terms of goal to achieve) were purposely edited that way to reflect the chaos that characterizes "contact situations."

In historiography, storytelling is not antinomic to representing the real or exposing the truth. On the contrary, it may be the form that enables one to learn about historical events and to make sense of them.[29] American historian Hayden White explains:

> Most of those who would defend narrative as a legitimate mode of historical representation and even as a valid mode of explanation (at least for history) stress the communicative function. According to this view of history as communication, a history is conceived to be a "message" about a "referent" (the past,

historical events, and so on) the content of which is both "information" (the "facts") and an "explanation" (the "narrative" account).[30]

In an article entitled "The Value of Narrativity in the Representation of Reality," White had already argued that narration was "the solution to the problem of how to translate *knowing* into *telling*."[31] He thereby confirms what Arthur Coleman Danto stated in his *Analytical Philosophy of History*, namely that "meaning can be conferred on events 'only in the context of a story.'"[32] Drawing inspiration from Aristotle's *Poetics* and ancient myths, Paul Ricœur similarly posits that "the *configurational arrangement* ["emplotment"] transforms the succession of events into one meaningful whole … which makes the story followable."[33]

In *Our War*, events follow a logical pattern. The platoon on which the episode focuses has a mission to accomplish: guaranteeing the locals' safety, securing a road, provoking a fight with the Taliban so as to lure their attention away from another target, preparing the country for a handover to the local government, and training the Afghan National Police. The platoon encounters obstacles and faces danger as it steps into enemy territory and exchanges fire with the Taliban, resulting in one or several of its members being wounded before the group is forced to retreat while organizing the casualties' evacuation by helicopter.

"Emplotment" however tends to turn individual soldiers into renewable characters and to present their stories not as past events but as an ever-recurring present (all the more so since the TV series was first aired while British troops were still fighting). Besides, due to its editing and production techniques (POV perspective, fast-paced action, sounds of gunfire and explosion, music, etc.), *Our War* shares many of the representational and aesthetic codes that are common in war fiction films and videogames whose action takes place in Afghanistan.[34] This is reinforced by the confession made by several soldiers that the Afghan landscape reminded them of "a spaghetti western" and that "it feels unreal."[35] Parallels between the reality of war as shown in the documentary and fictional accounts of the Afghan conflict are also drawn by journalists in their commentary.[36] This confusion even raised a controversy in 2013 when Prince Harry called his job as a co-pilot in an Apache attack helicopter a "joy" and compared shooting the Taliban to playing a videogame.[37]

Analyzing the representation of the war in Afghanistan necessarily implies the examination of its form (narrative) and of its purpose (discourse). Fusing together a repertoire of individual testimonies and events only experienced by a limited group of people (micro-narratives) so as to create a meaningful whole amounts to shaping a discourse (meta-narrative),[38] which linguist Benvéniste defines as "every enunciation which assumes a speaker and an audience, the first intending to *influence the other* in some way."[39] The targeted addressees were primarily BBC3's young audience, but the programme, also accessible on the internet (BBC website, YouTube, etc.) and on DVD, reached a much wider public. The speaker's identity is arguably plural; the soldiers freely express their views, but the series' producer had the final say on the editing of what remains a collaborative project with the MOD. In the end, does the documentary suggest a certain interpretation of the conflict? Does it contribute to better understanding what is at stake in geopolitical terms? Or does it reflect the ambivalent feeling about Britain's presence in Afghanistan that many share among civilians and even the military?

NEUTRAL OBSERVATION VERSUS MORAL JUDGMENT: A MULTI-LAYERED DISCOURSE

The avowed aim of *Our War* was to enable the soldiers to tell their own stories. They address their brothers-in-arms, the future recruits, their friends and families, and to a larger extent, British people at home.

One of the most recurrent elements in the accounts given by the soldiers in the interviews pertains to the feeling of comradeship and to the sense of purpose and achievement that they share – the belief that British presence in Afghanistan has a positive influence and contributes to make this country a better place:

> Having been to Sangin when it was under siege … when seeing a little thriving market town, full of people, full of shops, you know you've made a difference. That is the difference. Some kind of normalisation. Yeah. There's a bit of a sense of pride. It meant that we are doing good despite what the rest of the world thinks. We are actually the boots on the ground and we see it first-hand.[40]

> In Iraq, I felt that we were the problem. In Afghanistan, I really felt that when you spoke to the kids, and when you spoke to people – local people – you felt that you were making a difference. You felt that the lives that we lost had actually been [lost] for a purpose, that we'd actually done something worthwhile.[41]

Those two commentaries are quite revealing. They acknowledge the failure of the allied intervention in Iraq but claim that, despite widespread belief to the contrary, significant progress is being made in Afghanistan. This is highlighted by images illustrating the first statement that show Afghan people waving and smiling to the camera (and therefore to the soldier who filmed them), thereby validating what is being said. In episode three of the first season ("Caught in the Crossfire"), the emphasis is on education and the opening of schools. The behaviours and attitudes of the British soldiers are described as benevolent and humane, in contrast with the Taliban's barbarism, exemplified by stories of beheaded teachers and girls whose faces were burnt with acid for attending school. "If we didn't have 'courageous restraint,' we'd be as bad as the Taliban themselves," Lance Sergeant Chris Haworth concludes.

The documentary also offers some protagonists the opportunity to express feelings that they are aware might be difficult to understand or accept for people who have not shared their experience, like the thrill of being shot at,[42] the thirst for revenge after a friend's death,[43] or even the pleasure of killing an enemy: "I did enjoy it!" Sgt Panter confesses in episode one, season one.[44]

The audience may react differently to the aforementioned statements, according to their own feelings and moral judgments. In their interviews, the soldiers – be they officers or other ranks – may be equally critical about their own actions, doubtful about their mission, or frank about the trauma they have experienced.[45] Viewers are reminded that most recruits are between seventeen and twenty-one years old, and that the 9/11 attacks that justify their presence in Afghanistan are for them but a distant memory associated with their teenage years.[46] Finally, the parents of the soldiers killed in action are also heard in the series. The use of close-ups reinforces the proximity effect and may enable viewers who have lost a child in war to identify with them and to share their grief. Anger at the institutions and the alleged lies of the politicians is expressed as well.[47]

Even if the documentary relies mainly on first-person accounts, it also produces third-person commentaries on the soldiers' attitudes and behaviours, and passes indirect judgment on British intervention in Afghanistan. It is obviously the producer's choice to have selected, in the final edit, sequences showing heavily armed, shades-wearing soldiers being dependent on a translator to address poorly clad locals, entering a small shop to ask for a Coca-Cola in English, distributing pens and sweets to slightly bemused children, or wondering about the Afghans' "strange" customs.[48] In these scenes, British soldiers seem out of place and their attitude is somewhat reminiscent of that displayed by Western tourists in countries they deem poor. Dedicating a long sequence (season one, episode three) to the rescue of a three-year-old girl accidently shot by members of the ANP (Afghan National Police) produces the confused impression that, despite all the supposed goodwill and benevolence of the British, their mission is bound to fail for exogenous reasons (the Taliban's folly or the presence of corrupt officers among the ANP). Seeing young soldiers using a hammock as a stretcher to try and carry away one of their wounded comrades, while being screamed at by a threatening sergeant, conveys an idea of unpreparedness and amateurism.[49]

The series' discourse may take the form of an indirect question, leaving undecided which answer is privileged, as illustrated by the concluding commentary in the final episode of the first season: "It has now lasted ten years and questions are being asked about whether the war can be won, and if it has made the world a safer or a more dangerous place." The ambiguity of the message delivered by the series only reflects the ambivalent feeling most Britons have regarding the war in Afghanistan. Doubts about British intervention have been voiced by journalists as well as by diplomats and army officers.[50] Public opinion is mostly opposed to the war even if it still supports "the boys."[51] Similarly, the documentary praises the bravery of the troops[52] while questioning whether the mission assigned to the British contingent may be fulfilled regarding the conditions in which the war is waged and the lethal consequences this has for many soldiers. Finally, it may also be interpreted as a wake-up call for the political elite who are responsible for having started the war and for conducting it:

> This being a film that had – presumably – been sanctioned by the British Army, there were no official recriminations; just the

standard comments of "a job well done in difficult circumstances," "a good cause," and "paying the ultimate sacrifice." But unofficially there were plenty: the references to "an unwinnable war," "the army pulling out of Afghanistan in 2014," and, most poignantly of all, the sergeant from Arnhem company who had left the army after that operation saying he "just didn't know if it was worth it any more." As anti-war propaganda, *Our War* was on a par with anything made by Martin Scorsese or Michael Cimino; and when it's our own army who is making the film it's probably time for the politicians to pay attention and to start covering the armed services' arses rather than their own.[53]

Given the context, *Our War* could never have been a totally consensual programme. When questioned on the effects he thought the series may have had on its audience, producer Colin Barr answered that judging from the various public meetings in which he took part, a fairly equal number of young people said they were attracted or repelled. Some of them however claimed that watching *Our War* was instrumental in their decision to join the army.[54]

The documentary series *Our War* uses video testimonies as raw material to create narratives that contribute to the construction of a discourse. In doing so, it combines historiographical and political considerations. On the one hand, it takes part in writing the history of the war in Afghanistan as it may be remembered and told in the future. On the other, it questions the legitimacy of the war and queries the means provided to those on the frontline. This point of view shows through the selection and editing made from the footage recorded by the soldiers. Now, if one compares this approach with that of the historian, as described by Tzvetan Todorov, one may posit that "this work of selecting and combining is necessarily guided by the search, not for truth, but for the good,"[55] and that the discourse heard in *Our War* also includes moral considerations.

CONCLUSION: WRITING HISTORY AND SHAPING COLLECTIVE MEMORY

In *The Writing of History*, Michel de Certeau argues that history is a conflation of facts ("*materia*") and commentary that arranges and interprets those facts ("*ornamentum*"). Historiography thus establishes a relation "between two antinomic terms, between the real and discourse."[56] The TV documentary series *Our War* offers a first-hand video account of the reality of the war as well as a discourse on that reality so as to enable the viewers to make sense of what they are watching. Writing the series supposes that the raw footage collected from the soldiers has been selected, edited, and "emploted" so as to produce a linear, ordered narrative that can be told to a target audience who will react to it. This approach is reminiscent of the notion of temporality in history[57] and integrates the different stages of shaping collective memory: selection of facts, archiving, transmission, and appropriation.[58] Examining the forms and functions of a representation of the war in Afghanistan based on films made by British soldiers on the frontline pertains to questioning how the conflict may be interpreted today and how it might be remembered tomorrow. To some extent, *Our War* takes part in writing the history of the war. It is also revealing, in this regard, that the MOD has launched the *War Story Project* in collaboration with the Imperial War Museum.[59] This project also focuses on individual portraits (photographs and videos) with a view to give a more human face to war. In doing so, its purpose is also to hammer home the argument that Britain's involvement in Afghanistan is justified by the necessity "to protect our national security by helping the Afghans take control of their own."[60] British soldiers are giving their lives not only to reconstruct a faraway country but also to guarantee peace at home.

NOTES

1 Alexander Allan (captain), *Afghanistan: A Tour of Duty* (Third Millennium Publishing, 2009); Craig Allen (reservist paratrooper), *With the Paras in Helmand: A Photographic Diary* (Pen & Sword Military, 2010); Doug Beattie (MC), *Task Force Helmand: A Soldier's Story of Life, Death and Combat on the Afghan Front Line* (Pocket Books, 2010); David Blakeley (captain), *Pathfinder: A Special Forces Mission behind Enemy Lines* (Orion, 2013); Sherard Cowper-Coles (former British ambassador in Afghanistan), *Cables from Kabul: The Inside Story of the West's Afghanistan Campaign* (Harper Press, 2012); Leo Docherty (captain), *Desert of Death: A Soldier's Journey from Iraq to Afghanistan* (Faber & Faber, 2007); Richard Dorney (lieutenant colonel), *The Killing Zone: The Grenadier Guards Pushed to the Limit on Helmand's Front Line* (Ebury Press, 2012); Paul

"Bommer" Grahame (sergeant) and Damien Lewis, *Fire Strike 7/9* (Ebury Press, 2011); Graham Lee (officer in the Air Assault Brigade), *Fighting Season: Tales of a British Officer in Afghanistan* (Gerald Duckworth & Co Ltd, 2013); Russell Lewis (major), *Company Commander* (Virgin Books, 2012); Charlotte Madison (captain), *Dressed to Kill: The Remarkable True Story of a Female Apache Pilot on the Frontline* (Headline Review, 2010); Mark Ormond (royal marine), *Man Down* (Corgi, 2010); Sean Rayment (ex-paratrooper, now defence journalist), *Bomb Hunters: In Afghanistan with Britain's Elite Bomb Disposal Unit* (Collins, 2011); Paul Smyth (major), *Blogging from the Battlefield: The View from the Front Line in Afghanistan* (The History Press, 2011); Steve Stone (pen name of a former SAS officer), *Afghan Heat: SAS Operations in Afghanistan* (Lulu.com, 2014); Richard Streatfeild (major), *Honourable Warriors: Fighting the Taliban in Afghanistan – A Front-Line Account of the British Army's Battle for Helmand* (Pen & Sword Military, 2014); Chantelle Taylor (sgt in the Royal Army Medical Corps), *Bad Company: Face to Face with the Taliban* (DRA Publishing, 2011); Stuart Tootal (colonel), *Danger Close: The True Story of Helmand from the Leader of 3 PARA* (John Murray, 2010); Simon Weston, *Helmand: The Diaries of Front-Line Soldiers* (Osprey Publishing, 2013), foreword.

2 http://www.bbc.co.uk/programmes/poovhs86.

3 For further detail on the series (episode titles, storylines, duration, airing dates, names of the narrator and producers, etc.), see: http://www.bbc.co.uk/programmes/poovhs86/episodes/guide.

4 "Operation Herrick" is the name given to all British operations conducted in Afghanistan. http://www.army.mod.uk/operations-deployments/22800.aspx.

5 Interview with Colin Barr, the series' executive producer, on *British Forces News* (29 October 2010). http://www.youtube.com/watch?v=aJKVjxp-h2I. Colin Barr explains that he drew inspiration from a 2009 BBC1 documentary entitled *Wounded*. The two-part programme focused on two injured soldiers as they came back from Afghanistan and already made use, though in a marginal way, of videos filmed by the protagonists. "Making 'Our War' – Colin Barr," interview at Coventry University, 6 October 2011. http://coventryuniversity.podbean.com/2012/01/03/making-%E2%80%98our-war%E2%80%99-colin-barr/. For further detail on *Wounded*, see: http://www.bbc.co.uk/programmes/b00n0q05/episodes/guide.

6 Each one of them also granted permission to use the videos. The interviews used the "talking head" format with the interviewees addressing the camera (Colin Barr's interview at Coventry University). In some sequences, the split-screen technique allows the viewers to watch the action as it is commented upon by the interviewee. Subtitles are sometimes used to explain military slang and acronyms, or to compensate for the poor quality of the directly recorded sound. Digital images have been added to the final edit to show the respective positions and movements of the soldiers and their enemies. Archive footage (documentary, news bulletins, Taliban propaganda video, etc.) has also been used. In season two, episode three ("The Lost Platoon"), excerpts from Lt Mark Evison's diary are read in voice-over by actor Benedict Cumberbatch.

7 "Making the Second Series of BBC Three's *Our War*," interview with Colin Barr, BBC, 17 August 2012. http://www.bbc.co.uk/blogs/aboutthebbc/posts/making-the-second-series-of-bb.

8 Paul Ricœur, *Time and Narrative* [*Temps et récit*], vol. 1 (Chicago: University of Chicago Press, 1990); Also in Paul Ricœur, *Memory, History, Forgetting* [*La Mémoire, l'histoire, l'oubli*] (Chicago: University of Chicago Press, 2004), 238; On the concept of "emplotment," see Hayden White, "Historical *Emplotment* and the Problem of Truth," in *Probing the Limits of Representation: Nazism and the "Final Solution,"* edited by Saul Friedlander (Cambridge: Harvard University Press, 1992), 37–53.

9 http://edition.cnn.com/2013/10/28/world/operation-enduring-freedom-fast-facts/.

10 http://www.isaf.nato.int/history.html.

11 Paul Dixon, ed., *The British Approach to Counterinsurgency: From Malaya and Northern Ireland to Iraq and Afghanistan* (Basingstoke: Palgrave Macmillan, 2012), 8, 135.

12 Ibid., 29.

13 Executive producer Colin Barr explains: "It feels like you're in somebody's head. When they look left, you look left. When they look right, you look right. And when they run, you run." Quoted in Louise Coletta, "Life at War Captured through the Eyes of Soldiers," *BBC News*, 28 May 2011. http://www.bbc.co.uk/news/uk-13573611.

14 See Roland Barthes, "L'effet de réel," *Communications* 11 (1968): 84–90; In "The Discourse of History," the French semiologist adds that "the prestige of *this happened* ['*le prestige du* c'est arrivé'] has a

truly historical importance and scope." Barthes, "Le discours de l'histoire," *Social Science Information* IV, no. 4 (1967): 65–75.

15 Chris Harvey, "*Our War*, BBC Three, review," *The Daily Telegraph*, 7 June 2011. http://www.telegraph.co.uk/culture/tvandradio/8561833/Our-War-BBC-Three-review.html.

16 John Grace, "TV Review: Our War; Ian Brady – Endgames of a Psychopath," *The Guardian*, 20 August 2012. http://www.theguardian.com/tv-and-radio/2012/aug/20/tv-review-our-war.

17 Interview at Coventry University.

18 The interviews were not conducted by historians and the interviewees were asked to look down into the camera so as to maximize emotion. The beginning of episode two in the second season ("Return to Death Valley") offers a glimpse of the setting used to carry out the interviews. There is no guarantee either that several takes were not shot to meet the producer's expectations. For these reasons, it remains debatable whether the oral accounts given in the interviews may be considered as "testimonies" in the historiographical meaning of the term.

19 Renaud Dulong, "Récit autobiographiquement certifié d'un événement passé," in *Le Témoin oculaire : les conditions sociales de l'attestation personnelle* (Paris: EHESS, 1998), 43, quoted in Ricœur, *Memory, History, Forgetting*, 163.

20 Ibid.

21 Ibid., 162.

22 Ibid.

23 Ibid., 163–6.

24 Quoted in Coletta, "Life at War Captured through the Eyes of Soldiers."

25 Interview at Coventry University.

26 Only two women appear in the whole series: a medic (Private Stacey French in season one, episode three) and an unidentified young recruit who is seen very briefly in season two, episode two.

27 "Making the Second Series of BBC Three's *Our War*."

28 Interview at Coventry University.

29 See: Louis O. Mink, *Historical Understanding* (Ithaca: Cornell University Press, 1987); Mink, "Narrative Form as a Cognitive Instrument," in *The Writing of History: Literary Form and Historical Understanding*, edited by Robert H. Canary & Henry Kozicki (Madison: University of Wisconsin Press, 1978), 129–40, also published in Geoffrey Roberts, ed., *The History and Narrative Reader*

(London: Routledge, 2001), 211–20. See also Mink, "Representation and Narration," in Ricœur, *Memory, History, Forgetting*, 238–48.

30 Hayden White, "The Question of Narrative in Contemporary Historical Theory," *History and Theory* 23 (1984), reproduced in White, *The Content of the Form: Narrative Discourse and Historical Representation* (Baltimore: The Johns Hopkins University Press, 1987), 40; see also William Cronon, "A Place for Stories: Nature, History, and Narrative," *Journal of American History* 78, no. 4 (March 1992): 1349.

31 Hayden White, "The Value of Narrativity in the Representation of Reality," *Critical Inquiry* 7, no. 1 (Autumn 1980), reproduced in White, *The Content of the Form*, 1 (original italics).

32 Arthur Coleman Danto, *Analytical Philosophy of History* (Cambridge: Cambridge University Press, 1965), 11.

33 "*L'arrangement configurant transforme la succession des événements en une totalité signifiante [qui] fait que l'histoire se laisse suivre.*" Ricœur, *Time and Narrative*, 67.

34 *The Patrol* (directed by Tom Petch, 2013) was the first British feature film to deal with Britain's involvement in Afghanistan. For video-grames, see for example: *Heavy Fire: Afghanistan* or *Medal of Honour*.

35 Season one, episode one. There is also a reference to a "western movie environment" in season two, episode three.

36 See the two following examples:

"Our War was an extraordinarily powerful, even profound, insight into the nature of war and the character of the people who execute it. It was as gripping and moving as The Hurt Locker or Platoon, only with the added advantage that the raw emotion was real." Jim Shelley, "Powerful and Profound: Here Is 'Our War,' Here Are the Lives It Costs," *The Daily Mirror*, 26 August 2012. http://www.mirror.co.uk/tv/tv-reviews/powerful-and-profound-our-war-on-bbc-shows-1281242.

"This extraordinary view of the conflict, jerky, low resolution, with a restricted field of vision that recalled the claustrophobia of 'first-person-shooter' computer games, and with a soundtrack that distorted every time Panter [the sergeant who filmed the scene] screamed a command was not how we are used to seeing war on our screens. It was much more real." Harvey, "*Our War*, BBC Three, review."

37 Jon Boone, "Taliban Retaliate after Prince Harry Compares Fighting to a Video Game," *The Guardian*, 22 January 2013. http://www.theguardian.com/uk/2013/jan/22/afghanistan-taliban-response-

prince-harry. In 2010, then defence minister Liam Fox expressed outrage at a soon-to-be-released videogame, *Medal of Honour*, for it enabled players to take the role of Taliban fighters. "No Backing Down as Fox Takes on 'Un-British' Video Game," *Politics*, 23 August 2010. http://www.politics.co.uk/news/2010/8/23/no-backing-down-as-fox-takes-on-un-british-vi.

38 This draws inspiration from the distinction made by Émile Benveniste between narrative and discourse. The former denotes an oral or iconic account of past events, while the latter supposes the expression of a point of view on the events and can only be interpreted in a given context. See: Jean-Paul Desgoutte, ed., *La Mise en scène du discours audiovisuel* (Paris: L'Harmattan, 1999); Jean-Paul Desgoutte, *Le Verbe et l'image: essais de sémiotique audiovisuelle* (Paris: L'Harmattan, coll. «champs visuels», 2003).

39 "*Toute énonciation supposant un locuteur et un auditeur, et chez le premier l'intention d'influencer l'autre en quelque manière.*" Émile Benveniste, *Problèmes de linguistique générale*, vol. 1 (Paris: Gallimard, 1966), 241–2.

40 Sgt Simon Panter in season one, episode one ("Ambushed").

41 Lt Bjorn Rose in season one, episode one ("Ambushed").

42 The opening credits of the six episodes feature an extremely joyful and excited soldier who, amidst explosions and gunfire, addresses the camera and boasts: "This, ladies and gentleman, is fucking war!" Sgt Panter in season one, episode one admits: "Being in contact is like a drug. It's good fun. I know it sounds very, very strange, but being a soldier, there's nothing like being in contact, you know. It lets you know you're alive."

43 Lt Rose in season one, episode one: "I actually wanted to kill someone because I'd been there and they'd killed my man, and I wanted them to pay back for what they'd done. It's difficult to say that to people because you think: 'how would you want to kill another human being?' but it was very much an eye for an eye." Lt Jimmy Clark in season two, episode two: "Although obviously, you know, it's never nice to have to kill people, it was a good feeling for the platoon because we felt we'd been under attack, we were in a static location and it was a good way of showing them that we could fight back."

44 See also Sgt Simon Panter's portrait in Sean Rayment, "Fighting the Taliban in Afghanistan," *Daily Telegraph*, 30 August 2008. http://www.telegraph.co.uk/news/newstopics/onthefrontline/2652284/Fighting-the-Taliban-in-Afghanistan.html.

45 "Is it all worth it?" Lance Corporal Luke Langley wonders while admitting to drinking a lot and often looking for a fight when he came back home (season two, episode three). The same episode features another soldier talking about his alcoholism and the difficulty of being back home after being diagnosed with PTSD and discharged from the military. Season one, episode one includes the interview of a soldier explaining that he had to leave the army as he now suffers from epilepsy.

46 On the grounds of its members' young age, one of the platoons of the Princess of Wales's Royal Regiment was nicknamed "the kindergarten platoon." Season one, episode three ("Caught in the Crossfire").

47 See season one, episodes one and two.

48 Season one, episode three: "They smell different, they eat differently, they wear facial hair to a sort of extremes" (Lance Corporal Greg Staunton); "That's the way they are, and I respect the way they are" (Lance Corporal Robert Duncan about men praying on the side of the road); "The thing with the ANP was that 'courageous restraint' wasn't really a concept that they understood quite so well. I don't think it's really in their mindsets" (Capt. Neil Gow).

49 Season one, episode one ("Ambushed").

50 Dixon, ed., *The British Approach to Counterinsurgency*, 28–41.

51 In November 2001, 66 per cent of British respondents said they were in favour of the war. In March 2011, it was 31 per cent. Ibid., 122.

52 "The bravery of the British troops in Afghanistan has never been in question and it was fully in evidence here." Grace, "TV Review: Our War; Ian Brady – Endgames of a Psychopath."

53 Ibid. This quotation may also refer to the controversy mentioned in episode two, season one ("The Invisible Enemy"). In 2009, following the death of Jamie Janes, then Prime Minister Gordon Brown sent the soldier's mother a condolescence letter as is customary. The controversy arose from the fact that the letter contained several spelling mistakes and that G. Brown mispronounced the victim's name in a filmed parliamentary session.

54 Interview at Coventry University.

55 "*Ce travail de sélection et de combinaison est nécessairement orienté par la recherche, non de la vérité, mais du bien.*" Tzvetan Todorov, *Les Abus de la mémoire* (Paris: Arléa, 1995), 50, quoted in Ricœur, *Memory, History, Forgetting*, 86.

56 Michel de Certeau, *Writing History* [*L'Ecriture de l'histoire*] (New York: Columbia University Press, 1988), xxvii.

57 "History furnishes the empty frame of linear succession which formally answers to questions of *beginning* and to the need for *order*." Ibid., 12.
58 See also Paul Ricœur's analysis on "blocked memory" (in case of trauma), "manipulated memory" and "obligated memory" (including the duty of memory) in *Memory, History, Forgetting*, 68–92.
59 See http://www.iwm.org.uk/corporate/projects-partnerships/war-story.
60 See https://www.gov.uk/government/policies/establishing-stability-in-afghanistan.

17

Diary as Activism: The Case of *The Diary of an Unknown Soldier*

GEORGES FOURNIER

The Diary of an Unknown Soldier is a 1959 film by Peter Watkins. It follows a young soldier sent to France to fight in the First World War, on the last day of his life. The date is 1916. It recounts the last, desperate hours before he goes into combat. It dramatizes the traumas of war for volunteers, conscripts, and professional soldiers. The protagonist is not much older than eighteen, though the narration, which voices the inner thoughts of the boy, is from Watkins.

One of Watkins's documentary techniques is mind-reading, in its several guises, which he uses to show things as the boy sees and hears them. When the glorious morning atmosphere is shattered by the sound of mortar shells, he wonders whether the other men in his unit feel the same fear as he does, whether they are overwhelmed with it. He wishes he could appear cool, calm, and collected like some of the other men. He attempts to escape the reality of the situation, and comforts himself by thinking about the humorous qualities and characteristics that the other men exhibit. But fear returns when he realizes that his superior officer loves war and seems to be ignorant of the death and destruction that it causes.

Regarding the notion of the Unknown Soldier, it is closely connected with the First World War even though on the two sides of the English Channel the idea materialized in different ways and was brought to fruition at different times. Why an Unknown Soldier? Because of all the soldiers who fell victim to such violent deaths and could not be identified. There remained scattered pieces of their bodies that could not be reunited to determine their identity.[1]

As far as the film is concerned, the idea sprang from Watkins's contact with R.C. Sherriff's *Journey's End*,[2] a minimalist anti-war story that focuses on a soldier's thoughts and fears on the Western Front during World War I, and also from T.S. Eliot's poem, *The Hollow Men*.[3] Watkins explains:

> In the mid-1950s, I underwent compulsory military service in Britain ... I landed a clerical post in Canterbury, Kent, where I fortunately met a group of people running an amateur theatre group called "Playcraft" ... A drama student bitten by the "acting bug" in London before my military service, I acted in several of Playcraft's productions – including in R.C. Sheriff's anti-war drama, *Journey's End*, set in the trenches during World War I. Immediately following my release from the army, I was bitten by another – amateur filmmaking – "bug," and acquired a Bolex spring-driven 8mm camera.[4]

The filmmaker's involvement with film as a political medium is so important that the first two parts of this article are going to be devoted to how this trope characterizes his work; the other two developments are centred on the diary as a sepulchre and as a statement of self-assertion.

PETER WATKINS'S APPROACH TO THE FILMIC MATERIAL

The Diary of an Unknown Soldier is one of Watkins's first movies, a creation that laid the foundations for future TV productions connected with war, like *The Battle of Culloden* (BBC, 15 December 1964) and *The War Game* (BBC, 31 July 1985). It contains all the ingredients of Watkins's approach to the concept of "docudrama," which is defined as a well-documented piece of work, whatever the material, whether first-hand testimonies or historic events, that is combined with fictional elements to create a hybrid film. The notion of hybridity is already contained in the notion of diary in so far as it is a highly personal account that purports to testify to what the past – the narrator's present – was like. Even though it is fiction, a diary is meant to be a record and as such it has a testimonial dimension.

One of the main features of this hybrid form, called docudrama or dramadoc, is its dynamism. It is particularly well suited for a television audience that is not as captive as a cinema audience and whose attention to serious matters needs to be regularly rekindled with filmic devices, what Dai Vaughan calls "constantly shifting stylistic practices."[5] Its dynamism perfectly suits the demands of assignments by filmmakers who are politically committed. Its hybridity is a decided statement of intent designed to claim out loud that it is the filmmaker's vision of the topic and not a neutral one. Yet, it is not propaganda nor is it a devious attempt to gain support from an audience that would be tricked into believing that fiction is actuality. The filmmaker's commitment to the transmission of a point of view clearly classifies his work as fiction, which Dai Vaughan refers to as a legitimate and "creative response"[6] to existing material already circulating in the historical world. Originally, more than a genre, it is a series of techniques designed to elicit responses among viewers. Among such devices, recreation and re-enactment hold prominent positions, as does the filling of gaps with fictional segments that rest on remembrances or on hypothetical and conjectural elements. Watkins draws much of his inspiration from Sherriff's *Journey's End*. Memory, more than conjectures, is relied upon since Sherriff himself took an active part in the First World War as a private; his play is the compilation of many of his personal experiences. The promiscuity that prevails, the meaninglessness of the motives for which soldiers fight – like the fact that they rejoice over their spoils, among which is an area of 200 square yards of mud – the necessity to try and understand what others think and the way they behave so as to make sense of the insanity that prevails, all these elements infuse Watkins's film and are part and parcel of Sheriff's play.

The Diary of the Unknown Soldier is the filmic equivalent of all the letters soldiers would write and of all the sketches of the conflict they would draw; all these forms of testimony are attempts by soldiers to situate themselves among the horrors of the mass conflict. Watkins's real creativity lies in his capacity to bring the past to life and to make the narrator's experience alive, thanks to the work of imagination; it consists in giving visual representations to what was written and in suggesting what is missing in the original text but that can be conjectured. The filmmaker conjures up filmic images of what is provided and hinted at in the written material; the audience is afforded a visual representation of what life was like on the front, something which only filmic fiction can provide.

THE DIARY OF AN UNKNOWN SOLDIER AS MATRIX IMAGES

The images shot for *The Diary of an Unknown Soldier* became matrix images for Watkins's later films, and he used them in productions for television in the UK and abroad, whether for *The War Game* or for *Punishment Park*. As a matrix film, *The Diary of an Unknown Soldier* provides ample examples of the techniques the filmmaker was to use in some of the films he shot later and of the reactions they were intended to arouse among viewers. Watkins's docudrama style is designed to entertain and capture the attention of viewers on topics about which he felt highly committed and on which he intended to testify. The montage he uses in these films is both eye-catching and effective in creating the message and mood that he wants to convey. His recurrent use of close-ups allows for an intimate connection with the protagonists and provides access to their thoughts. In *The Diary of an Unknown Soldier*, Watkins's use of angled shots, in the montage, and perspective shots looking into the sky, is very efficient in so far as it gives viewers a glimpse of the sense of disillusionment that was felt by soldiers, especially those as young as the protagonist. The viewer is afforded a glimpse of the protagonist's feelings and Watkins's editing choices help show his distress. While the protagonist's fear reaches a peak, as he thinks of the impending doom that is soon to come, Watkins jumps from battle scenes of soldiers waging war, to shots providing information on the soldier's perspective, and finally zoom-ins on the eyes of the soldiers themselves. This montage is effective at rendering a feeling of extreme fear, excitement, and anxiety, which are feelings very similar to what those engaged in the battles would experience.

Watkins's willingness to bear testimony to the horrors of war and make explicit factual claims with fiction led him to tamper with the codes of the documentary. He pioneered the field of fictional images of war designed to document how mass destruction happened. His images became prototypes of how war could be seen by future generations since at the time images of war were not rife. So he offered paradigmatic images of war which, though fictional, had a documentary touch and were based on true stories, features which later defined docudrama.

Consequently, his films meet the requirements needed to have the title of committed films that became the main providers of authored television in Great Britain. With the notion of author comes the idea of point of view, and this is precisely what Watkins wanted to promote, not an unbiased approach to the issues he tackles, but, on the contrary, a highly personal and committed perception. However, images of memories, of things remembered, are inevitably highly subjective and lead to deeply emotional interpretations. As Derek Paget notes, docudramas are inclined to move away from a depiction of general historical narratives in favour of narratives based on the individual – on everyday stories of "ordinary citizens."[7] Yet, more than the exact daily account of life on the front, Watkins's film provides an assemblage of indiciary elements which offer a kaleidoscopic image of what First World War soldiers were going through.

Watkins defines a new genre here. He creates a "matrix," and his films become matrix films designed to engineer a new approach to historical issues. His films are activist films and pave the way for authored television with, among other features, the representations of dead bodies. Films, and TV films in particular, shy away from images of dead bodies because of the filmmakers' alleged respect for viewers and out of respect for human dignity. Yet, films discriminate between images of death. Images of dead enemies are allowed while images of dead fellow-soldiers are not. Another difference is that fiction can show dead bodies while news cannot. This feature alone accounts for the fact that thanks to hybridity, docudrama can bypass constraints and show what documentary and news cannot,[8] while at the same time providing evidential value to what is shown, as news and documentaries do.

By resorting to mind-reading and giving the viewer access to the thoughts and feelings of the characters, Watkins operates a disruption in the narrative mode which is conducive to reflections on both the themes of the film and on the filmic technique itself – how the latter works and the effects it has upon viewers. It stands in sharp contrast to the Hollywood way of filming with its continuous transitions which edit away insignificant details so as to achieve coherence and downplay the presence of the film crew.[9] Watkins's films act as forms of metadiscourse: they speak about war but also about film and in particular about film and politics. What should films purport to do? Shouldn't they "rock the boat"[10] and raise questions designed to challenge certainties?

THE DIARY AS SEPULCHRE

Watkins's attempt to try and help viewers regain control over the meaning of the things they are presented with bears a striking resemblance with the diarist's attempt to isolate himself from the chaos that soldiers have to endure so as to try and make sense of this prevailing state of insanity. Both are political endeavours.

Watkins's film is the equivalent of the Greek drama that would stage fear and death. *The Diary of an Unknown Soldier* is to be understood with Antigone in mind and the opposition between the state and the individual. *The Diary of an Unknown Soldier* stages the attempt of individuals to resist state terrorism, to resist the emptiness and the anonymity into which destruction drags them. The state celebration of the Unknown Soldier is the ultimate stage of cynicism, the ultimate cover up of mass destruction. Conversely, writing a diary is, for the Unknown-Soldier-to-be, like Antigone when she confronts Creon, posing a form of resistance to the system of destruction of the individual. It means creating something that will outlive the individual, like Antigone who fought the system by claiming a decent burial for Polynice, her brother. Phobos[11] prevails through Créon; Phobos rules, all-powerful, over others, like Reason of State which, in the First World War, ordered men to lay down their lives for national interests.

A diary is a challenge which is both individual and collective: it is individual since it is a very personal account of life on the front but also collective since it testifies on behalf of all the others who were unwilling or unable to testify because they neither had the skill to write nor the will to do so. Diaries have a universal dimension and so has the notion of the Unknown Soldier: the Unknown Soldier is everybody's soldier though at the same time the soldier of the nation. He cannot be the soldier of the enemy, yet his diary has a universal dimension.

Deciding to inform readers and viewers about what daily life was like on the front means replacing chaos with meaning. The diary corresponds to the attempt by the Unknown Soldier to try and regain control over his life by writing about it and thus keeping mass destruction at bay. The soldier's will to keep an account of what is going on and what he is going through then corresponds to a rational undertaking that goes against the violence of insanity. Writing a diary means refusing to be engulfed by the present and by the fear of mass destruction, that is to say trying to remain an individual who experiences emotions and who wants to relish these moments, to live them fully, instead of being robbed of them by fear. Writing a diary corresponds to an individual statement of self-assertion in an environment where death and massacre prevail. Writing a diary is producing meaning out of meaninglessness. It answers the need to assert life against the backdrop of destruction, to assert oneself and to confront death with life.

Hell is one of the terms that is most often used in *The Diary of an Unknown Soldier*, and the comparison between war and hell is common to describe the First World War. Hell is physical pain and extreme anxiety, but it is also madness, in all its forms. Fiction best renders the true atmosphere of what was going on at the time on the battlefields. Keeping a record of what soldiers were going through is an act of resistance against oblivion and against the impossibility for future generations to even envisage the fact that such a thing ever existed. The fiercest destroyer is time, which brings oblivion in its wake. Writing is then designed to provide testimonies against forgetfulness and against things that are hushed up or forgotten, even though, like docudrama, the diary is not an exact account of what happened and the writer is necessarily biased in his choice of perspective and of things to be kept for examination.

War means death and the diary represents an attempt at fending off death with the sublimation of individuality over the forces of destruction; it is an attempt at capturing a glimpse of eternity in an environment of death. The emptiness, void, and vacuity of death are challenged by the traces that are left by the diary.

The diary raises the question of how to think of sepulchre in a modern way; how the autobiographer or the diarist creates his own sepulchre and defines the terms on which he is going to be remembered; how the things he mentions are going to be approached. With the diary, the protagonist chooses to relate with precision the conditions in which things happened, which leaves little leeway for future second-hand narrations. It corresponds to a rational attempt to survive by imposing the words around which the memory of war is going to be arranged. The diary then becomes a sort of sepulchre – meaning the place where the remains of the dead are laid – which is conducive to mourning. The author, who is also the protagonist, chooses the way he wants to be remembered, and the diary becomes the locus of both mourning and celebration, which happen whenever the diary is opened for reading.

Unlike the sepulchre that allows for all types of interpretations, the autobiography of the dead provides only one presentation of reality. Reading an autobiography is a way of paying tribute to the autobiographer. It is both memory and celebration, the autobiography being the fictional locus of the dead, of his past life, both material and spiritual. The book is a spiritual sepulchre in so far as it contains the spirit of the author, his thoughts and feelings. The book is a receptacle, and words, in black standing out against the white page, are like bones in a window case. It synthesizes both spirit and place, both body and soul. Yet, unlike authentic relics of which there is only one instance, which exists in one place only, a book can be reproduced indefinitely and reading, as a celebration, can take place anywhere and as often as is deemed reasonable.

The relics stand as a transitional stage that allows the living to redefine and draw the contours of the deceased. It is the Greek pharmacon which is both the poison and the remedy. A hallucinatory stage is required that needs to be overcome but it can be fatal if it is not: settling into fantasy, into phantasm, is poisonous. Yet, the relic has an obsessive, even haunting, dimension because it haunts the place where it stands. Unlike a tombstone or a sepulchre, a book is nowhere and everywhere at the same time, and the memory of the dead can be revived at any time, unlike a celebration which takes place at defined places and at a specific time. With the Unknown Soldier's diary, a ghost-like figure stands out and whoever possesses it, in whatever form, whether book or film, possesses words without a body, something that is haunting. Diaries are memories and opening them means bringing back to life what was dead up until then. From the moment the reader opens a diary or the viewer plays a tape, the past is allowed to infringe upon the present. The word "diary" has the same etymology as the word "day" in the sense of today; it means bringing the past time into the present time and shedding light on it. Reading the diary of an unknown soldier is a private ritual that is linked to the social ritual of celebrating a battle and remembering the memories of the dead and the unknown. It is a foray into the past. So the diary is a sepulchre; thanks to his writing, the Unknown Soldier is no longer a dead man without a sepulchre, that is to say a ghost that would haunt the living, but a dead man whose literary legacy is conducive to remembrance.

Yet, the diary is also a sepulchre which opens onto the horror of the war. Unlike national celebrations of the field of honour which beautify things, the diary opens onto the field of horror; courage, national pride, and heroes are replaced by dismay, death, and decay.

The representation of closeness in a confined environment is conducive to the representation of day-to-day and nitty-gritty realities with which everyone can easily identify and which gives Sheriff's play and Watkins's film their testimonial and persuasive dimensions. Watkins's film is remarkably effective at conveying the nature of the fear that confronts the anonymous young man as symbolized by "the shattered branches that turn into sharp bayonets."[12] It shows the materiality and corporeality of the violence that is to come. As Léopold Lambert notes:

> The way the body is filmed and described in the script is remarkable as it heavily insists on the fact that war for privates – in opposition to high-rank[ing] officers – is essentially a matter of bodies: their movement, their combination with the bullets and bombs trajectories and their relationship to the ground – in that case, the mud.[13]

Since *The Diary of an Unknown Soldier* is a personal account from an anonymous person, it can be inferred that millions of other soldiers felt the same. By examining, from a behavioural approach, what the others feel, the protagonist affords viewers an insight into different ways of perceiving war. Daily life takes over: jokes and an atmosphere of amiability and friendliness permeate this society. Soldiers sing, they chat and are understanding with the others' shortcomings, in particular with Ginger Morris, who is afflicted, as are his closest compatriots, by persistent bowel disorders. Promiscuity is not far when it comes to closeness. Yet, the viewer can wonder about the use of such coarse and crude details. More than promiscuity, these details prove the will to show the body working in an environment of corpses, that is to say an environment made of skeletons and decaying bodies. It is the assertion of life, in its crudest form, as it stands in sharp opposition to death and defies it. Is the working of a living body more obscene than the decaying of a dead body on the battlefield? The body not only attests to sufferings, privations, and anxiety but it is also the object of the most ominous representations: it is envisaged as a "discarded … piece of offal"[14] and as "empty," "a void … nothing."[15]

More than a succession of accurate accounts of ordinary days, Watkins's fiction collapses into one day many of the elements that make up daily life on the frontline. There is always a metonymic dimension contained in this type of fiction, and whatever the soldier relates, there is always much more than what is actually mentioned. The choice of fiction is explained by the need to encapsulate all the experiences. It is also accounted for by the urgency caused by the narrator's knowledge that this day is his last day. His choice of information is carefully made and ordained and it is designed to account for his feelings towards war, towards the wait for the combat, and his relationships with fellow soldiers. Like fiction, this diary, like any diary, is not a minute record of days but the amalgamation into an ordinary day of the most salient features of life on the front. As is often in the case of diaries, which are highly personal and not necessarily designed to be read by others, the psychological dimension of the narrative is crucial. The soldier's confessions are actually comments on how men see the war and the waiting for the combat, as when the narrator comments on how they spend their days and the way they envisage their commitment.

THE DIARY AS AN EXAMPLE OF RESISTANCE TO EXIST

Drama being social and film being psychoanalytic, Watkins's *The Diary of an Unknown Soldier* is the recipient of personal discontent, of fear, and of anger. These feelings stand in sharp contrast to the ambient atmosphere which is marked either by "unconcernedness" or, on the other hand, by the will to fight, which in either case infuriates the narrator. He criticizes Ted Crompton because he rather "enjoys his war."[16] Crompton is the image of what a soldier should be and what the narrator is not, that is to say one who dissembles his feeling and puts on a brave face. More than being critical of Crompton, the narrator is critical of his apparent indifference in this hostile environment. He envies Crompton's will to fight, not so much for what it is as for the fact that he has turned war, as an object of violence and destruction, into an object of desire: Crompton tries to control the impact war has upon him. Crompton has managed to transcend what appears to the narrator as something violent and stupid, over which he has no control, into something which he possesses and even desires. Though Crompton fails to have complete control over war and over the violent assaults of the enemy, which take him by surprise, he manages to derive pleasure from war. The protagonist's anger at Crompton is a confession of his own failure to achieve peace of mind and of his failure to achieve it through his diary. Unlike Crompton, he has failed to come to terms with war and so with his destiny, as newly defined by the context of war. The diary means catharsis and the release of pent-up emotions. Writing is a form of escapism, something soldiers desperately needed.[17] The protagonist has opted for the introspective approach afforded by writing. Yet, writing does not help him come to terms with his feelings. Crompton remains an enigma that angers him and he envies his composure. Writing a diary is a step towards composure; it is an attempt at mastering one's own destiny by regaining control over it, by making sense of it and then being a man again, being human again. Crompton seems to have come to terms with the impossibility of having control over the situation and in the process he has ceased to grieve over his past life. Until then, he was haunted by death and there was no place for anything but fear and regret.

The diary is also a psychoanalytic attempt at trying to understand the impact of what is going on in the minds of the soldiers who are on the battlefield. It is an attempt at rationalizing the feelings that overcome soldiers when confronted with extreme situations of fear and closeness to death. Fear and terror are obstacles when trying to understand what is going on. Fear imposes the dictatorship of recurring images of horror and of pain, of suffering and of impending death. Fear and terror block any attempt at trying to understand what is going on, at making sense of war and trying to manage the way war affects each and every one. When overcome with fear and horror, the soldier can only remain subjected to these feelings; he remains overwhelmed by them and so fails to act upon them.

Writing is then an attempt to repossess one's life in an environment ruled by the daily rhythm of fear, death, horror, and suffering. It is an attempt to put things into perspective so as not to be swallowed by them. Fear obliterates everything and replaces all things with horror, which blocks any attempts to make sense of events; it replaces the rational approach with a sentimental approach and impedes attempts to be sensible. By trying to understand what is going on in the soldier's mind, the diarist also tries to learn from the others' survival techniques so as to retain common sense. People cannot help but predict the future, which is what the Unknown Soldier does by prying into others' thoughts. Prediction is a survival strategy. Decisions in life are made by assessing the future, by making wise guesses which take into account the information available, hence the need for the Unknown Soldier to have access to what others think. It corresponds to a rational attempt to bring light into the darkness of chaos. The writing of a diary corresponds to a strategy of survival, bearing in mind that on the battlefield there is the inescapable proximity of death. Conjecturing about what the others are thinking induces procrastination, which incidentally is one of the soldiers' main activities; it is trying to have access to different perceptions to other worlds. The protagonist once again wonders what the other men are thinking, whether they feel as distressed as he does. But there are as many reactions as there are men, even though he tries to convince himself that beneath the surface of things people are all the same and, for instance, he wonders if his commanding officer is really as hard as he claims he is, or if it is all a façade, and whether Tom, the veteran, has any fear at all, since he himself occasionally feels petrified.

The Diary of an Unknown Soldier goes against the national effort to boost patriotic feelings because it is synonymous with the fall of myths, of values related to war. Conversely, it corresponds with the birth of personal values as an extension of the romantic spirit that characterized the nineteenth century. The diary can be seen as a personal address to the nation. The Unknown Soldier is at the same time one particular soldier and all the soldiers. Being addressed to no one in particular, the diary is addressed to everyone. The narrator of *The Diary of an Unknown Soldier* not only rages at what he is going through but also at what may happen to him. He feels sorry for himself and indulges in self-pity. Viewers can only sympathize with him since the price to pay will be death. It suffices to justify what could be seen as moping self-pity, but which is actually a plea against the absurdity of war. Moreover, war is not described as a series of brave and heroic attacks but rather as waiting for the instructions. Most of the time the narrator sits and waits. He waits apprehensively for the messenger to come with the order to go to the front. Writing gradually becomes his favourite pastime since it helps him dispel this threat.

Affording an overview of the general feelings that prevailed at the time on the front reinforces simple ideas like fear and death, which were overshadowed by heroism once the war was over. The narrator looks to Tom for support; as a veteran soldier, Tom is supposed to be the one who brings relief and peace of mind. But he does not. The message is clear: no matter how long one has been a soldier, one never can never get used to war. The glorious hero is fearless and dauntless but the actual soldier is full of fear and regret and longs to live at all costs, a stand which is embodied by the narrator. The figure of the hero-to-be and of the ordinary soldier overlap and merge into the figure of the Unknown Soldier. Yet, the Unknown Soldier who will be remembered and celebrated after the First World War will not be the moaning, scared, and fearful narrator of the diary but a figure like Crompton who is among the few who have come to terms with their predicament.

A modern approach to *The Diary of the Unknown Soldier* would suggest a parallel with the videos made by kamikazes before dying. It is because modern kamikazes resolve to die for a cause that videos need to be made to explain their determination. In both cases, the anticipation of death brings about meaning. Predicting the future is a way to apprehend it and be rational about it. It means becoming familiar with it, so being less afraid of it. By pre-enacting the near future, the Unknown Soldier states that "this will happen" and so manages to come to terms with it. As far as suicide bombers are concerned, the reward is fame and recognition, which materializes the passage from anonymity to stardom. It means the rise to stardom of an individual who previously had not done anything worthy of it. In the case of the Unknown Soldier it is the opposite: fame and stardom are refused to an individual and instead granted to a community of soldiers who died unidentified. With the modern kamikaze, there is post-mortem glorification of the individual. The video records the sublimation that is the act of dying for a cause. It corresponds to the cult of the individual, which is just the opposite of the diary written by the Unknown Soldier. With the diary, the Unknown Soldier chooses to leave a trace but he also chooses to remain anonymous.

It is only when marching to the front that he becomes fully aware of the absurdity of it all. As the men proceed to the frontline, the protagonist happens to walk past the first German soldier he has even seen – an ordinary man, crouching with a bowl of soup in his hands. It suddenly dawns on him how very identical they are with only different uniforms on. Suddenly he is face to face with the man he has been trained to hate and to kill. Why so much anger, frustration, and fear for people who look so harmless? In an Orwellian way, he realizes that everything suddenly makes sense and that they have all been abused. For them, as soldiers, they have had to lay down their lives for a supposedly noble cause. As for the rest of the population, they will have to keep on living with the hatred of people they do not even know, just because they have been told to do so and out of respect for the memory of the dead soldiers. The film ends with a note of disillusionment that encapsulates the spirit of the soldiers as they get near the battle zone: "We are told, 'What a tremendous thing it is to die for one's country!'... Well tell it to those who do."

CONCLUSION

The Diary of an Unknown Soldier marks a major defeat for the spirit that had prevailed until the beginning of the First World War and that considered that progress meant happiness for humanity. Progress eventually turned its back on man, who paid a dear price for technological achievements. The need was felt to bear testimony to this turning point in the history of mankind through literature, drama, and cinema. Since little had been done to provide filmic representations of what had been going on at the front, Watkins's docudrama technique proved invaluable to help younger generations catch a visual glimpse of the horror that characterized the First World War.

These images became matrix images that were later used to represent other wars like the Vietnam War. In feature films and they proved invaluable for TV films about D-Day, for instance. For many, this film was also one of the first pleas against the war in Vietnam, which had started only five years before its release (1955–75). It helped Watkins achieve recognition for his artistic merit, but also for his anti-war messages. As an activist director, he has made an invaluable contribution to a more realistic and less glamorized perception of war. Watkins's *Diary of an Unknown Soldier* stands as a landmark in the history of films on war. It paved the way for other films which contributed to relaying Watkins's political message on the demystification of war.

NOTES

1 "The idea of a tomb of the Unknown Warrior was first conceived in 1916 by the Rev David Railton, who while serving as an army chaplain on the Western Front, had seen a grave marked by a rough cross, which bore the pencil-written legend 'An Unknown British Soldier.' In 1920, he corresponded with the Dean of Westminster proposing that

an unidentified British soldier from the battlefields in France be buried with due ceremony in Westminster Abbey 'amongst the kings' to represent the many hundreds of thousands who had died serving the British Empire. The idea was endorsed by the Dean and the then Prime Minister Lloyd George. There was initial opposition from King George V (who feared it might reopen the wounds of all the losses suffered by Britain in the Great War) and others but a [*sic*] outpouring of emotional support from the great number of bereaved families ensured its adoption and implementation." Henry Allingham and Dennis Goodwin, *Kitchener's Last Volunteer: The Life of Henry Allingham, the Oldest Surviving Veteran of the Great War* (London: Random House, 2011), 123.

2 Robert Cedric Sheriff, *Journey's End* (London: Penguin, 2000).

3 Thomas Stearns Eliot, *Poems, 1909–1925* (London: Faber & Gwyer, 1925).

4 Peter Watkins, *Media Crisis* (Paris: Homnisphères, 2004), 79.

5 Dai Vaughan, *For Documentary: Twelve Essays* (Oakland: University of California Press, 1999), 58.

6 Ibid., 202.

7 Derek Paget, *No Other Way to Tell It* (Manchester: Manchester University Press, 2011), 61.

8 Unlike documentaries, news capture images of dead bodies though they refrain from showing them for ethical reasons.

9 On the contrary, in *The War Game* Peter Watkins purposefully staged the presence of the journalist and of all his equipment, which acted as intrusions in the narrative designed to give a documentary touch and a political note to the film.

10 Peter Kosminsky, "Making Mischief? It's an Essential Part of the Job," *Independent*, 16 June 2008.

11 In Greek mythology, Phobos is the embodiment of fear. Helen Saul, *Phobias: Fighting the Fear* (New York: Arcade Publishing, 2004), 19.

12 http://geographicalimaginations.com/2013/07/16/unknown-soldiers/ (accessed 12 October 2014).

13 Ibid.

14 Words from the narrator (00:09:45).

15 Words from the narrator (00:13:38 – 00:13:45).

16 Words from the narrator (00:05:41).

17 Smoking was also another form of escapism. It was undeniably one of the most popular ways of getting away from the pressure of violence.

In the First World War, the horror of the conflict was such, the violence around men was so strong and death so obsessive, that smoking was vital to survive. It was required as a way to fend off death, a way to cover the pervasive smell of decaying flesh that would otherwise be suffocating.

18

Tunes of Glory or Jarring Notes?[1] Filming the Great War in Music: *Oh! What a Lovely War* (Richard Attenborough, 1969) and *War Requiem* (Derek Jarman, 1989)

NICOLE CLOAREC

As cultural and film historians have now well demonstrated, cinema has played a major part in how we "remember" wars and conflicts.[2] In the case of the First World War, films very soon established a set of recurring images and representational conventions that contributed to producing the dominant imagery of the war which still prevails today, a century after the historical events. Among these, the first which comes to mind is the trench, full of mud, infested with rats, drenched in perpetual rain, surrounded by tangled fences of barbed wire and relentlessly assaulted by artillery. Another is a disfigured, moon-like landscape strewn with craters filled with stagnant water and a few twisted trunks of dead trees. Pierre Sorlin calls these visual iconography "stereotypes," not because "they lie but because they restrict the memory of war to a few recurring pictures." In other words, they are "neither true nor false," only "partial and limited."[3]

Filmmakers and viewers alike readily acknowledge that when dealing with extreme experiences like wars, there remains an unbridgeable gap between reality and representation. Nonetheless, more than any other cinematographic genre, war films have been judged by the exclusive criterion of realism, even as the notion of realism itself has kept evolving over time.[4] Most films about war, be they documentary, propaganda, or fiction, claim they are depicting "the real thing." Whether to celebrate the valour of soldiers or to denounce the horrors of battle, filmic devices are used to physically immerse the viewers in the action and involve them emotionally, arousing all sorts of feelings, from the joys of victory to the dread of fighting or the pain of loss. Likewise, most popular or critical responses acclaim war films for their realism and authenticity, which led James Chapman to conclude that "The public at large have become conditioned to accepting the filmic representation of war as being like the real thing."[5]

Very few films dare challenge the realistic conventions to present war images for what they are: discursive and representational constructs, images that are elaborately staged before, during, and after war. The two British films studied in this paper are therefore most atypical in their representation of the Great War, insofar as they rely on distancing effects, literally *staging* the war as spectacles, and musical spectacles to boot. *Oh! What a Lovely War* (1969) turns the war into a music hall review; *War Requiem* (1989) is an adaptation of Britten's opera. Both films adopt complex narratives, using first-hand testimonies but departing from them. They are formal hybrids, mixing elements of stage performance with elaborate cinematic devices, shifting from surrealist fantasy or stylized symbolism to stark realism. From the outset they are conceived as a mediated representation of the war; rather than claiming to immerse the viewers into the "real thing," they adopt a historical perspective as they both investigate collective representations of the Great War through the prism of commemoration and memory.

Through this critical perspective, the films are clear damning indictments of war, but more importantly, they also reveal the ambiguities of the process of commemoration itself. Indeed, the dramatic contrasts and constant changes of stylistic modes that characterize these two unconventional works, while conveying disturbing shifts of mood, lay bare the tensions between a harsh satire of official patriotic discourses and a genuine tribute to the memories of the dead soldiers.

Richard Attenborough's directorial debut *Oh! What a Lovely War* was adapted from Joan Littlewood and Gerry Raffles's 1963 stage production,[6] which itself was inspired by Charles Chilton's *The Long, Long Trail*, an acclaimed radio program broadcast in 1961 which contrasted the songs of soldiers on the Western Front with those sung on the home front.[7]

The play is very much a product of the 1960s, which saw a resurgence of interest in the Great War due to the commemorations of the fiftieth anniversaries along with the beginning of what has come to be called the "decade of discontent," with growing anti-establishment and anti-war movements, lack of deference, and the questioning of traditional values and beliefs. In *British Culture and the First World War*, George Robb notes, "Not surprisingly this interest was reflected in a reflowering of the literature of disillusionment and in cynical, anti-heroic representations of the Great war. Popular histories of the war, such as Alan Clark's *The Donkeys* (1961), Barbara Tuchman's *The Guns of August* (1962) and A.J. Taylor's *The First World War* (1963) reinforced the negative images of the First World War as a cruel and futile slaughter."[8] In keeping with Marxist theory, Joan Littlewood was also keen to recast history from the perspective of the common man, but what was most unconventional was to use the device of a *Pierrot* show to represent the war.[9] As a critic from the *Times* noted in 1963, "What emerges from this research is the familiar view of the 1914–18 war as a criminally wasteful adventure in which the stoic courage of the common soldier was equaled only by the sanctimonious incompetence of their commanders and the blind jingoism of the civilians."[10]

This dual perspective remains central to the film, which is entirely built on a series of contrasts and tensions. Although ambitious in scope,[11] since the film encompasses the four years of the war, it remains necessarily partial, focusing exclusively on the Western Front and taking up a number of myths as defined by Dan Todman, including a selection of names, events, famous quotes and songs, objects, and artifacts that are all readily recognizable as they are now part of the shared "mythology" of the First World War.[12]

As in the play,[13] the film claims to be based on factual World War I data gathered in official records, memoirs, and newspapers and, above all, period songs which provide the narrative backbone of the film, weaving the scenes together. Just after the credits, a title card reads: "The principal statements made by the historical characters in this film are based on documentary evidence and the words of the songs are those sung by the troops during the First World War." However, while this claim to historicity might raise expectations of a realistic reconstitution, the first scene immediately contradicts this expectation, opening on a highly stylized set in which the historical characters perform an elaborate choreography. We soon understand the setting literally represents the stage of History where historical events such as the assassination of Archduke Ferdinand are played out like the shooting of a photograph,[14] or the complex game of alliances that ensued like a chess board representing the map of Europe.

Perspectives on the war are then sharply contrasted between the home front and the General Staff Headquarters, represented as an amusement fair located on Brighton Pier, and the reality of the Western Front, depicted in a more traditional realistic mode, where we follow the five brothers of the Smith family. War is first depicted as "the ever-popular war game – complete with songs, battles and a few jokes," with its ticket office run by Sir Douglas Haig, its shooting gallery, its carousel of French cavaliers, or its viewing machines named after the great battles of the Western Front.[15] The abrupt change of setting and mood is all the more unsettling as it comes within the same scene or even the same take. The wooden puppets of the merry-go-round are turned into actual French cavaliers on the plains of France who then come across a full-scale carousel that reveals broken dummies again after they are mowed down by machine guns. The curtain call that closes off the show on the pier opens back as a tent on a French camp full of wounded soldiers. Fireworks that are enlivening the evening of the upper class transmute into flares and mortars above the trenches. The mother who first watches her son, smiling, as the miniature train of the pier takes the new recruits away is then filmed alone and forlorn, standing on the platform of Waterloo Station. Perhaps the most spectacular instance from a technical point of view is the single take which starts showing one of the Smith boys aiming at the shooting gallery and, after the camera has panned around him, ends with the actor again in the same position but this time wearing uniform and tin hat, in a salient.[16]

This constant to-and-fro between vaudeville spectacle and realistic modes of representation highlights the staggering discrepancy between the glorious representation of warfare in patriotic discourses and popular culture and what the soldiers actually experienced. It also sets forth a fierce indictment against the carefree cynicism of the upper class,[17] drinking champagne and discussing business, the indifference of the church extolling the virtues of sacrifice,[18] and the callous incompetence of the high command,[19] depicted as irresponsible "donkeys," to quote the title of Alan Clark's popular book,[20] a group of aristocratic botchers, more preoccupied with prestige and backstabbing each other than with the fate of their men. Field Marshall

Sir Douglas Haig in particular[21] bears the brunt of the charge, depicted as blustering, bigoted, and stubborn, obsessed with launching full-scale offensives and convinced of his own destiny and God's favour. [22] It is no small irony that General Haig should be interpreted by John Mills,[23] known as the upright gallant hero of a dozen British war movies,[24] thus subverting casting expectations. However, pacifist discourse is not exempt from criticism either, as Sylvia Pankhurst's address, quoting from a letter by George Bernard Shaw, sounds only hyperbolically high-flown and patronizing, utterly out of touch with the ordeal of the common people that they call the "misguided masses."[25]

In this respect, the songs, while commenting upon the action, are the primary means by which the voice of these "masses" is heard. What is more, they set the tone of the film, underpinning the multiple shifts of mood within a scene as well as throughout the film.[26] The first enlisting songs thus capture the sense of bravado and gaiety with which so many people senselessly entered the war, then the songs become more and more ironical, showing in particular how soldiers used to parody famous songs and hymns.[27] By keeping the light-hearted mood of the original, the new words, depicting the deprivations of everyday life or the terrible ordeals of battle, only add to the poignancy while paying tribute to the soldiers' enduring valour and their sense of cheeky humour. The music hall song "Drunk Last Night and Drunk the Night Before" becomes "Gassed Last Night and Gassed the Night Before"; "Hush, Here Comes the Dream Man" is turned into "Hush! Here Comes a Whizz-Bang"; "Come My Lad, and Be a Soldier" into "I Don't Want to Be a Soldier"; "Sing Me to Sleep, Sergeant Major" into "Far Far from Ypres I Long to Be"; or Jerome Kern's "And When They Told Me How Beautiful You Are" becomes "And When They Asked Us How Dangerous It Was." Even hymns are not exempt from impudent rewriting as with "Onward Christian Soldiers" turned into "Joe Soap's Army," or "What a Friend We Have in Jesus" into "When This Lousy War Is Over." The latter provides one remarkable example of a genuine polyphony of voices, with the tenor voice of a soldier subverting the lyrics of the hymn sung by the chaplain during service.

To a large extent the songs contribute to the persisting tension between the fantasy of spectacle and some degree of reality. When a group of slouching ANZAC soldiers start singing "They Were Only Playing Leap-Frog," the high commanders who are inspecting the

British troops start walking in jerks. Later on, after digging a mass grave, soldiers are filmed going back to the front to the tune of "The Bells of Hell," while in cross-cutting Field Marshall Haig is filmed standing on top of his tower tapping on the balustrade as if he were beating the rhythm, implying he is the orchestrator of the whole massacre. However, period songs are also powerful emotional vehicles and in this respect they prove highly ambivalent; as outrage gives way to melancholy, their jarring irony and satirical edge become more blunted.[28] Thereby the film pinpoints the ambivalence of commemoration, which involves a degree of nostalgia and empathy in contrast to the critical distance on which the aesthetic strategies of the film are based.

Although the film takes up a familiar iconography of the Great War – including the spectacular final aerial shot that starts from a few white crosses to a field of crosses stretching as far as the eye can see[29] – it is most atypical in its absence of graphic violence and combat scenes. In keeping with the "ever-popular war game" advertised at the beginning, the staggering numbers of casualties are flaunted on cricket scoreboards.[30] The film also subverts one of the most enduring symbols of the conflict: the red poppy that keeps appearing throughout the film is used not as the traditional symbol of remembrance but as a foreboding sign of doom. Interestingly, most of the poppies are handed out by the same character (John Melia), who is first seen acting as the photographer giving a poppy to the archduke and his wife, then keeps reappearing throughout the film with different functions and uniforms, acting like the MC in a music hall revue. What is more, a number of times he looks directly at the camera and comments upon the action, breaking a virtual fourth wall as it were. The film actually adopts a number of Brechtian distancing devices, which, by breaking the viewers' suspension of disbelief, are meant to make them react. In this respect, the presentation of war as a form of entertainment may very well constitute a self-reflexive comment on the part war films as a genre have played in the building of what Graham Dawson has termed "the pleasure-culture of war."[31]

Thereby, the film questions the ability of any representation – be it symbolic or realistic – to suggest the actual experience the soldiers went through at the front. When the last of the Smith brothers is killed at the end, a blurred blot of red invades the screen. It takes a few seconds before the image comes into focus again and reveals the red blot in the foreground as a poppy. While the film stresses the hypocritical euphemism of this traditional symbol, which turns the shock and outrage of slaughter into a vision of death redeemed by nature and time,[32] the poppy also remains a simple yet potent symbol of heartfelt tribute. But the image is suddenly followed by a complete silence, as though to highlight its unreal, artificial quality. When the stillness is finally interrupted by the little girl asking her grandmother, "What did Daddy do in the war?,"[33] her grandmother can only remain silent. The answer eventually comes from the soundtrack with the last song "They'll Never Believe Us," stressing again the inability of the home front, then and now, to "imagine" the unimaginable.

Far from exploiting cinema's persuasive claim that it can capture a fragment of reality and give credit to the reconstitution of past events, *Oh! What a Lovely War* questions the very possibility of adopting any adequate critical outlook on the Great War. What remains is a deliberate backward perspective. As Dan Todman aptly observed, "The play ends with no hint that the war itself ever came to a conclusion; in contrast, the film views the war as history."[34] What some viewers were quick to spot as a faulty anachronism – namely the light sign that reads: "World War One" – should rather be a warning, inviting us to adopt a critical view in a film conceived from the onset from a memorial point of view.

A similar commemorative perspective characterizes Derek Jarman's *War Requiem*. The film is a visual translation of Benjamin Britten's eponymous work which was commissioned for the inauguration in May 1962 of the new Coventry Cathedral, built to replace the one destroyed by the air raids of 1940. Jarman was granted permission to use Britten's music provided it would be played with no alteration or interruption.[35] Notwithstanding, Jarman added a very short prologue showing a war veteran (interpreted by Laurence Olivier in his last role) wheeled about by a nurse (Tilda Swinton).[36] From the onset, the film is placed under the two notions of commemoration, as the old soldier displays his medals, and memory, when he shows the nurse the old photograph of a war nurse he has kept in his wallet near a poppy. However, although nurse and soldier are filmed chatting throughout the scene, no dialogue is heard. Sound is deliberately disconnected from image, clearly indicating that image and sound are set in a dialogic, not an illustrative, relationship, and creating a sort of echo chamber abstracted from any precise space and time. Instead we hear Olivier's voice-over reading Owen's poem "Strange Meeting."

The prologue thus underscores the centrality of poetry, following an opening card focusing on the poet, reminding us of his tragic death "in the last week of World War I" ("Wilfred Owen, the soldier poet whose words inspired Benjamin Britten's music, was killed in the last week of World War I at the age of 27"). Along with Britten's music, Owen provides a loose narrative thread[37] in a film which otherwise mixes various film material and cinematographic techniques[38] and eschews conventions such as continuity, dialogue, narrative causality, or characterisation.

Indeed, although Owen's poem "Strange Meeting" is the last of the nine poems quoted in Britten's *Requiem*,[39] there is no corresponding frame ending the film nor any connection with the main narrative. But significantly enough, the poem's reading ends halfway through, concluding with the lines:

> And of my weeping something had been left,
> Which must die now. I mean the truth untold,
> The pity of war, the pity war distilled.

By choosing to end with these words, recalling Owen's own famous preface,[40] even before he tackles Britten's work, Jarman makes his perspective clear: the object of his film is not to represent war but to convey "the pity of war," to offer a filmic expression of grief, commemoration, and memory.

Many scholars have commented on the tensions that underpin Britten's *Requiem* due to the insertion of Owen's poetry within the traditional liturgy of the Mass in Latin.[41] By foregrounding the figure of the poet whose work has become so prominent in shaping Britons' vision of the Great War as emblematic of the horrors and futility of all modern warfare,[42] Jarman builds on the jarring juxtapositions and even exacerbates them, questioning the Christian ideology of redemptive sacrifice and offering instead a harsh criticism of the Establishment and the Established Church in particular. As early as the first scene, which opens with the chorus of "Requiem Aeternam," the second line, *et lux perpetua luceat eis* ("and let light eternal shine upon them"), is undermined by the painful close-up of the nurse who covers her eyes with her hands while screaming silently. In the "Offertorium," the "holy light" of Archangel Michael is ironically depicted as fires and air bombs. Britannia is depicted as an ageing courtesan surrounded by cross-dressed soldiers dancing a can-can in a deliberately overexposed travesty of music hall entertainment which businessmen applaud. Perhaps the most striking indictment is the staging of Owen's "Parable of the Old Man and the Young" in which Abraham, dressed as a bishop, dismisses the angel and the ram and actually sacrifices his son "and half the seed of Europe, one by one" under the ecstatic eyes of grotesque overfed businessmen and with the approval of the state as represented by the archive footage of George V and members of the General staff in cross-editing.

As in Owen's poetry and most of his other films, Jarman reclaims the figure of Christ who embodies, in a context of futile sacrifice and extreme suffering, "all those cast out, like myself, from Christendom."[43] Here the imagery of Christ is displaced to the figure of the Unknown Soldier who, in the "Agnus Dei" section, is wearing a crown of barbed wire in lieu of thorns and is carrying Owen's dead body like a Pieta. In sharp contrast to the hypocritically merciless rituals of the Established Church, the truly sacred is to be found in the profane, the simple scenes of domestic life filmed on Super 8, tinged with soft edges and the golden glow of a paradise lost, depicting mundane and yet highly symbolic gestures like breaking the bread, sowing seeds, and hanging up or folding a white sheet. Rather than strictly adhering to the lyrics and music, Jarman favours the creation of structural patterns through repetitions and variations and most specifically through parallelism and contrast. In particular, one recurring stylistic device is cross-editing which, for example, links together the caring gestures and supervision of the nurse for the wounded in hospital, and of Owen for his men in the trenches, while the soundtrack evokes "the written book" (*liber scriptus proferetur*) of the Last Judgment in the "Dies Irae" section.[44]

Moreover, throughout the film, tension is visually conveyed through the disruptive juxtaposition of two radically different modes of representation that both problematize the representation of grief and commemoration from a collective and a personal perspective: one staging characters in *tableaux vivants* that evoke the aesthetics of memorials (what Dillon calls "the monumental"); the other dwelling on raw emotions through documentary footage or uncut sequences of emoting (what Dillon calls "performance").[45] On the one hand, solemn war memorials or pictorial allusions – of Henry Moore's "Sleeping Figures" and "Shelter Drawings" or Piero della Francesca's *Resurrection* – offer dignified images of redemptive suffering. On the other hand, the seven minutes of the "Sanctus" are accompanied by a single take of the nurse filmed in close medium shot, going through a myriad of emotional expressions while sitting in front of a bier, suggesting that such an amount of horror and suffering remains beyond the reach of any artistic representation or religious discourse.

Paradoxically, the limits of representation may be best illustrated through the inclusion of documentary footage. Following the perception that the First World War was the first modern technological war, introducing the use of ever more sophisticated weaponry, a number of sequences are montages of newsreel images of twentieth century wars. The eight-minute long "Libera me" section is the most remarkable in this respect. Starting with a field of skulls, it shows highly disturbing images of gruesome injuries, wounded men lying about or carried away, devastated cities and landscapes intercut with discharges from guns and cannons, and bombardments by ships and planes, all culminating in the apocalyptic images of atomic explosions. However, these raw fragments of "reality" are submitted to a degree of disfiguration and reconfiguration. Indeed, the documentary found footage was transferred onto video so it could be subject to various colour filters, electronic controls, and superimpositions, creating highly stylized visual effects with the final paradox of turning what is supposed to be unmediated figuration into nearly abstract painting. The outbursts of colours and the dissolving of outlines and shapes through superimpositions all undermine the integrity of the image to better suggest some of the conflagration that war represents.

While the film opens and closes with a burning candle in close up, the prevailing motif throughout is the image of a snuffed-out candle. Its smoke, along with the recurring fades to black that punctuate the film by focusing on literal and symbolic darkness, make visible the limits of figuration while celebrating cinema's powers of suggestion.

Oh! What a Lovely War and *War Requiem* provide two highly original approaches to filming the Great War, challenging realistic conventions and their claim of immersing the viewer within "the real thing." Although very different in tone, both films rely on distancing effects, presenting the war as a musical spectacle, thereby investigating collective representations of the war through the prism of commemoration and memory. While both ultimately pay tribute to the memory of the dead soldiers, what characterizes these two unconventional works is the unresolved tension between reverence and irreverence, heartfelt sympathy for the soldiers' sacrifice and harsh criticism towards patriotic discourses and popular representations of war. These tensions are expressed through dramatic contrasts and constant changes of stylistic modes, questioning the very possibility of representing such tragic experiences while conveying disturbing shifts of mood. The jarring notes have superseded the tunes of glory.

NOTES

1 *Tunes of Glory* is the title of a 1960 British film by Ronald Neame. The title is already quite ironic since the film, set in the aftermath of WWII, relates the confrontation between two senior officers vying for the command of a Scottish military regiment. Despite some comic scenes, the conflict ends tragically for both men.

2 The First World War proved a seminal event in the early development of cinema, with the involvement of government agencies, the huge demand for entertainment, and the American film industry starting to establish its dominance over the world in terms of production, distribution, spreading its mainstream narrative conventions, aesthetic codes, and values. See: Michael Paris, "Introduction" and Pierre Sorlin, "Cinema and the Memory of the Great War" in *The First World War and Popular Cinema: 1914 to the Present*, edited by Michael Paris (New Brunswick, NJ: Rutgers University Press, 2000), 1–4, 5–26; James Chapman, *War and Film* (London: Reaction Books, 2008), 125–8, 246–50.

3 Sorlin, "Cinema and the Memory of the Great War," 20.

4 See Chapman, *War and Film*.

5 Ibid., 247. Chapman also notes the irony of using feature films to illustrate historical programmes (for example using extracts from *All Quiet on the Western Front* to feature in TV programmes about WWI) "because they are more dramatic than the 'real' thing."

6 Joan Littlewood's stage production opened at the Theatre Royal, Stratford, East London in March 1963.

7 As Dan Todman notes, "The emphasis of *The Long, Long Trail* was on the valour, humour, and endurance of the ordinary front-line soldier: 'In spite of mud, blood, hell and high water they smiled – and carried on.'" Todman, *The Great War: Myth and Memory* (London: Bloomsbury, 2005), 63.

8 George Robb, *British Culture and the First World War* (New York: Palgrave, 2002), 224.

9 The stage productions, which were the result of collaborative work using live performances, relied on "Brechtian" distancing devices such as direct address to the audience, use of placards, and projection of slides, but the audience was also invited to participate in singing, thus merging agit-prop style with the tradition of British music hall, variety shows, and pantomime. Steve Lewis concludes that the distancing devices "presented within the added dimension of the *pierrot* show and the use of period songs are what gives *Oh What a Lovely War* its unique status as a musical-political-historical-documentary-entertaining drama." Theatre Workshop, *Oh What a Lovely War* (London: Methuen Drama, 2006), xxxvii.

10 *The Times*, 20 March 1963, quoted in Theatre Workshop, *Oh What a Lovely War*, lxvii.

11 James Chapman qualifies *Oh! What a Lovely War* as "the most ambitious yet least regarded" film about the Great War. Chapman, *War and Film*, 134. The film evokes the assassination of the archduke, the multiple games of alliance, Emperor Franz Josef's signing the declaration of war, the invasion of Belgium, the meeting of Sir John French with General Charles Lanzerac at Rethel in August 1914, the debacle of the French army, the Battle of Mons in August 1914, the first Battle of Ypres (October 1914), the fraternisation at Christmas 1914, Haig's replacement of Sir John French as commander in chief, the Battle of Loos (September 1915), the letter sent to the *Times* after the battle of Loos, Haig's diaries and dispatches, the conscription (1916), the ANZAC troops, the Battle of the Somme (July–November 1916), the Battle of Vimy Ridge (April 1917), the Battle of Passchendaele (July–November 1917), George V falling from his horse while inspecting the troops in France, the arrival of the Americans, the signing of the peace treaty, and the home front evolving from disbelief to cheerful patriotic feeling and to bitter disillusionment, grief, and mourning.

12 The film refers to many famous quotes that are all readily recognizable as they are now part of the shared "mythology" of the First World War (see Todman's definition in *The Great War*, xiii). To give a few examples: Edward Grey's famous remark at the outbreak of the war: "The lamps are going out all over Europe. We shall not see them lit again in our lifetime"; Wilhelm II's war speech to the guards at Potsdam: "The sword is drawn! I cannot sheath it again without victory and honour! All of you shall and will see to it that only in honour is it returned to the scabbard"; Lines from Rupert Brooke's poem *The Soldier*: "If I should die, think only this of me/That there's some

corner of a foreign field/That is forever England"; George Bernard Shaw's outcry, "The men of our country are being sacrificed by the blunders of boobies" (published in the preface of *Heartbreak House*, 1919); and Siegfried Sassoon's outcry: "The sons of Europe are being crucified on the barbed wire" (published in *The Memoirs of George Sherston*, 1937). Among the visuals, the film displays many posters of the time, including the famous recruitment poster featuring Lord Kitchener (designed by Alfred Leete), advertisements, and recruiting posters for women's contribution to the war effort in munition factories.

13 When the show was produced in New York, the program gave the following description: "Revue based on factual World war I data in official records, memoirs and commentaries including those of the Imperial War Museum, Kaiser Wilhelm II, General Erich Ludendorff, Field-Marshall Graf von Schlieffen, Marshal Joffre, Field-Marshal Earl Haig, Field-Marshal John French, general Sir Henry Wilson, Rt Hon. David Lloyd George, Philip Noel-Baker, Alan Clark, Engelbracht and Hanighen, Siegfried Sassoon, Sir Philip Gibbs, Edmund Blunden, Leon Wolff, Captain Liddell Hart, Barbara Tuchman, Herman Kahn, the London newspapers *The Times* and *Daily Express*; assembled by Theatre Workshop, Charles Chilton and members of the cast." Theatre Workshop, *Oh What a Lovely War*, xxi.

14 The photographer makes the pun explicit as he says to the different heads of state assembled for the "family" portrait: "Gentlemen! Gentlemen! Ready for the shot, if you please!"

15 The viewing machines are respectively entitled: "Mons" (August 1914); "Ypres" (October 1914); "Loos" (September 1915); "Vimy Ridge" (1917). The next machine into which the young boy is eager to peer remains blank but the next shot shows a line of soldiers filmed in high angle as if watched from above and we soon figure out they are marching towards the Somme. It is significant that the scene, although set at the beginning of the film, refers to major battles throughout the entire war, clearly indicating that the film adopts a retrospective perspective.

16 Richard Attenborough commented on this technical choice: "It was in a way cumbersome but in terms of emotion it took the audience absolutely with you. The easiest thing obviously would have been to dissolve or to cut … it reinforced, I think, the fact that statements made in the pier were just as pertinent and just as important as the actual reality so I wanted desperately to do it in a single movement." Andy

Dougan, *The Actors' Director: Richard Attenborough behind the Camera* (London: Mainstream Publishing, 1994), 15.

17 To give a few examples: Enjoying a glass of "real champagne" while discussing potential contracts for tin hats, young aristocrat Stephen (Dirk Bogarde) comments on the "chaps at the front": "The men at the front simply adore the war. I had a letter from Julian the other day. He said it's like a great big picnic. Nobody grumbles at him for getting dirty"; Sir John is seen being driven, eager to go grouse shooting and reluctantly inquiring about one of his wounded tenants he meets and whose first name he keeps forgetting; during the ball of the General Staff, a lady announces she has just volunteered for the VAD because "the uniform is so becoming."

18 Before performing church service in a Red Cross camp on the eve of the Battle of the Somme, the chaplain announces: "Dear beloved brethren. I'm sure you will be glad to hear the news from the home front. The Archbishop of Canterbury has made it known that it is no sin to labour for war on the Sabbath. And I'm sure you would also like to know that the Chief Rabbi has absolved your Jewish brethren from abstaining from pork in the trenches. Likewise, his holiness the Pope has ruled that the eating of flesh on Friday is no longer a mortal sin."

19 To give a few examples: Sir John French – the first commander in chief of the British Expeditionary Force – is shown refusing any interpreter for his meeting in August 1914 with French General Charles Lanrezac, although the latter spoke no English while the former hardly spoke any French at all: "Don't be ridiculous, Wilson! The most vital consideration at the moment is to maintain absolute secrecy." Later on, a senior officer inspecting the trenches delivers hollow-ringing cheering words in a very posh accent: "Any way, we're all here … well not all of us of course, and that gas of ours was rather nasty, damn wind changing. But these mishaps do happen in war and gas can be a war-winning weapon. Anyway, so long as we can all keep smiling, you're white men all."

20 Alan Clark is one of the secondary sources that were used by Joan Littlewood and Gerry Raffles. His book *The Donkeys* was published in 1961 and soon became a popular source on the war. Dan Todman comments: "Many of the anecdotes that Clark retailed have been taken up by subsequent authors and entered into folklore; perhaps the best known is the book's title and epitaph, taken from the supposed comment of the German general Hoffman that 'the British soldiers

fought like lions but were led by donkeys.' The book's tone is highly sarcastic and Haig is repeatedly condemned out of his own mouth with a series of quotations from his diaries and letters (edited or taken out of context), which is also the case in the film." Todman, *The Great War: Myth and Memory* (London: Bloomsbury, 2005), 99–100. One case in point is when Clark implies Haig was more concerned about George V's fall from his horse during a visit to France than with the fate of his army. This point is taken up in the film when Haig is shown writing his diary and reading in voice over: "Yesterday, the King inspected the troops. Trouble was that the men waved their hats instead of flags as His Majesty rode by. The King did clutch the reins too firmly. Correction. The King did clutch the reins rather firmly, no reflection on His Majesty's horsemanship. The grass was very slippery, and the mare moved backwards. I'd exercised her every day for a year. So unfortunate it had to be my horse that threw the King."

21 As Todman notes: "Few issues in modern British military history have inspired so much writing as the quality of generalship in the First World War, and while Haig was to become the iconic general of the War, he has remained a most controversial figure." Todman, *The Great War,* 83. B.H. Liddell Hart, considering Haig's reputation in his book *Through the Fog of War* (1938), writes: "The figure of Haig has enfolded in a dual legend – one might describe it as a 'Jekyll and Hyde' legend. On the one hand there has grown the conventional picture of a great commander – far-sighted, profound in reflection, quick of decision, unshakeable in resolution, moved solemnly by a sense of duty. On the other hand, there is the picture of a soldier moulded to a different yet less popular pattern – short-sighted, dull, slow, obstinate and callous." Quoted in Todman, *The Great War,* 93.

22 Haig is shown repeatedly praying for victory, especially "before the Americans arrive," yet he confidently believes God is on his side: "I feel that every step I take is guided by the divine will." He is shown writing in his diary or dispatches of "complete victory" despite all evidence to the contrary as with the third Battle of Ypres known as Passchendaele: "The attack is a great success. Fighting has been severe but that was to be expected … First reports from the clearing stations state that our casualties are only some 60,000, mostly slight. The wounded are very cheery indeed." To demonstrate to a doubtful officer that his "policy of attrition" is the best possible solution, he explains, using *reductio ad absurdum* reasoning: "We must grind them down. You see, our population is greater than theirs, and their losses are

greater than ours. In the end, they will have 5,000 men left and we shall have 10,000 and we shall have won."

23 John Mills was actually one of those behind the film project; he wrote the script along with Len Deighton (who later had his name removed from the film credits because he objected to what he felt was Richard Attenborough's over-glamorized adaptation). John Mills then asked Attenborough to direct the film. As Richard Attenborough jocularly explains: "Mills explained they could go for someone who knew everything and had vast experience and in the process take the risk they might be doing things that had been done before, or they could go for somebody who knew absolutely bugger all and would perhaps open some new doors and introduce fresh ideas." Quoted in Dougan, *The Actors' Director*, 14.

24 For example, John Mills starred in *Forever England* (aka *Brown on Resolution*) by Walter Forde (1935) based on C.S. Forester's First World War adventure in which after his ship has been sunk by the Germans, he escapes, wounded, and manages on his own to neutralize the crew of a German cruiser until the Royal Navy arrives.

25 "Now before I talk to you I should like to read you a letter from George Bernard Shaw to my mother: 'The men of our country are being sacrificed by the blunders of boobies, the cupidity of capitalists, the ambition of conquerors' ... The sons of Europe are being crucified on the barbed wire because you misguided masses are crying out for it!"

26 Actually, this change of mood is intimated as early as the opening credits which are composed of a series of close shots of memorabilia on a white background: from colourful kitschy objects that suggest the grandeur of "King and Country" (a tea cup, a biscuit box adorned with portraits of royalties, medals to the effigy of kings and queens, etc.) to drabber and drabber objects characteristic of a soldier's everyday life like a shabby shoe, a gas mask, a bayonet, some barbed wire, etc. Meanwhile the cheerful music becomes much more subdued and sadder.

27 The film features more than thirty musical numbers. Patriotic and enlisting songs include: "Belgium Put the Kaibosh on the Kaiser" (performed by French actor Jean-Pierre Cassel); "Are We Downhearted? No!"; "It's a Long Way to Tipperary"; "Rule Britannia"; "We Don't Want to Lose You"; "I'll Make a Man of You" (performed by a teasingly alluring Maggie Smith); "Send for the Boys of the Girls' Brigade"; "Over There"; Ivor Novello's famous "Till the Boys Come

Home." However most of the songs are "Tommies' songs" ("Oh, It's a Lovely War"; "The Long, Long Trail"; "We're Here Because We're Here"; "Pack Up Your Troubles"; "Goodbye-ee"; "Never Mind") and they are often parodies of famous songs of the time: "Gassed Last Night" is sung to the tune of the music hall song "Drunk Last Night and Drunk the Night Before"; "Hush! Here Comes a Whizz-Bang" to the tune of "Hush, Here Comes the Dream Man"; "I Don't Want to Be a Soldier" to the tune of "Come My Lad, and Be a Soldier"; "They Were Only Playing Leap-Frog" to the tune of "John Brown's Body"; "Joe Soap's Army" to the tune of "Onward Christian Soldiers"; "When This Lousy War Is Over" to the tune of "What a Friend We Have in Jesus"; "The Bells of Hell" to the tune of "She Only Answered Ting-a Ling-a-Ling"; "Far Far from Ypres I Long to Be" to the tune of "Sing Me to Sleep, Sergeant Major"; "They Didn't Believe Me" to the tune of Jerome Kern's "And When They Told Me How Beautiful You Are."

28 When the film was first released, a number of critics noted how in the film grief superseded the play's political passion. Margaret Hinxman considered that the film "was moved not so much by a cynical outrage as by a desperate sadness." "A Lovely War for British Film," *Sunday Telegraph*, 6 April 1969, 6. Likewise, Philip French concluded: "We are left with a sense of wasted lives, a feeling of impenetrable sadness, of unassuageable grief." "Oh! What a Lovely War," *Sight and Sound* 38, no. 2 (Spring 1969), 94, quoted in Todman, *The Great War*, 64.

29 Richard Attenborough explained in an interview: "The end shot was the first scene I thought of. Everybody said it was completely out of the question. You have to remember that was 1969, which is 25 years ago, and there were no computers and the possibility of high-tech special effects like digital matte shots simply did not exist if that is indeed what you wanted to do. But I didn't want to do that. I wanted to start on that boy's grave, that one cross, and then pull back … In those days there was only one way to get a shot like that and that was by using a helicopter." Eventually Attenborough had to have 15,000 holes drilled in the Sussex Downs as it was impossible to hammer the crosses into the chalk. Quoted in Dougan, *The Actors' Director*, 15–17. White crosses were a recurring motif of First World War films: *Verdun* (Léon Poirier, 1928), *All Quiet on the Western Front* (Lewis Milestone, 1930), and *The Wooden Crosses* (Raymond Bernard, 1932) all close with a haunting image of the landscape covered in white crosses. See Chapman, *War and Film*, 125.

30 Successive boards read: "1914: Total allied loss 1,500,000 men"; "Battle: Loos/British losses: 60,000/Total allied losses: 250,000/Ground gained: 0 yards"; "1916 Battle: the Somme/Losses: First day: 60,000/Ground gained: 0 yards"; "1917: Battle: Passchendaele/British losses: 244,897." The Great War is remembered for the unparalleled number of British casualties. It is estimated that over 750, 000 British died during the war and over one million ex-servicemen were in receipt of postwar disability pensions.

31 See: Graham Dawson, *Soldier Heroes: British Adventure, Empire and the Imagining of Masculinity* (London: Routledge, 1994); Michael Paris, *Warrior Nation: Images of War in British Popular Culture 1850–2000* (London: Reaction Books, 2000).

32 The use of a field of poppies at the end of the final episode of the 1989 BBC TV series *Blackadder Goes Forth* raised similar debates: some castigated the note of deference it reintroduced in an otherwise highly irreverential vision of the war. See Todman, *The Great War*, 146.

33 This seemingly "innocent" question is a sarcastic reference to Savile Lumley's war poster "Daddy, what did YOU do in the Great War?" which was meant to shame the men who would not enlist. It shows a little girl sitting on her father's lap and asking him the question while the father looks ashamed.

34 Todman, *The Great War*, 64.

35 See: Rowland Wymer, *Derek Jarman* (Manchester: Manchester University Press, 2005), 122; Joseph A. Gomez, "The Process of Jarman's *War Requiem*: Personal Vision and the Tradition of Fusion of the Arts," in *By Angels Driven. The Films of Derek Jarman*, edited by Chris Lippard (Westport, CT: Praeger, 1996), 86. Despite these constraints, *War Requiem* clearly answered the filmmaker's enthusiasm for Britten's music which he repeatedly listened to while completing *The Last of England* (1988), his interest in poetry and his political agenda, describing *War Requiem* as part of "the reclaiming of the Queer Past." Derek Jarman, *Dancing Ledge* (London: Quartet Books, 1991), 7.

36 The fact that the same actress (Tilda Swinton) plays the nurse in the prologue that frames the film in the present as well as the nurse and Owen's sister in the past narrative recalls Powell and Pressburger's *The Life and Death of Colonel Blimp* (1943) in which Deborah Kerr plays three different women, yet fulfils a similar key part in the life of the main protagonist.

37 In his published journal on *War Requiem,* Jarman wrote he had conceived "a loose story around Wilfred Owen, a Nurse, and the

Unknown soldier." Derek Jarman, *War Requiem: The Film* (London: Faber and Faber, 1989), i.

38 The film actually uses conventional 35mm but also Super 8 sequences and documentary found-footage re-filmed on video. In the same journal, Jarman concluded his film was "a collage. A cut-up." Ibid.

39 The nine poems are "Anthem for Doomed Youth," "Voices," "The Next War," "Sonnet: On Seeing a Piece of Our Artillery Brought into Action," "Futility," "The Parable of the Old Man and the Young," "The End (after the blast of lightning from the east)," "At a Calvary near the Ancre," and "Strange Meeting."

40 Owen's preface reads: "This book is not about heroes. English poetry is not yet fit to speak of them. Nor is it about deeds, or lands, nor anything about glory, honour, might, majesty, dominion, or poser, except War./Above all I am not concerned with Poetry./My subject is war, and the pity of war./The Poetry is in the Pity." Wilfred Owen, *The Collected Poems of Wilfred Owen* (New York: New Directions, 1964), 31.

41 See: Melvyn Cooke, "Owen, Britten and Pacifism" (Cambridge: Cambridge University Press, 1996), 1–19; Gilles Couderc, "The *War Requiem*: Britten's *Wilfred Owen* Opera." http://www.awpreview.univ-paris-diderot.fr/IMG/pdf/1.1_2_coudercrevised1novbrittenwar.pdf. One major problem, though, is that unless one is familiar with the text, the lyrics, whether in Latin or in English, remain extremely difficult to grasp, thus limiting the possible understanding of these tensions.

42 In 1963 Philip Larkin noted: "In the end Owen's war is not Sassoon's war but all war; not particular suffering but all suffering, not particular waste but all waste." Larkin, *Required Writing: Miscellaneous Pieces, 1955–1982* (London: Faber and Faber, 1983), 162–3. Dan Todman analyzes how since the 1960s Owen has come to stand out as the symbol of war poetry in British culture, gaining the status of "the celebrity poet of the First World War." See Todman, *The Great War*, 161–72.

43 The quote appears near the end of the published script: "In my heart I dedicate my film of *War Requiem* to all those cast out, like myself, from Christendom. To my friends who are dying in a moral climate created by a church with no compassion." Jarman, *War Requiem: The Film*, 35.

44 Cross cutting occurs in the "liber scriptus" passage, showing alternately the nurse and Owen both carrying a lamp on night guard, both

covering the wounded or the soldiers with blankets. After "the Next War" passage, nurses preparing bandages alternate with men preparing their weapons. Likewise, letters link both the nurse and a soldier. In the "Agnus Dei" section, the Unknown Soldier carrying Owen's dead body while wearing a crown of barbed wire alternates with the nurse who covers herself with wet earth and raises a similar crown.

45 "Jarman stages his own version of a requiem through a visual dialogue between monumentality and performance." Steven Dillon, *Derek Jarman and Lyric Film: The Mirror and the Sea* (Austin: University of Texas Press, 2004), 120.

PART FOUR

"With Due Reverence": Remembering the Forgotten Fighters

19

Integration Politics and the New Zealand Army: The Fate of the Maori Battalion in the Wake of the Second World War

CORINNE DAVID-IVES

The involvement of native peoples from the British dominions in both world conflicts was not simply predicated on loyalty to the nation. The "price of blood" was expected to provide significant political leverage for indigenous peoples, and often contributed to a large extent to changing the status and the perception of indigenous minorities in the aftermath of the conflicts. It became "the price of citizenship," an idea which was notably expressed in New Zealand by Maori politician Sir Apirana Ngata, who in 1914 and in 1940, together with prominent Maori leaders, successfully lobbied for the incorporation of distinct Maori units into the New Zealand army.[1] The New Zealand (Maori) Pioneer Battalion of the First World War was therefore set up essentially on a native basis in 1914 and became a combat unit in 1916.[2] Its 1940 successor, the 28 (Maori) Battalion, was a distinct indigenous unit organised on a tribal basis, with Maori officers and even a Maori commander – a unique case in the British Commonwealth. Participation was massive, even though conscription had not been imposed on Maori. Recruitment was organised on the home front by tribal committees. New Zealand therefore constituted a major exception, in that it allowed its indigenous minority a large degree of autonomy in managing the war effort.

The mode of participation of native peoples in the World Wars can certainly be analyzed as an indicator revealing the position occupied by the indigenous part of the population in the different nations across the British Empire.[3] Thus, the Maori Battalion and its First World War ancestor the Maori and Pioneer Battalion organized the visibility of the indigenous minority in the military. In the last few years, historians have taken a renewed interest in this and they have explored the way the Maori War Effort Organization sought to renegotiate the national pact between Maori and New Zealanders of British descent (Pakeha).[4] However, little has been said about the complete turnaround that took place only fifteen years after the Second World War. The legacy of the Maori Battalion was to be short-lived. As memories of war started to fade, the New Zealand government adopted a new policy of integration which resulted in the phasing out of distinct Maori units in the national army.

How could such a change be accepted? This article will seek to analyze the implications of integration from the late 1950s on the New Zealand military. It will focus on the generational gap between the Maori veterans and the younger generation of Maori soldiers. Far from anecdotal, the case of integrated troops in New Zealand provides a revealing example of the shift in the postwar narrative of identity. Integration will be analyzed as yet another brand of assimilation, focusing on the individual rather the group, and reducing a collective visibility that had been much enhanced by the World Wars Maori Battalions episodes.

THE DUAL NATIONAL PACT AND THE NEW INTEGRATION POLICY

The history of Maori in colonial New Zealand had always been that of a constant struggle for empowerment and for the enforcement of the rights that had been granted to them from the foundation of New Zealand under the Treaty of Waitangi in 1840. The episode of the Maori Battalion is in line with this long tradition. The creation of specific military units regrouping indigenous soldiers gave visibility to Maori, proved their loyalty to the nation, and was also to have a significant impact on Maori unity rising above tribal divisions.[5] The presence of Maori not as individual soldiers but as a collective force had always been the goal of Maori national leaders and politicians because it enhanced the specificity of Maori across tribal differences. As noted later in *The Official History of New Zealand in the Second World War 1939–1945* about the main architect of the formation of the Maori Battalion, Sir Apirana Ngata, "Ngata was jealous that his race be not submerged in a New Zealand at war any more than it had been submerged in a New Zealand at peace."[6] The war provided a new opportunity for Maori to be clearly identified once again as one of the founding peoples of the nation. From the point of view of the dominion's government, the creation of a distinct Maori unit embodied the dual nature of the New Zealand identity. It reinforced the official discourse on racial equality in New Zealand. Far from the American model of segregated troops, the Maori Battalion was the perfect illustration of the racial harmony that supposedly reigned in New Zealand. Evidence of this unique egalitarian model was to be found in the promotion of Maori high-ranking officers.[7]

The Maori Battalion came home to New Zealand in January 1946 to a national welcome. The glorious epic of the battalion had received national news coverage and been a source of pride for all New Zealanders.[8] Popular enthusiasm was real and the war news had enhanced Maori image in the country. All the archive footing of the time emphasized the distinct identity of those troops, as noted in the *Official History*: "The troops assembled on the wharf and were met at the Aotea Quay gates with all the ceremony pertaining to *the return of a war party in pre-pakeha days*."[9] The battalion had symbolically provided the opportunity for Maori to regain their full status of warriors from before the onset of colonization. The reports showed traditional welcomes and *hakas* (war dances) for the soldiers, receptions throughout the country on the *maraes* (meeting houses), and sometimes reported on the return home to a village or *pa* (fortified village). National recognition was afforded in the form of medals and war citations, sometimes posthumous, including the most prestigious Victoria Cross.[10]

During the war and in the first years of peace, the "price of citizenship" – the price of blood – was paid in the form of political decisions taken by the Labour government. Maori veterans had been receiving the same pensions as Pakeha veterans since 1915, but legislation was introduced to facilitate the rehabilitation of veterans, improving pension rates and eligibility.[11] The Maori Social and Economic Advancement Act was also passed as early as 1945 to further the improvement of Maori social conditions, which were still markedly inferior to those of the Pakeha majority. More symbolically, in 1946, the Ministry of Native Affairs became the Ministry of Maori Affairs, placed under the direct authority of Labour Prime Minister Peter Fraser.[12] The Ministry of Maori Affairs was going to play a strategic role in the postwar period, in particular by opening its doors to a number of veterans. The term "native," with its derogatory connotations, was officially abandoned in 1947 for any future official references to Maori. The New Zealand authorities thus appeared to make sure that the principles of equality that were so paramount in the national discourse were upheld.

However, the aftermath of the war also opened perspectives onto an uncertain future. On the political level, the ministry and the government were wary of Maori nationalism; they rightly interpreted the Maori War Effort Organization as its prime vehicle, with its network of tribal committees. Maori self-government was not on the New Zealand government agenda in 1945. Economic equality was the aim of the Labour government, and Fraser worried that anything more might prove divisive for the nation. There was therefore a planned move to somehow re-colonize the Maori War Effort Organization and to incorporate its structures into the Ministry of Maori Affairs, in order to defuse its radical potential and regain control.

But this behind-the-scenes battle was to be over-shadowed by a new phenomenon partly triggered off by the war: the onset of massive Maori migration towards the cities. Until then, the Maori population had been largely rural, often living in relative isolation, in particular in poor areas such as the Far North. The war effort had not only sent soldiers to the front, but it also contributed to exposing large numbers of Maori youngsters to Pakeha society, as young men and women were massively recruited to work in factories and strategic sectors of the economy. In the same way, a number of veterans chose not to return to their farming communities and settled in towns. This was the first step toward a major shift to the urban areas.[13] The social upheaval experienced by traditional Maori society within the next decade was to lead the New Zealand government to reconsider its Maori policy.

THE CHOICE OF INTEGRATION: NEW VALUES FOR NEW CHALLENGES?

Intensification of contact between Maori and Pakeha glaringly revealed the mythical nature of a supposed absence of racism in New Zealand. "Prejudice," as it was referred to by the national press at the time, expressed itself fully in the immediate aftermath of the war, as veterans were first exposed to the difficulties of finding work and accommodation in the cities from which most Maori were traditionally absent. As Major K.T. Harawira, former chaplain of the Maori Battalion, observed in 1944, "The Maori people are fighting and shedding blood to achieve equality in New Zealand, but the wretched colour bar remains," he said. "There is no doubt that it exists in New Zealand, so let us air it, instead of keeping these things behind closed doors."[14]

Although racist incidents reported in the press seemed to give rise to righteous indignation, the government rightly sensed that this was the prelude to more significant problems. The national pact might be placed under increasing stress. Confidential "race relations files" started to be put together at ministry level to monitor the situation and to deal discreetly with incidents on a case-by-case basis.[15] Peter Fraser himself found it necessary to spell out the standards of behaviour required of Pakeha civil servants towards Maori colleagues within the Ministry of Maori Affairs. In rather blunt language, he recalled in a confidential memo, "I do feel that discrimination does exist among certain people, and I would be very sorry to see it creep into our Department. A term that has come to my notice recently is: 'A typical Maori.' I must confess that I have never seen such a Maori any more that I have seen a typical Scotsman."[16]

However, the Conservative National government elected in 1949 was going to switch to a more subdued approach. The idea was to preserve at all costs the image of a racially tolerant New Zealand, which had been so useful in defining the nation's identity. The Conservative Minister of Maori Affairs E. Corbett thus continued to affirm publicly that "It is true ... that New Zealand can be shown as an example to many countries of how two races can live side by side in perfect understanding."[17] Defusing tensions and avoiding scandal and international exposure at all costs made up the core of the Conservative government's Maori policy. Incidents continued to be dealt with away from the public eye; no general policy statement was ever made, no piece of legislation introduced to put an end to discrimination. However, as major social change was experienced by the country at large and by Maori in particular, it became clear that a change of approach was needed.

The 1961 Hunn Report would provide the basis for a new policy better suited to new times and new challenges.[18] The visibility of Maori as a people within a nation would give way to an individualistic approach which was to ease the integration of Maori individuals within Pakeha society, in particular in urban settings. Named after its author, a senior civil servant whose personal career would culminate with his appointment as defence secretary in 1964, the Hunn report dealt with the necessity of facilitating the adaptation of Maori to their new socio-economic conditions in a manner which would limit clashes with the non-Maori population. In reality, the ideas developed in the Hunn Report were a revamped version of the old assimilationist approach.[19] Resolutely paternalistic and Eurocentric, the report measured progress with Maori in proportion to their adoption of Western ways. Although the eradication of Maori culture was not the final goal envisaged in the report, its survival was viewed in terms of a selection of a few valuable traits – once again an old idea. The need for Maori to practice their own culture was considered necessary in order to operate a smooth transition into a world that until then had been unknown to most. However, this was conceived in terms of recreational practice, which would take place in the private sphere. Tribal connections and collective identity were to dissolve progressively.

The Hunn Report became the blueprint for the Conservative government's Maori policy. It provided the guidelines for social policy, in particular in the sensitive field of social housing.[20] Education was targeted. Integration became the rallying cry of the government. Its principles were spelled out in various documents destined to the public, insisting on the ideal of a racially mixed society.[21] The next step was its application to the armed forces.

INTEGRATION POLITICS IN THE NZ ARMY

Maori had been overrepresented in the army since the Second World War. After 1945, young Maori recruits continued to join the armed forces, while a number of Maori veterans joined the Ministry of Maori Affairs. The very special world of the armed forces was a particularly sensitive target for integration; Maori had used the successive wars to prove their potential in terms of autonomy. The Maori Battalion had provided a tremendous opportunity to get the whole nation to focus on distinct Maori identity. In this context, even fifteen years after the battalion had come home, the switch to integration was a challenge for the government, and certainly a national policy well beyond the jurisdiction of the Ministry of Maori Affairs.

However, the Ministry of Maori Affairs could bring its support to the reforms and comment on them. Since 1952, the ministry had been publishing a magazine destined to the Maori readership: *Te Ao Hou/The New World*.[22] The publication provides an excellent testimony to the atmosphere of the time. It gave advice and information on the major social changes experienced by Maori in the 1950s, accompanying the transition to a more Western way of life. The articles generally sought to accommodate Maori cultural practices and identity with the economic imperatives of life in the cities in a way that would not disrupt the latter.[23] *Te Ao Hou* covered the topic of integration within the armed forces through a series of articles between 1961 and 1964. Although relaying the official discourse on integration, the magazine bears witness to the tensions and debates surrounding the topic of the status of Maori within the armed forces. Of course, the ultimate goal was to persuade Maori readers of the merits of integration. However, dissent was also apparent because of the substantial number of Maori veterans involved with the Ministry of Maori Affairs and with the publication.

The new policy of integration was in complete contradiction to the veterans' aspirations. In this sense, integration was also very revealing of the government's will to resume control and in particular to check once and for all a form of Maori nationalism deemed potentially dangerous. An article published in *Te Ao Hou* in December 1961 about the veterans' yearly congress expanded on "this strong feeling of Maori nationalism" still very much alive with the veterans.[24] Maori veterans continued to represent an important and influential group at the national level, supporting Maori aspirations for more justice and equality. But their hallmark was their defence of Maori cultural integrity. They insisted in particular on the fundamental role of the Maori language as the preferred vector of a living culture: "These men, too, proved that no Maori can best express the innermost feelings of his heart or his *hinengaro* except through the medium of his mother tongue. It was one of the revelations of the reunion."[25] This view was in direct opposition to the New Zealand government's efforts to promote English as the key to economic integration. The veterans thus placed themselves in the long tradition of Maori leaders who had consistently resisted acculturation.

Aware of the danger looming in the army, the 1961 Veterans Congress voted a motion to present to the government, recommending the creation of a permanent separate Maori unit within the New

Zealand army on the model of the wartime Maori Battalion. Anticipating criticism, they insisted that this should not be seen as segregation, but "common sense":

> Did not the authorities agree to the formation of Maori Battalions in World Wars I and II? Was it segregation then? Did not Sir Apirana say, "Your martial forbears will march, eat, sleep and fight with you?" How best can the Maori people unite itself against a foe except through a fighting unit of its own? ... Surely, he concluded, we have proved our right to have our own way in this matter.[26]

This was the perfect illustration of that "Maori nationalism" as it had come to life during the last war. The argument that was developed shed light on the ambiguous position of the New Zealand government, which was clearly more worried about this Maori nationalism than about some potential problem of segregation within the armed forces. But the veterans' voices were going to find it more and more difficult to be heard.

While the New Zealand government made the choice of integration, the New Zealand armed forces offered interesting career prospects for young Maori. They were building on their reputation for enforcing equality amongst servicemen. As a new generation of Maori joined the army, Maori veterans would come to be identified with an older generation out of touch with the modern world. The Ministry of Maori Affairs cleverly relayed the change through *Te Ao Hou*. In 1961, the magazine reported on army life in Malaya, where New Zealand forces were supporting the British in their efforts to control the colony's future and its aspirations to independence. In an article entitled "Why Maoris Choose the Army," published soon after the Hunn Report, the magazine insisted on "one remarkable feature of the battalion," that is "the way in which Maoris and Europeans have been welded together *into an integrated whole*."[27] The article focused on the complete absence of distinction between Maori and non-Maori troops: "There are 300 Maoris, including four officers and quite a number of NCO's. This is about the same proportion as in previous Malayan contingents. *The Maoris form no unit of their own but are spread throughout the battalion*."[28]

This of course was the result of an official policy and was in complete contrast to the situation that had prevailed during the Second

World War and to the ideal that the Maori Battalion had embodied. Instead, the author stressed the benefits of integration which made it possible to erase the differences between Maori and Pakeha. The expression of Maori culture was apparently welcome, but in the form of a "Maori club." Far from organizing life in the battalion, Maori culture was relegated to recreational activities.[29] It is important to note also that there was no reference whatsoever to tribalism, whereas tribalism had provided the framework for the organization of the Maori Battalion during World War II. The result of this new approach was presented in a positive light, since the new arrangements seemed to make the Malaya contingent very popular. It attracted many young Maori recruits, "four times as many Maoris as one would expect from the size of the Maori population." And very significantly, Maori were "happy with the excellent race relations in the battalion."[30]

The system was therefore described as the best possible environment the army could offer to young Maori soldiers. Moreover, it provided an excellent opportunity to paint an idyllic picture of race relations in New Zealand. This was expanded upon in yet another article published in 1962 about the troops stationed in Malaya.[31] This time, there was a lengthy interview of a young Maori soldier from this "roughly half Maori half Pakeha Battalion," who stated that "The Asians used to express surprise and pleasure at the mixing of the two groups on leave and at work and in our concert party." Of course, the New Zealand army appeared as very progressive in the context of the time, not only because of "the lack of any segregation in the unit" noted in the article, but also because "the sight of Maori Officers and N.C.O.'s commanding pakeha troops as well as vice versa seemed to them a practical demonstration that in New Zealand we try and practise what we preach."[32] In other words, the New Zealand Army would promote indigenous soldiers to commanding ranks almost always reserved for whites elsewhere. Once again, this enabled New Zealand to capitalize on an image of racial harmony. The Malayan theatre functioned as a showcase for the New Zealand government, which wished to appeal to the multicultural nations of the new Commonwealth. The appointment in 1959 of a former colonel of the Maori Battalion as New Zealand's High Commissioner in Malaya had been another political move supporting New Zealand's diplomacy in this respect.[33] In an international context that insisted on racial equality, that had witnessed a general outcry against apartheid in South Africa leading to the forced withdrawal of the old dominion from the Commonwealth, New Zealand could be singled out as a model while defusing indigenous nationalism, somehow killing two birds with one stone.

These new developments were far from being greeted with the same enthusiasm by all. However, the dissent expressed by the veterans of the Maori Battalion was presented as very inopportune. The campaign launched by the Veterans Association for a new Maori Battalion was met with embarrassment at best, and more often with slight annoyance, as the following comments show:

> When we came home we read that the Maori Battalion old boys are agitating for an all-Maori unit in the army. This makes me sad. Of course the tradition of my race tells me I must listen with respect to our elders. Yet age does not always bring wisdom and the elders are not always right. They often think with their hearts and not their heads.[34]

The young recruit's interview testified to the generational gap that seemed to have opened between young Maori who were apparently satisfied with the government's new policy and its enforcement in the army, and the previous generation who came across as being cut off from modern realities and completely out of touch with Maori youth. This tactic was a clever way to point out divisions within the Maori community and to discard nationalistic aspirations as things of the past.

The author of the article also insisted on the friendship that could develop between Maori and Pakeha in a perfectly well integrated environment such as the army. Constant interaction was suggested as the best way to fight against racism from both sides:

> Before I went into the army I do not mind admitting that I had never learned to mix with Pakeha. I thought they were different in more ways than skin colour. Well, now I have lived with them we all know one another. For the first time in my life I have really close Pakeha friends. The other chaps and I have learned a lot off the Pakeha and I like to think that they have learned a lot off us. They respect us. Many of the Pakeha in the battalion sing our songs and some can do a pretty good haka.[35]

This was a discourse in which the army provided an ideal model of what New Zealand should be as a perfectly integrated society. It gave evidence that integration constituted a very positive experience for both sides. The young recruit also warned against the dangers of segregation within the army which, ironically enough, was bound to attract fierce criticism. He finished with this scathing remark: "These old boys should use their energies to encourage Maoris with more education than I to become officers instead of wanting *racial segregation in the army*."[36] This was going to become the final argument against any prospect of resuscitating the Maori Battalion. The general aversion for the segregationist model would be used to prevent any return to separate institutions that had yet always been associated with experiments in Maori self-government in New Zealand. Maori autonomy would ironically be checked in the name of the fight against racial discrimination.

The controversy that raged between the army and the veterans culminated in 1964 during the yearly Veterans Congress at which Jack Hunn himself was invited as a keynote speaker, in his new capacity as defence secretary. *Te Ao Hou* reported on the congress and on the confrontation between the veterans and the man who was, after all, the main architect of integration in New Zealand. Feelings ran high and according to the author, "He made what many thought, a very provocative address."[37] Although subjected to fierce criticism on the part of the successive Maori orators, Hunn conceded nothing at all on the subject of a new Maori Battalion which, according to him, would be "a blow to the integration of the two races."[38]

Although the author concluded the report with the hearty prospect that "the meeting ended as it did three years before in Rotorua, with the firm resolve to continue to fight for a separate Maori Unit," this fight would peter out with time. The aging veterans no longer had the same political clout as they did right after the war. It was much easier for the New Zealand government to resist their demands in time of peace than it had been in time of war. The New Zealand Army would from now on be perfectly integrated. The glorious memories of the Maori Battalion would fade as years went by, maybe in the same way as tribal connections weakened all throughout the years of integration in the 1960s and 1970s amongst young urban Maori.

CONCLUSION

It is interesting to note that the Maori leaders' efforts to obtain a special status within the New Zealand Army were only successful in time of war. Both Maori battalions were disbanded in peace time.

After World War II, integration policies clashed with the very notion of separate units within the army because the strategies of integration focused on the individual rather than the group. Strong collective Maori identity was considered a potential political threat on one hand, and on the other hand it was perceived as a hindrance to the final process of assimilation which was expected to follow integration. The army was a symbolic place in which to impose integration not only because of the Maori Battalion episode, but also because of the weight of Maori recruits, well over the percentage of Maori in the population. The government's strategy was to present resistance to integration policies in the army as resistance to modernity on the part of an older generation of Maori veterans. The argument was reinforced by the fact that the army continued to attract young Maori men, in spite of or rather *because of* integration, according to the official discourse. Certainly, many young Maori made a choice based on socioeconomic factors; the army seems to have offered opportunities that were not so readily available to young Maori in New Zealand civil society. Socio-economic indicators have consistently pointed out at discrepancies between Maori and non-Maori; in contrast, the army functioned as a social leveler. Its egalitarian tradition offered a suitable environment and the possibility of promotion. This however went in hand with the acceleration of assimilation. Maori cultural practices became recreational activities. Although the *haka* is still performed today on special occasions by all New Zealand troops and remains the hallmark of the New Zealand military, it is also because it conveniently continues to convey the traditional message of the dual origins of the nation, rather than being the expression of the distinct character of the indigenous participation in the defence of the nation.

Maori today continue to represent a sizeable percentage of the New Zealand armed service proportionally to their share of the population.[39] Significantly, between 2006 and 2011, the chief of the New Zealand force was Maori.[40] This seems to be more of a testimony to New Zealand's image as the champion of race relations than the expression of genuine power sharing that was the ideal of the old Maori Battalion. The last dozen or so Maori veterans still alive chose to bow out two years ago. The Maori Battalion Association was formally wound up at an official ceremony on 18 December 2012. Memories of war certainly continue to linger, with tributes to all those who paid "the price of citizenship." Very little however is ever said about the process that led to the complete phasing out of specific Maori units.

NOTES

1 Apirana Ngata, *The Price of Citizenship: Ngarimu, Victoria Cross* (Wellington: Whitcombe & Tombs, 1943).
2 Pugsley, *Te Hokowhitu a Tu: The Maori Pioneer Battalion in the First World War* (Auckland: Reed, 1995).
3 Winegard, *Indigenous Peoples of the British Dominions and the First World War* (Cambridge: Cambridge University Press, 2011).
4 Soutar, *Nga Tama Toa/The Price of Citizenship: C Company (28) Maori Battalion 1939–1945* (Auckland: David Bateman Ltd, 2011).
5 "The war did undoubtedly promote mutual understanding of tribal points of views. The tribal representatives became more tolerant of each other … Undoubtedly present day Maori leadership owes much to this change." Anonymous, "Italy: After Ten Years," *Te Ao Hou/The New World*, no. 5 (Spring 1953), 28–64, 29.
6 J.F. Cody, "28 (Maori) Battalion" in *The Official History of New Zealand in the Second World War 1939–1945*, edited by Howard Karl Kippenberger (Wellington: Historical Publications Branch, 1956) 1.
7 The most famous was Lieutenant-Colonel E. Te W. Love. "Lieutenant-Colonel E. Te W. Love, of Wellington, Appointed to Command the Maori Battalion," *New Zealand Herald*, Volume 79, issue 24307, 23 June 1942, 5.
8 See for example "MAGNIFICENT FIGHTERS: Men of the Maori Battalion, Who Covered Themselves with Glory by Their Fighting in Thermopylae Pass," *New Zealand Herald*, volume 78, issue 23955, May 1941, 9.
9 Cody, "28 (Maori) Battalion," 485. Italics added.
10 Lt Te M. N. Ngarimu. See Ngata, *The Price of Citizenship*.
11 "The War Pensions Act 1943 improved pension rates and made it easier for war veterans and their families to receive compensation for death, disability or financial disadvantage." "Veterans' Assistance – War Pensions," *Te Ara – The Encyclopedia of New Zealand*. http://www.teara.govt.nz/.
12 Peter Fraser also appointed Tipi Ropiha as Under-Secretary of Maori Affairs, the first Maori senior civil servant to occupy the position.

13 "At the end of the war, three-quarters of the Maori population still lived in the country, in areas where there were relatively few Pakehas. By the mid-1970s, three-quarters of the Maori population was urban, over a fifth living in Auckland." Dunstall, "The Social Pattern" in *Oxford History of New Zealand*, edited by Geoffrey W. Rice (Auckland: Oxford University Press, 1992), 451–81, 457.

14 "The Colour Bar: Evidence in Dominion," *The New Zealand Herald*, 17 October 1944.

15 This practice was initiated in 1947 under Prime Minister Peter Fraser. The resulting "Colour Bar Files" mixed confidential memos, newspaper clippings, and ministry correspondence dealing with various incidents or topics relating to "race relations." Ministry of Maori Affairs, "Colour Bar Files," Wellington National Archives, Archives Ref M A 1, 36/1/21, Part 1–4.

16 Peter Fraser, "Memorandum for: The Under-Secretary, Native Department, 5 June 1947, Ministry of Maori Affairs, "Colour Bar Files."

17 E. Corbett, "The Colour Question in Africa," 24 November 1950, Ministry of Maori Affairs, "Colour Bar Files."

18 J.K. Hunn, *Report on Department of Maori Affairs* (Wellington: Government Printer, 1961).

19 This was readily admitted by Hunn himself: "The British (Celts, Britons, Hibernians, Danes, Anglo-Saxons, Normans) are an assimilated society. In the course of centuries, Britain passed through integration to assimilation. Signs are not wanting that that may be the destiny of the two races in New Zealand in the distant future." Hunn, *Report*, 15.

20 The government's obsession with the need to avoid "ghettoization" notably led to the ill-famed policy of "pepper-potting," which tried to prevent Maori families from regrouping in certain neighbourhoods.

21 "A well-integrated, racially mixed community would be composed largely of people who have achieved a cultural balance suitable to their particular environment and the make-up of the local population." Department of Maori Affairs, "Integration of Maori and Pakeha," *Series of Special Studies, Race Relations: Integration and Segregation*, no. 1 (Wellington: National Archives, 1962).

22 "*Te Ao Hou* is intended as a magazine for the Maori people. Pakehas will, we hope, find much in it that may interest them and broaden their knowledge of the Maori, but this publication is planned mainly to provide interesting and informative reading for Maori homes. *Te Ao Hou* should become like a 'marae' on paper, where all questions of

interest to the Maori can be discussed." Anonymous, "Editorial," *Te Ao Hou/The New World*, no. 1 (Winter 1952), 1.

23 "The Maori, in general, earns his living in the same way as the Pakeha. Life on the *marae*, sports, *haka*, arts and crafts therefore have to wait until times of leisure and relaxation. Yet, if these recreational and artistic interests are developed, they will make life in a predominantly Pakeha world more satisfying. They can, in fact, be the basis of a Maori culture in which his identity will be preserved." *Te Ao Hou*, 1.

24 Ted Nepia, "A People of Warriors," *Te Ao Hou/The New World* no. 37 (December 1961), 50–2, 51.

25 Nepia, "A People of Warriors," 51.

26 Ibid.

27 E. G. Schwimmer, "Why Maoris Choose the Army," *Te Ao Hou/The New World*, no. 36 (Sept. 1961), 7–8. Italics added.

28 Ibid.

29 "In the recreational programme, the Maori element is important. The two main clubs in the battalion are the sports club and the Maori club." Schwimmer, "Why Maoris Choose the Army," 7.

30 Ibid., 8.

31 Arena Kahi, "Maori Soldiers in Malaya," *Te Ao Hou/The New World*, no. 40 (September 1962), 21–2, 21.

32 Ibid.

33 It was Coronel Bennett. The appointment was commented upon shortly after by Cameron in *New Zealand: The Modern Nations in Historical Perspective* (New Jersey: Prentice-Hall, Inc., 1965), 8.

34 Kahi, "Maori Soldiers in Malaya," 21.

35 Ibid., 22.

36 Ibid. Italics added.

37 Ted Nepia, "Reunion of 28th Maori Battalion Association," *Te Ao Hou/The New World*, no. 47 (June 1964), 45–6, 45. Note that this is the same author as the one who had reported on Maori nationalism in 1961.

38 Ibid.

39 Statistics showed in 2012 that Maori represented 17.4 per cent of the regular forces for a proportion of 14.6 per cent of the total population of New Zealand (2006 census). "Story: Armed Forces: Defence Force Personnel by Gender and Ethnicity, 2012," *Te Ara – The Encyclopedia of New Zealand*. http://www.teara.govt.nz/.

40 Sir Jerry Mateparae was appointed governor-general of New Zealand in August 2011, the second Maori person to hold the office after Sir Paul Reeves.

20

Remembering the Black Diggers: From "the Great Silence" to "Conspicuous Commemoration"?

ELIZABETH RECHNIEWSKI

Inattention on such a scale cannot possibly be explained by absent-mindedness. It is a structural matter, a view from a window which has been carefully placed to exclude a whole quadrant of the landscape ... We have been able for so long to disremember the Aborigines that we are now hard put to keep them in mind even when we most want to do so.

W.E.H. Stanner[1]

There is an issue as to whether we are facing an excess of commemoration, or perhaps what might be called conspicuous commemoration, in Australia.

Joan Beaumont[2]

Despite the obstacles that were put in the way of their enlistment, and despite the discriminatory policies to which they were subject, hundreds of Australian Aboriginal volunteers ("Black Diggers")[3] served in the First World War and thousands in the Second. Their service, which contradicted the tenets and ideology of "White Australia," was long overlooked by the official and civil institutions that preserve the nation's war memory. But in the last fifteen years or so there has been a dramatic reversal of the "great silence" concerning the role of Aboriginal servicemen, with a surge in many forms of recognition and commemoration: monuments, ceremonies, publications, and films. This article seeks to understand both the long decades of neglect and the recent rediscovery of the role of Black Diggers as responses to the changing national context, as White Australia aspired to become a multicultural nation. In so doing, it questions the political significance of the current upsurge in commemoration.

The Federation of Australia in 1901 was intimately bound with the aim to acquire the legal means to ensure a "White Australia," a policy aimed in part against the presence of Chinese and other foreign workers such as the Kanakas. It also entrenched the subordination of Aboriginal peoples that had allowed progressive annexation of their land from the earliest days of settlement. Upon the outbreak of WWI, Aborigines were not citizens (though a few had the vote because of particular state legislations), were often forced to live on missions, and were subject to the control of the "Protector" of Aborigines. They experienced daily discrimination, exclusion from public places and services, and occasional violence.

Before WWI both the government and the armed services opposed Aboriginal military service for reasons that ranged from their supposed unsuitability to claims that the white soldiers would refuse to serve alongside them. The prejudice against Aborigines was compounded by the racial fears attached to a possible invasion from the north by Japan. A number of recent works have drawn attention to the widespread fictional representations and nonfictional predictions relating to a Japanese invasion that preoccupied Australians from the late nineteenth century, fears that intensified after Japan defeated Russia in 1905.[4] The more lurid predictions suggested that the Aborigines, seeking to throw off the British colonial yoke, might aid the Japanese. It was against this background that persons who were not "substantially of European descent" were excluded from the Universal Training Scheme in the Defence Act of 1909 and subsequent acts, although in the early years of the war a few voices were raised advocating the open and official recruitment of Aborigines.[5] Thus when war broke out in 1914, many Aborigines who tried to enlist were rejected on the grounds of race, although some slipped through the net, either because the criteria were not made clear to the recruiters or because a blind eye was turned to the enlistment of "half-castes." By March 1917, however, when recruits were harder to find and one conscription referendum had already been lost, official restrictions were cautiously eased and in May 1917 active recruiting began in Aboriginal communities. The new Military Order 200 stated: "Half-castes may be enlisted in the Australian Imperial Force provided that the examining Medical Officers are satisfied that one of the parents is of European origin."[6]

Because the recruitment of Aborigines had been unofficial and "British" names were sometimes allotted to or adopted by the recruits, records of their true origin were poor and it has not been easy to estimate the numbers of Aborigines who enlisted for the war or to identify whether they were included on war memorials.[7] Robert Hall puts the figure of serving soldiers at 300 to 400, noting that "there were at least 300 from Queensland, New South Wales and Victoria," and suggests that probably about a third of the Indigenous soldiers who served overseas were killed in action or died of wounds or disease.[8] The Australian War Memorial has recently revised the total number of Black Diggers who served to over 1,000 out of an estimated population of 93,000 in 1901.[9] At least three were captured: Private Douglas Grant, 13th Battalion, captured at Bullecourt in 1917, was of particular interest to German scientists and anthropologists.[10]

The development of forms of war commemoration – monuments and ceremonies, official and unofficial practices of mourning – in the years following WWI has been well documented. The participation of Aborigines, however, was usually overlooked in the official accounts of the war; their names often omitted from honour rolls, they disappeared from official memory. Timothy Wineguard writes that apart from four brief articles in the journal of the Returned Servicemen's League, *Reveille,* in 1931–32 (to which I refer later), "The service of Aborigines in the Australian Imperial Force (AIF) was wholly neglected until the late 1970s."[11] Of the seven types of forgetting that Paul Connerton identifies, the forgetting of the participation of Indigenous soldiers in WWI might most closely be classified as "repressive erasure."[12] Drawing however on the framework of analysis proposed by Timothy Ashplant et al., who highlight how the interplay of the "agencies, arenas and narratives of articulation" determine the forms of war memory,[13] this article will argue that the "forgetting" of Aboriginal service was less the result of deliberate erasure than of the confluence of a number of factors: institutional amnesia, ideological dissonance, and conflict over material interests, all underpinned by the inequality of social, economic, and political power between the Europeans and the Indigenous peoples. The recent "remembering" of their service is the result of a similarly complex array of factors – political, ideological, and social – to which must be added the important role of the new "modes of articulation" of memory: the internet, social media, film, and television.

THE SURVIVAL OF VERNACULAR MEMORY

The recent remembering and commemoration of Aboriginal service presupposes that it was "forgotten"; it is important to recognize however that this "forgetting" refers only to the official agencies and histories of White Australia. That the memory of the Australian Indigenous veterans was kept alive in the communities concerned is revealed by the occasional article in the mainstream press of the 1920s and 1930s. A *Sydney Morning Herald* reporter on Cape Barren in 1938 wrote: "There is [*sic*] still a number of returned men on Cape Barren who talk reminiscently of the war, and they refer with quiet pride to those who made the supreme sacrifice."[14] There are also occasional references in the press to the participation of Aboriginal veterans in official commemorations. Giving an account of the Anzac Day March in Sydney in 1935 – which took an hour to pass – the reporter notes a number of Aborigines among the Light Horsemen as "unexpected types among the marchers."[15] The reporter's surprise at their presence reveals much about the ignorance at the time of Aboriginal service. In fact, so many Aboriginal stockmen had joined the Light Horse in 1917 that the 11th became familiarly known as the Black Watch.

The *Sydney Morning Herald* carried an article in 1935 about the mission at Caroona that mentions the initiative of the local Aboriginals in erecting their own memorial to their veterans, the Gate of Memory: "At the gateway to the school we find the 'Gate of Memory.' This, the first of its kind in Australia, was unveiled early this year." On the tablet inserted in the wall is the following: "This tablet was erected in honour of those men resident on this station, who served abroad with the A.I.F. during the Great War, 1914–1918." This Gate of Memory was built by the Aboriginals on the station, and on Anzac Day a special service was held.[16] These are rare references though.[17] The articles about Aborigines in the mainstream press during the interwar period are far more likely to discuss their status as a race on the verge of extinction.

In the few newspapers written by and for Aborigines, vernacular memory of service is not only recorded but marshalled in support of political claims to citizenship, or for access to the rights accorded to other veterans. The May 1938 issue of *Abo Call: The Voice of Australian Aborigines* contains several accounts of Aboriginal returned soldiers denied the relief granted to other veterans: housing relief for a "returned soldier Aboriginal at Moonah Cullah," and the case of Private Thomas Robinson of the 11th Battalion, who was wounded in the war and whose wife had been denied the maternity allowance because she was an Aboriginal.[18] A few Black Diggers received exemption certificates that released them from the control of the State Aborigine Protection boards, though at the cost of severing relations with their Aboriginal relatives. Nicholas Petersen and Will Sanders write that "only a tiny handful" of former soldiers were concerned by this measure that also gave them access to some benefits.[19]

THE AGENCIES OF OFFICIAL MEMORY

The ability to determine what is to be remembered and what is to be excluded from official collective memory is vested in modern societies in a set of powerful institutions that Timothy Ashplant et al. identify as the "agencies of articulation" of memory: "Institutions through which social actors seek to promote and secure recognition for their war memories."[20] They include the official bodies of the nation-state, its ministries, departments of veterans' affairs and the national systems under its control such as the education system, and institutions of civil society such as associations of war veterans. The role of the state in promoting or neglecting the memory of events is crucial, its interventions ranging along a scale of intensity from highly directed, coercive forms, to those that involve merely the organisation of symbolic gestures. Paul Connerton describes state-imposed forgetting as "repressive erasure": the suppression of memory that results from the censorship of inconvenient truths and perhaps the persecution of those that bear those memories. On a lesser scale the state plays a key role in what we might term "institutional amnesia" by foregrounding versions of events that concur with its national priorities and neglecting others, often responding to pressure groups, constituencies (in the broadest sense), and communities who lobby for their experiences to be remembered, recognized, and perhaps even compensated. Aboriginal veterans however lacked the necessary access to the federal- and state-controlled institutions to impose their presence on official memory or to press for recognition. And not only were the state and federal government institutions closed to

Aboriginal influence, but the institutions of civil society were of little help, as the notable example of the RSSILA (Returned Sailors' and Soldiers' Imperial League of Australia) demonstrates. The state and city RSSILA clubs sometimes called for equal rights for Aboriginal veterans. In the case of Private Robinson referred to above, the Sydney branch of the RSSILA passed a motion: "That all men of Aboriginal blood who served in the AIF be granted full citizens' rights and all social services be made available to them." (This was not awarded until after WWII.) The New South Wales branch of the RSSILA assembled a roll of the Aboriginal and part-Aboriginal members of the First AIF who served from Queensland, New South Wales, and Victoria that was published in the RSSILA journal *Reveille* in 1931 and 1932 and lodged with the Australian War Memorial. The attitudes of country RSSILA branches were, however, generally less welcoming, as Heather Goodall illustrates in her account of Collarenebri, where the Aboriginal veterans were allowed to march on Anzac Day but not to enter the club. Their names were not inscribed on the official honour roll, nor were their graves identified with the usual plaque recording war service.[21]

The institution that was charged with preserving the nation's war memory was the Australian War Memorial (AWM). A janus-faced institution – part memorial, part museum – conceived by Charles Bean, who oversaw its collections during the interwar period (it was opened in 1941), the AWM reflected the emphases he wished to give to war memory and the assumptions and prejudices of the time. There is little doubt that the AWM offered throughout the twentieth century a perspective on Australian national identity and nation building that was closely aligned with a British colonial heritage, offering a field for what Ghassan Hage calls the "rituals of White empowerment."[22] The only sculptural presence of Aboriginals at the memorial were the stone carvings of the faces of an Aboriginal man and woman, included amongst representations of Australian native fauna on the walls of the Roll of Honour cloisters. A plaque to commemorate the service of Aborigines in war, paid for by private donors, was placed in 1988 in bushland some ten minutes' walk behind the memorial.

The Black Diggers were thus unable to promote their private memories in the broader public "arenas of articulation" of war memory, where struggles take place "to extend, or alternatively to limit, the arenas within which specific memories are able to circulate."[23] And they had no control over the narratives that were recounted about them, over the ways in which they were represented, included in, or indeed excluded from, the accounts of war.

NARRATIVES OF NATIONAL IDENTITY

Official memory is conveyed in "narratives of articulation,"[24] the stories that are developed around the war events that structure and give meaning to individual and collective memory and may play a role in the construction of national or racial identity. The dominant, hegemonic narratives that structured the mindset of post-WWI Australia, those concerning national and racial identity and citizenship, were inimical to the recognition of Aboriginal war service.

In colonial settler societies, argues Ann Curthoys, national identity is built on "the exclusion of Indigenous peoples from the foundational historical narratives."[25] Representations of the "struggle to tame the land," of the hardships and sacrifice of the early settlers, serve to obscure the sufferings of the displaced Indigenous peoples. In the case of Australia, the myth of Gallipoli, representing the sacrifice of the iconic figure of the digger, a legend to which the journalists Ellis Ashmead-Bartlett and Charles Bean contributed heavily, laid the foundation of post-federation national identity. To remember the contribution of Aborigines to the war would be to undermine the symbolic significance of this figure and this myth: "For the association of white Australia with the Anzac legend to retain its narrative and symbolic power, those who fought in the First World War ought to be white Australians, and this is in fact how they are largely remembered."[26]

Many commentators have emphasized the essentially masculine nature of the Australian identity forged in the trenches: "a glorified and heroic martial masculinity."[27] Aborigines on the other hand were often seen as part of a "'feminised' nature, sometimes passive, sometimes capricious or wild, but always to be invaded and possessed."[28] Unlike the Maori, who had forced the New Zealand settlers to recognize their martial qualities through battlefield confrontations that the whites recognized as constituting a "war," the Australian Aborigines – who adopted guerrilla tactics for the most part, including raids, night attacks, and ambushes – were not considered a warrior race.[29] To recognize their military prowess would be to undermine these convenient and longstanding representations and the distinctions they installed between settlers and colonized.

Charles Bean and others (notably the Australian Prime Minister Billy Hughes) argued that by shedding their blood on the battlefield the ANZACS (Australian and New Zealand Army Corps) had earned for the whites the right to inhabit Australia: "The final right to claim the land for colonists had been won."[30] In his 1918 tract *In Your Hands, Australians*, Bean exhorts his fellow countrymen and women to complete the work begun on the battlefields, to create "the greatest and best country in the world,"[31] an "Anglo-Saxon nation of free, happy, brilliant people."[32] There is no room (and indeed no mention) in his vision of Australia for the Aborigines.

That the whites had earned the right to belong to the land – and indeed for the land to belong to them – from their military service illustrates the close relationship that had existed between citizenship and military service since the nineteenth century.[33] Many politically aware Aborigines no doubt hoped and believed that the participation of Aborigines in WWI would facilitate their access to full rights, and they used this argument in their campaigns for citizenship in the 1930s. The Aborigines' Progressive League launched several campaigns for citizenship based on war service, echoed in the short-lived *The Australian Abo Call: The Voice of Aborigines*, which editorialized in June 1938:

> The time has now come for all Aborigines and persons of Aboriginal blood to join the Aborigines Progressive Association in the coming fight for Citizen Rights. Many Aborigines and Halfcastes joined the Australian Army (AIF) in the last war "for freedom." Hundreds of these have died to uphold the fair name of Australia. Yet today, Aborigines and Halfcastes and all persons having "any admixture of Aboriginal blood" are treated as dingoes and as outcasts in the land of their ancestors.

This front page editorial (by J.T. Patten) was accompanied by a platform of demands printed on the same page calling for "full Citizen rights" and that the Aborigines be treated as "ordinary Australian citizens."[34]

Ashplant et al. write that "Demands for inclusion [in war commemoration] may expose a profound contradiction within or between dominant narratives, where failure to recognise the involvement of marginalised groups in war draws on a longer history of silence or omission."[35] We might describe these contradictions as founded in ideological dissonance, where the facts (the service of Black Diggers) were at odds not only with the official hegemonic narratives of war but with the dominant belief systems of the society. One of those systems was the belief in racial hierarchy and the superiority of Europeans, the basis of the theory and practices of White Australia.

The ANZAC soldiers had, so Bean and others reported, proven themselves worthy members of the "British race," destined to rule over Australia as Britain ruled over its own empire. The early 1920s saw racialist theories and eugenic policies at their height in the white dominions, in Europe, and in America. Lake and Reynolds catalogue the obsession with preventing the racial decline of the white race that would be brought about through miscegenation and even association between the races, theories that were widely shared by politicians, intellectuals, and scientists, the latter seeking to prove through fanciful experiments the superiority of the white race.[36] In the hierarchy of races, Aboriginal Australians were generally believed to occupy the lowest rung. There was, according to Wineguard, a common belief in the dominions that the condition of their Indigenous peoples was one of "stagnation," "which manifested itself in the characteristics of lower intellect, an imitative childlike demeanour and a penchant for violent and erratic outbursts."[37] According to the Social Darwinism of the time, the Aborigines were generally believed to be unable to compete or survive in the modern world, to be a "dying race," a description widely used in the press of the period as it was in "scientific" and political discourse. Their imminent extinction might be the subject of lamentation, there might be calls for the languages and stories of this "prehistoric race" to be preserved and expeditions mounted with this aim,[38] and there might be calls for them to be better treated in their decline, but the assumption that they were dying out was very rarely questioned. They belonged to the past and could therefore have no part to play in the construction of the nation whose present and future was "in the hands" of the whites.

Underpinning the relations between settlers and Aborigines was the ongoing, indeed intensifying, conflict over land. Much of the best farming land in Aboriginal reserves was confiscated after WWI for soldier settlement blocks and awarded to white veterans.[39] The loss of land to the soldier settlement scheme accelerated the dispossession of Aboriginal land, continuing a trend since the early twentieth century for the resumption of land granted to Aborigines known as the "second dispossession."[40] Only one Aboriginal soldier is known to have received a soldier settler's block in New South Wales.[41] The interwar years saw a marked deterioration in other aspects of the Aborigines' situation. Each state passed new protection acts that effectively deprived Aboriginal people on reserves of freedom of movement, freedom of association, the right to control property and earnings, the right to drink alcohol, and the right to vote. The Aborigines Protection Board acquired the power to remove children from their parents and to move Aboriginal families between reserves. Violent conflict persisted in some areas: in 1928 a WWI veteran, Constable W.G. Murray, who had served at Gallipoli as a Victorian Mounted Rifleman, led a punitive expedition that shot perhaps a hundred Aboriginal people at Coniston in the Northern Territory after a white dingo trapper and station owner were attacked. A court of inquiry ruled that the Europeans' actions were justified.[42]

It is beyond the scope of this article to trace the service of Aboriginal soldiers in WWII other than to record that some 3,000 served in fighting units, many others as coast watchers and in other war-related roles, despite the continuation of the policy of not enrolling those "not substantially of European origin or descent."[43] Robert Hall argues that the war changed attitudes both of Aborigines and of whites towards Aborigines;[44] however, changes were slow to be reflected in their legal status although ex-servicemen did acquire the right to vote soon after the war. In 1946 the annual congress of the Returned and Services League (RSL) asked the federal government to grant the franchise to all Aboriginal ex-servicemen, arguing that "a man who was fit to fight in the front-line was fit to vote,"[45] a right that was granted in 1949. Discrimination remained widespread in the RSL clubs, however, particularly in rural areas, until well after WWII, whether because of exclusionary policies or perhaps due to the Aborigines' self-exclusion.[46] Writing in 2001, Heather Goodall noted that the Collarenebri RSL club had still not agreed to the inclusion of Aboriginal names on the Honour Board.[47]

REMEMBERING ABORIGINAL SERVICE

Recognition of Aboriginal service followed broader social, political, and ideological change, and above all the campaigns for rights and recognition that took up and amplified pre-war demands: the Freedom Ride through rural Australia in 1965 closely followed by campaigning for the 1967 referendum that removed discriminatory provisions from the Australian Constitution; the Land Rights movement for recognition of prior ownership of land from the mid-1960s; the Tent Embassy in Canberra from 1972; the breaking of the "great Australian silence" with a flood of books on the impact of European settlement on the Indigenous people by a younger generation of historians inspired by anti-colonial struggles;[48] and Aboriginal protests in 1988 at the bicentennial celebration of the British landing. This all increased the visibility of Aborigines and brought to light many aspects of their contribution to Australian society.

Demands to recognize Aboriginal service came later, influenced almost certainly by the resurgence of interest in Australia's military past from the 1980s onward, and in particular the promotion of Anzac Day and of Gallipoli as the birthplace of the nation.[49] Once again Indigenous individuals and organisations often led the way in drawing attention to the role of Black Diggers through campaigns, films, and documentaries. Richard Frankland's thirty-minute documentary, *Harry's War* (1999), recounting the story of his uncle Harry Saunders in the South Pacific campaign in WWII, won many awards in Australia and overseas and has been extensively shown in schools. Glen Stasiuk's *The Forgotten* (2003) recounts the service of Aborigines and Torres Strait Islanders in WWII and in Korea, the Persian Gulf, and East Timor. Both filmmakers are of Indigenous origin and their work and that of others in film and television contributed, James Bennett writes, to "decolonising the screen"[50] and allowing for the first time an Indigenous perspective on their own history to be widely broadcast. The Aboriginal and Torres Strait Islander Veterans and Services Association (ATSIVSA) was founded in 1999 as an advocacy group to work with the RSL and the Australian War Memorial. John Schnaars, an Indigenous Vietnam Veteran, established *Honouring Indigenous War Graves Inc.* in June 2005 in Western Australia to place headstones on the graves of Aboriginal soldiers. The "Coloured Diggers Project," based in Redfern, the suburb of Sydney traditionally home to urban Aborigines, has organized a separate ANZAC Day march for Indigenous servicemen since 2007. The importance of new "modes of articulation" of war memories must be emphasized as Black Diggers scattered across the country were able to record and share their experiences through social media platforms, and to campaign for recognition.

In a dramatic reversal of their previous neglect, the official institutions at federal, state, and city levels that for so long overlooked

Indigenous service have, in the last fifteen years or so, begun to promote their memory in a major and sustained way. The guardian of the nation's war memory, the Australian War Memorial has developed an education resource for schoolchildren highlighting the role of Aboriginal soldiers, and has held several major exhibitions including "Too Dark for the Lighthorse" that toured the regions in 2000–2001. It has also planned an extensive programme to commemorate Black Diggers over the Anzac Centenary period: their website lists a suite of projects that includes "providing input into some 15 documentaries and programs," compiling a roll call of Black Diggers, and collecting individual stories of Indigenous personnel that will feature in the redeveloped galleries.[51] A major government-funded project, "Serving our Country," brings together researchers from the ANU, the Department of Veterans' Affairs, the Australian Defence Force, and the Memorial to research the history of Aboriginal and Torres Strait Islander service in the ADF.[52]

The monuments dedicated to Aboriginal and Torres Strait Islander soldiers that Ken Inglis described in 1998 as "few, modest and late"[53] have greatly increased in number,[54] and while those dedicated in the 1990s were often small local memorials or plaques, the more recent ones have been much more ambitious and prominent. In Adelaide, a monument dedicated by the governor in November 2013 lays claim to being the first national memorial. Another, designed by Aboriginal artist Tony Albert, was inaugurated in April 2015 in central Sydney's Hyde Park, near the existing war memorial. The words of the WWII Aboriginal serviceman Reg Saunders were added to a memorial adjacent to North Bondi RSL in Sydney, dedicated on 27 November 2011. The RSL has partnered with city authorities including Sydney and the Federal Department of Veterans' Affairs (under its "Wartime Legends" initiative) since 2007 to hold annual commemorations during National Reconciliation Week. The ultimate cultural consecration was accorded in January 2014 with the performance of *Black Diggers* at the Sydney Opera House, the principal theatrical production of the Festival of Sydney. Directed by Wesley Enoch of the Queensland Theatre Company, himself of Indigenous origin, it tells the stories of Black Diggers who served in WWI in sixty mini scenes; nine Aboriginal actors play multiple roles as recruitment officers, British commanders, grieving mothers, and soldiers of the empire. It met with considerable critical acclaim and popular success and toured major Australian cities in 2015.

CONCLUSION: RECOGNITION OR *RÉCUPÉRATION*?

Who could cavil at this extensive, if belated, official recognition of the role of Black Diggers? And yet what are the dangers of the *récupération* of their service in the interests of a kind of "soft reconciliation" that downplays the reality of Indigenous experience for the vast majority of the Aboriginal population before, during, and after the war? In vogue amongst the left during the May 1968 events, the French term *récupération* refers to the danger of "the Establishment," government, or political party seizing on an issue and opportunistically turning it to its own ends. An illustration can be found in the recent *récupération* of the service of troops from France's colonies who fought in the World Wars. For a long time relatively sparsely commemorated in France (although many monuments were raised in the colonies themselves),[55] in recent years their service has been the object of sustained presidential attention. In 2006, President Jacques Chirac unveiled at Douaumont a memorial to Muslim soldiers who died at the Battle of Verdun. In 2012, President Nicolas Sarkozy inaugurated a temporary plaque at the Great Mosque in Paris dedicated to the memory of Muslim soldiers who were killed in 1914–18. In February 2014 François Hollande, the current president, inaugurated two permanent plaques at the mosque to Muslim soldiers who died in both World Wars. The dedication speeches given by the presidents make clear their hope that this recognition will contribute to reconciliation with the second and third generations of Maghrebian immigrants (the "Beurs") and to their integration into French society.

There are many important differences between the conditions under which the French colonial troops were recruited (often conscripted) and served, and those of Aboriginal soldiers from Australia. And yet the politically charged commemorative agenda of the French presidents is a reminder of that well-established trope in the social sciences that commemoration is far more about the present than the past, and that the official commemoration of formerly excluded groups is rarely an apolitical restoration of justice for past omission, but rather serves contemporary functions. It may reflect the evolution in social and political power and influence that allows formerly marginalized groups to claim greater recognition. It may also be the result of political calculation by governments to accord symbolic recognition where other forms of recognition and inclusion are lacking, a kind of internal memorial diplomacy.[56] It may play a part in history wars where groups vie for an interpretation of the past that favours their version of history.

All these elements may be in play in the commemoration of Black Diggers. Thus in the early 2000s, when the "Black Armband" view of history (history that highlighted the violence exacted against the Aborigines) was being condemned by a Conservative government, the inclusion of Black Diggers in the commemorative framework of the World Wars offered a pacified representation of a nation united in a common struggle. Even if such recognition does not result from a conscious political strategy, it "exclude[s] a whole quadrant of the landscape," and it obscures the long history of inequality of treatment and displaces the focus towards a putative shared struggle. South Australian Liberal Senator David Fawcett asserted in his 2013 Remembrance Day speech that "The fact that so many [Aboriginal] people served when so many barriers were put in their way is, I think, a testament to their love of country – they actually wanted to serve their people and their nation."[57] His comments illustrated the kind of claims that can be made about the significance of Aboriginal war service in order to promote a pacified vision of European/Indigenous relations.

The commemoration of Black Diggers accords with the revised dominant narratives of national identity, contributing to the adaptation and modernisation of the Anzac myth for contemporary Australia: multicultural Australia requires a multicultural Anzac, with examples of "Anzac Diversity" now illustrated on the Australian War Memorial website.[58] The Anzac narrative has been extended to incorporate groups who were formerly marginalized or forgotten. Not only Aborigines but Chinese diggers have been rediscovered, illustrated by the memorial to Chinese-Australian diggers raised in Sydney's Chinatown in 2004 and the renewed interest in Billy Sing "The Assassin," a renowned sniper at Gallipoli.[59] The presence of many Russian soldiers amongst the Anzacs has also recently been highlighted by Elena Govor.[60] Commemoration of war service holds out a hand to these groups as to the Aboriginal community, encouraging them to see themselves as part of the narrative of nation building based on war service and with the laudable aim of refashioning the mono-cultural representations of the young Australian nation in order to acknowledge its (albeit limited) cultural diversity.

However, the representations of a more multicultural ANZAC force leave largely untouched the mythology that now surrounds this war, simply including within it a broader range of actors. As Celeste Liddle wrote in the *Guardian* in July 2014, perhaps the Indigenous perspective on war should also be about challenging the grand narrative of nation building through military sacrifice that now holds sway in Australian national life.[61] Rather than recuperating the Black Diggers and soldiers from minority communities into the "militarisation of Australian history,"[62] perhaps we should use their experiences to cast a different perspective on war, to complicate the assumptions about why men enlisted for example, to talk about the post-war neglect of veterans, both white and black, and the terrible impact of war on individuals and communities. Instead, in Joan Beaumont's words, an "excess of conspicuous commemoration" feeds a "national obsession with Disneyfied images of war" that, a former Australian army officer writes, misrepresent the experience of past and present soldiers and distort the priorities of government policy.[63]

Commemoration of the nation's military engagements proceeds at a quickening pace in Australia, where one of the latest projects is a Boer War memorial to be added to the many monuments that line Anzac Parade in Canberra. Projects to identify individual Indigenous solders who served in Australia's wars also proliferate: a plaque was unveiled in Perth at Karrakatta cemetery on 20 April 2013 to Pte Robert John Searle, an Indigenous soldier who served in the Boer War.[64] And yet the Aboriginal people have a war narrative uniquely their own, not as soldiers in an imperial force but as resisters to white settlement. The question of official commemoration of this protracted and deadly struggle has occasionally been aired in relation to the collections and displays at the Australian War Memorial: What room, if any, is there in the memorial for an exhibition about the early wars between Aborigines and white settlers?[65] The question has thus far met with a resounding rejection by the memorial board, suggesting the extent to which the memorial is still associated with a particular perspective on the nation and national identity, and the journey that still has to be made in Australia towards recognition of the wars that "made the nation" long before Gallipoli.[66]

NOTES

1 In 1968, the anthropologist W.E.H. Stanner delivered the second of his Australian Broadcasting Commission's Boyer Lectures entitled "The

Great Australian Silence." This and other essays were republished in W.E.H. Stanner, *The Dreaming and Other Essays* (Collingwood, Vic: Black Inc Agenda, 2009).

2 Joan Beaumont is quoted in Adrienne Francis, "'All Commemoration is Political': Historians Lead Charge against Gallipoli 'Myth,'" ABC News online, 14 April 2014, http://www.abc.net.au/news/2013-11-11/war-and-memory-australians-experiencing-commemoration-fatigue/5081544 (accessed 23 April 2014).

3 "Digger" is the term commonly used to refer to Australian soldiers.

4 See for example Peter Stanley, *Invading Australia: Japan and the Battle for Australia, 1942* (Sydney: Viking, 2008).

5 The formation of a military corps composed of Northern Territory "half-castes" is recommended by Mr Beckett, the chief inspector of Aborigines, in a letter to *The Argus*, 4 March 1915, 12.

6 Timothy C. Winegard, *Indigenous Peoples of the British Dominions and the First World War*, (Cambridge: University of Cambridge Press, 2011), 161.

7 See Ken Inglis, *Sacred Places: War Memorials in the Australian Landscape,* 3rd Edition (Melbourne: Melbourne University Press, 2008), 356.

8 Robert A. Hall, *The Black Diggers: Aborigines and Torres Strait Islanders in the Second World War* (Sydney: Allen & Unwin, 1989), 1.

9 https://www.awm.gov.au/encyclopedia/aborigines/indigenous/(accessed 12 October 2014).

10 One German scientist described Grant as "an unmistakable figure" who was appointed by his fellow prisoners to take charge of relief parcels because of "his honesty, his quick mind, and because he was so aggressively Australian." Grant returned to Australia on 10 April 1919. He died in 1951. AWM website: http://cas.awm.gov.au/item/P01692.001 (accessed 23 April 2014).

11 Winegard, *Indigenous Peoples,* 8.

12 Paul Connerton, "Seven Types of Forgetting," *Memory Studies* 1 (2008): 59–71.

13 Timothy G. Ashplant, Graham Dawson, and Michael Roper, "The Politics of War Memory," in *Commemorating War*, edited by Timothy G. Ashplant, Graham Dawson, and Michael Roper (New Brunswick, NJ: Transaction Publishers, 2004), 3–86.

14 "They contributed their quota of 21 men to the A.I.F., and are spoken of in the highest terms as front-line soldiers." R.S. Rolph, "Cape Barren Islanders: A Community Apart. Dusky Citizens of the Sea," *Sydney Morning Herald*, 3 September 1938, 5.

15 "The March Watched by Large Crowds," *Sydney Morning Herald*, 26 April 1935, 11.

16 A.E.F., "The Gate of Memory: Raised by Coloured Folk," *Sydney Morning Herald*, 17 August 1935, 11.

17 To research this article I carried out several searches for the inter-war period in the National Library of Australia's Trove digitized archive of Australian newspapers. I looked for articles with the co-occurrence of words such as "Aborigin/" "veterans," Aborigin/and "memorial."

18 "Returned Soldier Victimised," *The Australian Abo Call*, May 1938, 2. Six issues of *The Australian Abo Call: The Voice of Aborigines*, each of four pages and priced at 3d, were published monthly between April and September 1938.

19 Nicholas Petersen and Will Saunders, *Citizenship and Indigenous Australians: Changing Conceptions and Possibilities* (Cambridge: University of Cambridge Press, 1998), 12.

20 Ashplant et al., "The Politics of War Memory," 17.

21 Goodall writes: "For a small community, Collarenebri Murris had sent an extraordinary proportion of young men to fight Australia's foreign wars. There are four veterans of World War I buried in the Aboriginal cemetery and three from World War II. Through the 1930s and 1940s these men were invited to march in the town parade on Anzac Day, which some of them did to support old comrades. But they were refused access to the segregated Returned Servicemen's Leagues Club for the rest of the year, their names were not inscribed on the Honour Board inside the Club recording those who had fought, and this local RSL had refused to recommend that their graves be identified with a special plaque in the manner usually accorded returned service people." Heather Goodall, "Mourning, Remembrance and the Politics of Place," *Changi to Cabramatta: Places and Personality, Public History Review* 9 (2001): 87.

22 Ghassan Hage. *White Nation: Fantasies of White Supremacy in a Multicultural Society* (Annandale, NSW: Pluto Press, 2008), 241.

23 Ashplant et al., "The Politics of War Memory," 17.

24 Ibid., 17.

25 Ann Curthoys, "National Narratives, War Commemoration and Racial Exclusion in a Settler Society," in Ashplant et al., *Commemorating War*, 132.

26 Ibid., 133.

27 Stephen Garton, "Longing for War: Nostalgia and Australian Returned Soldiers after the First World War," in ibid., 227.

28 Alison Blunt and Gillian Rose, *Writing Women and Space: Colonial and Postcolonial Geographies* (New York: Guilford Press, 1994), 177.
29 Rachel Standfield, "'These unoffending people': Myth, History and the Idea of Aboriginal Resistance in David Collins' *Account of the English Colony In New South Wales*," in *Passionate Histories: Myth, Memory and Indigenous Australia*, edited by Frances Peters-Little, Ann Curthoys, and John Docker (Canberra: ANU Press, 2011), 136–7.
30 Garton, "Longing for War," 224.
31 Charles Bean, *In Your Hands, Australians* (Melbourne: Cassell and Company, 1918), 9.
32 Ibid., 46.
33 Citizenship "was tied less to owning property than it was to loyalty, your willingness to sacrifice your life if necessary to protect the cultural and political values of the nation." *Oxford Handbook of Afro-American Citizenship, 1865–the Present* (Oxford: Oxford University Press, 2011), 429.
34 *The Australian Abo Call*, 3 June 1938, 1.
35 Ashplant et al., "The Politics of War Memory," 21.
36 Marilyn Lake and Henry Reynolds, *Drawing the Global Colour Line: White Men's Countries and the Question of Racial Equality* (Melbourne: University of Melbourne Press, 2008).
37 Winegard, *Indigenous Peoples*, 36.
38 The *Brisbane Courier* joined with the *Adelaide Advertiser* to send a "trained scientific investigator" on one of these expeditions. "A Dying Race. Scientific Expedition. Research among Aborigines," *Brisbane Courier*, 10 August 1932, 12.
39 For example, two areas of land totalling 1,410 acres at Warangesda near Darling Point that had been gazetted in the 1880s as Aboriginal reserves were revoked on 16 April 1926. Winegard, *Indigenous Peoples*, 249.
40 Heather Goodall, *Invasion to Embassy: Land in Aboriginal Politics in New South Wales, 1770–1992* (Sydney: University of Sydney Press, 2008), 148.
41 Farrier Quarter Master Sergeant George Kennedy of the 6th Light Horse Regiment who drew a 17,000-acre block at Yelty seven miles outside of Ivanhoe. www.awm.gov.au/education/box/03_res_book (accessed 24 April 2014).
42 David Day, *Claiming a Continent: A New History of Australia*, 4th edition (Sydney: Harper Perennial, 2005), 22.
43 William Cooper, the Secretary of the Australian Aborigines' League, argued that Indigenous Australians should not fight for White

Australia. Cooper had lost his son in the First World War and was bitter that Aboriginal sacrifice had not brought any improvement in rights and conditions. https://www.awm.gov.au/encyclopedia/aborigines/indigenous/(accessed 20 June 2015).

44 Hall, *Black Diggers*, 3.

45 *The Mercury*, 2 November 1946, 1. The motion was passed unanimously.

46 An Adelaide RSL official observed to the reporter that "Few Aboriginal ex-servicemen visited the club except during the Anzac Day period." *The Advertiser*, 29 May 1951.

47 Goodall, "Mourning, Remembrance," 87.

48 Dirk Moses, "Genocide and Settler Society in Australian History," in *Genocide and Settler Society: Frontier Violence and Stolen Indigenous Children in Australian History*, edited by D. Moses (New York: Berghahn Books, 2004), 9–10.

49 Elizabeth Rechniewski, "Quand l'Australie invente et réinvente une tradition: l'exemple du débarquement de Gallipoli," *Vingtième siècle* 101, January–March (2009): 123–32.

50 James Bennett, "Lest We Forget Black Diggers: Recovering Aboriginal Anzacs on Television," *Journal of Australian Studies* 38, no. 4 (2014): 1–19.

51 http://www.awm.gov.au/1914-1918/Indigenous-commemoration/ (accessed 1 October 2014).

52 http://www.ourmobserved.com (accessed 1 October 2014).

53 Inglis, *Sacred Places*, 421.

54 Some early and recent examples include:

Burleigh Heads Aboriginal War Memorial (rock inscription): Erected by the Kombumerri Aboriginal Corporation for Culture with support from the Gold Coast City Council, April 1991;

RSL Aboriginal Memorial, East Victoria Park (WA): A black granite rock with a memorial nameplate and flagpole flying the Aboriginal flag, February 2002;

Australian Indigenous War Veterans Memorial, Toomelah (NSW): Plaque listing the names of twenty-one Toomelah and district Aboriginal veterans who served in both World Wars and the Vietnam War, February 2009;

Aboriginal War Memorial Plaque, Warrnambool (VIC): Plaque honouring Aboriginal service personnel from southwestern Victoria, November 2010;

Memorial wall at Karrakatta Cemetery, Karrakatta (WA): Commemorates Aboriginal servicemen killed in conflict during World Wars I and II, January 2012.

55 Robert Aldrich, "Memorials to French Colonial Soldiers from the Great War" (2007). www.crid1418.org/doc/textes/aldrich.pdf (accessed 20 September 2014).

56 The term "memorial diplomacy" is used by Matthew Graves in "Memorial Diplomacy in Franco-Australian Relations," in *Nation, Memory and Great War Commemoration: Mobilizing the Past in Europe, Australia and New Zealand,* edited by Shanti Sumartojo and Ben Wellings (Oxford: Peter Lang, 2014), 169–87.

57 Senate Adjournment Debate, Tuesday, 12 November 2013: http://www.openaustralia.org/senate/?id=2013-11-12.39.1 (accessed 24 August 2014).

58 http://www.awm.gov.au/education/schools/resources/anzac-diversity (accessed 30 September 2014).

59 John Hamilton, *Gallipoli Sniper: The Life of Billy Sing* (Sydney: Pan Macmillan, 2009). A documentary "Forgotten History: Untold Stories of Chinese Anzacs Remembered" aired on SBS on 16 July 2014, and an exhibition in Melbourne's Chinese Museum was held from August to December 2014.

60 Elena Govor, *Russian Anzacs in Australian History* (Sydney: UNSW Press, 2005).

61 Celeste Liddle, "We Must Remember Indigenous Warriors Who Fought War Itself," *Guardian* online, 11 July 2014. http://www.theguardian.com/commentisfree/2014/jul/11/we-must-remember Indigenous-warriors-who-fought-war-itself (accessed 28 July 2014).

62 Marilyn Lake and Henry Reynolds, eds., *What's Wrong with Anzac: The Militarisation of Australian History* (Sydney: UNSW Press, 2010).

63 James Brown, *Anzac's Long Shadow: A National Obsession* (Sydney: Black Inc Publishing, 2014).

64 www.bwm.org.au/site/John_Searle.asp (accessed 7 October 2014).

65 The issue has been raised on several occasions by Ken Inglis: on the launch of his book *Sacred Places* in 1998 and again on publication of the 3rd edition in 2008. In 2009 a discussion took place on the ABC that raised a number of the issues addressed here. It was between John Coates, prominent Aboriginal academic Gordon Briscoe, Geoffrey Blainey, Ken Inglis, and Peter Stanley on the one side, and RSL president Bill Crews on the other. http://www.abc.net.au/7.30/content/2009/s2502535.htm (accessed 24 April 2014).

66 Insofar as there has been commemoration of these wars, the memorials tend to record the Aborigines as the victims of massacre rather than as fighters. Consultation of the list of memorials with Indigenous relevance reveals that a majority of the twenty-five identified concern

massacres of Aborigines. These are mostly very recent: the Myall Creek Memorial, 2001; the Aboriginal Massacres Monument, Port Fairy, Victoria, 2011; and the Appin Massacre, 2007. Only a handful of the memorials refer to "battles." http://monumentaustralia.org.au/themes/conflict/indigenous.

21

The Return of the Native: Remembering the Circle in Joseph Boyden's *Three Day Road*

LORIE-ANNE DUECH-RAINVILLE

Scott sniffed. "I'm surprised at how you keep on using the word 'survivors.' Admittedly an Indian school could be a difficult place for children, but it's not as if they'd been through the trenches serving their country in the Great War."

"Isn't it?" I said.

He stared at me. "No. It isn't."[1]

The above epigraph, taken from Montreal writer Mark Abley's recently published book, *Conversations with a Dead Man: The Ghost of the Ottawa Poet and Bureaucrat Duncan Campbell Scott (1862–1947)*, contains the parallel that sustains Joseph Boyden's first novel *Three Day Road* (2005). By sending off two young northern Ontario Cree men to fight in the battlefields of France and Belgium, Boyden counterbalances two different wars with, on the one hand, the Great War, the official military war overseas upon which the world's attention was focused, and, on the other, the one he calls the "quiet war" or the "insidious battle"[2] going on in Canada with its detrimental colonization measures (namely, the strategic implementation of reserves and residential schools) endured by First Nations back home, obscure to the public eye. *Three Day Road* is thus a two-dimensional historical novel that weaves together two different stories, both fuelled by domination and resistance, involving possession of territory that belongs to someone else.

The beginning of the twentieth century was a decisive period for the Ojibwe and Cree of northern Ontario with the pursuit of the government's colonizing mission to obtain more land. In the case of the James Bay region, this led to the signing of Treaty No. 9, also known as the James Bay Treaty, in which more than forty-five First Nations communities agreed to cede ancestral lands in exchange for a number of benefits, which they believed would save their people.[3] Boyden draws a parallel between the plight of the James Bay Cree and the world conflict through the two Cree soldiers who participate in the war. The Cree story also resonates in the World War thanks to the name of the surviving war hero, Xavier Bird, a young Cree raised by his aunt Niska in the northern Ontario bush who goes off to war with his friend Elijah. If Boyden's fictive Cree snipers, Xavier and Elijah, are inspired by the real-life legendary Ojibwe war hero and sniper, Francis Pegahmagabow (from a reserve near Parry Sound, in the near north of Ontario), the fictive Xavier Bird shares the very same name as one of the Cree Indians who served as a witness to the signing of the James Bay Treaty. On 3 August 1905, the real-life Xavier Bird signed Treaty No. 9 in Fort Albany, and signed it with his X mark (significantly, "X" becomes Xavier Bird's war nickname in the novel).[4]

Boyden pulls Xavier Bird, the Cree signatory of Treaty No. 9, out of oblivion by giving him, in name at least, a role as hero in WWI. In doing so, the writer brings to the foreground the issue of land and thus of identity, for tribal identity is inseparable from land rights in Aboriginal Canada. The name "Bird" is anchored in the history of the James Bay area.

The focus of this study is not on history, however, but on the dynamics of memory. Native history is kept alive through memory. Memory recalls the past despite past attempts to disconnect First Nations from their heritage. Memory combats the forgetfulness imposed on Natives through colonizing missions such as the reserves and the residential schools. Memory drowns out the genocidal motto "kill the Indian in the child."[5] The war memories that come to the surface in *Three Day Road* are rooted in two distinct conflicts – one international, the other national – that merge together thanks to Boyden's two Cree war heroes.

"RETURNING" ... "HOME": THE CIRCULAR PATTERN OF THE NOVEL

Three Day Road begins with the return from battle of the wounded Xavier Bird, a James Bay Cree, who will be nursed back to life by

Niska, his only remaining relative. If put side by side, the titles of the opening and closing chapters read "'Returning' ... 'Home,'" underlining the typical war trope of the veteran's homecoming, a trope that emerged from the beginnings of WWI literature, as explicitly announced in Rebecca West's 1918 novel *The Return of the Soldier*.[6] "Home" here is not, however, typical mainstream society, but the marginalized, remote, and vast James Bay area in northern Ontario, which is Boyden's literary home ground. Far from being "home" to the majority of Canadians who live in urbanized centres, it is home mostly to the Ojibwe and Cree, and has been so for thousands of years. Once they ceded their lands to the government in the James Bay Treaty, they began settling on reserves. It is to this region that the surviving hero returns, a region which is often referred to today as Canada's "Third World"[7] – a direct result of the colonizing process which was in full gear during the turn of the twentieth century.

Through the eyes of his three main characters who are Cree Indians from this region, Boyden, of Anishnabe descent himself, has his readers embrace a Native point of view of WWI. In this way, the author joins acclaimed Native American writers Scott Momaday of Kiowa descent and Leslie Silko of Laguna Pueblo descent who, in the late 1960s and 1970s, published their WWII novels – *House Made of Dawn* (1968) and *Ceremony* (1977) – now classic works of Native American literature. Like *Three Day Road*, both *Made of Dawn* and *Ceremony* relate the return of a Native solider. These three novels by three different writers of different Native descent share several common points, amongst them bringing their physically wounded, culturally dislocated, and psychologically fragmented character full circle, back home, on a "circular journey toward identity."[8] Scott Momaday has explained how he sees his novel as a circle: "It ends where it begins and it's informed with a kind of thread that runs through it and holds everything together."[9] The cyclic pattern provides a literary means for contemporary writers of Native descent to re-enact on a narrative level the fundamental shape of the circle. Traditionally, the circle represents "the concept of reciprocation" which "is at the heart of everything going on in the world."[10]

Like Momaday, Boyden has pointed out on multiple occasions the circularity that structures his own novel, explaining how he reshaped the original linear narrative of the first draft into "a more Native style," through a "circular kind of telling"[11] that invokes the shape of the circle which informs spiritual, social, and cultural beliefs of various Native American nations dispersed throughout the continent.

Dwelling on what was missing in the original draft of the novel, Boyden recalls that for the Cree and Ojibwe, life evolves around a circle:

> The earth, the sun, the moon are all round, and we live our days according to their dictation. The seasons travel through spring, summer, autumn, winter and back to spring again. The teepee and the wigwam and the shaking tent and the fire ring are circular structures. And so I decided to begin this story near the chronological end and then trace through the circle around to where I started. Niska knows that the circle can't be broken and fights as hard as she can to keep Xavier alive so that one day he may have his own children and keep the cycle intact.[12]

These words echo Black Elk's famous words, calling attention to the loss of his people's power, which coincided with the loss of the meaning of the circle once his people were forced to live in "square boxes" on the reservation. In the 1930s the Sioux leader said:

> Everything an Indian does is in a circle, and that is because the Power of the World always works in circles, and everything tries to be round. In the old days when we were a strong and happy people, all our power came to us from the sacred hoop of the nation, and so long as the hoop was unbroken, the people flourished ... The sky is round, and I have heard that the earth is round like a ball, and so are the stars. The wind, in its greatest power, whirls. Birds make their nest in circles, (and so on) for theirs is the same religion as ours.[13]

In the spirit of the circle of reciprocation, Boyden's narrative moves back and forth from WWI memories to the memories of colonization measures in Canada. The circular pattern of the novel intensifies this spirit. By abandoning chronological linearity, in which A leads to B, in favour of a circular pattern, in which A does not connect with Z alone but with several other narrative elements in between, Boyden reconsidered the composition of his novel by "seeing it with a Native eye."[14] It is a pattern he had already adopted in *Born with a Tooth*, where he arranged his stories into four sections, each one representing a cardinal direction, thereby recalling the shape of a sacred hoop or a Medicine Wheel. To quote the distinguished Native historian

Donald L. Fixico, "'Indian thinking' is 'seeing' things from a perspective emphasizing that circles and cycles are central to the world and that all things are related within the universe[15] … 'Seeing' is visualizing the connection between two or more entities or beings, and trying to understand the relationship between them."[16]

If, from a Native perspective, all things are related and interconnected, then these two worlds, however opposed, must balance out and fuse to some extent to be integrated within the larger circle of the universe. In the aptly entitled chapter "Turning," Xavier is "left wondering what connection there might be between their world and mine."[17] I wish to explore these connections and relationships between things, events, and characters, between "us" and "them" – the two opposed cultures, "the white linear mind" and the "traditional Indian mind"[18] – as well as the narrative strategies deployed by Boyden to depict them.

To illustrate how complex these connections are I shall focus on the beginning of the novel, the first two chapters (respectively entitled "Returning" and "Arrival"), when Xavier comes back from the war overseas and arrives at the same northern Ontario train station from which he had departed with Elijah a few years earlier. Just as the titles of these two chapters reflect each other, so too do the two wars, and a contrapuntal analysis reveals how Boyden connects the two story lines together. While the chapter "Returning" centres on Xavier's return to northern Ontario, seen from Niska's point of view, the next chapter centres on Xavier's "Arrival" on the battlefield, seen from his own point of view. Even though sequential time is immediately disrupted in the novel by the four-year gap, connections are established between the two wars through the two distinct Native points of view.

THE TRAIN OR "THE LINE": THE ENCROACHMENT OF WESTERN SOCIETY IN NORTHERN ONTARIO

The train is the first and central symbol in the opening chapter. This train follows the newly built line of the Canadian Pacific Railway tracing through northern Ontario country, opening it up to a greater number of newcomers. This line not only foreshadows the death of the Cree way of life but also the reality of the battlefield, which is also conceived in terms of lines with its trenches and "Hun lines,"[19] as well as the army's trio of reserve lines, support lines, and front lines.[20]

All of these man-made lines, including the traplines back home, point to death. Barre Toelken notes that lines are contra-natural to Native patterns. He argues that "there are very few straight lines in nature," and explains that the preferred spatial system in technological cultures is indeed linear, with its imposition of "straight lines and grid patterns" on nature so as to control the landscape and "to put things in order."[21]

The Canadian Pacific Railway that now cuts through the north was known as "The Line" (with a capital "L"), as the commissioners of Treaty No. 9 observed in the summary of their 1905 treaty tour.[22] This line is one of the main reasons that led to Treaty No 9,[23] after which there would be no turning back to the traditional Cree lifestyle. The arrival of the train brought commercial competition to the existing fur trade for the Hudson's Bay Company and for the Native trappers who now had to compete with the increasing number of white trappers. In the novel, the French-Canadian trapper is one such trapper. He has a devastating effect on Niska when he attempts to take her power away. After getting Niska to drink beer at the trading post and making love to her in the church across the street from the residential school, the trapper finally laughs at her: "'I fucked you in a church … I fucked your *ahcahk*, your spirit. Do you understand that?'"[24] The references to the three major steps marking colonization – the trading post, the church, the residential school – point to the political treachery underlying the treaties signed with First Nations. The relationship between Niska and the French-Canadian trapper is based on a phase of seduction followed by one of betrayal. It serves as an allegory of the betrayal of colonization, which was facilitated by better access to First Nations territory thanks to the railway.

As a symbol of colonial expansion, the train announces a new civilization that is coming into being, one that is on the way of defeating and conquering the old one. This is suggested from the very beginning of the novel with the image of nature surrendering to the arrival of industrialization: Niska sees the spruce trees "across the tracks" as "blackened by soot," "bend[ing] in defeat."[25] This train pulling in, bringing Xavier back from the war, represents the destructive appetite of modern society expanding northward into traditional lands.

WWI IN COUNTERPOINT

The relationship between war and colonization is established from the outset in the train station scene, for Niska's description of the northern Ontario town announces the first war memories Xavier has of Belgium. It is clear that, in Niska's eyes, the town into which the train is pulling to bring Xavier back "home" from the war is not perceived as home.[26] The town is foreign territory to her, even enemy territory in which she needs to "hide" (the verb is repeated four times on the first page), reflecting how Xavier and Elijah needed to hide during the war. She is easy prey in this town, "an Indian animal,"[27] "afraid of this place," just as the rabbits are.[28] Having no significance in Niska's world, this town (most likely Cochrane) remains nameless. She refers to it as an "ugly town … a place to which I will never return."[29] Niska's perception of the town describes impressions that Xavier already experienced four years earlier upon his arrival in Flanders: "I want to be home and not in this ugly place."[30] Once Xavier sets foot in this northern Ontario town, he still needs to be "protect[ed]"[31] by Niska because the small urban community that has sprouted with the arrival of the train is not their home. "Home" can only be reached after a three-day canoe journey along another line, one drawn by nature, the only life-giving line in the novel, the line of the river leading further north beyond the man-made railway line. The novel opens with a man-made line but closes with a natural line that is drawn by the river, "the black line" "heading north"[32] as if to re-establish the natural rights of the landscape.

As a symbol of colonial expansion linked to linearity, the train is something unfamiliar to Niska – something that she cannot easily identify. She first describes the train as an indefinite "it,"[33] a "thing,"[34] and then as a sound ("the call"; "It whistles like a giant eagle screaming"), as something that "the old ones call … the iron toboggan,"[35] but that Niska sees as a foreboding, predatory "beast"[36] that "sniffs the track"[37] as if searching for prey to devour. The motif of the war – the war seen as a voracious beast[38] – is used contrapuntally, and so it too is already at work in the train station scene. During his first war battle, Xavier perceives the attacking enemy shells in identical terms; he sees the war as the cannibalistic *windigo* that inhabits the legends of his land: "The shells creep a little further away with each boom and shudder, like they are live beasts sniffing and pounding the dirt in search of men's flesh to rip apart."[39] Quoting Eric Leed's *No Man's Land*, Herb Wyile explains how the war came to be seen as a "gigantic, incomprehensible, and malevolent beast,"[40] a trope that Boyden revitalizes by viewing it through the prism of the *windigo*, one with a cannibalistic appetite. As Xavier remarks, "It [the war] has sucked the life from Saint-Eloi and left it like this, has moved on in search of more bodies to fill its impossible hunger,"[41] words which, once again, replicate Niska's when she talks about the *windigo* legend "of people who eat other people's flesh and grow into wild beasts twenty feet tall whose hunger can be satisfied only by more human flesh."[42]

The repetition that circulates in the novel from the outset shows that Boyden has skilfully woven repeated images into his narrative to create unity between Niska's and Xavier's stories. Xavier picks up on the images his old aunt uses. Moreover, he often sees the enemy soldiers as a singular, inhuman, monolithic, threatening entity, as "the German line"[43] with "no faces."[44] The aunt and the nephew see things with the same eye, speak the same language, imagery included. They know the value of the timeless legend of the *windigo*, and so they resort to it, to understand and make sense out of the respective horrific events that they face.

"ELIJAH CROSSED THE LINE"

This is not the case with Elijah, a victim of the residential school, whose connections with his people and culture have been severed. As Xavier observes: "The front line. That is his home."[45] In the eyes of his fellow soldiers, Elijah comes across as a "warrior of the highest order,"[46] but unwittingly embodies the fearsome *windigo* that Xavier alone detects in him: "To me he is mad. I am the only one now to know Elijah's secrets, and Elijah has turned himself into something invincible, something inhuman."[47] Elijah, with his Cree trickster's name – Weesageechak – has indeed tricked his fellow soldiers into believing that his actions are the result of bravery: "Elijah. He fools everyone but me."[48] Elijah has crossed over from the trickster to the *windigo*.[49] Like the foreboding mechanical train, like the modern war, Elijah, the colonized Indian, is a *windigo*, "an other-than-human" creature.[50]

In the Western world of lines, lines can be crossed, and Xavier observes that "Elijah crossed the line, crossed it long ago."[51] In the war, Elijah crossed the line from soldier to killer, from sanity to madness, just as "long ago," in residential school, Elijah crossed the line separating innocence from the experience of colonization. It is as an already damaged man that Elijah goes to war. The initial cause of Elijah's disorder stems from his childhood wounds of sexual abuse by Sister Magdalene during his residential school years. Boyden thus reveals how the residential school accomplished its mission of killing the Indian in the child that Elijah once was. Indeed, the "first dead body" that Xavier sees in Flanders is that of "a small boy" with "a great chunk of his head gone,"[52] an image suggestive of Elijah's cultural death and impending insanity. By "killing the Indian" in the child to "save the man," the process of assimilation has not led to saving Elijah's soul, which has become increasingly sick ("Elijah is mad"[53]), nor has it led to saving the man, for Elijah is, in the end, "inhuman."[54] As Louis Bird, an Omushkego (Swampy Cree) storyteller explains, there are several types of "wihtigos," one of which perfectly describes Elijah's case:

> Another wihtigo was created when a person was driven extremely insane. People lost their human consciousness and were driven to become a wihtigo by another human's abuse – if, for example, a man had a wife who he abused, and beat, and starved. There is a certain point when the mind cannot tolerate any more and when that limit is reached it turns chaotic, and then it turns really crazy. A person turns crazy. Sometimes the person actually became another-than-human and he was not normal anymore. Automatically such a person would want to retaliate and hurt or kill someone. A person who got that way was very dangerous.[55]

Elijah's dangerous behaviour is so great that Xavier grows fearful of his best friend,[56] and is led to kill him. In his obsession to impress others, to be seen as superior to others, Elijah demonstrates the "white linear" way of thinking based on hierarchy. As Xavier kills Elijah, the narrator tells us that all that is left of his boyhood "trickster grin"[57] is a "thin line"[58] across his mouth. His mouth turns out to be similar to his childhood persecutor's, to Sister Magdalene's mouth, which was described as "a tight line across her face."[59]

Elijah's story is one in which the spirit of the circle has been broken. He has become dissociated from his past, from his language, from Niska and Xavier, his relations whom he dismisses as backwards "bush Indians"[60] and "heathens."[61] Elijah's identity as a colonized Indian is best illustrated in his mastery of the English language; he can speak "in an English accent"[62] even "like a lord" (a simile which likens him to the colonizer), but cannot "speak in his old voice even if he wanted to."[63] He has even become dissociated from his own family name. The Hudson's Bay Company traders have also contributed to killing the Indian in Elijah by anglicizing his Cree trickster name "Weesageechak" into "Whiskeyjack" (also called the Canada jay or the grey jay), "making his name a name without a family."[64] Elijah seems oblivious to the Cree stories allowing him to remain grounded in his identity. He has not learned any of the teachings of the innumerable trickster stories, stories that can only be told in the winter when he was away at the Christian residential school. The story of "Wesakechak and the Medicine," for instance, would have warned him of the danger of abusing morphine, while the story of "Wesakechak Wants to Fly" would have taught him the limits to one's powers. This is a story that Xavier seems to know, for despite his own explicit family name, "Bird," he has "always known men aren't meant to fly."[65] Elijah has lost touch with the Weesageechak in him. This explains why Elijah has no trouble killing the barn swallow that brings Xavier comfort, claiming it is "just a bird."[66] Elijah kills the little bird spirit left in him. Elijah's indigenous identity has no future. Only his Christian name, Elijah, the name of a prophet, looks towards the future. If his Biblical name carries any prophetic weight, it is in the destructive effects of colonization and its attempts to transform Natives culturally, inside and out.[67]

Xavier Bird's story is read as a contrast to that of Elijah. In its connection to the animal, the name "Bird" is tied up with the idea of survival. Xavier Bird's only remaining relative, Niska, helps her nephew save the spirit of the circle by restoring him to wholeness during a healing ceremony in the sweat lodge that unifies past, present, and future. Xavier does indeed save the spirit of the circle from being broken. Niska's final vision connects past to future through recollections of the youthful friends, Xavier and Elijah, uniting them with Xavier's future offspring. The Bird cycle remains intact.

LOUIS BIRD'S VOICE

In *Three Day Road,* Joseph Boyden not only honours the legendary war sniper Francis Pegahmagabow and all other Native soldiers, as he explains in his page of acknowledgments, but he also honours the name Bird itself. The name Bird may be rich in the universality of its symbolic resonance, but it is especially a name that is steeped in local Cree history, as I indicated at the beginning of this paper with reference to the Treaty No. 9 signatory Xavier Bird. However, Boyden's fictional Xavier Bird slips out of the framework of further colonization that was set up by the treaty by following the river home to return to his "bush Indian" lifestyle further north. Boyden's Xavier Bird can thus be perceived as thumbing his nose at the 1905 James Bay Treaty, the terms of which have not been respected.

Another Cree Indian whose family name was Bird signed the Winisk adhesion to Treaty No. 9 in 1930: John Bird, the grandfather of Louis Bird, a Cree storyteller and friend of Joseph Boyden's.[68] For years now, Louis Bird has been recording legends and stories to save them for the younger generations.[69] His first stories are autobiographical; they are stories about his family, about trapping with his brother Xavier (another Xavier Bird!), and about his early childhood memories. In keeping with Boyden's traditional narrative structure of circularity, I will end my study of *Three Day Road* with Louis Bird's very first childhood memory, which will bring us back to the beginning of this study and to Niska's fear of the train. The presence of Louis Bird's voice permeates Boyden's narrative, especially the opening of the novel. Louis Bird explains that his first recollection is of a dream he had at the age of three, about a frightening "monster." This "monster" that scared him turned out to be the manifestation of the rapid advance of white civilization, for it was, according to his mother's explanations, none other than "the train that we were waiting for in 1936 on the Moosonee railway station."[70]

In conclusion, we can see how "the sharp blade of survival"[71] that Xavier resorts to in *Three Day Road* is double-edged: the survival of a Cree soldier during a war being waged in foreign lands, and the survival of his people back home on their ancestral native land. By bringing the name Xavier Bird back to life, Boyden retrieves Native Cree history, their stories, their beliefs and the historical events imposed on them by the colonization process in their region. Boyden infuses his novel with a strong sense of the land, of its people and their stories. In his depiction of Xavier Bird, the author has created a fictional character true to the spirit of the circle that looks at one and the same time towards the historical past of northern Ontario and towards the future with Xavier Bird's descendants in his next novel, *Through Black Spruce* (2008).

NOTES

1 Mark Abley, *Conversations with a Dead Man: The Legacy of Duncan Campbell Scott.* (Madeira Park, BC: Douglas & McIntyre, 2013). The extract is an imaginary conversation between Montreal writer

M. Abley and Duncan Campbell Scott, who played a key role in the signing of the Numbered Treaties (1905–06) and in the Indian residential school system across the country in the 1920s and 1930s. Scott was a key figure in the cultural genocide.

2 Interview with Herb Wyile, "Pushing Out the Poison" in *Speaking in the Past Tense: Canadian Novelists on Writing Historical Fiction* (Waterloo: Wilfrid Laurier University Press, 2007), 221.

3 The treaty terms were not fully explained to the First Nations, who believed they would be sharing the land, not ceding it. For the deceit and manipulation details behind this controversial treaty, see John Long, *Treaty No. 9: Making the Agreement to Share the Land in Far Northern Ontario in 1905* (Montreal: McGill-Queen's University Press, 2010).

4 The treaty texts can be read on the Canadian Government's site of Aboriginal Affairs and Northern Development: http://www.aadnc-aandc.gc.ca/eng/1100100028863/1100100028864#chp5 (accessed 31 May 2014).

5 The phrase "kill the Indian in the child," attributed to Duncan Campbell Scott, was inspired by the American military officer Captain Richard Henry Pratt's phrase, "Kill the Indian, save the man."

6 Rebecca West's novel *The Return of the Soldier* (Penguin, 1998) was first published during WWI in 1918.

7 For example, in several interviews, Teresa Spence refers to the region as Canada's "third world." For the shocking conditions that First Nations endure in northern Ontario reserves, see Andrée Cazabon's documentary film *Third World Canada* (2010).

8 Louis Owens notes: "Though like his predecessors, he focuses upon the agony of the Indian seemingly trapped between worlds, with this circular journey toward identity, Momaday establishes a new pattern that will continue to inform Native American novels up to the present time." Owens, *Other Destinies: Understanding the American Indian Novel* (University of Oklahoma Press, 1992), 25. Other common aspects include Native inarticulateness, tension between Native and Euro-American cultures, dislocation from one's cultural roots, healing ceremonies, and the importance of storytelling.

9 Owens, *Other Destinies*, 95.

10 Barre Toelken, "Seeing with a Native Eye: How Many Sheep Will It Hold?" in *Seeing With a Native Eye: Essays on Native American Religion*, edited by Walter Holden Capps (New York: Harper & Row Publishers, 1976), 17.

11 In interviews and during several of his talks. See for example: Herb Wyile's interview "Pushing Out the Poison" in *Speaking in the Past Tense: Canadian Novelists on Writing Historical Fiction* (Waterloo: Wilfrid Laurier University Press, 2007), 236; and the talk given by Joseph Boyden at the Université de Caen Normandie in March 2014, http://www.unicaen.fr/recherche/mrsh/forge/2699 (accessed 31 May 2014).

12 In interview for Penguin: http://www.penguin.com/read/book-clubs/three-day-road/9780143037071 (accessed May 31, 2014).

13 John G. Neihardt, *Black Elk Speaks: Being the Life Story of a Holy Man of the Oglala Sioux* [1932] (Lincoln: University of Nebraska Press, 1979), 194.

14 The expression is from the title of Barre Toelken's essay "Seeing with a Native Eye" in *Seeing with a Native Eye: Essays on Native American Religion,* edited by Walter Holden Capps (New York: Harper & Row Publishers, 1976).

15 Donald L. Fixico, *The American Indian Mind in a Linear World: American Indian Studies and Traditional Knowledge* (New York: Routledge, 2003), 1.

16 Ibid., 2.

17 Joseph Boyden, *Three Day Road* (London: Phoenix, 2006), 278.

18 Fixico, *The American Indian Mind*, xii.

19 Boyden, *Three Day Road*, 35. All subsequent parenthetical references are to the Phoenix edition.

20 Ibid., 277.

21 Toelken, "Seeing with a Native Eye," 15–16.

22 In their report to the Superintendent General of Indian Affairs, dated 6 November 1905, the commissioners (amongst them Duncan Campbell Scott) describe their arrival at the English River Trading Post: "This is a desolate post of the Hudson's Bay Company, in charge of Mr G. B. Cooper. There are very few Indians in attendance at any time; about half of them were assembled, the rest having gone to 'The Line,' as the Canadian Pacific railway is called, to trade." The report is accessible online: http://www.aadnc-aandc.gc.ca/eng/1100100028863/1100100028864#chp1 (accessed 31 May 2014).

23 The commissioners' report on Treaty No. 9 explains that it was necessary to establish a treaty with the Indians living on the unceded lands of northern Ontario due to the "increasing settlement, activity in mining and railway construction." See report online.

24 Boyden, *Three Day Road*, 197.

25 Ibid., 4.

26 Ibid., 3.

27 Ibid.

28 Ibid.

29 Ibid., 23. In the chapter entitled "Betrayal," Niska will say the same thing of Moose Factory, "vowing a thousand times never to return to that place." Boyden, *Three Day Road*, 198.

30 Ibid., 14.

31 Ibid., 7.

32 Ibid., 432.

33 Ibid., 3.

34 Ibid., 4.

35 Later in the novel, Xavier sees the war tanks as "great iron monsters" (223) and the German U-boats as "great iron fish." Boyden, *Three Day Road*, 208.

36 Ibid., 6.

37 Ibid., 4.

38 Herb Wyile, "Windigo Killing: Joseph Boyden's *Three Day Road,*" in *National Plots: Historical Fiction and Changing Ideas of Canada*, edited by Andea Cabajsky (Waterloo: Wilfrid Laurier Press, 2010).

39 Boyden, *Three Day Road*, 19.

40 Ibid., 86.

41 Ibid., 81

42 Ibid., 49

43 Ibid., 36

44 Ibid., 37.

45 Ibid., 307.

46 Ibid., 395.

47 Ibid.

48 Ibid., 356.

49 Significantly, the shift from trickster into *windigo* becomes apparent to Xavier in the chapter that bears Elijah's last name, "Weesageechak," subtitled by the ambivalent English word "Hero," leaving the reader wondering whether Elijah is a war hero or a culture hero, the Trickster who shares his name.

50 In Cree, the word "windigo" means "other than human" as Cree storyteller Louis Bird explains in *The Spirit Lives in the Mind: Omushkego Stories, Lives, and Dreams*, compiled and edited by S.E. Gray (Montreal: McGill-Queen's University Press, 2007), 112.

51 Boyden, *Three Day Road*, 394.

52 Ibid., 15.
53 Ibid., 356
54 Ibid., 395.
55 Louis Bird, *Telling Our Stories: Omushkego Legends & Histories from Hudson Bay*, edited by Jennifer S.H. Brown, P.W. De Pasquale, and M.F. Ruml (Peterborough, ON: Broadview Press, 2005), 112.
56 Boyden, *Three Day Road*, 363.
57 Ibid., 120.
58 Ibid., 417.
59 Ibid., 472
60 Ibid., 65, 183.
61 Ibid., 360.
62 Ibid., 86.
63 Ibid., 156.
64 Ibid., 174.
65 Ibid., 11.
66 Ibid., 292.
67 Xavier remains the traditional Indian throughout; he does not shed off his past identity when immersed in the Western world. When Xavier and Elijah take the train to join the army, Elijah, the false prophet, goes dressed "like a preacher" (160) while Xavier keeps his Indian moccasins on (183), to the embarrassment of Elijah. Boyden, *Three Day Road*.
68 In a personal conversation (June 2014), Joseph Boyden spoke of his endearment of Louis Bird as a friend.
69 Read S.E. Gray's presentation of Louis Bird in the preface of *The Spirit Lives in the Mind*.
70 "Our Voices: Louis Bird's Autobiography," recorded by Louis Bird on 14 July 1994, transcribed in April 2001, site housed by the University of Winnipeg: http://www.ourvoices.ca/filestore/pdf/0/0/0/1/0001.pdf (accessed 31 May 2014).
71 Boyden, *Three Day Road*, 21.

Contributors

JOAN BEAUMONT is professor of history, Strategic and Defence Studies Centre, Australian National University, Canberra. She is author of the critically acclaimed *Broken Nation: Australians and the Great War* (2013), which was joint winner of the 2014 Prime Minister's Award for Australian History and winner of the 2014 New South Wales Premier's Award (Australian History). She is also joint editor of *Beyond Surrender: Australian Prisoners of War in the Twentieth Century* (2015).

STÉPHANIE A.H. BÉLANGER is associate scientific director of the Canadian Institute for Military and Veteran Health Research (CIMVHR), a unique consortium of over forty Canadian universities dedicated to researching the health needs of military personnel, veterans, and their families. She is co-editor-in-chief of the *Journal of Military, Veteran and Family Health* (University of Toronto Press, 2015), and co-editor of *Beyond the Line: Military and Veteran Health Research* (McGill-Queen's University Press, 2013), of *A New Coalition for a Challenging Battlefield* (Canadian Defence Academy Press, 2012), of *Shaping the Future* (Canadian Defence Academy Press, 2011), and of *Transforming Traditions: Women, Leadership and the Canadian Navy* (Canadian Defence Academy Press, 2010). Member of the College of New Scholars, Artists and Scientists of the Royal Society of Canada, she is professor at the French Department of the Royal Military College of Canada where her research focuses on war testimony and soldier identity, as well as moral injuries. She also specializes in military ethics and the representation of the warrior through just war theories, a topic on which she published the monograph *Guerres, sacrifices et persécutions* (Paris: Editions L'Harmattan, 2010). An active researcher, she co-chairs the annual CIMVHR forum as well as the War Memories International Conference series. She completed her PhD degree at the University of Toronto in 2003. She has been co-chair of the Kingston Garrison Diversity Advisory Group for Persons with Disabilities since 2010 and she has served in the Royal Canadian Navy as a reservist since 2004.

GILLES CHAMEROIS is senior lecturer at the University of Brest, France. He is a former student of the École nationale supérieure Louis-Lumière, and has published texts on Thomas Pynchon and on cinema, including articles on Robert Kramer, Ken Loach, John Huston, *King Kong*, Jacques Rozier, and more. He has co-authored two books on adaptation published by Éditions Atlande. He has also edited or co-edited two collections of essays on Thomas Pynchon.

SUBARNO CHATTARJI is associate professor in the Department of English, University of Delhi, India. He has also taught in Japan and the UK. He was a Fulbright Senior Research Fellow at La Salle University, Philadelphia (2004–05) and the recipient of a Kluge Postdoctoral Fellowship at the Library of Congress in 2008–09. His publications include: *Memories of a Lost War: American Poetic Responses to the Vietnam War* (Oxford University Press, 2001); *Tracking the Media: Interpretations of Mass Media Discourses in India and Pakistan* (Routledge, 2008); co-author with Suman Gupta, Richard Allen, and Supriya Chaudhuri, *Reconsidering English Studies in Indian Higher Education* (Routledge, 2015).

NICOLE CLOAREC is senior lecturer in English at Rennes 1 University. She is the author of a doctoral thesis on Peter Greenaway's films and a number of articles on British and English-speaking cinema. She has edited two collective volumes on letters and the insertion of written material in films and recently co-edited *Social Class on British and American Screens: Essays on Cinema and Television* (2016). Her latest research focuses on questions of transmediality, adaption, and documentary.

CORINNE DAVID-IVES is currently senior lecturer at the European University of Brittany – Rennes 2, France. Her research work is in the field of Commonwealth Studies and deals with identity politics and the place of indigenous peoples in the former British colonies of settlement, with a focus on New Zealand. She is working on the strategies used nationally and internationally by indigenous peoples for recognition and empowerment. She has published several studies in France and abroad on reconciliation politics and the representation of indigenous minorities.

JEFFREY DEMSKY is a historian of politics and culture. His research agenda focuses on American Holocaust memory. He has authored various articles, book chapters, and encyclopedia entries. He has presented conference papers in Britain, France, Holland, Canada, and numerous American cities. In addition to his teaching duties, he has served as a manuscript referee for the *International Journal of Press and Politics*, and as a consultant with secondary schools teaching the Holocaust and Genocide Studies curriculum.

RENÉE DICKASON is currently professor at the European University of Brittany – Rennes 2, France. Her research work is in the field of British cultural history, in particular the visual media and the representation of contemporary British society through television fictions, political communication, and government advertising. She is interested in the phenomenon of war memories and in the representation of the "real" and the shaping of reality in films, documentaries, and comedy series. She has published several studies on these topics in France and abroad. In 2003, she created *Revue LISA/LISA e-journal* (http://lisa.revues.org/), which is hosted by Revues.org (CLEO, CNRS, EHESS) and is part of the Presses Universitaires de Rennes. She has written *British Television Advertising – Cultural Identity and Communication* (University of Luton Press, 2000), *Radio et télévision britanniques* (Presses Universitaires de Rennes, 1999), *Vers la paix en Irlande du Nord: communication politique et publicité télévisuelle, 1988–1997* (Presses de la Sorbonne Nouvelle, 2000), and *La Société britannique à travers ses fictions télévisuelles : le cas des soap operas et des sitcoms* (Ellipses, 2005). She has edited *Expériences de guerres, regards, témoignages, récits* (éditions Mare et Martin, 2012), *Mémoires croisées autour des deux guerres mondiales* (éditions Mare et Martin, 2012), and the special topics section: "Propaganda," *Symbolism*, vol. 11 (AMS Press, 2010). She co-edited, with Xavier Cervantes, *La Propagande au Royaume-Uni, de la Renaissance à l'Internet* (Ellipses, 2002), with Benoît Raoulx, *Screening Social Spaces* (Coll. Les Cahiers de la MRSH, Caen, PUC, 2007), with Karine Rivière-De Franco, *Image et communication politique. La Grande-Bretagne depuis 1980* (Coll. Psychologie politique, Paris, L'Harmattan, 2007), with David Haigron and Karine Rivière-De Franco, *Stratégies et campagnes électorales en Grande-Bretagne et aux Etats-Unis* (Coll. Psychologie politique, Paris, L'Harmattan, 2009), and with Rüdiger Ahrens, *Screening and Depicting Cultural Diversity in the English-speaking World and Beyond* (Coll. Anglo-amerikanische Studien/Anglo-American Studies, Frankfurt am Main, New York, Oxford, 2013).

LORIE-ANNE DUECH-RAINVILLE is associate professor in the English Department at the Caen University, Normandy, France, where she teaches literature of the English-speaking world. She is the author of *James Joyce: Dubliners & A Portrait of the Artist* (Ophrys, 2005), and has published articles on Margaret Atwood, Alice Munro, and Jane Urquhart. Her current work focuses on First Nations and Canadian writing.

SAM EDWARDS is senior lecturer in American history at Manchester Metropolitan University. His research engages with transatlantic relations, commemoration and memory, and the cultural history of conflict. He is co-editor of a volume exploring the place of D-Day in international remembrance, entitled *D-Day in History and Memory: The Normandy Landings in International Remembrance and Commemoration* (University of North Texas Press, 2014). He has recently published his first monograph, entitled *Allies in Memory: World War II and the Politics of Transatlantic Commemoration* (Cambridge University Press, 2015). Edwards is lead editor for a new volume exploring the use of film and television as historical sources, entitled *Histories on Screen: The Past and Present in Anglo-American Cinema and Television* (forthcoming, Bloomsbury Academic, 2017). He is co-editor of another volume examining the post-mortem legacy of Thomas Paine in the transatlantic world, under contract with Pickering and Chatto. Edwards is a fellow of the Royal Historical Society, a senior fellow of the Higher Education Academy, and a former Fulbright Distinguished Scholar at the University of Pittsburgh.

GEORGES FOURNIER is a researcher at the IETT at the Jean Moulin University in Lyon, France, and an associated researcher at the ACB at Rennes 2 University. His research interests are the British media, the representations of the political and social issues in Great Britain, and the cinema of the English-speaking world. He is a member of *InMédia*, for which he has published articles and supervised issues. He has written articles for *Revue* LISA/LISA *e-journal* and also for foreign publishers. He is currently collaborating with a team of seven European researchers on the representations of political and social issues on the European television screens.

ANNIE GAGIANO is professor emerita in the Department of English at the University of Stellenbosch (South Africa). She is the author of *Achebe, Head, Marechera: On Power and Change in Africa* (Lynne Rienner, 2000) and *Dealing with Evils: Essays on Writing from Africa* (Ibidem-Verlag, 2008; second edition co-published by Columbia University Press, 2014) as well as numerous essays on a wide range of African fiction. Gagiano's research focuses on the postcolonialism of the present, engaging with issues of power, gender, and the plight of children, often adopting a comparative reading perspective.

DAVID HAIGRON is senior lecturer in English at Rennes 2 University, France. His PhD thesis was entitled "The British Conservative Party's Televised Political Broadcasts (1974–1997): Mutations, Strategies, Images" (2006). His current research focuses on political ideology and communication in the United Kingdom and in the Republic of Ireland. He is also interested in social representations in cinema and television productions. His publications include: *Social Class on British and American Screens: Essays on Cinema and Television*, which he co-edited with Nicole Cloarec and Delphine Letort (McFarland, 2015); "The UK's Political Landscape in the 21st Century: Players, Strategies, Achievements," *Revue* LISA/LISA *e-journal* (vol. 12, no. 8), which he edited in 2014 (http://lisa.revues.org/6932); and *Stratégies et campagnes électorales en Grande-Bretagne et aux États-Unis*, which he co-edited with Renée Dickason and Karine Rivière-De Franco in 2009.

JUDITH KEENE is associate professor in the Department of History at the University of Sydney, Australia. Her research focuses on the cultural history of twentieth-century war, including art and cinema, and the formation of individual and collective memory. She has published on the Spanish Civil War and World War II and is currently writing a history of memory and the Korean War. She is also part of a research group, funded by the Australian Research Council, to examine the transnational uses of the past in the post–Cold War world.

MELISSA KING has specialized in the study of survivorship, memory, and youth activism in the Armenian-American community. She received her doctorate in anthropology from the University of California, Riverside, in 2013, and her research was funded in part by a Summer Institute Scholarship at Columbia University through the National Endowment for the Humanities. She has published short pieces in *American Anthropologist* and *Anthropology and Humanism*. She has been an instructor at San Bernardino Valley College since 2013, where she teaches courses in all subfields of anthropology.

CHRISTINE KNAUER is currently affiliated with the Eberhard Karls University Tübingen while finishing her second book. From 2011 to 2015, she was a postdoctoral fellow in the Cooperative Research Center 923 "Threatened Order – Societies under Stress" at the University of Tübingen, where she worked on lynching narratives in the US South after 1945. She received an MA from Brown University and an MA and PhD in history from the University of Tübingen. Her dissertation investigates the African-American fight for the integration of the American military from World War II to the Korean War. It was published as *Let Us Fight as Free Men: Black Soldiers and Civil Rights* (University of Pennsylvania Press, 2014).

LILIANE LOUVEL is professor emerita of British literature at the University of Poitiers and specializes in contemporary British literature and word/image relationship. She has written numerous articles on the subject and published five books on the interrelationship between word and image: *L'œil du texte* (Toulouse PUM 1998); *The Picture of Dorian Gray, Le double miroir de l'art* (Ellipses, 2000); *Texte/image, images à lire et textes à voir* (PUR, 2002); *Le tiers pictural* (PUR, 2010); *Poetics of the Iconotext* (Ashgate, July 2011). She has also edited three collections of essays published in *EJES*, *La licorne*, *Word/image*, *EJES*, including: *Like Painting…* (*La licorne*), *Actes du colloque de Cerisy: Texte/image nouveaux problèmes* with Henri Scepi (PUR); *Actes du colloque de Cerisy Littérature et photographie* with Jean-Pierre Montier, Philippe Ortel and Danièle Méhaut (PUR); *Intermedial Arts*, with Leena Eilitta and Sabine Kim

(Cambridge Scholars Press); *Musing in the Museum*, with Laurence Petit and Karen Brown, *Word/Image* (Taylor and Francis, May 2015).

MICHELLE P. MOORE graduated in spring 2013 from the Royal Military College of Canada with a master's degree in War Studies. She obtained a bachelor's degree with honours in psychology from Brock University in 2008. In line with her interests in psychology, her research has focused on the influence of military culture on soldiers' behaviour. She serves as an intelligence officer in the Royal Canadian Navy (Reserves) and currently works as the personnel investigations and workplace relations coordinator at the Canadian Army Doctrine and Training Centre.

JOHN MULLEN is professor at the University of Rouen, France. He has published widely both on the history of trade unions and the history of British popular music. His articles include a reflection on "ethnic" music festivals and immigrant identity in Britain (1960–2000), and on racial stereotyping in music hall songs from 1880 to 1920. His full-length work on popular song in Britain during the First World War was published in French by L'Harmattan in 2012, and in English by Ashgate in 2015. His most recent work is about the British music industry in 1900, and about the use of voice in British wartime music hall.

ELIZABETH RECHNIEWSKI is honorary senior lecturer at the University of Sydney. She has published widely on remembrance of twentieth-century wars in Australia, France, and New Caledonia, including on the commemoration of the role of Indigenous soldiers from these countries. Her recent publications on this topic include: "Forgetting and Remembering the Darwin Bombings," *Revue électronique d'études sur le monde anglophone* (9:3, 2013); and "Contested Sites of Memory: Commemorating Wars and Warriors in New Caledonia" in Ben Wellings, ed., *Nation, Memory and Great War Commemoration: Mobilizing the Past in Europe, Australia and New Zealand* (Oxford: Peter Lang, 2014). She is currently chief investigator on the Australian Research Council Discovery Project "Judging the Past in a Post-Cold War World" with special focus on decolonization in Cameroon and the long silence concerning the internal repression that accompanied it.

RAPHAËL RICAUD is associate professor at the University of Montpellier III, France. In 2012, he defended his dissertation on the theories, practices, and effects of American public diplomacy, under the supervision of Pr Pierre Guerlain. He has recently published a number of articles on American public diplomacy and propaganda, among them: "De la vérité comme propagande sous l'Administration Truman," *Revue Française d'Etudes Américaines* (2012:3); "The Advent of New Media and the Conduct of Public Diplomacy," in Abrioux et al., *"Naming and Narrating," Transferts critiques et dynamiques des savoirs* (Collections patrimoniales de l'université Paris 8, 2014); "John L. Brown's Epistolary Wit,, *Angles* 1 (2015); and "John Lackey Brown, public diplomat par excellence," *Caliban* 54 (2015).

LAURA ROBINSON is professor and dean of arts at the Royal Military College of Canada. She has published articles about Canadian children's literature, Canadian women writers, and *The L Word*, in addition to many articles on L.M. Montgomery's work. Her current project examines Montgomery's depiction of friendship and sexuality.

ISABELLE ROBLIN is assistant professor at the Université du Littoral-Côte d'Opale, France. She specializes in contemporary anglophone literature and is currently working on literary and cinematographic rewritings of the British and American literary canons.

Index